WHAT YOU'LL LOSE
IF YOU DON'T READ THIS BOOK . . .

The next time you want something from someone, will you get it? Or will you get nothing because you haven't mastered the techniques in this book?

"But I'm not selling anything."

If that's what you believe, that's why you aren't getting your way more often—why you aren't persuading more people to accept your opinion. That's why your advice isn't sought more often—why your influence doesn't reach further and cut deeper.

The truth is, you're constantly trying to sell quite a number of ideas, beliefs, and goals, aren't you? You want your point of view to win more often with members of your family, with friends, associates, and neighbors, and with the world in general, don't you? Are you pleased with how well you're doing all this? Would you like to improve your performance at the gentle, satisfying, and profitable art of selling?

Maybe you don't like the word *sell*. Let's say "persuade" and "dissuade"—better yet, "talk into" and "talk out of." You also need to motivate, instruct, encourage, and reassure people from time to time. And you want to achieve your goals so that you can get what you want from life.

You care intensely about—what? A special person, your family, your religion? A political, social, or environmental cause? You're heavily involved with life in many ways; you have concerns, interests, challenges, and opportunities galore—so many, in fact, that you have to ration your time, money, and energy among them. Have you ever considered what an enormous waste of time failure is? When there aren't enough hours in our days to save all the successes we're capable of achieving, why should we give so much time to preventable failure? So much failure is avoidable when we know how. Preventing failure—any kind of failure in personal, business, or public life—starts with understanding *Why don't I do what I know I should do?*, which is the title of Chapter 5.

But it isn't failure that hurts us most—*fear* of failure does the greatest damage. Failure is in the past; fear of failure can destroy our future. That's why this book puts so much emphasis on methods that beat down our fear of failure, on methods that banish our fear of rejection. Use this book to learn how to waste less of your time on failure and fear. When you're doing that, you'll automatically enjoy life more.

Every technique in this book has proven its value on the firing line of sales work. Almost every one of them can add a new dimension of effectiveness and excitement to your private life. They work when you work; they work when you play; they work when you cope with life. Use them to help make good things and fewer bad things happen. Use them to oil the rough spots around the house or where your friendships are squeaking.

Look over the contents a couple of pages further along, then decide. Can you afford to face tomorrow without all the aid this book gives you?

If you want more attention paid to your needs,
If you want to achieve more in your personal life,
If you want to enjoy people more,
If you want to have more impact on your community,
If you want to influence your family more,
If you want more people to value your ideas and beliefs,
If you want to sell more of your products and services,
If you want to make more money,

Take this book home with you tonight.

Tom Hopkins

HOW TO
Master the Art of
SELLING

Fully Updated and Revised

TOM HOPKINS
THE NATION'S #1 SALES TRAINER

GRAND CENTRAL
PUBLISHING

NEW YORK   BOSTON

This Grand Central Publishing edition is published by arrangement with Tom Hopkins International, Inc., Scottsdale, AZ 85251.

Grand Central Publishing
Hachette Book Group
1290 Avenue of the Americas
New York, NY 10104

www.HachetteBookGroup.com

Grand Central Publishing is a division of Hachette Book Group, Inc.
The Grand Central Publishing name and logo are trademarks of Hachette Book Group, Inc.

The Hachette Speakers Bureau provides a wide range of authors for speaking events. To find out more, go to www.hachettespeakersbureau.com or call (866) 376-6591.

The publisher is not responsible for websites (or their content) that are not owned by the publisher.

Printed in the United States of America

First Grand Central Publishing Edition: October 1982
Revised and Updated Edition: May 2005

Printing 19, 2021
LSC-C

Library of Congress Cataloging-in-Publication Data

Hopkins, Tom.
    How to master the art of selling / Tom Hopkins.— Fully updated
and revised.
        p.   cm.
    Summary: "A revised and updated edition of How to master the
art of selling, which educates on how to succeed in sales, including
new information on using the latest research techniques and using
e-mail and online resources to generate deals more quickly and
efficiently"—Provided by the publisher.
    Includes bibliographical references.
    ISBN 978-0-446-69274-8
        1. Selling.   I. Title.

    HF5438.25.H66   2005
    658.85—dc22   2004026385

Book design and text composition by Ellen Rosenblatt/SDDesigns
Cover design by Brigid Pearson

To my parents,
Les and Kathy Hopkins,
with gratitude, respect, and affection

Acknowledgments

This volume exists because thousands of the people who attended my sales seminars went on to become Champions of Selling. Their success after learning this material convinced me that it should be published in book form and kept current to the times.

Hundreds of people have contributed to my knowledge of selling. I'll be able to single out only a few here, but my gratitude goes to them all. To begin with, the Edwards family—Doug, Jerry, and their son, Jay—have been an unfailing source of encouragement and support. Danielle Kennedy, herself one of the nation's great sales trainers, proved to me that any price is worth paying to make your dreams come true. I am indebted to Art Mortell for much of the basis for chapters 5 and 6.

And for countless well-dones, my thanks go to every member of my staff. Their energy, competence, and loyalty have made our company's growth and this book possible.

Contents

Introduction, by J. Douglas Edwards • xix

1. What the Profession of Selling Really Is • 1

The Myth of the Natural-Born Sales Wonder • The Seven Basics That'll Make You as Great as You Want to Be • Money Study: The Learning-to-Earn-Fast Fivesome • Your Primary Tool

2. The Twelve Sources of Sensational Selling Success • 16

Why You Can't Fail • How to Develop Desire • SPR Is the Difference Between Have and Have-Not • The Purchase Path

3. Question Right and Sink Your Teeth into Sales Success • 32

Twelve Pointers on Question Technique • Questioning 101—The Basics • The Standard Tie-Down • The Inverted Tie-Down • The Internal Tie-Down • The Tag-On Tie-Down • Tagalong Questions • The Alternate of Choice • The Porcupine Technique • The Involvement Question • Making These Strategies Yours • Make Two Right Turns to Sales Success • Use Both Barrels: Discovery Questions and

Leading Questions • How to Take Command with Leading Questions • The Three Principles of Question-Asking Power

4. Creating the Selling Climate • 58

Sell the People Who Can Buy • Don't Sell Logic—Arouse Emotions • Catch the Change on the Move • Replace Rejection Words with Go-Ahead Terms • The Triad Concept: How to Multiply Your Effectiveness • The Senses That Sell the Emotions

5. Why Don't I Do What I Know I Should Do? • 93

How You Get Depressed • The Motivators • The Demotivators

6. Learn to Love No • 120

How to Reject the Negative Effects of Rejection • The Five Attitudes Toward Rejection • The Creed of the Champion

7. Finding the People to Sell • 133

Know Your Ratios, and Strive to Improve Them • Four Ways to Hover Until You're Ready to Fly

8. Nonreferral Prospecting Methods • 149

The Itch Cycle • How to Determine the Itch Cycle for Your Product or Service • Orphan Adoption • Technical Advancement • Your Local Newspapers • Claim-Staking • Swap Meet or Leads Clubs • Selecting Strong Salespeople for Your Swap Meet • Service Your Service Department • Community Involvement

9. Referral Prospecting, or The Art of Getting Quality Introductions • 171

Card Referral System

10. How to Find Fortune and Felicity with the Phone • 182

Incoming Calls • Outgoing Calls • The Phone Survey • Finding Good Lists • Telephone Scoring Systems

11. A Spectator Sport, Buying Is Not • 197

Three Formats for Selling Interviews

12. Put Champion Selling Power in Your Presentations and Demonstrations • 205

Glamour Words • Words to Replace • Learn Many Different Lingoes • Keep Clients Mentally and Physically Involved • Handle Interruptions Calmly • Give the Entire Body of Your Presentation in Less than Seventeen Minutes • A Champion Plans Every Presentation in Writing • How to Preplan Your Presentation in Writing • Working with the Preplanning Form • The Corporate Sales Preplanner • When Do You Plan? • Visual Aids • Seventeen Minutes Are All You've Got • How to Make Visual Aids Pay Off for You • Testimonial Letters • How to Use Printed Literature • Models • Video Equipment

13. Finessing the First Meeting • 237

The Referred Lead • The Nonreferred Situation

14. Qualification Is the Key to Quota Busting • 246

The Six-Step Qualification Sequence • Focusing Them In with the Triplicate of Choice • The Uh-Price Nontechnique

15. The Objection Connection • 257

Make the Handling of Objections an Integral and Expected Part of Your Selling Sequence • What Is an Objection • What Is a Condition? • Two Don'ts and One Do That Every

Champion Lives By • The Objection-Handling System •
Four Shock Treatments for Concerns

16. Closing Is Sweet Success • 273

Test Closes • How to Steer Safely Through the Most
Dangerous Closing Time • The Crash-and-Burn Close •
Moving to the Major Close • What the Actual Close Is •
Close with Empathy • Likes and Dislikes • Close
Through Their Eyes • When Do You Close? • Where Do
You Close? • The Anatomy of the Close • The Fourteen
Most Important Words in the Art of Closing • You Wear the
Suit of Lights

17. Sixteen Power Closes for Aspiring Champions • 292

The Basic Oral Close • The Basic Written Close, aka the
"Let Me Make a Note of That" Close • The Benjamin
Franklin Balance Sheet Close • The "I Want to Think It
Over" Close • The Reduction-to-the-Ridiculous Close •
The Sharp-Angle Close • The Secondary-Question Close •
Bridging • The "My Dear Old Mother" Close • The Puppy-
Dog Close • The Similar-Situation Close • The "It Isn't in
the Budget" Close • The Economic Truth Close • The "I
Can Get It Cheaper" Close • The Competitive Edge Close •
The Higher Authority Close • The Lost-Sale Close

18. A Clutch of Moneygrabbers • 322

Turn Little Dollars into Big Dollars • The Power of Thank-
You Notes

19. How to Perspire Less and Profit More from Paperwork • 337

Company Paperwork • Follow-Up Paperwork

20. Fortune Building Starts with Time Planning • 344

21. How to Sell Your Way Out of a Slump • 352

22. The Most Necessary Skill of All • 363

23. How to Sell to the Most Important People You Know • 372

To Maximize Your Results
From This Book . . .

This book is written to show you how to make money in sales and to get more out of life. I encourage you to do more than just read this book. Take notes, use a highlighter pen to mark the book in any manner you see fit, or do anything else that makes this book a more effective tool for increasing your income.

AUDIO PROGRAMS

It is imperative that you try as rapidly as possible to get my techniques into your subconscious mind so they become part of you and come out automatically in your own words. In today's hectic world, many of us don't have the time to read as often as we would like. Because of this, many of the top salespeople we train absorb the material easier by listening to audio recordings while doing other activities. If you have trouble making time to read, I heartily suggest you consider our audio training program, *How to Master the Art of Selling Anything.* It's available in compact disc from our home office in Scottsdale, Arizona, or on our Web site at http://www.tomhopkins.com.

This program was recorded in lecture format with a live studio audience. They cover all the basics of the profession of selling. Topics covered are:

1. The Profession Called Selling
2. What Is a Champion?

3. Control with Questions
4. Minor Reflexive Questions
5. Emotions, the Triggers of Selling
6. How to Handle Failure and Rejection I
7. How to Handle Failure and Rejection II
8. Referral Prospecting
9. Nonreferral Prospecting
10. Telephone Techniques
11. Preplanning your Sales Presentation
12. Contact
13. Qualification
14. The Visual Aid Presentation
15. Presentation Demonstration Tactics
16. Objections—Premise
17. Objections—Solution
18. Test Closing
19. Anatomy of a Close
20. Power Closes of a Champion I
21. Power Closes of a Champion II
22. Turning Little $ into Big $
23. Time Planning Organization
24. Goal-setting

MOTIVE

My primary concern in telling you about these audio programs is your success. I know personally how lonely and frustrating the life of a salesperson can be. When I started, I was as much a failure as anyone until I was able to get the proper training to ensure my success. At that time, I swore if ever I could share my success with others, I would do it with high quality and at an investment that anyone could afford. You may feel that I am trying to sell you something—and that is true. I'm in the business of selling just like you. However, if you know something is good, you have an obligation to offer it to your client. You will make a small investment for this audio program and that constitutes one sale for me.

But it may mean hundreds of sales in your career and thousands of dollars for you and your loved ones. In this way, I hope that my company can play some part in your continued success. Thank you.

Tom Hopkins

Introduction

James Buchanan Brady could borrow millions on the strength of his name. Before he was thirty, he was creating a legend. Brady hobnobbed with the leading industrialists and financiers of the day. Lillian Russell, the most glamorous actress of the Gay Nineties, was his great friend and frequent companion.

You know this man by his trademark. Diamond Jim walked around wearing more wealth than most banks held in their vaults. His cufflinks, watch, cane, and every finger glittered with diamonds.

Why am I telling you about this man? Because Diamond Jim Brady was a salesman. He made more money selling railroad equipment than he could get rid of as Broadway's biggest spender. Brady was a superpro.

Selling itself goes far back beyond that. We know that Stone Age men traveled great distances to trade for goods they couldn't get where they hunted and gathered food. There's reason to believe that barter is older than war, that we're all descended from peaceful traders—salespeople, because barter requires salesmanship—rather than from violent marauders who lived on plunder.

The next development in selling was the open-air marketplace. But before history dawned, the exposed marketplace was pretty much obsolete. Merchants were moving inside and selling from permanent stores. Wandering traders were now carrying less merchandise on their backs and more on animals and ships. Then development stopped except for details, and this ancient system for distributing goods came over to the New World.

In the early 1800s, a revolutionary development took place and selling, as we now know it, was born. It happened very quietly. The owners of a small woolen mill in Massachusetts decided they wanted more business than the traders were giving them. With New England directness, they went straight to the heart of the matter. They hired a man to take their samples to shops in distant places and get orders for future delivery. This seems painfully obvious now, but it was a startling innovation in those days. It took intelligence to conceive that idea, courage to try it, and persistence to make it work. And work it did. Within a few years, the new system had spread to other mills and other industries, and the distribution of goods has never been the same.

During this period, the first railroads were being built. The new way of getting around suited the new way of selling perfectly. Traveling salesmen with their bulky sample cases became a familiar sight wherever the rails ran. But they weren't called salesmen yet. Everyone called them drummers, after the old-time peddlers who beat drums to attract an audience as they drove their wagons into small country towns.

The man who was to become the first superpro of sales was born in 1844. John H. Patterson was still a young man when the railroads connected our two coasts, but by that time his career had already been meteoric. Patterson created the first national sales force. He was the first man to organize sales training, the first man to have a fully organized sales staff with regional and district managers throughout the nation. He set the first sales quotas. And he was the first to guarantee exclusive territory to his salesmen. Before Patterson, many companies pitted two salesmen against each other in the same territory and let them fight it out selling the same products to the same customers. This practice died out after Patterson revealed its folly.

In 1895, a young man joined Patterson's company. This man, Thomas J. Watson, was destined to become another superpro of sales. After he worked his way up to become one of Patterson's top assistants, they parted ways. Watson went on to become the driving force behind one of the most dynamic companies the world has ever seen—IBM.

Watson's finest contribution to the profession of selling was his concept that no one should ever be out of training. This is a very profound idea. You don't have to go to school today to continue your training, to keep on learning. There are books, audio programs, lectures, seminars, magazines, videos, online courses—the list of training and learning sources goes on and on. If you stop training and learning, you start sinking. Nobody can float: You're either rising or sinking. It's been this way for a thousand years. The only difference is that you can rise, or you'll sink, a whole lot faster now.

The next superpro was H. W. Dubiski. When he arrived in this country right after the turn of the twentieth century, Dubiski had just turned fourteen and couldn't speak English. Four years later, he was a chalk boy posting prices in the New York Stock Exchange. Only three years after that modest beginning, he opened his own securities firm. More than any other man except Watson, Dubiski understood the opportunities that Patterson had discovered. Feeding off Patterson's concepts of selling, Dubiski perfected mass training. He perfected the prepared sales talk. He perfected the inspirational sales meeting in an age when it worked. And he developed the original philosophy that securities could be sold during one call. Dubiski was the master of staging what we used to call—well, never mind what we used to call it—the Shot in the Enthusiasm meeting. Every morning his salesmen (they were all men in those days) got together for a session of chanting, cheering, and singing that, in a commercial way, had almost the fervor of a religious revival meeting. Nobody got a sales management job in that firm unless he could give the men a motivational shot every morning and lead them through the company songs and cheers. After Dubiski's salesmen were pumped up to the bursting point with enthusiasm and determination, the managers would turn them loose on an innocent world. Barely a dozen years after he reached this country, Dubiski sold out and retired with five million dollars in government bonds. In 1914, that was an awful lot of money to have earned by the ripe old age of twenty-six.

Twenty years later, I started looking for work. I went into sales because, in the bottom of the Great Depression, sales work was the only kind available. My first job was with a traveling sales crew. The system was easy to understand. If you didn't sell that day, you didn't eat that day. I mean that literally. We sold personal stationery to schoolteachers and secretaries. They were making about $4.00 a week and our stationery was $3.75. That was a tough sell. We closed because it was the only way we could survive.

We were gypsies then. When we found something better, we changed. You name it, I've sold it. After the Second World War, I became the sales manager of an aircraft distributor. We sold three thousand planes in one year, a record that's never been approached by anyone else. Then the bottom fell out of the aircraft business. Demand for airplanes vanished. The industry augered itself into the bottom of the earth.

I went into the information business with a very bright outfit that was advising businesses on taxes and regulations. I almost walked away from it when they wanted me to learn their canned sales talk. Fortunately, the man hit the right note with me. He asked if I knew everything I needed to know about sales, and I had sense enough to admit that I didn't. So I got involved for the first time with a formal sales presentation in a situation that forced me to learn how to sell. In three months, I was a marketing executive with that firm, and then I met the man who was to become my mentor. Bob Barber was a sales genius, a superpro, and to him I owe my foundation in the profession of selling.

Later, Barber, I, and some other people formed a company to market the first magnetic wire dictation machine. That venture was very successful, and we soon sold out for a nice figure. Suddenly, I had nothing to do.

For years, I had been aware that there was a hole in the rapidly developing field of selling. Researchers and business consultants we had, but no sales consultants. I decided to create a new profession out of whole cloth. That's what I did, though it turned out to be a lot tougher job than I'd bargained for. The biggest problem was that, despite my sales skills, I couldn't go out and sell my services, for the same reason that doctors and lawyers struggle to peddle theirs. So I started speaking to any group that would hear me. Slowly, from my audiences, I started building my professional sales consulting career. My first client paid me twenty-five dollars a day, which was the smallest amount of money I'd made in many years.

My first real break came after I recruited and trained a sales force for the local agent of a major insurance company. When corporate headquarters saw the results, I acquired my first national account. At last, I was on my way.

In 1959, I released an LP recording titled *Closing the Sale*. That recording broke new ground. For the first time, the art of selling was broken down into specific tactics and techniques and made available to anyone who wanted to learn them. That recording became the best-selling business recording ever produced, and at my speaking engagements people started introducing me as "the father of modern selling."

Around this time, I met Tom Hopkins. I remember the occasion well. At a training seminar in California, I noticed a young man sitting in the front row. I couldn't help noticing him because he was wearing a high school band uniform. Never in my life have I seen anyone take notes as fast and thoroughly as he did. He seemed to be trying to snatch the words before they got out of my mouth. I marked him as a man to watch.

The next time I saw him, he met me at the Los Angeles airport. I was there to consult with the firm he worked for. Tom was wearing a new suit and driving a new car. Back at their headquarters, the president told me that Tom had memorized my techniques, and then he had taken off like a rocket.

Tom went on to become the greatest real estate salesman who ever lived. Then he went into sales management for a few years. The next thing I knew, he was living next door to me and pursuing his goal with the kind of zeal that would have impressed all the sales greats of old. Tom adapted and refined and added to the material I gave him just as I had adapted and refined and added to the material that was given to me.

Since then, Tom Hopkins has spent years advancing the profession of selling with his seminars that teach and inspire, and with his audio and video programs that carry his message where he can't be. And then there's this book, the culmination of a century of development in sales training, written by a true superpro, Tom Hopkins. Everyone who aspires to success must read it.

J. Douglas Edwards

Seeing's believing, but feeling's the truth.
—*Thomas Fuller*

All excellence is equally difficult.
—*Thornton Wilder*

That you may be strong be a craftsman in speech,
for the strength of one is the tongue, and the speech
of one is mightier than all fighting.
—*Written five thousand years ago by Ptahhotep*

HOW TO
Master the Art of
SELLING

1. What the Profession of Selling Really Is

I learned a long time ago that selling is the highest-paid hard work—and the lowest-paid easy work—that I could find. And I also found out another exciting thing about selling—the choice was mine, all mine. By myself, I could make it the highest-paid hard work, or I could let it be the lowest-paid easy work. I discovered that what I'd achieve in my selling career was entirely up to me, and that what anyone else wanted wasn't going to make much difference. What anyone else would or wouldn't give me wasn't going to make much difference, either. The only thing that really mattered was what I did for myself, and what I gave to myself.

Will you agree with me on that? I hope so, because the whole point of this book is that the skills, knowledge, and drive within you are what will make you great, and that these qualities can be expanded and intensified—if you're willing to invest time, effort, and money in yourself. Is there any better investment than in yourself? Most of us know there isn't, but many of us don't act often enough, or decisively enough, on that belief.

You are your greatest asset. Put your time, effort, and money into training, grooming, and encouraging your greatest asset.

Let's talk about some of the advantages of selling.

The first advantage and the reason I love selling is its freedom of expression. Sales is one of the few professions left in which you can be yourself and can, in essence, do what you want to do. This freedom you've won for yourself by successfully competing where

1

resourcefulness and perseverance are demanded and highly val-ued. No activity is more vital to the economy's health than selling; no activity is more dependent on individual initiative than selling.

The second advantage of selling is that you have the freedom to become as successful as you'd like to be. In this profession, no one limits your income but you. There are no income ceilings.

You may question this statement. You may think the limit is the highest income anyone has yet made selling for your company. Does that mean it's not possible to earn more? Of course not. But it does mean that all the salespeople in your company who aren't earning the highest income aren't applying all the strategies and techniques of the Champion.

The third advantage of selling is that it's a daily challenge. You can go into almost any business and have no challenge. That's never the case in selling, where every day you're confronted with new chal-lenges. Let that fact refresh you, not weary you. Glory in it. Our over-regulated and highly organized society provides few lucrative work activities where the end of each day isn't known before that day dawns. You are privileged to be involved in one of those precious few activities where freedom and challenge aren't rarities, they're constant companions. In sales, you never know what opportunities the day will open up, what prizes you can win—what catastrophes may befall you.

To the salesperson, every day is an adventure. Working at this profession, we can go from the heights of exhilaration to the depths of discouragement within forty-eight hours—and climb back to the heights again the next day. Isn't that exciting?

Say yes.

Every morning, tell yourself that challenge is exciting, it's fun, and you look forward to it. Tell yourself that—and mean it. Psych yourself up to enjoy challenge. Then go on the prowl for it, find it, and overcome it. If you want to be better than average, do that. If you aspire to greatness, you won't hesitate. The shortest route to high earnings goes straight through the challenges you'll encounter.

The fourth advantage of selling is that it offers high potential re-turns from a low capital investment. What does it cost to gain entry into this profession that has no income ceiling? Compare whatever you think that cost is to the investment required for one of the fast-food franchises that have been so successful. Typically, owners of a new location invest three hundred thousand dollars or more, work long hours, and pay themselves a small salary. All of this is done in the hope of a sixty-thousand-dollar return on invested capital the second year.

You can launch yourself into a sales career for a tiny fraction of the franchiser's investment and, by applying the systems in this book, have greater earning power sooner. This enormous leverage on the small investment that getting into selling requires has always fascinated me. What an exciting prospect!

The fifth advantage of selling is that it's fun. Do you know how many people aren't having fun with what they're doing for income? My philosophy is that if it's not fun, it's not worth doing. Life was meant to be fun, and there's no reason not to have some of it while you're earning a nice income for your family.

The sixth advantage of the selling profession is that it's satisfying. You feel good when your client owns your product. It's a thrill to know you've helped people when you go home at night and can say, "I got another family happily involved in what my company provides."

When an executive or official approves your purchase order, it's exciting and satisfying to know you've helped that organization carry out its purposes, save money, make more money, or provide its employees with better benefits. The people you serve benefit in direct proportion to your ability and skills. The better you are at sales, the more you benefit others—your clients, your family, and the nation's economy.

No one limits your growth but you. If you want to earn more, learn more. That means you'll work harder for a while; it means you'll work longer for a while. But you'll be paid for your extra effort with enhanced earnings down the road.

Most people in this world have jobs and professions—existences—that can't fulfill their potential. The scope of their labor is confined to narrow limits; their toil hinders rather than fosters their growth; they dislike everything about their employment except the sense of security its familiarity has bred in them. So instead of venturing into what they don't know and might love, they allow themselves to be trapped by what they do know and don't like.

Professional salespeople recognize no limits to their growth except those limits that are self-imposed. They know that they can always reach out for more. They know they will grow in direct proportion to their competence. And they have little fear of the unknown in change because overcoming the unknown is their daily work. That's the seventh advantage of being a professional salesperson: It stimulates your personal growth.

To earn more, develop more competence. Study this book's sales skills. Study your product or service. Study your customers and your territory. Keep up with technology—at least those aspects of it that help make you more productive. Practice growing your skills at every opportunity. Do what you know you should do. Follow that program, and you can't fail to push your earnings to a much higher level.

That's my purpose in life—to help you make more money. Please don't let me down—develop more competence, earn more money, get your share of life's good things. Developing competence is the only way. I know many salespeople making several hundred thousand dollars a year, and some making more than a million dollars a year, and I'm always intrigued by the variety of their backgrounds, the diversity of their personalities, and the range of their interests. Yet they have many things in common, foremost of which is this quality: They are competent. They know exactly what they are doing. This book, like my seminars, is aimed at helping you learn how to become competent.

Please notice that I said *learn*.

There's an obstacle to learning how to become competent that we meet with here.

THE MYTH OF THE NATURAL-BORN SALES WONDER

So many of us believe in this that we've come to look on it as an old friend. It's a tempting devil. It lets us avoid taking full responsibility for our own performance. This common fallacy is a destructive idea that I'd like to eliminate from your mind right now.

Having trained more than three million salespeople on five continents, I've met a lot of strong individuals who are on the fast track. I've met with large numbers who haven't put their foot on the lowest rung of their potential yet. And sadly, many of these people never will climb very high on their potential's ladder because they are firm believers in the myth of the natural-born sales wonder.

The myth cuts two ways.

A few believe they're naturals. That's great for confidence, but it's often the source of raging overconfidence. When this overconfidence persuades people that they don't have to bother learning to be competent like ordinary mortals, they trap themselves far below their potential.

Many more people believe they're not naturals, think it's hopeless to work at becoming competent—and trap themselves far below their potential.

"I'm just not a salesperson by nature. Wasn't born with the golden touch like Joe Whizzbeau over there. If I'd been born with his wit, charisma, and bear-hug personality, I could tear 'em up, too. But I wasn't, so I'm never going to make it big in sales."

Don't be too quick to say you're free of this myth. I hear it far too often from my seminar audiences to take it lightly. In fact, I'm convinced that most salespeople who operate far below their potential suffer from it. Let's attack this dangerous idea now and get rid of it.

There never has been a great salesperson who was born great. Imagine a woman in the delivery room. Her newly born infant is saying, "Make yourselves comfortable, folks, and if you have any questions, please feel free to ask me." Pretty silly, isn't it? The little feller has a long way to go before he can even start learning how to walk, talk, and operate without diapers. He's got a lot to learn, and if he's going to be a great salesman, he's got it all to learn. Psychologists still argue whether it's instinct or learning that causes us to jump at a sudden loud noise, but they agree that everything about selling is learned.

So stop excusing yourself from the hard work of learning how to be competent in your sales career. It doesn't matter whether you think you're a wonder or a nonwonder; you still have to pay the learning price.

And you never stop learning and reviewing. Professionals work on the basics once every year. That's where we're going to start.

THE SEVEN BASICS THAT'LL MAKE YOU AS GREAT AS YOU WANT TO BE

What so few of us are willing to accept is this fundamental truth: Great salespeople, like great athletes, simply do the basics very well. Some of us would like to believe that there's a shortcut around the basics; that, if we could only find it, there's a secret formula out there somewhere for just sitting back and letting the money roll in. The sooner you get rid of that illusion, the sooner you can get on with reaching the heights you want to reach through effective use of the basics.

1. **Prospecting.** If you're like most of the people in my seminar audiences, just hearing the word *prospecting* makes you a little nervous. Don't think that way. If you don't like to prospect, it's because no one has taught you the professional way to do it. I'm going to.

2. **Making original contact the professional way.** We all meet new people all the time—in social situations, at events for our children, at church, in nonsales business settings. The key to success in selling is to refine your skills during these initial contacts to become memorable to the other folks and to remember as much about them as possible so you can impress them even more on your second meeting— which, hopefully, will be a selling situation.

3. **Qualification.** Many salespeople spend most of their time talking to the wrong people. If you do that, it doesn't matter how eloquently you present your service or product. Your earnings are going to be low. I'll show you how professionals make sure that they invest their time with the right people who can make yes decisions, instead of expending it on the wrong people who can only make no decisions.

4. **Presentation.** After you qualify and know that this person has a need for your product or service, it's time to move on to the fourth basic, which is the presentation or demonstration. You must present your product in such a way that your prospects see it's just what they had in mind all along.

5. **Objection handling.** The fifth basic method of developing your competence is to learn how to handle objections effectively. Maybe you've had prospects who want to wait and think it over; prospects who already have one of whatever it is you're selling; prospects who've been doing business with your competitor for years. Have you ever heard any of these things? If you've been in sales longer than a week, you undoubtedly have. Read on. You'll find material that'll make you smile the next time you hear these objections. You'll smile, bore in—and close a delightful number of such sales. But there's a price to pay for that smile: You've got to learn the concept, adapt the idea to your offering, and learn the words that make it work.

6. **Closing the sale.** Many average-to-good salespeople prospect, make contacts, qualify, present, and handle objections so well that they manage to get by without learning to close competently. And that, of course, is what keeps them from being great. Closing contains elements of both art and science, and those elements can be learned.

7. **Referrals.** After you've satisfied the needs of your client and closed the sale, you have earned the right to your next prospect. By that I mean getting referral business from each and every client. That is the seventh and final basic. If they're happy, they'll want someone else to be happy, too. I'll teach you simple steps to getting solid, qualified referrals every time, if you're willing to learn.

But many of us have forgotten how to learn, so let's quickly review the steps to learning that apply not only to everything in this book, but to anything you choose to study.

MONEY STUDY: THE LEARNING-TO-EARN-FAST FIVESOME

Money study—I call it that to emphasize how vital it is to learn how to acquire new knowledge quickly and thoroughly. Knowing how to learn fast is the key to rapid personal growth and quick sales success. As adults, it's easy to fall into the habit of skimming over new knowledge, of avoiding any organized effort to grasp and hold new knowledge. That's no good at all. That's how you achieve the status of being average. Superior earning ability grows out of the superior performance that superior learning makes easy. The place to start being superior is to acquire and use a superior learning system. Here it is:

1. Impact. You've noticed that the more you're interested in a subject, the more easily you remember details about it. To learn something with greater thoroughness and speed, first take a few moments to psych yourself up. Dwell on how much the knowledge is going to help you; visualize the benefits you're going to get from possessing it. Form a clear and vivid picture in your mind as to why you're learning this material. Then, each time you start to study it, take just a second or two to recall that vivid picture of the benefits you're seeking. Do that, and you'll intensify the impact of the material, and make it yours faster.

2. Repetition. Repetition is the mother of learning. Repeat anything often enough and it will start to become you. All the great salespeople I know started with words they knew worked. They tailored those words to their own products and services and molded them to their own personalities. Having done that, they proceeded to repeat and review the statements until they controlled those words. Then they delivered them with conviction—and the results they wanted were there.

In four words, *they used repetition effectively.* What is effective repetition? It's far more than bleary-eyed singsong in the middle of the night. Effective repetition means your review is wide-awake and intensive. Effective repetition means you cut the material apart and sew it back together to fit you. Effective repetition means you hear it, write it, read it, and speak it. Effective repetition means you dramatize the material and make it dance in your head. Effective repetition means you pay a good price in an effort to make good material yours.

These first two steps are vital. They're the foundation and the floor of a powerfully constructed selling career. But don't stop when you've completed them—don't even slow down—because you can't live in a house with no walls. Push on immediately to the next step of learning.

I frequently return to cities where I've already given my sales seminar, and on these occasions, I always see dozens of Champions who are coming back through the program again. The ones who tell me they've doubled or quadrupled their incomes say that this happened because they worked energetically through the next step.

3. Utilization. The basic law of possession is *Use it or lose it.* This law applies to all learning, and it applies with special force to sales skills. Use them or lose them.

There's a wonderful truth about skills and knowledge: They don't wear out with use. Quite the contrary. Knowledge takes on greater depth and meaning through hard use; skills become strong and tough through hard use.

And the hard use of sales skills and knowledge is the only road to high earnings. Learning for the mere sake of learning is sterile. It's a form of play. For any kind of learning to have meaning, it must not only be capable of utilization, it must be used. Unused learning is fertilizer left in the sack.

Bring out your skills and knowledge; spread them on the fertile soil of your territory. Let them bloom.

Discover the golden hours when your offering sells best. Then get in front of as many people as possible during that time. Put the strategies, words, and phrases to use. If you use them properly, they'll work. You'll earn money while honing your skills for the next presentation.

Get in front of the executives considering corporate jets, computers, or whatever you're marketing. Meet with the families in need of your appliances. Get into the kitchens of the people now wasting the money they should be ensuring the futures of their loved ones with. Now is the time to use the powerful sales statements you've organized for the benefit of others. You've turned yourself into a sales machine; now turn that machine on. Produce results.

The moment you get into high gear and start using your material efficiently, you'll glimpse your bright new destiny. At that moment, you'll be ready to break out above average and join the ranks of the excellent. You'll be ready to fly higher and farther because of your newly learned abilities. You'll be ready to take the fourth step toward learning and toward greatness.

4. Internalization. This occurs when you've exploited impact, when you've molded the standard material to your needs and made it yours, when you've made your new skills strong through hard use. You've utilized them so efficiently that your first good results generate the energy to accelerate you into superperformance. All of a sudden, these new concepts stopped churning within you and a new reality was born: You and the concepts are one. They have literally become you. You have become them.

I've had Champions bring their spouses to my program to say hello. In a few minutes, the spouse says, "My husband [or wife] sounds just like you."

But it really isn't that way. They aren't hearing their spouses imitate my words and manner of speaking; they're hearing their spouses express themselves with the language of achievement that's common to both of us. We have been using the same techniques. Now we voice the similar experiences of success that have grown out of the shared knowledge we've both internalized.

Internalization is the next-to-last step to completing any learning. When the day comes that you can truly say you've internalized all the concepts of this book, or have internalized all the concepts of any other body of learning you aspire to, then and only then are you capable of greatness with that learning. In the case of the learning we're primarily concerned with here, you'll be capable of going on to greatness in sales—and you'll also be in great danger of sliding back into average performance. That's where step 5 comes in to play.

5. Reinforcement. When you achieve the status of superprofessional salesperson, you'll be tempted to despise the very labors and methods that put you there. When you're still struggling upward, you'll find it easy to say, "Oh, no, not me. When I get there, I won't forget how I did it." But you will, and some of that is good. You don't want to dwell on past difficulties except to laugh about them. Still, the toughest task I have as a trainer always is with the superprofessionals who are slipping. They don't want to believe that the explanation for their troubles is that they've stopped doing what made them superprofessional in the first place. Can there be any other reason for them to slip back into average performance? You might say, Maxie Kwotabuster's sales are down because of his three-martini lunches, because of his three-hour handball games during the golden hours, or because of the manner he's adopted since becoming successful. But when old Max was fighting his way clear of being average, his lunches were businesslike and left him refreshed for an effective afternoon; he guarded his golden hours jealously and used them effectively; he treated people cordially. And you can be sure that when Max was making his first run at success, he found the time necessary to effectively perform all the basic functions of sales work.

When you entered the profession of selling, you learned your product. You learned some sales techniques, you got out there among your potential clients and put your knowledge to work, and you started to make some money. Then all of a sudden, you got smart. You quit doing what your company asked you to do. And you started to slip.

You might finish reading these words, put this book down, and in six months double your income. Then you'll stop doing what I've asked you to do. You'll stop doing the things that caused your income to double. Your income will begin to fall, and you'll wonder why. There's a way to keep that from happening.

Don't stop.

Instead, do what professional athletes do. There's a lot of similarity between the professional athlete and a professional salesperson.

You know that high school teams practice. That doesn't surprise you—the kids have to learn the game. You know that college teams practice. Okay, they're still quite young. But before every season starts, the pros are out there sweating it up. The first string is out there. The star quarterback is out there. He's making a chunk of money but he's running. He's perspiring. He's spending some of his time on new plays, certainly, but most of the time he's drilling on fundamentals. Reviewing the basics. In fact, what's interesting is that the more professional and talented an athlete is, the more that athlete—man or woman—practices and trains. This comes back to that neat little thing called discipline. It calls into play that business of making yourself do what you know you should do.

Jump ahead in your calendar. Put a note there to review this book a year from now. When the time comes, I know there's a good chance you'll say, "I'm not going through that stuff again. I know it. I've milked it for everything it's worth."

I hope you won't say that. I hope you won't limit the effectiveness of your learning. I hope you won't put a ceiling on your income-earning potential. I hope you won't decide to slip back into the quagmire of mediocrity. Reinforce your learning. Do it at least annually. Preserve your hard-won skills. Enhance your knowledge. Add to it.

Reinforce.

Keep your greatness.

Instead of letting your greatness wither, fertilize it regularly to make it grow. You'll find this true of all learning that's important to you: Every time you review the material in depth, you'll see things you never saw before and discover concepts you weren't ready to use before. Whenever you review effective knowledge, you reinforce your previous insights with richer insights.

YOUR PRIMARY TOOL

Let me ask you a question. If the professional golfer uses a club, the tennis player a racquet, and the carpenter a hammer, what do we professional salespeople use?

We use something that's gotten us in lots of trouble, don't we? But is there a pro on the golfing circuit who hasn't used his club to drive the ball into a sand trap? Is there a tennis player who hasn't used the racquet to feed an opponent a sure winner? Is there a carpenter out there who hasn't used a hammer to smack her thumb?

Is there a salesperson who's never used his primary tool to say something that lost an account?

Your primary tool—the opening in your face called a mouth—

must be used with confidence. But it can malfunction. The words you speak can destroy sales as well as create them. That's why you should think of your mouth as a sharp-edged tool that has to be used intelligently if it's going to do you more good than harm. But set reasonable goals. You can't reasonably expect to never say the wrong thing to prospects and clients.

Hitting the ball wrong in tennis is much like saying the wrong thing in sales. Every year at Wimbledon, the eventual winners use their racquets to feed a few easy shots to their opponents, and they lose the point every time they do. But far more often, they use their racquets to hit winning shots for themselves.

In both activities, you can learn to avoid making the common mistakes. But in the profession of sales, you're constantly involved in new and unique situations, which means that you're faced with a steady stream of opportunities to make new and unique mistakes— usually by saying the wrong thing.

The good news is that if you learn enough right things to say, and if you concentrate on warmly saying them to your prospects and clients, there'll be very little time left for saying things you'll regret. And there'll also be less chance that you'll lose any vital point if you do happen to let out an unfortunate remark. Work toward having the relaxed, cheerful, and confident manner that comes from dwelling on what you know you'll say right rather than worrying yourself into a tense, gloomy, and fearful attitude be- cause you've occasionally blundered in your choice of words or topics. Accept the fact that what you say will sometimes come out badly. Then cultivate an honest respect for all people, and learn all the right statements to make. Do that and you'll never cut yourself with the sharp edge of your tongue.

Accentuate the positive through knowledge. That's my program for developing your primary tool into a reliable instrument for win- ning success in the profession of sales.

My life is working with people who have the desire but not the skills to earn more. Usually I work from a seminar stage—just now I'm working in a quiet room on this book—but the object is the same: to deliver that needed training. After I've done that, it's up to you. I know that I can do my part because I've been fortunate enough to have trained thousands of the top salespeople in this country and abroad. They had the desire but not the training or the income. They came to the seminar. They learned the material. They used it daily. And then, all of a sudden, they not only had the desire and the training, but also had the income they wanted.

The highlight of my life comes when people take my training, go out with it and win whatever amount of success they need, and then tell me about it.

Now let me tell you about some of the Champions who've done that. Here's a Champion whose actions may startle you. Until he was eighteen, Robert Burns worked on his father's ranch. It was dependable work, but he wanted more from life than he could lift with a pitchfork, so he decided to enter the profession of selling. He took my training. When Robert celebrated his twenty-third birthday, his sales earnings were headed over the half-million mark for the year. I don't know any better word for it than *excitement*. It's exciting to know that if you learn the material and then go out and do what you know you should do, there's no ceiling on your income. People often tell me that they're too young for sales. Robert Burns wasn't too young. Today, he's a major developer and multimillionaire.

And other people say they're too old. Let me tell you about Gertrude Nunn. I met her years ago, not too long after her former employer had said that she was getting too old for the job and should retire. She walked out, puttered around for a month, and decided that she wanted to be where the action is. Gertrude had no background in sales, but by happy accident she heard about our training and took it. At seventy-five years young, she was earning more than a hundred thousand dollars a year.

Jimmie Walker is another Champion. He started learning about professionally selling insurance when he was sixteen. He dedicated himself to greatness in the field and succeeded. How many people do you know at any age—let alone their early twenties—who earned enough money to acquire a major professional sports team? Jimmie Walker did.

Our next Champion, David Bernstein, became one of the top four in luxury car leasing at a very young age. For years, I've preached the importance of sending thank-you notes, but I'd never seen anyone use this technique more effectively than David Bernstein did. Within a week of meeting him as a prospect, a member of my staff and I received four of these notes from Bernstein, all of them well-written, sincere, personal notes that made a solid impression. David Bernstein, a true Champion.

Aside from being graduates of my training, what do all four of these people have in common?

The twelve characteristics of a Champion are what they all have. In the next chapter, we'll take a careful look at these marks of the Champion.

2. The Twelve Sources of Sensational Selling Success

I'm often asked for personality traits or characteristics of the top people in selling. Those new to selling or veterans wanting to boost their incomes are smart to ask about qualities they can develop within themselves in order to succeed. I've gathered a list of twelve that seem fairly common to those who achieve Champion status in selling. They're interwoven. All twelve overlap. You can't improve in one of these characteristics without helping yourself improve in all the others; you can't ignore one of them without damaging your potential over the whole range. As we cover these twelve areas, think about how you would rate yourself in each area on a scale of 1 through 10, with 10 meaning that you've got it. You don't even need to think about improving in that area. Any trait in which you'd rate yourself less than a 7 will need some thought and dedication to develop.

One. You know the Champions when they walk in the door. Whether they're dressed conservatively, clad in clothes that are ahead of the latest fad, or wearing anything between those extremes, they project the unmistakable stamp of competence with their attire and grooming. Just by looking at them, you know that you're in the presence of a powerful force—people who have a purpose and are ready to carry it out to the fullest. They reflect a sense of unique individuality and a solid consciousness of worth that's far more impressive than mere good looks. Whatever nature gave them and time has let them keep, they've molded into a commanding, memorable appearance.

Two. The Champions we've trained take tremendous pride in the profession of selling and in themselves as human beings. They base that pride on the serious way they've met their responsibilities and capitalized on their potential. They are proud, not only of what they do for a living—helping others—but also of their companies, their products, and the service they provide. And they do this without feeling a need to look down on anyone who is less effective than they are. No one is a Champion without achieving an honest pride.

Three. Champions radiate confidence. If you're new in sales, you might ask, "How can I be confident when I don't know what I'm doing?"

I agree that you should be wary of feeling confident in any situation where you don't have a clear idea of exactly what you're doing. Overconfidence will float you down the river and over the falls nearly every time. If overconfidence is a challenge for you, a few hard drops will quickly put you in step with your knowledge. And there'll be no real harm done; you'll simply get some opportunities to develop your sense of humor and practice your techniques.

Coming down with a permanent sense of underconfidence is another great danger. Potential clients will sense your uncertainty and, even if you do a reasonably good job of presenting your product, buy from someone else. Every day, as you gain skill, you must practice being more and more confident. Remember that your clients and prospects look to you for only the very narrow area of expertise that thorough knowledge of your product or service represents. The people you come in contact with are moved by your belief, by the conviction and confidence you display in your offering. When you finish this training, you'll have every tool necessary to help people make the yes decision, you'll have faith in your worth, and you'll radiate confidence.

Four. The top people close warmly. You may find that confusing, especially if you have any tendency to regard the profession of selling as essentially being the business of separating people from their money.

Let's talk about this idea, because it's out there, and it has some reality to millions of people. It arises from the actions of the minority of salespeople who believe that selling is purely and simply aggression. Eventually, all such vultures will be driven out of sales by the new breed of enlightened salespeople who qualify their prospects, care about their customers, and make sure their clients get benefits from their purchases that outweigh the prices paid.

The change is already in the works. Trained salespeople, who neither want nor need to stoop to unfair practices, are gradually taking the place of the *get-'em-for-all-you-can* crowd. Admittedly, it's a slow process, and we'll wait a long time to see it completed. But it's happening. I'd like to enlist you in fighting the good fight for sales integrity.

We've all heard people say, "I used to sell, but I wasn't pushy enough." The ex-salespeople who say this don't realize they never learned how to prospect, contact, and qualify professionally. In fact, many of them never even learned the sales meaning of the word *qualify*. So, in desperation, they tried to close prospects they knew in their hearts shouldn't be closed on their particular product or service. That made these ex-salespeople feel like crooks. Because they were basically honest people, they had to escape the guilt; instead of getting into sales training, they got out of sales work.

Champions don't have this problem because they never close people they know shouldn't be closed. Champions don't push people with warmth. They are sincere in their desire to help clients have better lives, more fun, save money, or whatever the benefit is that their product or service provides. Their techniques are such that they lead people smoothly to the decision that'll benefit them—with genuine concern and warmth.

Five. Most Champions look to only one person for their self-assurance, and that one person is themselves. They realize that we live in a world where many people really don't care. People are apathetic even about their own welfare beyond immediate satisfactions. Champions know that they can't change the prevailing culture all by themselves. So they float through life without being overwhelmed by problems they can't solve. They concern themselves with helping their customers and their loved ones through the skills they develop in the profession of selling. Many of them are active in other causes as well, but they're always careful to put their efforts into activities where they can be most effective. In everything they do, they believe in themselves and act with assurance.

Six. Champions want to get rich. That's right, rich. Champions want the high income that'll provide the capital for investments to make them financially independent. There's nothing wrong with getting rich as long as the people you serve along the way benefit. True Champions shape their values and organize their lifestyles to achieve their objective of getting rich.

Seven. A quality I can't measure, but I know it's always present in Champions, is the burning desire to achieve. For years, sales managers have said, "If we could only measure how much desire each person has, we'd have the whole problem of selecting salespeople solved. We'd know who'll keep on working despite challenges and disappointments, and who'll sit down and give up. No more sweating it out with capable-looking people who've got all the tools except desire, so in the end they fizzle out." Sales managers think it would be wonderful if they could, but there's no way to measure how much desire another person has. Only you can measure how much desire you have, and here's how you do it. Ask yourself these questions:

How much pain can I handle before I quit?

How many problems can I put up with before I stop, go home, and lie down?

How many no's am I willing to accept on my way to success?

If you have the potential to be a Champion, your answer will be that you don't quit no matter how much pain and how many challenges you encounter, because those things are nothing compared with your desire.

Eight. I've discussed this point before, and I'll discuss it again because it's the very lifeblood of success. Champions learn what their fears are, and often that's not easy since we're all so good at concealing them from ourselves. But the Champions persevere in this. They learn what they fear. Then they attack what they fear, and overcome it. Once they've done that, they radiate the confidence that comes only from overcoming fear.

Nine. A lot of salespeople are only up when everything else is.

Their enthusiasm depends on other people and outside events. Are you that way? If you are, let me ask you to think deeply about why you allow yourself to be knocked this way and that by the fickle fumblings of fate. Why think of yourself as a mere passenger on your voyage through life? You can take the helm and steer any course you choose to anyplace you want to go.

Why should you only feel good when things are going well? That's what the salesperson does whose idea of selling is to stand around until someone comes in and demands to buy. When you're with Champions, you can't tell whether things have gone well or poorly for them the previous hour, day, week, or even month. How can they hide their feelings this way? Well, in the first place, they aren't hiding their feelings. They are excited about life. They know they'll have challenges—if not this week, then next week. They know that over a five-year period, some seasons will be better than others. They live very much in the present but they don't forget that tomorrow is coming right on schedule. They know that no matter whether they're having good or bad luck today, it will change—but what won't change is their superior performance regardless of circumstances. They bring their own sunshine. They make their own luck. They don't let little things bother them. If they have an irate client, they handle it. They solve the problem. Then they move on.

And Champions know that no matter how good they get, they're still going to fail some of the time between their successes. It's all a part of the game we call selling. So they don't have to hide their true feelings while they're failing, because they're still filled with enthusiasm.

Ten. The top people I train get emotionally involved with the folks they serve. Champions really care about their clients, and this true feeling comes through loud and clear to the people they're selling. That's why Champions get so many referrals to other potential clients. I don't think any salesperson ever made much money without a rich flow of well-deserved referrals. I'll show you the techniques to use to get a lot of referrals because most people won't think of these by themselves, but the secret behind the techniques is caring.

When the buyer of your offering sees the cash register behind your eyes ringing up your earnings if he says yes, he'll automatically fight you. He'll see that you care more about making the sale than making him happy. Instead of giving him a powerful emotional reason to want to do business with you—because he can see that you really care about his welfare—you've given him a powerful emotional reason for *avoiding* doing business with you.

You may find this hard to believe, but I've met a few salespeople who hate other people. Out of the millions in sales, there are a few thousand who can't stand their fellow humans. And some of them manage to make fairly good money in this business. But I never knew one who wasn't always scrambling from job to job, because people haters make enemies faster than money. Champions, on the other hand, tend to stay with what they're doing for a long time. And they use some of the generous money they're making to build their clientele. It all comes about because they're experts not only in sales but also in caring.

Eleven. Do you take rejection personally? Maybe a client you're working with—someone to whom you've made your entire presentation—decides to talk to your competitor and says he'll call you next week. Not only does he fail to call you, he doesn't answer the number you have for him. When you find him the following week, he's already bought from your competitor.

Or you meet someone who says, "I'm really interested," and when you arrive a week later for your appointment, she calmly informs you that she's been enjoying another brand of your product since the day after your meeting. Has something like this ever happened to you? If it hasn't yet, keep on plugging—it will.

That's sales. That's the business world.

You can't prevent situations of this kind from happening, but you can train yourself to take them in stride. These prospects haven't rejected you as a person. They've rejected your product. Champions don't take rejection personally.

Twelve. This final characteristic of great salespeople is also true of their companies. They all believe in continuing education. They study technique. They learn new skills. The company managers encourage their salespeople to go to seminars, to listen to educational audio programs, to watch video training programs, and to read books on selling and people skills.

You never have to push Champions to invest in their minds. If you're a Champion, you know that when you put better ideas into your brain, better performance will come out. You know that the place to start improving your environment is inside your own skull. Invest more time, money, and effort into your mind, and finer things will start gravitating to you. You'll take more enjoyable trips, live in a more comfortable and prestigious home, and have more of the goodies that money buys, if that's what you want for yourself. I'm not giving you a new idea. Benjamin Franklin said, "Empty the coins in your purse into your mind and your mind will fill your purse with gold."

WHY YOU CAN'T FAIL

Even though I've seen it happen over and over, I'm still amazed when I return to a city and see the same people sitting there in the front row at my seminars busily taking notes. I had a little fun with this at one of my seminars where about fifteen hundred people were in the audience. A gentleman sitting in the front row looked familiar. I said to myself, *I'll bet he's been here five years in a row.*

I talked to him from the stage and found out that I was right. So I asked him, "Did you bring all your people?"

He said, "Tom, I'm the top salesperson in my company, so you'd think what I say would carry some weight. I told everybody about this seminar and talked it up, but only a few of our people are here— and they're all strong salespeople. It's the same every year; the people who need it most never come."

It's amazing what people choose to spend their money on before investing in themselves. I'm proud of you for investing in this book, but its cost is only a small fraction of the time you'll have to put in if you're going to acquire its knowledge. Although you can get the money you spent for this book back thousands of times over in your sales work, you still have to invest the time to extract its knowledge.

There's no way I can give you that time back. It isn't ever going to be today again. That's why I try to make my message as powerful as possible. That's my obligation, and it's a heavy one. Yours is just as heavy: You have to provide the desire to succeed and the effort to make this training work.

Since you're reading these words, you either already have all the desire you need to succeed, or you want to develop that desire. That's why you can't fail—you want to succeed badly enough to invest time, money, and effort in becoming a more productive person.

But we live in a distracting culture, don't we? There's always something that demands our attention: Monday football, Tuesday TV, Wednesday bowling, Thursday poker, Friday TGIF party, Saturday night fever, Sunday brunch, game, and last fling at the weekend. How do you find time to study the knowledge and practice the skills of competence?

Desire finds the time. It cancels your reservations at the time-blasting spectator sports and puts you on the field playing the most exciting sport of them all when you play it to win: the great game of your life.

Maybe you want to play that game, and play it hard, but you're afraid that you may be a bit deficient in the desire department. That's understandable. Desire is a learned response, but it's one of great and subtle complexity.

HOW TO DEVELOP DESIRE

Here are three methods of developing the burning desire to succeed that can't be denied. They work—if you want them to.

1. The greatest obstacle to developing desire is our conviction that we'll never be able to satisfy it, so the safest course is to discourage the desire and avoid the frustration. John Galbraith calls this process "accommodating to poverty," and points out that people always choose the economic level they'll accept—it's never thrust on them. You are constantly in the process of schooling yourself to accept the level of prosperity that you have, or you are exerting extra effort to get more.

If you've been coasting along on the idea that your ship will eventually get blown into port by itself, this can be scary stuff. A lot of us just aren't willing to face the fact that our ship ain't movin' until we climb aboard, sweat the sails up, and start steering. Many of the Cubans who escaped Castro with nothing in the 1960s are now prosperous. The boat people from Asia who practically swam the Pacific to get to the United States are making it, so what's your excuse?

The fact is that there isn't any excuse for not achieving success in America today. There hasn't been since Peter Minuit traded the Natives for Manhattan. If you don't have a burning desire to better your life, you're cheating yourself and your loved ones with phony excuses. You're choosing a level of life that's poor compared with what you could have with the extra exertion you're capable of. It's all on your shoulders, and there's no way you can shift a bit of the responsibility to anyone else.

I know former migrant farm workers who've come out of the fields and made themselves wealthy. Do you think they did that without first believing they could succeed at something better paying than picking fruit? If your sunshine wants far outstrip your cold morning desire, have a talk with yourself. Then have a lot more talks with yourself. Convince number one that you can succeed— and you will succeed.

2. Focus on the specific things you want. Make agreements with yourself: *If I do this, I get that.* Don't try to make yourself work for nothing.

3. Take it in steps. If you've never made more than the minimum wage, don't aim for half a million the first year. Always aim for the earnings level that excites you a lot and only scares you a little. The essential element is faith in yourself.

You have a deep obligation to yourself and your loved ones. That obligation is to commit yourself to learning the material in this book. Make that commitment, complete it quickly, and then start operating at your full potential. Unless you do this, you won't achieve the quality of life that is within your reach.

SPR IS THE DIFFERENCE BETWEEN
HAVE AND HAVE-NOT

Right now, you're as good as your R's and no better. But your R's might not be very good because you haven't taken a good P yet. The thing is, it's almost impossible to take a good P unless someone gives you a good S.

My job in this book is to give you an eloquent S, and to give it to you with such excitement and enthusiasm that you'll take the P necessary to develop your own effective R's.

Let me explain.

What I just gave you is called the stimulus, pause, and response theory. If you walk into your den tonight and, failing to see your cat, step on its tail, you'll give your cat a stimulus. Your cat will have an immediate response. It won't pause and think, *All right, I'm going to get even later, but first I'd better make a noise and get out from under.* The animal's instant reaction is S–R, stimulus-response.

We humans possess an enormously greater ability to respond to stimuli. We can receive a stimulus, pause to consider what our best response will be, and then respond.

In selling, the pause is essential, even after you've mastered the response to every stimulus. Responding too quickly to a stimulus, such as an objection, clients may get the feeling that you've answered this question many times; that you're too slick. In other words, it may raise doubts in their minds about your motivation for talking with them. So even when you know the answer to an objection right off the top of your head, take a moment to pause before giving it. The pause will make it seem as if you're considering the best answer. That you're with them in the moment—not in the thousand other moments you had to deliver the same answer to the same objection. The pause remains critical after you've mastered the responses.

On a piece of paper, write down the formula for our human reaction: S–P–R.

This stands for stimulus–pause–response. Now draw an arrow

from the P straight down, and write three words that can make the difference for you, three words that can make your pauses effective:

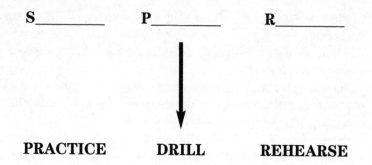

S_____   **P**_____   **R**_____

PRACTICE   **DRILL**   **REHEARSE**

At anything you choose to do, you'll be as good as the practice, drill, and rehearsal you go through before you actually perform the action. The toughest thing I have to do with new salespeople is to convince them that if they don't know what they're going to say and do until they're in front of the customer, it's too late.

Salespeople like to wing it. That is to say, average salespeople like to wing it. Champions like to make money. So they don't wing it—they prepare. Intensively.

One of the reasons many new salespeople think they can wing it and win has to do with the faulty image they have of the sales process. They think of the selling situation as a slow-paced affair where there's plenty of time for telling jokes, chatting about sports and the weather, and winging their way through any unexpected challenges. What these new salespeople don't realize is that, even in such a leisurely interview, the brass-tacks business part of it goes very, very fast.

And some purchasing agents are notorious for keeping the trivia going with any salesperson they don't know and favor in order to avoid hearing the presentation. Many buyers will do that. If you sell a product or service that's regularly bought by a purchasing agent—industrial supplies, for example—you can be sure that some of those agents have favorite salespeople they work with. Unless you develop a unique, interest-catching plan to beat that game before you walk in the door, the favorite players will finesse you every time.

I am not a great tennis player. I understand the game and played a good bit when I was younger, but haven't played in several years now. Imagine what would happen to me if I went on the court with a tennis pro after saying I was going to beat him.

I'd plop my serve over and back it would come, headed wherever I'm not. I'd see the ball coming and think, *Okay, hustle over there and hit it backhand.* By that time, of course, the ball and the point would be long gone. I received an expected stimulus, but had to pause to think about how to respond. By the time I came up with the right response, the moment had passed.

Considering the sorry state of my preparation, my response may have been quick, but it wasn't anywhere near quick enough. The difference, of course, is that the tennis pro has hit ten thousand balls for every one I've hit. The pro has conditioned responses to tennis situations that I do not have.

But let's say we can roll back time to the first day that tennis pro ever hit a tennis ball and end his tennis career right there—he takes up swimming instead, while I go out for professional tennis. Never mind how well or badly I'd do on the pro circuit, I still hit ten thousand balls for every one the fellow who took swimming instead of tennis does. Then put us on the same court today. I've been engaged in tennis full-time for many years, and he's been swimming all those years. He hardly knows a racquet from a banjo. What would happen? I'd blow him off the court, natural ability notwithstanding. The point is that thorough preparation, including psyching up and confidence building, is the decisive factor in the overwhelming majority of cases. In sports, in sales, anywhere, superior preparation rarely tastes defeat.

What factor is common to all types of superior preparation?

Speed.

Superior preparation develops reflexive responses. When you respond reflexively, the quality of your response automatically improves. This doesn't happen only because your responses always come quick enough to count; in addition, you're not rushed, so you have time to choose your best response and to deliver it smoothly. And while you're doing that, you'll also have time to think about your next move. If you're trying to wing it, you simply can't keep up.

Champions collect sales objections. They like to hear them from other strong salespeople, read them in books, and think them up themselves. They enjoy finding new objections anytime—except when they're with customers. And you can be sure that as fast as the Champions find new objections, they develop their best responses to them. But they don't stop there. They practice, drill, and rehearse their best responses. Before they ever hear the new objection in a sales situation, they're ready to instantly fire their best answer at it because they've practiced, drilled, and rehearsed the answers to all the objections they have already heard. That's professionalism. That's the type of thinking and action that brings in the big money.

Along about now, you may be wondering, "If it's that simple, how come every salesperson in the world hasn't already succeeded?"

The theory is simple, but its application is demanding, specialized for every product or service, and in a constant state of evolution. You don't just learn a few objections, memorize the answers, and then turn your mind off the subject of objection–response forever. Constant alertness for new objections and for better responses to old objections marks the Champion.

Could your prospects say any of these things about your product or service?

- "Three years ago we tried it [or, we had one of those], but we were disappointed at how it worked out."
- "You know, we're just not the type of people who jump into decisions like this. Your camera is great; we love it; but we're going to look around."
- "Your price is too high."

Now, you can look at those common objections and say, "Someday I'll make a study of how to respond to them, but for now I'm getting by all right winging it. When I'm in front of the customer, the adrenaline's going, and sometimes I come up with some real good stuff."

Sure you do. That's why you're breaking all those sales records. Oh, you aren't breaking any sales records? Then possibly one reason you're not is that you're winging (improvising) your responses to objections instead of practicing, drilling, and rehearsing them. No one ever became great in sales without first becoming great at handling objections.

When you turn pro (which means that you decide to stop playing the game for free, and go for the prize money), you come up with an effective response to objections without pausing or thinking.

In the chapter on objections, I'm going to give you proven responses to the basic objections that are common to a wide range of sales situations. Then, after you're through with practicing, drilling, and rehearsing your responses to those standard objections, you'll be familiar with the method. You'll be able to devise effective responses for the objections that are unique to your offering at this time in your territory.

Work these standard objection responses thoroughly. You hear most of them every day of your sales career. If you've never studied them, you must still be unaware that all successful sales interviews follow the pattern shown in this diagram:

THE PURCHASE PATH

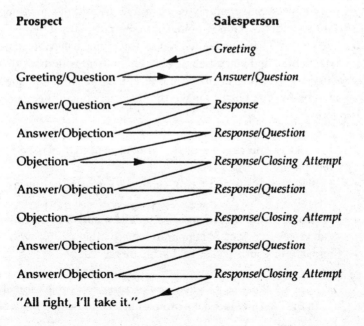

Prospect	Salesperson
	Greeting
Greeting/Question	*Answer/Question*
Answer/Question	*Response*
Answer/Objection	*Response/Question*
Objection	*Response/Closing Attempt*
Answer/Objection	*Response/Question*
Objection	*Response/Closing Attempt*
Answer/Objection	*Response/Question*
Answer/Objection	*Response/Closing Attempt*
"All right, I'll take it."	

Of course, the diagram is highly simplified. The greeting phase, for example, might include lengthy getting-acquainted small talk to establish rapport. Unless you're selling something over a counter, you'll have to ask more questions and respond well to many more objections than I've shown. But the essential elements are there, and it's the concept that's important. It expresses the simple essence of sales. The function of the professional salesperson is to know what a prospect might ask or object to, what information and responses will best meet the expected questions and objections, and what closes will guide the prospect toward approving the purchase. It boils down for a while to them saying this, you answering that, and then they walk out carrying the camera you've persuaded them was just right for them. Why did that happen?

Because you learned exactly what they would say and what you should say.

And that brings me back to the importance of practice, drill, and rehearsal. The techniques that have worked for more than a million salespeople are in this book. The objections and responses. The closes. But you can't just read through them and expect to apply this mass of material smoothly when you're in front of a customer in his office with the phone ringing, or in your display room talking to a husband and wife while their kids are scuffling. Give this material a quick read and you won't be able to come up with more than a fraction of it during even the most relaxed and uninterrupted sales interview. You have to make the material yours. This means that you:

- Practice the precise words that you'll use until they're second nature.
- Drill yourself on delivering them with clarity and conviction.
- Rehearse delivering them in as lifelike a situation as you can create, working in cooperation with other people who care about your success in this business.

When you've done that, when you've prepared professionally, you'll earn the high income that a professional commands—because when you're in front of buyers and they give you a stimulus, you give back the immediate response that moves you toward closing the sale. You'd like to do that, wouldn't you?

Then do it. It's just that simple. Prepare professionally and you'll earn a professional's income. But don't delay. Make a strong start today.

These words sound familiar, don't they? They've been used over and over for many products and services to present benefits that will help people achieve their goals. You've invested your hard-earned money in my book, but now will you own my concepts? Will you invest the time and effort that's required if you're to make them yours?

It's your life and your decision. I hope you'll make the right one.

3. Question Right and Sink Your Teeth into Sales Success

One of the things I find in most salespeople is that they have a tendency to talk too fast, too much, and try to control every conversation. That's probably where the stereotypical image of a salesperson as pushy originated. Champion sales professionals are just the opposite. They understand that God gave us two ears and one mouth and that those two organs should be used in that proportion. To be successful in selling, you need to learn to listen twice as much as you talk.

As we get into the types of questions professional salespeople use, it's important that you realize why you need to master questioning skills.

TWELVE POINTERS ON QUESTION TECHNIQUE

First, you ask questions to gain and maintain control. Rather than letting potential clients take control of the conversation and provide important details in a random fashion, you gain and maintain control of the selling situation by asking questions that help you determine the best solution to the clients' needs. Your questions must build on one another so the clients will follow your lead.

Second, you ask questions to indicate the broad areas they are interested in where you might be of service. You ask more questions to isolate the narrow area that is your best opportunity to serve them. Then you ask more questions to pinpoint the exact item you can provide, or the specific service you can render.

Third, you ask questions to get the minor yeses that will start the stream of minor agreements that will swell into the major river of acceptance of your proposition. If you get enough minor yeses, it will be tough for buyers to change course and say no to your product when it's time to make the final decision.

Fourth, you ask questions to arouse and direct their emotions toward the purchase. Chapter 4 covers this in detail.

Fifth, you ask questions to isolate objections. Only in rare cases will a qualified and properly handled prospect voice all the standard objections to your offering; only a few objections will occur to, or be important to, any one client. By isolating the objections that are important to an individual client, and by handling those objections in a professional manner, the Champion knows that a qualified client won't continue to come up with objections until every one ever dreamed of has been voiced. There will almost always be some objections. Knowing that, the Champion seeks them out with eagerness instead of avoiding them with fear.

Sixth, you ask questions to answer objections. Unquestionably, the finest way to answer an objection is with a question that, when the client answers it, affirms that the objection is of no consequence—or even is an advantage to the client.

Seventh, you ask questions to determine the benefits that the prospect wants to own. Yes, that's right, benefits. People don't really buy products and services; they buy the benefits they expect to receive by owning those products or services.

Eighth, you ask questions to acknowledge a fact. If you say it, they can doubt you; if they say it, they must believe it to be true.

Ninth, you ask questions that will confirm that (a) they are going ahead, and (b) you should now go on to the next step in your selling sequence.

Tenth, you ask questions that involve them in ownership decisions about your offering.

Eleventh, you ask questions to help your clients rationalize decisions that they want to make. You do this because *you* want them to make those decisions, too. Aren't we all looking for someone to tell us that we need that fancy new car, that we deserve the bigger house, that we'll benefit from and be complimented on that new four-hundred-dollar dress or suit? When we see that new electronic marvel, that glittering gadget, that sleek boat, aren't we hoping someone will come along and explain to us how necessary it is that we have it? Don't we all want someone to help us rationalize our desires and work out the logic that will prove our desires are sound? When our emotions shout, *I want it*, don't we all crave support? Yes, ask questions to help your clients rationalize the decisions they want to make—and also make clear and firm statements to that effect.

Twelfth, you ask the questions that close them on the purchase. All the closes in chapter 17 depend on your question-asking ability for their potency. Don't make the mistake of concentrating solely on what you're going to *tell* clients. Don't overlook the vital importance of asking the right questions, and varying your methods to fit their answers.

QUESTIONING 101—THE BASICS

Before you ask anyone a question, be sure it's a question they'll know the answer to. If they don't know the answer, they may feel threatened by it and you. For example, if you help people make buying decisions on computers, don't assume they know every bit and byte of information about computers. Begin by asking them questions that will be easy for them to answer. "Jim, most people who are looking for a laptop do so because they move around a lot. Do you travel mostly in town where it will be with you in your car, or will you be primarily taking it on airplanes?" He'll know that answer. If you had asked, "What weight of machine were you looking for?" "What type of carrying case will you need?" Jim may have not known because he doesn't even know what the choices are.

There are basically two types of questions to ask: open and closed.

Open questions. Open questions are those that require thought on the part of the person you're asking. They have to think about their responses. Remember in school the WWWWWH questions that teachers wanted answered in reports? Who, what, when, where, why, and how. That's what we're talking about here.

When you ask a question beginning with one of those words, prospects can't give you a quick or reflex answer. They have to think and give you some bit of information that will be helpful to you in your sales presentation.

"Who will be using the new laptop the most in your household, Mr. Johnson?"

"What is the most important feature you need this new machine to have?"

"When would you expect to have the new unit installed?"

"Where do you see yourselves spending your retirement years?"

"Why are you interested in replacing the old air conditioner just now?"

"How do you see this machine impacting your business?"

Because they require thought and get the conversation going, you need to build at least two or three open questions into your presentation. Depending on your product, you might need to use all of the W's.

Take a moment right now to jot down at least six open questions as they relate to your product or service. It's best to think about the answers you need to get in order to write the question in just the right manner.

Closed questions. Closed questions are aimed at getting a specific answer. Normally, the answers to closed questions are fairly short. They could even be simple yes-or-no questions, the answers to which allow you to move the sales process forward. There are several types of closed questions that work effectively in selling situations. Let's review them now.

THE STANDARD TIE-DOWN

A tie-down is a question at the end of a sentence that demands a yes. The tie-down is hung on the end of the sentence, as in: "Fuel economy is very important today, isn't it?"

If what you said represents truth as prospects see it, won't they respond by agreeing? And when they agree that some quality of your product or service meets their needs, they've moved closer to buying it, haven't they? When you say, *Isn't it?* smile warmly and gently nod your head yes. Since it's not a threatening question in any way, shape, or form, prospective buyers will likely agree with their own nod or yes answer.

Here are eighteen standard tie-downs that you'll find useful:

Aren't they?	Don't we?	Isn't it?
Aren't you?	Shouldn't it?	Isn't that right?
Can't you?	Wouldn't it?	Didn't it?
Couldn't it?	Haven't they?	Wasn't it?
Doesn't it?	Hasn't he?	Won't they?
Don't you agree?	Hasn't she?	Won't you?

There are others, of course. Put them nicely on the ends of your sentences and you'll gather thousands of minor yeses. Selling is the art of asking the right questions to get the minor yeses that allow you to lead your prospect to the major decision. It's a simple function, and the final sale is nothing more than the sum total of all your yeses.

Now, to succeed with this strategy, I want you to work with me. Professional salespeople do many things at once. While delivering their presentation, they're thinking about upcoming benefits and objections and reviewing what has already been said to build on it for the rest of the presentation. The whole process flows smoothly. In order to reach that level of operation, you need to make this strategy natural to your speech pattern.

Start reading the sentences below and, as quickly as you can, write the appropriate tie-down on the blank line. Then read the sentences out loud to yourself. Do this exercise before a mirror, checking from time to time to make sure that you're nodding sympathetically as you say the tie-downs. Professionals do more than one thing at a time, don't they?

Here are the tie-down exercise sentences:

"Many progressive companies are using wireless computer systems today, _____?"

"Family security is something we're all concerned with, _____?"

"They're fun, _____?"

"It just takes practice, _____?"

"They're coming out naturally, now, _____?"

"Quality is important, _____?"

"You'd like to retire and dine on the delicacies of civilization someday, _____?"

"We've got to learn how to do several things at once, _____?"

"After you've practiced awhile, the tie-downs certainly pop out, _____?"

"Over a period of time, you could develop hundreds of questions that will lead your clients toward the decision to enjoy the benefits of your product or service, _____?"

"At any time, Champions should be able to write fifteen tie-down questions for their offering, _____?" *(Even though you'd never use fifteen in one single presentation.)*

"She's chosen some lovely colors, _____?"

"This will add nicely to your investment portfolio, _____?"

"Safety is an important consideration for all of us, _____?"

"You're doing this exercise well, _____?"

That's the standard tie-down. Before we go on to the other types, be sure to take a solid grip on this idea:

Wait for buyers' positive stimulus before using tie-downs.

If you tie them down without waiting for the positive stimulus, you could tie them down to a negative factor. For example, my product is office copiers and I have an appointment with the office manager of Makebux Corporation.

I've decided to sell one of my company's new SuperPow models to Makebux. Not only does the SuperPow make great copies fast, it also separates and collates fast. I want to sell this model because (a) it carries a bonus, (b) it gives me extra points in the sales contest, (c) there isn't a single SuperPow in that part of my territory, and I'm certain that getting one into Makebux will break the ice. All these reasons are excellent ones, but they're my reasons, not theirs.

When I drive into their parking lot after a long trip, the only copier I have in the back of my van is a SuperPow. I don't need any other because I'm going to sell them that model. I've already made the decision: They're going to buy it. Not only do I have the Super-Pow strapped to an easy, roll-in transporter, I also have a beautiful presentation folder titled, "What SuperPow Will Do for the Make-bux Corporation." I'm supercharged for SuperPow. I'm gonna do it.

As soon as the interview gets started, I say, "You want a copier that doesn't just make copies like all the rest, don't you? You'd like one that also separates and collates while it copies, wouldn't you?"

The office manager shakes her head. "No, we never collate anything in this building. Our subsidiary across the street has a complete printing plant that does that for us. All we want here is a compact, trouble-free machine that just makes high-quality copies."

See how I've destroyed myself?

I didn't ask, I told. I didn't wait for the prospect's positive stimulus before committing myself totally to the one course that raced me straight for the Dumpster. Professionals close on the *buyer's* positive stimulus, not on their own positive stimulus. As badly as I need to place a SuperPow in that part of my territory, as much as I want to win that sales contest, as fervently as I desire that bonus, Makebux isn't going to buy a SuperPow. In half the time I spent selling nothing, I could have closed them on our desk model, the SuperPup.

I could have done that had I only ascertained their needs on the phone before the appointment. If that wasn't desirable or possible, I should have structured my presentation so I could switch to whatever model did meet their needs.

THE INVERTED TIE-DOWN

For variety and for more warmth, I recommend using the tie-down in an inverted position. With this strategy, you put the tie-down at the beginning of the sentence to suggest a yes. Before you decide that this is too simple to practice, consider that I'm talking here about the habits of speech you'll make a career of using in the fast and demanding arena of sales. A good mixture of the four tie-down types won't find its way into your sales presentations by accident. Champions use all four types smoothly, and without lessening any of their concentration on the client. Such a high level of skill demands rehearsal.

Use the tie-down exercise sentences on pages 36 and 37 for inverted form practice. Read through them quickly, recast each sentence as you go, and say it aloud in inverted form. Sometimes changing an extra word or two helps to smooth the sentence out. The first example is, "Many progressive companies are using wireless computer systems today, aren't they?" That inverts to "Aren't a lot of progressive companies using wireless computer systems today?" Try it with the rest to smooth out your delivery.

THE INTERNAL TIE-DOWN

The smoothest way to hide a tie-down is to drop it into the middle of a complex sentence. This is much easier than it sounds. Let's spread one example over three forms.

Standard form, with the tie-down last: "Once you get the feel of it, you can really control it well, can't you?"

Inverted form, with the tie-down first: "Can't you really control it well once you get the feel of it?"

Internal form, with the tie-down in the center: "Once you get the feel of it, can't you really control it well?"

Another variation on the internal form is more obviously a tie-down: "You really can control it well, can't you, once you get the feel of it?"

To change any simple tie-down sentence into the internal form, all you need to do is hang a phrase on the beginning or end of it. Take the shortest of the tie-down exercise sentences: "They're fun, aren't they?" Hook a phrase on the front, and you've got a complex sentence and an internal tie-down:

"When you get used to them, aren't they fun?"

This isn't a difficult technique, and using it will keep your tie-downs hidden. Practice with the tie-down exercise sentences. Run through them, recasting each one as a complex sentence with the tie-down coming in the middle of, before, or after the phrase you've added. Many of these phrases will bear some relation to time:

"Now that we've eliminated that challenge, aren't you glad . . ."

"Next week when you take delivery, isn't your wife going to be delighted that . . . ?"

"Once you have this new model in your home, can't you just see . . ."

"In these days of heavy inflation, aren't you happy that you chose to . . ."

"When you . . ."

"After we . . ."

"Since you're planning to keep your next _____ a long time, won't it be great that . . ."

Practice, drill, and rehearse fifteen tie-down questions of your own creation. Then go on to fifteen more. Keep a good mixture of all three types. You'll soon find that tie-downs have become an effortless speech habit that's lifting your sales, your spirits, and your bank account.

THE TAG-ON TIE-DOWN

Our last tie-down technique is used in a variety of ways. In its simplest form, you tag your tie-down onto any statement your prospect happens to make that's positive to the sale.

PROSPECT: "Quality is important."
YOU: "Isn't it?"

He said it, so it's true. Every time prospects say something helpful to the sale, if you tie it down, you get a minor agreement. Don't you?

The tag-on technique is especially effective in tying down helpful points with strong-willed prospects who want to dominate the discussion. Ignore every statement they make that's negative to the sale unless you're forced to correct some misinformation they have. Concentrate on guiding the prospect into making positive statements that you can tag a tie-down on.

PROSPECT: "Your models are too boxy looking."
YOU: *(avoid agreeing with the negative statement)* "You've been looking at our standard line, sir. If you'll step over

here, I'd like to get your opinion on our new Barrier-
buster."

PROSPECT: "Now, that's what I call style."

YOU: "Isn't that right? Tell me, do you get the same feeling I do
seeing it sit there?"

PROSPECT: "Yeah, it looks like the speed of light just holding
your floor down."

YOU: "Doesn't it? How do you think it would handle?"

PROSPECT: "Well, I don't know—but I'd like to find out."

How you proceed with the prospect from this point depends on
whether you've already qualified him and on your policy regarding
demonstrations. However, by skillfully using tie-downs to set up
tagalong questions, you've been able to get three minor agreements
and put yourself in scoring position. That's coming a long way fast.

TAGALONG QUESTIONS

A tagalong question is something you ask about a remark made
by the client that allows you to carry the comment farther toward
the sale. Here's an example of tagalong questions working off tag-
on tie-downs. When the prospect comes into your showroom, the
matter of color immediately comes up.

PROSPECT: "I like green."

YOU: "Isn't green a wonderful color? We're offering a choice
of three new shades of green on our latest models. Which
do you prefer, Bali Mist, Irish Sea, or Acapulco Spring?

PROSPECT: "I go for Bali Mist. It looks like the most restful
shade."

YOU: "Doesn't it?"

Continue with another tagalong question that'll lead your prospect
closer to purchasing your product. Use any conversation to practice
setting up tagalong questions. Casual talk is great for this purpose.
And don't overlook the splendid opportunity you get to sharpen your
techniques every time you buy something for yourself.

THE ALTERNATE OF CHOICE

The alternate of choice is a question that suggests two answers, both of which confirm that your prospect is going ahead. The answer to your alternate of choice question gives you a minor agreement leading toward the major decision. It's best used for time of appointment, location, installation date, type of investment, and money amounts.

If, instead of asking an alternate of choice question, you ask one that suggests a yes-or-no answer, which will your prospect usually pick?

If you're like 99.9 percent of my students, the client will pick no.

We have something in common here—we all think it's easier and safer to say no than it is to say yes. That's why the professional uses the alternate of choice method to avoid asking questions that put "no" into the prospect's mouth.

In most kinds of sales work, it's almost impossible to make the sale without first making the appointment with the buyer. Generally speaking, more appointments mean more sales—will you agree with that?

So it's vital that you don't lose appointments unnecessarily, and get stopped before you can start. That's why the professional never asks, "Could I come by this afternoon?"

What answer does that suggest to most buyers? "No, I've really got a heavy schedule today. I'll call you when I have more time." Yes, he will. Sure.

A professional gives two options: "Mr. Johnson, I'll be in your area this afternoon. Which would be more convenient, should I stop by around two o'clock, or would you prefer that I wait until about three?"

When he says, "About three would be better," you have the appointment. You got it by suggesting two yeses instead of a no that he would have jumped on.

These alternate of choice questions are beautiful. If you were to use this question form as a closing tool, we would then call it the alternate advance. It would be advancing your presentation toward the close, not just confirming an appointment or helping the buyer choose a color. It's called the alternate advance when you are asking for a deposit or establishing a delivery date or any other detail that is required in order to close the sale.

"Mr. and Mrs. Johnson, we have to set up a delivery date. Which would best suit your plans, the first or the fifteenth?"

"Oh, we need it by the first." When they say that, they own it, don't they?

If your sales require some type of deposit, don't ask them how much of a deposit they'd like to give you. Put it in the form of an alternate advance. You have to design the question to fit your product and company policy.

If you were selling jets, you could say, "What type of deposit would you like to give me?"

The old boy might show you a picture of Abe Lincoln and say, "Well, I've got a fast five bucks here. Gimme the plane."

You have to structure all of this material to your product. You'd probably say, "As you know, we have a substantial purchase here. Which would you prefer, a 5 or a 10 percent deposit?"

What are they going to leap on?

Five percent.

Hopefully, that's what you wanted. If not, rewrite the question. So the alternate advance is any question that gives your prospects two alternatives, but neither of them is no. Both alternates confirm that they are going ahead.

Suppose you provide one of the most fantastic services there is to sell: insurance. After all the publicity this product has had over the last century, it's astonishing that average folks still don't know they need insurance. The main reason they don't know is that they've never met a professional insurance salesperson who could help them understand and make the right decision.

If I were sitting in front of you (and had fully done everything you're learning in this course), I would smile and say, "Mr. Johnson, will your wife be the beneficiary, or do you have a family trust?"

That's an alternate advance. If he says, "I want my wife to be the beneficiary," he now owns the insurance that he needs. The alternate advance—either way, they go ahead with the purchase of your product or service.

THE PORCUPINE TECHNIQUE

Of the minor closes, this is the most potent. Imagine a little porcupine snuffling around in the brush with all its sharp, long quills sticking out. If somebody put one in a sack and threw it at you, what would you do?

You'd throw it right back.

The porcupine is the technique of answering a prospect's question with a question of your own that maintains your control of the interview and allows you to lead into the next step of your selling sequence.

You may ask, "Won't prospects be annoyed unless I give them specific answers to their questions?"

Here's my porcupine answer: "Why are you so fearful of annoying prospects when your main concern should be to help them make wise buying decisions so they can enjoy the benefits of your offering?"

In any type of sales work, you'll constantly encounter questions that you can answer yes or no—and have nothing. You'll also constantly be asked to give information that you can give—and have nothing. In both products and services, "When can we get it?" is a common question, one that's usually perfect for throwing the porcupine back to the buyer.

PROSPECT: "Could I take delivery by the first of the month?"

You can answer, "Oh, sure, that's no problem," and have nothing. What do the pros do when a prospect asks this question?

They smile and say, "Does taking delivery by the first of the month best suit your needs?" Professionals answer in this way because they know that if the prospect says yes, the sale is made.

Believe it or not, some prospective buyers aren't looking for rapid delivery. Maybe they want to delay or spread out their investment and avoid the costs of warehousing or installing your product until the last possible moment. If so, the porcupine will smoke out their true feelings about delivery, won't it?

Let's look at two more porcupines:

PROSPECT: "Will this insurance policy have a cash value?"
YOU: "Is having cash value in the policy important to you?"
PROSPECT: "Definitely not. I don't want to pay anything extra for cash value."

Isn't it vital to find out things like that? With this prospect, if you go on selling cash value as though she understands its worth, you're going to sell yourself down the river. Cash value isn't something that this person will pay money for because she doesn't see it as a benefit. Make her a satisfied client. Sell her term. But the prospect may say, "Cash value is a necessity as far as I'm concerned." Then you know how to shape the rest of your presentation, don't you?

PROSPECT: "Can we get this one in pink?"
YOU: "Would you like it in pink?" Or, "Is pink the color that best suits your decorating scheme?"

The Champion understands how warmly the porcupine can be used, and how important it is to ask the porcupine questions with an air of friendly interest. The value of the porcupine is destroyed if it's overused, if it's thrown back at the prospect in a challenging put-up-or-shut-up tone. But if you use the porcupine with discretion, it'll coin a lot of gold for you.

THE INVOLVEMENT QUESTION

You may already be using this question regularly without realizing that this is an important technique with a name and a long history of success. If the involvement question came to you naturally, that's great. Let your previous success with it encourage you to work this winning method even harder. Design involvement questions into all your sales interviews and you'll find yourself in more closing situations.

What is an involvement question?

An involvement question is any positive question about the benefits of your product or service that buyers ask themselves after they own it.

In other words, an involvement question is an ownership question. You're taking them mentally into the future, to a place where they own the product. If they respond positively to an involvement question, they're seeing themselves owning it. When your clients ask an involvement question before they own your product or service, they confirm that they're going ahead. Let's try this on a business owner who is considering the purchase of a three-million-dollar jet aircraft from you.

"Mr. Kirkham, do you think you'll be using the plane for your own employees only, or would you possibly consider leasing it out?"

That's an alternate advance, isn't it? But on another level, it's an involvement question. Mr. Kirkham can reduce his cost of ownership considerably by chartering the aircraft out when it isn't needed for his own operations. You want him to be fully aware of this option before he makes his decision on the purchase, and you also want him to be thinking ownership thoughts.

Involvement questions can be created for every product and every service. You have both a challenge and an obligation to develop involvement questions for your offering—a challenge because not every product lends itself to this technique with ease; an obligation because you can't operate at your most effective level unless you create involvement questions to help your prospects own your product or service.

Your opportunity with the involvement question and all the other techniques in this book is to create something you can acquire wealth with—a set of skills that you enhance with your God-given talents and personal wisdom. Put the stamp of your unique personality on your sales methods. Create, take your creations to the people—and grow rich.

MAKING THESE STRATEGIES YOURS

When you read my words, my tie-downs, my involvement questions, my versions of the classic closes, don't sit there in your chair and tell yourself, *I couldn't say those lines. I couldn't use those words. They just aren't me.* Of course they aren't. You must be willing to take the strategy and write out what does work for you, and for your product. If you read my words and think you'd have to say it differently, that's great. That means you think there are better ways of saying more effective things, and stronger points to be made.

One of the great challenges in training salespeople—and perhaps in all education—is to provide an effective framework of techniques, theories, methods, and knowledge without stifling the creativity of those who learn. It's a challenge that's often not met, and the reason it isn't lies as much with the trainees as it does with the trainers. Most of us, when we approach a learning situation, want two incompatible things:

- We want to be shown exactly what's the right way, the best way, the only way, to do what we're studying.
- We don't want to have any rigid system forced on us just because we put ourselves in the learning mode.

Think about that. From this book, you want to learn exactly how to master the art of selling what you sell, but you don't want to parrot someone else's words in sales situations where those words aren't natural to you.

At times, you might think it would be terrific if everything could be spelled out for you in sixty simple steps to sales success. But you know that if such a thing could be done—if folks could read a book and become top-earning salespeople without deeply and intensely involving their own backgrounds and talents, and their own originality, drive, and enthusiasm—then anyone could do it. Effective sales work would become as poorly paid as day labor.

You don't want to be like me, to talk like me, or to sell like I do. You want to be you, talk like you, and sell like you. The power and the satisfaction of acquiring new knowledge and new skills lies in putting your own mark on them. That's my goal in writing this book, to have you tell yourself, *Now I've got the techniques and the concepts that'll allow me to become a professional. I'm going to write my own words for those techniques and make them mine.*

If you're sincere about becoming an effective high earner in sales, you'll create your own finished product of effective sales methods from the raw material that's in these pages.

The process is simple. Learn my words, embed these concepts in your mind, and then develop that material into your own special systems for success. When you learn the material that's in these pages, you've made a good beginning at becoming a Champion. So you've got a challenge to go much farther. Learning these minor closes is just the start of the process of making them your own.

MAKE TWO RIGHT TURNS TO SALES SUCCESS

Many salespeople who haven't yet reached the professional stage think professional selling is exactly the opposite of what it really is. When you entered the selling field, you may have thought, *Now my job is to talk and talk and talk.*

So off you go. "Here it is, folks. Won't ravel, rust, or rip. Can't blister, break, or drip. Oh, you're going to love it. You'd better buy it right now."

The professional salesperson, the true Champion, realizes that people have two ears and one mouth, and each should be used equally. This means that after talking for ten seconds, you switch your mouth off, switch your ears on, and listen for twenty seconds. This means that instead of overwhelming your prospects with words, you encourage them to talk. Let's compare the two methods.

Average salespeople speaking:

- "This is the best there is. Nothing on the market can touch it. We've got the best products because we're miles ahead of the competition. You'd better get it."
- "This insurance will do more for you than anything else you can find. You'd really better hurry and get it."
- "These items are on sale. Why waste your time shopping around? You can't get them for less."

When "salespeople" use such methods, what are they doing?

They're pushing, aren't they? They're arguing. They're telling people things they might not want to hear. They're trying to ram obviously self-serving statements down the throats of potential buyers. In effect they're saying, *I'm out to make you buy something. The only reason I'm doing that is to put money in my pocket, and I don't care whether what you buy helps you or not.*

Such tactics quickly drive off everyone except the few who love to argue.

Professional salespeople, on the other hand, never give prospects the impression that they're pushing—for the simple reason that they never push. But they do lead.

By not talking all the time, by listening most of the time, by asking artful questions, Champions lead their prospects from the initial contact to happy involvement in owning the product or service. In all this alert and pointed questioning, true professionals maintain a friendly attitude of interest and understanding that encourages prospects to open up and give the desired information freely.

Have you ever bought something from a professional salesperson? You may never have had this experience because truly professional salespeople are in short supply—which is another reason why they earn large incomes. If you did buy something from a true professional (before you got into sales yourself), you may not have realized it. That salesperson was so smooth, relaxed, and skillful that you merely felt you were working with someone who was well informed and friendly. But a Champion? That thought probably didn't occur to you.

Have you ever been surprised at how freely you've talked to certain salespeople before buying from them? They were alert and interested; you felt comfortable with them. Recalling those conversations, you may think that you were leading and the salesperson was following. Superficially, that was true—at first. In a deeper sense, however, that professional salesperson was leading all the way and you were following all the way.

How did that happen?

Having a variety of products or services to offer you, pros encourage you to start off. Once you set your direction, they get smoothly in front and begin to lead you toward any of several open paths to a purchase. When artful questioning reveals which of the several paths is best, pros guide you smoothly and warmly to it. The halter goes over your head so softly that you never think about bucking. Instead, you buy.

USE BOTH BARRELS: DISCOVERY QUESTIONS AND LEADING QUESTIONS

Professional salespeople use two basic types of questions: discovery questions and leading questions.

And of course, these highly skilled professionals often ask a single question that both leads their prospect *and* discovers more information. They can do that because they are fully aware of the dual role their questioning must play if the sales interview is to be successful.

Discovery questions are so simple and obvious that we tend to overlook their pitfalls.

"May I help you?"

"No, I'm just looking."

Many salespeople on the retail level ask that question and get that answer fifty times a day for years—and never stop asking it. That's why they're still selling pins and ribbons. The day they decide to stop asking that say-no question is the day they qualify themselves for a more advanced selling position.

YOU: "Good morning. If you have any questions, just let me know. In the meantime, please feel free to look around all you'd like."

PROSPECT: "Uh—I was wondering. Do you have . . ."

Sometimes the best discovery question in a given situation doesn't end with a question mark. It comes out like a statement but it gets the answer the salesperson wants more often than the bald question will. If you're in outside sales, you may never run into situations where you might be tempted to say, "May I help you," but you'll constantly be exposed to opportunities to ask say-no questions.

"May I quote on your next month's requirements for #10 Gunk?"

"No, we've got all we need for quite some time."

Instead of a say-no question, isn't it far better to ask a true discovery question?

"Do you use #10 or #12 Gunk?"

"Would you prefer that I quote on a monthly, quarterly, or annual basis?"

The first rule of discovery questioning is:

Never ask a say-no question.

This is an important concept, so I'm going to give it one more whack. What is a say-no question?

A say-no question is any question that can be answered by a yes or a no.

If you give prospects that choice, you stack the odds against yourself. People will pick no over yes between 51 and 99 percent of the time when they're given that choice by a salesperson.

HOW TO TAKE COMMAND WITH LEADING QUESTIONS

Let's think about truth for a moment. What is it? That question has been debated for thousands of years and there's still no agreement. I'm not going to try to solve this problem in a philosophical sense. All I want to do is emphasize that, in everyday matters, truth is what people believe it is. If you believe that Snortfire High Octane is the only gasoline that's fit to put in the sports car you love like a sweetheart, you'll go out of your way to get it. You'll be willing to pay more for it. The reality may be that a dozen other brands are better for your car; the truth is that you won't put anything in your tank except Snortfire—not if you can help it.

So let's agree that as a practical matter, truth is what we believe it is. I'm not being cynical; I'm simply being pragmatic. We may have the best product for our customer. Not only is it more durable and less costly, it has features no other make has. We know he needs our product's exclusive features. That's the reality. What's the truth? That he won't buy our better product unless he believes all these things.

How do we get him to believe what we know is true?

We can tell him. We can ram the facts down his throat whether he wants to listen or not. We can let him know how stupid we think he is because he won't admit the truth of our statements.

We can do all that and he's still not convinced. Why? Because we've told him. The professional salesperson operates on a different concept, one that's simple and effective. Here it is:

If I say it, they tend to doubt me;
if they say it, it's true.

That's the bedrock concept of professional selling. It's also the underlying concept for the successful use of leading questions. Salespeople who are guided by this concept never make their prospects think: *You silver-tongued devil salesperson, you. I know why you're telling me that—to make me buy your proposition. Well, I just don't have any faith in what you're saying because I know your kind. You'll say anything to make a sale.*

When you're standing there pumping out the facts to prospects, and you're telling them how fantastic your product is, and you're laying it on about features and the warranties—have you ever noticed how they're pulling back? Have you seen their faces harden, their arms cross over their chests, their eyes start to dart this way and that? Have you noticed them either take a step backward, or lean backward in their chairs?

When that happens, you're sending but they're not receiving. You've lost them—they just haven't vanished yet.

When professional salespeople talk, their purpose is to encourage prospects to say the things and ask the questions that will advance the sale. Let's try a few:

"You're interested in quality in the product you're looking for, aren't you?"

Now that, of course, is a yes-or-no question, but it's not a say-no because people don't reply, "No, don't give me quality. I'm looking for something that's a real piece of junk."

Here's another: "If you needed it, you'd like everything on the warranty to happen, wouldn't you?"

"Certainly." Is anyone going to say, "Oh no, I usually burn up warranties anyway. Who needs 'em? Just as long as it lasts till I get it home, I'll be happy."

"A reputation for professionalism is important, isn't it?"

How many prospects will disagree with that? "Oh no, I don't want to do business with professionals. I'd rather buy from someone who doesn't know what he's doing."

"Working with suppliers who value their reputations for reliability and integrity is important, isn't it?"

"What? You have integrity? Get out of here." People aren't going to say that, are they?

That's why professionals don't tell people things, they ask questions. But let's be careful. Don't drop this book, dash out, and start firing queries at every breathing thing you see that might be a prospect.

Control your enthusiasm long enough to read the rest of this chapter.

As a general rule, it's better to ask than to tell. But using questions powerfully is a bit more complicated than that.

Here's what's really effective and moneymaking-good:

- Ask the discovery questions that will reveal the benefits they'll buy. That way you'll know what specific products or services to close them on, and how to do it.
- Ask the leading questions that will cause them to affirm their belief in what you want them to believe about your offering. If you say it, they tend to doubt you; if they say it, it's true.

THE THREE PRINCIPLES OF QUESTION-ASKING POWER

Principle number one: *I always establish a bond before I go for control.* How much time this will take will vary widely, but keep this point in mind: You'll stack the odds against making the sale if you instantly try to lead every prospect.

Principle number two: *I ask questions that are designed to give me the answers I need and keep the sale moving forward.* What does this take? Preparation. Practice, drill, and rehearse so you can keep the excitement growing by keeping things moving fast. Also practice, drill, and rehearse how you'll recover from wrong answers the prospect may give you. Some of these answers you can ignore; others will force a change of course on you. Plan it all out in advance.

Principle number three: *I can't lead people to decisions until I make them.* Do your clients know all your products? If you have several products or services to offer, how many of them will your average client usually select?

Just one.

Many salespeople have lines of fifty to five hundred products; one sample of each would fill several moving vans. Even those with much smaller lines can't carry everything they sell with them. The chances are that you can't, either. You don't have to; you shouldn't want to even if you could.

Your job as a professional salesperson is to make decisions for clients. If you don't make decisions, why do they need you?

They don't. So they'll remain prospects to you and become clients to someone who can, and will, make decisions for them.

You may have difficulty with that one. I've been telling you to discover what benefits people want, and then to sell them something that will provide those benefits. So where does *your* decision making come into play?

Let me illustrate the answer to that question. Suppose tomorrow morning you wake up with a high fever. You can hardly move and you know you're really sick. So you force yourself out of bed and stagger into the nearest doctor's office. She smiles at you and says, "Hi. Nice of you to come in. You look terrible. Any idea what you've got?"

"Not a hint."

"Well, no problem. There's a hundred books on the shelf behind you. Sit down, make yourself comfortable, and take a run at those books. I have to play some golf now and, hopefully, by the time I get back you'll have figured out what's wrong with you. If you can

do that for me, I'm sure I can find a cure for what ails you right off."
She's incompetent, isn't she? No matter how sick you are, you're
going to crawl out of there and find yourself another doctor.

What would you do if your architect asked you to prepare the
detail drawings for your new house? If your attorney asked you to
outline your own case? You wouldn't use any of these people, because they aren't professional. They aren't solving problems for
you; they aren't making decisions for you; they aren't discovering
opportunities for you.

Professionals have expertise that they use to solve problems
and create opportunities for their clients. Doctors cure disease
problems and create opportunities for people to be healthy and active; architects solve space problems and create opportunities for
their clients to expand their lifestyles; professional salespeople
solve product or service problems and create opportunities for
their clients to increase their productivity, happiness, security, income, and status, and to enjoy a host of other benefits.

In every case, the professional must have a larger fund of knowledge than any one client can use. This means that the professional
must also have a means of discovering what part of that knowledge
will best serve the client's needs. Professionals make this discovery
through an organized, practiced consultation routine. A vital element in every professional's success is the ability to isolate, understand, and define the problems (opportunities) that each client has.
This is true of architects, attorneys, consultants, salespeople, and all
kinds of professionals. To help them isolate, and then understand,
their clients' problems and opportunities, some professionals have
developed a consultation routine that's deceptively casual. It seems
to have no structure. Why do they use this system? Because they've
found that it's the most effective. They get more and better information from their clients with a relaxed, offhand manner than they do
by direct grilling. Other professionals prefer—and have the skill to
use successfully—a highly structured and very visible method.

Whether the method is subtle and indirect or briskly to the
point, professionals control the consultation interview. They know
what information they must learn from each client, and they proceed to get it. Basically, it's no different for the doctor, the lawyer,

the salesperson, the management consultant—if these people are competent, they have more to offer than the client facing them at the moment can use. They control the interview to conserve their own and their client's time, and they make decisions for that client.

Take a moment and think about how many salespeople put themselves face-to-face with a possible buyer—through either referrals or prospecting—and then let their prospective buyer control them throughout the consultation interview. If they manage to move on to the demonstration or presentation step, it's due more to luck and the prospect's determination to buy than any skill they've displayed. And then, when they present or demonstrate, they again allow the prospect to control the proceedings. The result is that their prospective buyers rarely obtain the benefits of their product or service. What a shame.

Such people tend to blame their troubles on their offering. "We're just not competitive in this market," they're inclined to say. But if anyone in their company is happily involving lots of people in that same offering and making lots of money doing it, how can it be the offering that's at fault? If anyone in the sales force can do it, everyone in the sales force can do it. Nothing will destroy your sales future faster than falling into the habit of blaming the product or service you sell for your own lack of professionalism.

An accountant must know taxes and business procedures; an architect must know construction and design; all professionals must know their field—so what must you know?

You must know all these things in depth: your product or service; your professional systems for obtaining prospects; your professional procedures for diagnosing your prospects' situations and for isolating their needs and opportunities; and your professional techniques for surmounting objections, for demonstrating or presenting, and for closing.

It all starts with your intimate and detailed knowledge of what you're selling. You can't prospect with strength unless you know your offering; you can't demonstrate or present with strength unless you know your offering; and you can't close with strength unless you know your offering—which is the product or service that you're selling.

Take every opportunity to learn more about your offering. Go beyond that. Make opportunities to learn everything about the uses, benefits, and opportunities that your product or service provides, and also learn everything you can about its limitations and challenges. Every product or service provides its benefits within narrow limits, and is ineffective outside those limits. Every product or service has problems; if you attempt to ignore them, your ignorance will quickly be exposed in circumstances you won't enjoy or profit from.

Your first priority must be to acquire a formidable bank of expertise about what you are offering. That knowledge will include an adequate understanding of the competition and a superior knowledge of what qualifications your buyers must have. Without such knowledge, how can you intelligently decide, for both yourself and the other person, whether any given prospect can—or should—become your client? It's impossible. From product knowledge springs the expertise to work with clients in the effective and professional manner that earns high income.

What does a doctor do when you come in sick? She starts by asking questions. Then she uses her diagnostic equipment to gather more information. Only when she has eliminated a multitude of illnesses, and zeroed in on one, does she decide on the treatment.

Isn't that what you should do? You start by asking your prospect questions. Then you use your diagnostic equipment—which may be a calculator and a pad of paper, a measuring tape, a computer, or simply your brain—and gather more information. Now you're ready to zero in on the exact product or service that will solve your new client's problem or open up a new opportunity for that person.

Let's turn the page and explore how to create the conditions that are most favorable to sales.

4. Creating the Selling Climate

C hampions sell only the benefits and features that the prospect they're working with wants to buy. For years, I've monitored this point, and I'm convinced that it's critical to success: Don't sell what you want, sell what they want.

It's astonishing how many salespeople only talk about, explain, and try to sell the features of their offering that they like.

- "Oh, I just love the fact that it slices grapes." Meanwhile, the prospect doesn't give a hoot about what you love.
- "You know, I've got this same policy in my own investment portfolio." Of course, the prospects don't see what that has to do with their investment decision because your circumstances are different from theirs.
- "When you step on the gas in this beast—look out. It's gonna ram you back in the seat. It's gonna peel rubber." And the prospect is a conservationist who worries about the high cost of fuel and wants an economy car.

Champions don't sell benefits before finding out what benefits the prospect wants. Average salespeople plunge into selling benefits from the start and, inevitably, they have the prospect sitting there thinking, *None of this stuff I'm hearing is important to me.* Keep that up for a little while and the prospect leaves if he's on your premises, or you do if you're on his. I'd like to be sure that we're together in this area. Who pays for your product or service, you or the buy-ers? Of course, the buyers do. Then you should give them what they want. Doesn't that make sense? You should sell them the features that will give them the benefits they want.

How does this fit my teaching that you should make decisions for your clients?

Neatly. People want more than they can get. Money is only one of the great limitations that we all have. Time is another. People want their cars to be larger on the inside and smaller on the out-side, their meals to be more delicious and less fattening, their in-vestments to have higher return and lower risk. They want it all but you know they can't have it all, so you have to decide, among your many products and services and their many desires, what specific item will work best for them.

In most cases, you can't afford the time to show them everything or lead them step by step over every square foot of your knowledge to the one item they'll buy. That's not efficient, not professional, not moneymaking. The purpose of your consultation interview (which might be a few quick questions on the phone to prospects, or a longer face-to-face interview in someone's office) is to diagnose their challenge and determine what their opportunities are. Following that interview, you decide how to proceed. This process requires that you decide *not* to discuss with them a wide variety of possibilities that you have the professional expertise to know they won't buy any-way. Part of your service is to save their time as well as your own.

SELL THE PEOPLE WHO CAN BUY

Many salespeople spend endless hours with people who can't say yes. In commercial/industrial/government sales, this is an ever-present problem. Typically, you can't walk in and talk to the person who is in charge. In many cases, you'll be told that no one individ-ual will make the decision; you see, all such decisions are the sole prerogative of the board of directors, trustees, a committee, or whatever. When you're told that, you'll almost always be given to understand that every member of the decision-making group is away and unavailable. In essence, they are unreachable.

What you're hearing is the truth—it's just not all the truth. The committee exists. It meets regularly. It can make decisions. All important decisions are approved by it. And its members are, for all practical purposes, unavailable to you. Under the law, or in the by-laws, all the power in that organization is given to that group.

However, such unreachable committees rarely exercise any power that's important to you. They have it, but they don't use it because there's too much complexity and too little time. Willingly or not, the directors, trustees, and various boards of this and that have to rely on the nameless gnomes in the back rooms for recommendations that they will likely approve or disapprove. Of course, the gnomes are nameless only in the sense that they don't sign annual reports or get mentioned on cornerstones. But their signatures activate purchase orders.

There are few situations in sales that are more complex and easier to botch than the unreachable committee. In no other area will your sensitivity to small clues and the subtle nuances of power be better rewarded.

Organizations have purchasing procedures that involve several people, much time, more paperwork, and they all move through clearly defined and tidy channels in complete conformity to law and the dictates of their governing bodies or owners. That's the face the organization shows to the world, and it has the paperwork in its files to prove that everything has been done according to its book.

In reality, though, very little is done according to its book, and the real decisions are made outside the tidy channels. The paperwork to justify those decisions is then created after the event.

Flexibility is vital in these situations. Rigidity is dangerous to your success. Keep the ideas that follow in mind when you work with the unreachable committee situation and they'll frequently help you find your way—follow them blindly and they'll sometimes take you off the road and over the cliff.

- The gnomes in the back room are insecure, and they're jealous of the power wielded by the whim of the committee. Make the gnomes feel important. Never let a gnome suspect that you're anything but delighted that you can work with him instead of whoever has the title and the official authority.

- Have faith in the value and importance of your offering to that organization. You need this faith, but don't let it blind you to the fact that most of the unreachable committee will be too involved with their own pet projects to care very much about yours. Never hint that you'll try an end run around the gnome to the committee unless you're willing to accept the gnome's enmity. Unless you can somehow reach the unreachable committee and sell it on your proposition, you probably need the cooperation of the gnome to close that organization. Keep this in mind from the first moment you think about selling to them.

- Make sure you're working with the right gnome, not some chair-warmer whose main job is getting rid of the salespeople the right gnome thinks he doesn't want to talk to.

- There are two kinds of gnomes: those who relish displaying their power by committing themselves, and those who'll never commit themselves. Never try to get an ironclad commitment from a reluctant gnome—it can't be done.

- If you can't sell the gnome within a reasonable time, and if you think that organization is worth more of your time, try the end run. If you can't find a way to reach somebody on that unreachable committee through friends, via political connections, or by direct and persistent pursuit, go over the gnome's head to anyone strong enough to push your proposition past him. You risk making an enemy of the gnome, but what do you have to lose? You've already lost—or failed to gain—his support. Now you have no way to go but over his head.

In chapter 14, I'll show you strategies to overcome the problem of discovering the right person to work with. Bear in mind that difficulties in choosing the right person to sell aren't limited to organizational sales. The same challenge plagues retail and family sales.

Let's suppose that you're working with married-couple buyers.

You're getting along great with one of them—you're selling that person like crazy—but the reality is that the other half of the couple will give the real yes that makes the decision. Your job is to find out which one of the pair has the power to say yes on your particular sale and then to get that yes without inciting the second person to say no.

In retail sales, you'll frequently encounter three kinds of families:

- Single parent.
- Nuclear family—mother, father, and children.
- Extended family—nuclear family plus relatives.

Unless you're a member of an extended family or acquainted with one, you may not realize that their influence is still very much with us. The quiet oldster with the young couple may have the keys to the vault and be the real decision maker.

DON'T SELL LOGIC—AROUSE EMOTIONS

Many of us try to sell our products through logic and only through logic. Highlight this:

Seldom do people buy logically.
People buy emotionally, then defend
their decisions with logic.

Some of us think that many things are bought and sold totally without emotion. For example, who gets excited about pork bellies, cocoa beans, and baled cotton? Speculators do; they're betting heavily that they can outguess the future. Producers do; they worry about oversupply and falling prices. Users do; they worry about undersupply and rising costs. Even in the most unglamorous products and services, fortunes and reputations are being made—and lost—based on emotion.

What about standard shelf items that meet established specifications?

A lack of difference among competitive offers means that the emotional factors are very likely to be magnified, not diminished. When awarding orders, buyers can indulge in favoritism, score settling, or just plain whimsy without fear of creating problems for themselves. The role of sales and service in these situations takes on a greater importance and a changed aspect.

CATCH THE CHANGE ON THE MOVE

What is the emotional process that leads to a purchase? It begins with a new development in buyers' self-image. That is, buyers see themselves in a new way. If the projected purchase is small, that change need only be small, but if the purchase is a large one in relation to buyers' income, the change in self-image that makes the purchase possible will be large. Such a change can come about very quickly. It can take place within a few minutes or even within a few seconds. Champions are adept at spotting these changes in self-image as they occur during sales interviews. They are quick to reinforce buyers' new idea that they can have and enjoy, will look good in and be complimented on, deserve, need, and are worthy of the marvelous new goodie they like. When you see that hang-back eagerness, reinforce their self-image. Do this and they won't just like your product, they'll want it, need it, realize they can't get along without it, and then they'll buy it.

A few words of caution are in order here, because this is selling's most common and most abused technique. It's automatic in the Oriental bazaar, overused in the boutique, and heard too soon almost everywhere that apparel and accessories are sold at retail.

"It really looks good on you," they say—about everything you try on. Sometimes they'll say it without even glancing at you.

It's sad when a fine technique is beaten into a total turnoff by insincerity and carelessness. Yet when used right, this is a powerful technique. It requires attention; it requires discipline, but given that, it delivers the results. Here's how to do it:

First, be genuinely interested in doing your best for clients, and show this interest by asking questions that will tell you what they're seeking to accomplish. Rise above the limitations of your own taste and preferences. Recognize that what's right for you isn't right for everyone, and make an intense effort to see the world through your clients' eyes.

Second, use your expertise to guide clients to the best solution for them that your inventory provides.

Third, wait for positive stimulus from clients. When you get it, if you believe they've found something that helps them achieve whatever effect they want, reinforce their image about that purchase. Avoid the worn-out phrases they've heard a thousand times; stay away from the words they stopped believing years ago. Concentrate on your customers. Say sincere and positive things that reflect your customers' uniqueness, and you'll not only make that sale but also create clients who'll send you referrals and buy from you again in the future. The key is to discipline yourself to wait for their positive input. Unless you do that, you'll find yourself bragging about something they don't like and, before you know it, you're caught in a web of obvious insincerity.

I had retail sales in mind when I wrote that, but the principles carry over to every kind of sales work because the one constant is that you're selling to people. Machines don't buy much.

If you stick to the facts, if you constantly work on your buyers with logic and avoid arousing their emotions positively, what will happen?

The mere fact that you're a salesperson will arouse their negative emotions, and they'll start fighting you. Your prospects are either emotionally for you, or against you—and you can divide your chances of selling them by a hundred if they're against you.

At my seminars I ask my audiences to give me emotional reasons that cause people to buy. Things like this will usually be suggested first:

"They can afford it."

"It's the right size."

"Prices are going up."

"It meets their needs."

Most audiences will give me several logical reasons why people should buy before they'll give me a single emotion that will make people buy. This makes me believe that salespeople in general put too much emphasis on fact and too little on emotion. If we weren't the jangling bundle of emotions that we all are, everybody would buy everything based solely on logic—and then wouldn't the world be a dull place?

"They can afford it." They'll never think about whether they can afford it or not until you get them emotionally involved in wanting it.

"It's the right size." What does it matter if they don't want it?

"Prices are going up." Yes, they are, and that's a strong emotional reason for buyers to hang on to their money and not buy anything they don't want.

"It meets their needs." It may meet what you think they need, but the fact remains that they're going to buy what they want.

Emotion. That's where it's at. Unless you're arousing positive emotions, you're raising negative emotions—and you've lost the sale. Again I ask, what are the positive buying emotions?

At one of my seminars, a bright young woman who's going far as a salesperson said, "Style," and I jumped on it.

"We all have to wear clothes in our society, don't you agree? That's the logical reason for spending money on clothes. But do any of us buy the cheapest stuff that'll keep us warm, dry, and covered? Certainly not. We buy the style our self-image tells us to buy. We buy emotionally."

Another young lady said, "Color."

"Certainly color is one of the buying emotions. In clothing and home furnishings, it's commonplace for people to want their choice of color more than they want a particular product, and that attitude carries over to some degree on most purchases of things that will be seen. Colors make statements about the people who wear them, drive around in them, and sit among them in their homes and offices. We all have feelings about colors, and we buy the ones we want."

I asked for another buying emotion, and a man said, "Pride of ownership."

"Of course," I answered. "Human beings love to own things. Pride of ownership is, in reality, pride in oneself. This is not only a potent buying emotion, but also an easy one to arouse. That's what the salesperson does who says, 'Your friends will know you've really arrived when they see you drive up in this car, won't they?' Plain transportation is all that we really need on the surface. In the deeper senses, many of us need and want all the status that we can squeeze out of owning an automobile. And we buy what we want if we possibly can."

To get a thorough education in the emotions that sell, sit down with your children some Saturday morning and study the commercials on the programs they watch. You'll see advertising that grabs right at the emotions. It goes something like this:

Seven-year-old Stevie is sitting there when a commercial plays. On the tube, Johnny Powerful speaks directly to the boy. "You want to be like Johnny Powerful, don't you? Then have Mommy get Ookie-Gookies for you. You need Ookie-Gookies to be like Johnny Powerful," and he flexes his muscles. That happens over and over on every show.

Now here's little Stevie walking along a supermarket's aisle with his mother, and Stevie is looking around for something interesting. Suddenly he sees Ookie-Gookies. Stevie doesn't say "Let's look at the ingredients listed on the box before we decide to buy it. All right, thiamin, riboflavin, niacin—hey, it's loaded with exactly the stuff we need more of."

Little Stevie doesn't do that, does he? He sees Ookie-Gookies and big Johnny Powerful flexing his muscles at the same time. So little Stevie yells, "Mom, *I need Ookie-Gookies!*" Stevie was sold not logically, but emotionally.

Logic in sales is a gun without a trigger. You can twirl it all you care to but you can't fire it. Emotion is another gun in sales, and this one has a trigger. You can hit the target with it. Every time you generate another positive emotion, you're pulling the trigger on another accurate shot at closing the sale. Let's list the most widespread, effective, and powerful buying emotions:

Color and style	Peer pressure (keeping up
Pride of ownership	with the Joneses)
Vanity	Self-improvement
Security	Health
Prestige and status	Love of family
Ambition	Family getting larger
Employment change	Family getting smaller

No skill that you can acquire in sales will enhance your earning power more than learning how to arouse these emotions in your buyers in ways that are positive to the sale you're seeking. The exact words that you use will depend on your offering, your personality, your buyers, and market conditions. Study each of the selling emotions given above and develop a list of emotion-evoking questions you can ask your buyers. If you're selling luxury cars, you should be able to come up with several approaches for several of the buying emotions. But if you sell plastic pipe to landscape contractors, you'll have difficulty coming up with useful emotion evokers on anything except security.

You see that new bauble, that new neatarooney. There's no reason for you to have it other than the fact that all of a sudden you want it. Then you emotionally come up with reasons, urgent reasons, for getting it. But do those reasons explain why you want it? Certainly not. Their function is to prove that you need it—to your own satisfaction, at least. And it's amazing how fast you'll do this if the new goodie is good enough.

Put this item among your key notes, and review it often:

Positive emotions trigger sales; negative emotions destroy sales.

As you work at developing the skill to evoke emotions in your customers, always keep this concept in your mind. You can destroy sales as rapidly as you can create them through the clumsy use of, or the lack of control over, the emotional setting. Also remember that your actions and manners, your words and how you say them, and your grooming and clothes are all things that trigger emotions in your prospects—whether you want them to or not. People will react emotionally to you. I'm not being facetious when I say that it's important not to have them react with fear, anger, or disgust. To see some salespeople approach prospects as though these potential buyers had just fallen off the turnip truck, you'd swear they don't realize that prospects have feelings, too. Prospects suffer the effects of fear when a salesperson comes on too strong; prospects get angry when a salesperson patronizes them; prospects feel disgust when a salesperson is nonprofessional in any way.

Let me give you an example. Picture yourself walking into a showroom with your spouse. The salesperson on duty meets you. "Hi, I'm Pat Swifty. Nice of you to come in, sir. Hello, nice of you to join in, ma'am. You are husband and wife? Good-looking couple. How are you today?"

If a stranger opened up on you like that, would you feel a touch of fear, anger, and disgust? *Uh-oh,—this crocodile is out to get us. What business of his is it whether or not we're married? And who needs his phony compliments?*

Your sales interviews don't need any more fear. Your chances of success won't be improved by an injection of anger. Your prospects can't be closed if they're feeling contemptuous or disgusted.

I'm leading you through dangerous territory right now. On the one hand, it's vital that you be keenly aware of how easily negative feelings can be aroused, and of how hazardous they are to your sales hopes. On the other hand, it's equally vital that you not become tense about it, or your tension will impact negatively on your prospects and destroy your chances of closing them. The solution to this is to understand it. With understanding, you can make the right moves, work with the odds always on your side, and close on positive feelings rather than be defeated by negative feelings that you've aroused.

Everything you say to prospects creates images in their minds. That is, if you use words they understand, and if your prospects are listening and hear what you're saying—considerations that many of us aren't as concerned with as we should be—then your words will create images in their minds. Since life is complicated and varied, those images will be complicated and varied. Enormously so. But we're looking at this wide variety of images from the single viewpoint of closing the sale, and that makes matters simple: Every image that your words create in the minds of prospects either helps or hurts your chances of selling them. By this standard, all images are either positive to the sale or negative to it.

Let's explore the relative strength of negative and positive images. Are they very nearly equal in power? That is, will ten negative images balance out ten positive images and leave you still in there swinging? Or will a single positive image offset five or ten negative images?

The truth is, one negative can wipe out many positives. If you're satisfied you can spray all the negatives on prospects that you care to because you're smarter than they are, and if you're sure you can always save the sale by pouring on more positives when the mood strikes you, think about the dry forest that's destroyed by a single lighted cigarette thrown from a car. The power of the negative is enormous. The Champion doesn't fool around with it. Making just one thoughtless comment to prospects can destroy your chances of selling them. As I stated earlier, this is dangerous territory—but it's ground you have to cover every time you work with prospective buyers.

Understand the challenge. When you're working with strangers, you can't know where their sensitive spots are, and if you try to guess, you'll guess wrong more often than you'll guess right.

So play the odds. Greet them with a pleasant but unforced smile and a soft attitude. Don't pay them compliments; don't ask them personal questions; don't welcome them with a bootlicking manner. Look again at the imaginary Pat Swifty's words a few paragraphs back. Did it shock you when I said that those words aroused fear, anger, and disgust?

Pat would claim he was just trying to be nice. Not honest, maybe—just nice. But what did his words and manner convey to the couple who walked into his showroom?

His action told them very clearly that he thought they were suckers for a fawning compliment and a false smile. They were smart enough to instantly grasp how he really felt. Most people are that smart. They may not think it all out. They don't have to: Logic plays no part in this, and the emotions work fast. You lose all chance of selling people by meeting them with negative images. Before you realize what you've done, these folks are gone, and you won't ever get a chance to repair the damage. In fact, with most people in most sales situations, there's only a slim possibility that this kind of damage can be repaired once it's done.

Play the odds. Always be professional when meeting new people.

Do that and you'll close more sales. Champions realize that they must eliminate the fears their prospects brought with them without introducing new fears. They must arouse positive emotions without arousing negative emotions. Finally, they must provide the logic that will back up their buyers' emotional decision to buy from them. Champions know that they'll never get to that last phase unless they create positive images that will triumph over the negatives.

One way to make this happen is to avoid the rejection words. Many of us don't realize how often we destroy sales by using certain words that ignite fear in the minds of our prospects. Learn how to inspire confidence instead of anxiety when you talk to buyers.

REPLACE REJECTION WORDS WITH GO-AHEAD TERMS

Hundreds of thousands of salespeople don't know about rejection words, or—and this is far worse—they know, but they keep on using them to drive dollars from their pockets. Let me define what I'm talking about:

A rejection word is any term that triggers fear, or reminds prospects that you are trying to sell them.

When prospects hear rejection words, their responses often run something like this: "Oh no, I'm just looking." "We're in no hurry." "We're just killing time."

If you're deeper into the selling sequence when you let a rejection word slip out, your prospects will say things like, "We'll let you know." "We'll sleep on it." "We're just gathering information now." "We'll call you when we're ready."

Rejection words work well. They let you scare your prospects so much that most of them will reject you and your proposition. If you're using rejection words, you don't need enemies—you've got yourself. Here's a horrible handful of these words and what to replace them with:

Appointment. In business-to-business sales, you may be able to use this term. In consumer sales, however, you might want to make a change. When consumers hear the word *appointment*, they often think of time spent with doctors, dentists, mechanics, and so on. None of those situations is necessarily a pleasant adventure. So replace the term *appointment* with:

Meeting
Visit

By asking for a time to meet or visit with someone, you sound more like a person who cares rather than an impersonal appointment situation. The term *meeting* puts the time you spend with them on a more even footing. You meet with people to share ideas. With appointments, usually the other person is in charge. When you visit, people think of having a nice little chat—not a two-hour sales presentation. Now, if your presentation does take two hours, you are obligated to let potential clients know that's how long you expect to be with them before closing them on the time. However, you'll find you get farther into conversations with people about arranging meetings and visits before bringing up the amount of time required.

***Cost* or *price*.** Every time one of your prospects hears you give value information in these ways: "The price is ninety-nine thousand dollars," or "It costs eighty-five dollars," they know what's coming. You're going to put the pressure on, push them for a decision, try to sell them. That's why the pro calls it:

Total investment
Total amount

What do you do when you invest?

You put money to work in ways that will bring income or other benefits back to you, isn't that right?

What do you do when you pay a price or pick up a cost?

You spend money, don't you? You pay for dead horses and white elephants, incur expenses, run up bills, and shovel money out that you'll never see again.

The professional's favorite term here is *total investment*. But as with any other word or technique, it can be overused. Here are several alternatives that'll allow you to banish *cost* and *price* from your selling vocabulary forever:

Value, valued at
Available for, available at
Offered for, offered at
Worth

To avoid confusion and questions you don't want, use these alternatives with care. If you say, "This model is worth $975," your prospect may be inspired to reply, "Okay, but how much less can I buy it for?"

How you get around this depends on your selling procedures. If you quote prices from a printed list and your customer knows that your company has a one-price policy that eliminates bargaining, you can glance at the list and say any of these things:

"That model is worth $975."
"We show $975 for that model."
"That one is valued at $975."
"It's available for $975."
"We offer it at $975."

Write out exactly how you'll use these terms and role-play the situations you usually encounter when prices are discussed. If you think this is too much trouble, you think being professional is too much trouble. In that case, what are your chances of earning a professional income?

List price, listed at. These two terms are taboo except in resale situations where there's a retail list price and a lower wholesale price. To everyone else in our discount-happy society, if you say *list price* or *listed at* they'll think you're telling them to ask for a price cut. Talking about *list price* and saying *listed at* is even more destructive if you've made it clear that your prices are firm. In this case, every time you say these nasty words, you remind your listeners that they'd better check your competition before ordering from you because they might give a discount.

Use the same go-ahead terms to avoid *list price* and *listed at* that you use to avoid saying *price* and *cost*.

Down payment. If you're looking for a term that will strike fear into every prospect's heart, *down payment* is a splendid choice. But if you'd rather reduce fear than increase it, talk like a professional. The correct terms are:

Initial investment or initial amount

Monthly payment. Here's another term that's extremely effective at doing exactly what you don't want to do, which is to magnify fear in your prospects. Most people are petrified of monthly payments. They have enough already. When you see those two words, what flashes through your mind?

All your bills. You see yourself looking at the pile of paper that eats up your paycheck every month. "Dang it all, I'm sick and tired of that payment. I wish it was over with. Never should've bought the fool thing in the first place."

Monthly payment is a bookkeeper's term, and it's a favorite with bill collectors. Professional salespeople say,

Monthly investment or monthly amount

Contract. When most people hear the word *contract*, what clicks in their minds? Lawsuits. Courtrooms. Judges deciding their fate. Attorneys sending them bills. Deep trouble.

Champions don't call it a contract. They call it:

The agreement
The paperwork
The form

Rejection words aren't unusual terms that you might only use once a month or so, are they? I've been attacking your everyday vocabulary, haven't I? Now I'm going to take a shot at an even more basic word.

Buy. Please realize that no one wants to buy; they just want to own. Some salespeople plaster their presentations with sayings that go something like this:

"Once you buy from us, we can sure get it to you fast."
"When you buy our product, you'll be happy with it."
"The people who buy from me get terrific service."

What do prospects feel when those words hit them? "If I buy it, I'll have to spend money and I don't want to spend any money. All I want to do is have it. What I'm looking for is more benefits and less trouble."

Professionals know that people want to own things, so they frequently talk about owning. Buying is the pain, owning is the pleasure. So eliminate *buy* and go with:

Own

Let's rewrite the three sentences quoted above to replace their buying pain with selling power:

"If you decide to own it, we can get it to you fast."
"When you own our product, you'll be happy with it."
"When you own one of our models through me, you also own
    a piece of me because I feel very strongly about giving top-
    notch service to my clients."

The desire to own is a deep-seated urge. It's a compelling force that's too important to let your use of it depend on what you'll snatch from the charged air of a sales interview by chance. Professionals plan and practice exactly how they will tie the image of owning directly to every strong selling point that's available. This means that Champions sit down and write out the sentences that will accomplish this aim smoothly by repeating only the idea of ownership while varying all the other elements. What you don't want to singsong is: "When you own our product, you'll be happy with its exclusive crossover feature. When you own our product,

you'll be happy with our service. When you own our product, you'll
be happy with its durability."

Design a set of ownership image builders that will allow you to
continually reinforce this potent buying force without continually
reminding your prospects that your purpose is to sell them. It won't
take long to write out the sentences that will keep your technique
from being too obvious. In a few minutes, you can drill yourself on
those selling sentences until they're second nature. But however
long it might take you, doing so will put more money in your bank
account than bantering with the other salespeople around the coffee urn.

Here are some more ownership image builders to add to the
three recommended above as having selling power:

- "This crossover feature is exclusive with our company,
  and it's built into all our models. So when you pick the one
  you want to own, you can be sure that you'll be taking a
  crossover home with you."
- "All of us here are proud of our company's reputation for
  service. It's as important to us as it is to our owners and,
  when you're one of them, I know that you'll be delighted
  with the way we carry out our concept of total commitment to the service needs of our owners."
- "Since the profitability of your operation depends on one
  machine, durability is vital, isn't it? When you own one of our
  Workhorses and are depending on it, durability is just one of
  its qualities that you're going to be very pleased with."
- "I hope to show you a product today that will greatly enhance your opportunities when you own it." Before "when
  you own it," you can add, "for higher profits," or any other
  sales point that you want to emphasize with this wording.
- "When you find the model you'd like to own—and I'm confident that we have it in stock here right now—you're going
  to be delighted at how low the initial investment is." Tailor
  it to your product or service: "When you find the model
  you'd like to own, you're going to be delighted with our
  warranty." If you sell a service, you might cast the sentence

in this form: "When you choose the service you want to own, you'll be delighted with how much costly managerial time you'll free up for other, more important duties."

Every worthwhile sales point you can make about your offering can be welded to an image of owning. If you can't make the connection between the benefit and the joy of owning, either that point isn't important enough to mention or you're not enthusiastic enough about your product or service. In some cases, of course, you'll have to connect in a negative way: "If you own our security system, you won't have to worry about . . ."

Maximize your selling power. Tie your strongest sales points to the basic and very human love of owning. Of course, you won't slam these sayings at them one right after another. You'll sprinkle your ownership image builders throughout each of your sales interviews, incorporating them smoothly into other aspects of your selling sequence. I'm reminding you again of the dangers that are involved when you overuse any technique and allow your prospects to notice it. Every time that happens, they're tempted to pit their sales resistance against your sales skill—and whenever it's fun for your prospects to fight you, you'll lose.

You can help camouflage the ownership image-building technique by reserving the strongest word—*own*—for your strongest sales points. For less important points, you can substitute one of the words or phrases given below in italics:

- "When you find the design *you want to put in your living room*—and I'm positive we have it in our huge inventory right now—you're going to be impressed with our wide range of finishes."
- "When *it belongs to you*, you're going to be tickled pink with the way it impresses people."
- "When *you have this pattern on your walls*, you'll be delighted with the aura it imparts to your home."
- "After *you've installed this model in your office*, you'll be very pleased with how much time it'll save you."

- "If *you make this service yours*, you'll be very satisfied with the performance improvement in your shipping department."
- "If *you choose our service*, you'll find that you've added an important asset to your company's net worth."
- "When *you put this beauty in your garage*, you'll . . ."
- "As soon as *you take this model home*, you'll . . ."
- "When *you acquire this service*, all your worries about breakdowns will be over."
- "When *you've got our service on your side*, you can count on . . ."
- "When *it's yours*, you'll know your problems with overload are a thing of the past."
- "When *you have* our staff on your team—but not on your payroll—you'll be amazed at the credit you'll get for saving your company money." This selling method for fee-basis service is easily adapted to many products—just substitute the name of your cost efficient machine for *staff*.

The last technique given above aims two separate emotional appeals at salaried people working for companies they obviously don't own. The second of the two is the more powerful because it speaks to the most important emotion driving salaried employees. This emotion is expressed by a question that's in their minds every hour they work: *How can I increase my prestige, security, and power?* Its name is ambition.

On the gut level, this comes out as, *What's in it for me?* I'm not speaking of bribery. Few buyers for organizations are on the take, and nothing is more disastrous than offering a bribe where none is wanted. You're on your own if you're willing to carry the bag because I'm convinced that no job is worth the ignominy of having to give bribes to hold it. There are some things in this life that you should never tamper with, and one of the foremost of these is your own integrity.

But most executives, officials, and other buyers, though honest, are driven by ambition, by this *what's-in-it-for-me?* emotion. Why should they approve the purchase of your product or service today instead of referring your proposal to a committee, taking it under advisement, or zapping the whole thing into file thirteen as soon as you're out their door? Because there's something for them in your offering by way of company benefits that they can gain some glory by ordering. Develop the ability to tie the purchase of your offering to your buyers' personal advancement, and you'll be amazed at how many more sales you'll close. All that's required is sensitivity, subtlety, and effort.

Important as this is, don't overlook the power of the other emotional appeal in the sentence last quoted. It's vital to remember that most buyers respond strongly to properly worded owner image builders even though they don't own the company or organization they're buying for. This fact has its roots in a sort of tribal instinct. To some degree, everyone who works for an organization feels this pull of the group, this loyalty, this sense of *it's-us-against-them*. *Us* is everyone who works here; *them* is the rest of the world. There's the elementary force holding every group together that's going to survive for long, whether it's a family, a company, or any other organization. The higher in rank that people are, the stronger this feeling is. Since all those who buy for an organization have some status, you can be sure that they'll respond to owner image builders because they feel a strong loyalty to the group even though they may complain to you about their job.

Sell **or** *sold*. It's not likely that anyone will fix a happy smile on you and say, "Wait till you see what a salesman sold me today." No, you'll never hear that spoken in earnest, though you frequently will hear, "Wait till you see what I *bought* today." On the emotional level, *bought* is more than the past tense of *buy*—it's the present tense of *own*. Buying is dieting; owning is being slim. Describing what you just bought is a sneaky but safe way to boast of what you own because, though bragging about possessions is frowned on, it's socially acceptable to get wildly enthusiastic over a new acquisition. And people love to do it. In fact, this is an important emotional need that buyers are always seeking to satisfy, though few of them realize it and even fewer would admit it. If your product or service is right for this technique (almost all are), do the homework that's necessary to fold this zinger into your selling sequence. It's a powerhouse.

When people talk about what they bought today, they're really saying, *Wait till you see the new status raiser that I own as of today.* They've done something. Now they want everyone to admire their wisdom, style, and power—and they won't willingly share the glory with the salesperson who closed them. Why? Because they don't want to admit that anything entered into the choice except their own desires and decisions. Keep this firmly in mind whenever you speak with anyone known personally to one of your buyers. Avoid saying things like "I sold it to him." When you say *I sold*, you're the hotshot who pulled the buyer off the street and pushed him into signing on the line you had to check in red so he could find it. This is poaching on buyers' territory. Take all your glory from the people on your end, and let the buyers have all the glory on their end.

Some salespeople will tell prospects, "You're probably wondering who else has our service. Well, I'd like you to know that last week I sold our service to the Martunian family right down the street."

What does that make them think? "You might've sold the Martunians but you ain't selling me, buster." They're fighting you because they don't want you to do anything to them. If anything is done, they want to be the ones to do it.

Sell has a similar effect. The word throws an image of slick "fellers" in flashy shoes talking people out of their money. Professionals never sell anyone anything. They get people happily involved. Still, you can get different people happily involved all day long, but if you hit the same person with that phrase over and over, you'll raise welts. Eliminate *sell* and *sold* by playing variations on these themes:

Happily involve
Acquired (bought, ordered, purchased) through me
Help obtain
Counsel or consult
Worked with me on the arrangements
Aid (or assist) the buyer by eliminating difficulties

Providing expertise, or supplying
(vital, necessary, useful) information

Had the honor (privilege, pleasure, challenge) of
acting as agent, representative, or intermediary

Developed the opportunity

Worked out the details

To avoid sounding pompous or flippant, match what you say to your type of sale. "I had the privilege of consulting on that acquisition" is laughable if you're selling unpainted furniture at the discount store, but not if you sold the store. If you say that you "helped with the details" on a multimillion-dollar purchase, people may think you're a clerk.

Let's put a few of these phrases to work to highlight how they can smooth your daily performance:

"You're probably wondering if anyone nearby has our service. Do you know the Martunian family right down the street? Fine. They are happily involved with our Plan Six. I know because they worked with me on the arrangements. Would you like to give them a call right now and confirm how they're enjoying our service?"

To a new plant manager at one of your old accounts: "Mr. Klein, this is Frank Macy at Lift-Trucks-for-Less. Your company acquired a Gruntless Marvel through me two years ago. I'm calling to see if it's still doing a top job for you."

To a referral calling you for the first time: "Yes, I had the privilege of developing a fine opportunity for Mr. Raiche last month."

Compare those statements with "Yeah, I sold it to him." Then practice the phrases that will make the most money for you because they build confidence rather than fear and antagonism.

Customer. Let's go back to the Martunian family for a moment. Now that they have gotten happily involved with our product, are they now our customers? No. Don't use the word *customer*. This one isn't quite as critical as some of the other negative words I'm covering, but you can make something more positive out of it. Don't call your existing clients customers, call them:

Clients
People we serve
Families we serve

Now the image you've put forth is one of being involved with flesh-and-blood people, not a list of obscure names on a sales report. "We have so many families we serve right here in the local community." "The Smiths are one of the families we have been fortunate to serve with our fine product." Feel the difference? So will they.

Prospect. Along the same lines, don't refer to the people you hope to involve in your product next as prospects. They are:

Potential clients
Future clients

By envisioning them in your mind's eye as future clients, you'll find yourself treating them as clients even before they have the opportunity to acquire your product. It will be different than if you think of them as one of many prospects who either buy or move on. It will make a difference in the number of people who purchase from you and/or refer others your way.

Commission. At some point, you are bound to talk with potential clients who will blatantly refer to the money you make on the sale of your product or service. They might even ask, "How much do you make on one of these?" Rather than get into a discussion about mark-up, say these words: "John, our company does have a fee built into all of our transactions. However, I can assure you the service you will receive over the years from our firm will far outweigh any fee. And that's what you really want, isn't it?" Your goal is to change their thinking from that of your earning a commission to the value of their paying a:

Fee for service

Problem. Right now, stop thinking of anything that comes your way that might stall or prevent a sale from happening as a problem.

Problems bring things to a halt. Problems negatively impact relationships. Problems are terrible. From now on, look at anything that slows down the sales process as a:

Challenge

They give you an objection and you warmly say, "Other clients of ours had that same challenge and we were able to find a satisfactory solution that truly met their needs." Or, "It's my goal to see that there aren't any challenges as we proceed with the details of this agreement."

Besides projecting a more positive image to the client, the word *challenge* helps you feel better. You're not being stopped by a brick-wall problem. That wall is now seen as a challenge to break through or hurdle over.

Objection or *objections*. If someone you're talking with gives you an objection, be happy! You're probably thinking I'm nuts right now, but I'm not. Very few people will waste their time objecting to something they aren't feeling motivated to own. In other words, if they object, they're starting to want it and are a bit afraid of making the decision and so will try to slow things down. Like the difference between *problem* and *challenge*, you'll now start referring to objections as:

Concerns
Areas of concern

"John, I can appreciate that concern." Then you address the issue, calm his fears, and move toward the final decision.

Cheaper. Please never tell anyone that your product is cheaper than that of your competition. What comes to your mind when you hear that word? I see something that's of less value, perhaps poor quality. Even though people want to pay the least amount possible for things, they still want the highest quality possible. So if your product is less expensive than that of your competition, tell them it's:

More economical

Economy is a good thing in the mind of most people. They seek it out and feel good about acquiring something in an economical manner.

Pitches and ***deals.*** The profession of selling has been my life for nearly four decades. I love it. But I don't love hearing about pitches and deals. Some people in our profession insist on projecting the worst stereotype ever hung on us: that of the cold smiler who thinks like a shark, talks like a carnival barker, and struts around making pitches and deals.

"Yeah, I gotta go out on another pitch tonight."

"Lemme give you the pitch on this terrific little number."

"After you hear my pitch, you'll know I've got the best deal in town."

When you choose to express yourself with negative terms, you put yourself down. What you say decides how you feel about yourself.

Let's not make pitches. Be eager to have your people hear your presentation or watch your demonstration. And don't offer them deals. If you do, you'll focus their attention on price, and you'll raise expectations that you'll have to beat down later—if you can—to make the sale. Invite people to:

Hear the presentation I've developed for your company

Participate in the demonstration

Get involved in the wonderful opportunity we have for you

Consider this interesting transaction

If you don't believe that words create mental images, arouse emotions, and cause things to happen, sales is the wrong line of work for you. *Pitch* and *deal* are verbal garbage, and slinging them not only casts powerful images into the minds of those who hear you but also reinforces old images, precisely where they'll do the most damage—in your own mind.

How you feel about what you do determines much of how you feel about yourself.

How you feel about yourself is the image that determines how effectively you will work.

How effectively you work determines how much you will earn.

Stop talking about pitches and deals. Start asking people to hear your presentation, watch your demonstration, and consider the opportunity that you're offering. In other words, start showing respect instead of contempt for your work and the prospects you work with. Make that change and you'll make more money.

To achieve change, you have to ban those two words from your thoughts, from all conversations no matter how casual, and especially from your talk with other salespeople. The last will be the hardest, but your new attitude will make clear to your associates that you're in the business of succeeding, not failing. That will push you toward the winners and away from the losers—something that's always a good move. Here's my suggestion. It's a simple one. The very blood of sales is the power that words have to create favorable mental images. Use that power. Take a few moments now to form three positive images in this manner: Relax, close your eyes, and picture yourself dressed and groomed to your business ideal. Then imagine that you're: (a) giving a smooth presentation; (b) conducting a well-organized demonstration; and (c) offering your wonderful opportunity to people who want, need, and can afford it. Make all these positive images bright and specific in your mind, and name them *presentation*, *demonstration*, and *opportunity*.

Whenever you hear or think (of course you'll never say) *pitch* or *deal*, immediately throw that image out of your mind and replace it with the proper positive image:

- Now I'm giving this terrifically effective presentation.
- Here's me presenting my polished demonstration.
- What a beautiful opportunity I have for these people.

This method can be applied to a wide variety of negatives. Take charge. Use the good to drive out the bad.

But it won't happen overnight. Give it a month. If you say one of the words, or even think of one without instantly replacing that negative image with a positive one, start over. Stick with it until you've controlled the images for thirty consecutive days. Then count how much money your deliberate use of positive images has made for you.

Sign. Our last rejection word is the nastiest of all because it sinks your boat so near home, you can smell the biscuits baking and hear your old dog snore. For the salespeople who constantly hit the cold water because of this word, the worst part is that they never figure out what keeps knocking their planks loose.

The trouble starts without warning when you've sailed right up to your big close and dropped anchor. You've covered everything. It's gone well. You've finished filling out the agreement your prospect must approve if the sale is to go through—and now you get excited. But you conceal your excitement, turn the agreement around, and slide it across the desk to her. "There we are. Now, just sign right here and we'll get the wheels turning for you right away."

Suddenly your prospect's smile loses truth. She stares at the agreement for a moment. Then she clears her throat and mumbles, "Uh-huh, yeah, well, ah—my daddy always told me to read the fine print before signing anything."

The trouble is, that's exactly what her daddy—and her grandmother, her attorney, and her husband—did tell her. So when you say *sign here*, you trigger an automatic defensive response that makes her think, *If I'm not careful, I'll nail my fanny to the barn door with a ballpoint pen. Well, that's not going to happen, because I'm not signing anybody's one-sided company contract before I scrutinize every dot in it.*

And that's just what she proceeds to do. One of the first provisions reminds her of a tax angle to check out, and then she spots something she wants to talk to her attorney about—and all at once there's no chance she'll okay the paperwork during this meeting with you.

You follow it up energetically, of course. But things happen that you can't control. To begin with, her attorney is on vacation. The day he gets back, you're far away working the year's most important trade show. Before you're through explaining to and negotiating with her advisers, there's a new development. Something happens in the economy, your price goes up drastically, or a new trend shakes her industry—and now the emotional climate is wrong. Delay and change have robbed your opportunity for the buyer of all its freshness and excitement, and suddenly it doesn't look opportune to her anymore. Then it's time to say good-bye to the sale that would have been yours if you hadn't said *sign here* several weeks before.

Even if your sales agreement is a simple order form, *sign* is still a scare word. Champions never even hint that their clients will be expected to sign anything. Instead, they ask prospects to:

Okay the paperwork
Approve the form
Authorize the agreement
Endorse the file copies

There's a small but important item to watch when you turn your sales agreement around, smile warmly at clients, and say, "If you'll please okay the paperwork for me, I'll get your order moving right away for you."

Make sure they write their name, not just the word *okay*.

I hope you'll invest the time necessary to own this section. Forming the habit of using terms that are truly positive in an emotional way will give you potent force in every sales situation.

THE TRIAD CONCEPT: HOW TO MULTIPLY YOUR EFFECTIVENESS

Many of us have one sales message. Because it's successful with some of our prospects, we overlook the fact that our single message falls flat with the rest of them.

Let's suppose that your basic presentation takes about five minutes. Of course, you vary it slightly to fit each prospect's situation, but basically you give the same presentation in the same way to everyone. The style that you always use might be described as brisk, businesslike, and pleasant.

Very good. You've chosen a style that's effective between 30 and 60 percent of the time. (Effective in the sense that it'll allow you to make the sale if everything else is right.) Now let's go after the other 40 to 70 percent who are turned off by brisk, businesslike, and pleasant types with their shiny shoes and cheerful smiles.

"Wait a minute," you might be saying at this point. "Wild-eyed funny folks don't buy my product. I work with substantial people only."

Maybe so, but some of those substantial people have been talking to brisk, businesslike, and pleasant types several hours a day for twenty years and now they've got combat fatigue. They feel like shooting themselves in the foot to get away from the front lines every time another salesperson exuding the standard manner comes through their door. So they send distress signals—tell jokes or sad stories—and hope that you hear and understand their message: *Please do something different!*

It rarely happens.

The average salesman has his signal-receiving antenna raised high every time he goes in for any kind of a sales interview, though he doesn't hear much besides static because he's thinking too intently about himself and what he's going to say. So he misses the message, plods doggedly ahead with his standard presentation, and soon is trudging away without the order.

The Champion also has her antenna up. The message to her comes through loud and clear because she's giving all her attention to the prospect. She knows what she's there to say much too well to give any thought to it when she's face-to-face with opportunity. In fact, the Champion knows three versions of what she's there to say. Having her mind clear, she easily gets the message, goes with the version of her presentation that best fits this prospect's attitude, and soon is flying away with the order safely tucked in her briefcase.

Be a Champion. Use the triad concept. Design and practice three variations on every aspect of your selling sequence. You may be varying your approach to some degree now, but you'll enormously increase your ability to fit your words and actions to each prospect if you'll consciously work at creating triple-headed responses.

Let me explain further, because I'm not simply telling you to devise three answers to every objection (although that's certainly not a bad goal). I'm recommending that you practice three ways of phrasing every good answer that you have to each objection. One phrasing might be slangy or homespun, another might be lofty or long-worded, and one should be clearly stated in standard English.

The triad concept doesn't stop here. Each of these three phrasings of the single answer can be said fast, at medium speed, or slowly. You can speak softly, in normal tones, or loudly. Your attitude can be subdued, friendly, or somewhat forceful. That's eighty-one variations on a single answer to an objection ($3 \times 3 \times 3 \times 3 = 81$). When you apply this idea to every aspect of your selling sequence, you'll quickly develop such a huge inventory of responses that finding the perfect fit for every prospect will be easy. (Perfect in the sense that if there's any way the sale can be made, you'll make it.)

Start with your basic presentation and devise three variations. Here's one set of possibilities:

1. Casual, relaxed, and alert.
2. Brisk, businesslike, and pleasant.
3. Intense, candid, and personal for the large number of people who automatically fend off company parrots, working only with fellow human beings on an intimate one-to-one basis that recognizes their individuality.

The above are variations on emotional focus. Now let's look at content. Again, it's easy to think in terms of three.

1. Technical. This treatment puts heavy emphasis on the technological innovations your product has. Explore tax aspects and cost effectiveness if these apply. Appeal to the emotions in very businesslike terms.

2. Even Mix. A moderately technical approach that uses strong appeals to emotion made in standard English.
3. Gut level. A straight appeal to the emotions in down-to-earth language, with only a few pinches of technical detail to salt the meat.

The triad above applies to what you say. How you say it provides another great opportunity to gain sales power by being able to adapt to any situation instantly. To accomplish this, develop three moods of delivery:

1. Light. You can be easy without being careless, and you can be funny without getting hooked on it. I've known salespeople who'd rather get a laugh than make a sale. Do some of your laughing on the way to the bank by using humor in sales situations to further sales, not to amuse yourself.

   If humor isn't your forte now, don't worry; it'll come in time. Meanwhile, cultivate a relaxed approach that'll ease you into closing position with the more informal of your prospects who can't stand the all-business attitude.
2. Medium. A cordial, alert, matter-of-fact stance gives you the safest start with old customers who have volatile temperaments and with new prospects you don't know yet.
3. Heavy. Be prepared to talk fast and concisely in high-pressure situations. Nothing works well here except bone and muscle delivered in short, crisp sentences. No jokes, no flowery phrases, no confusing technicalities. Practice this one hard and you'll be surprised how often you'll use it, and delighted how often you'll win with it.

That's the triad concept. It sounds complex, but it isn't. All you have to do is train yourself to think in terms of three: three routes to every treasure, three solutions for every problem, three chances at every opportunity.

Do this and you can't fail to multiply your effectiveness, reduce your frustrations, and expand your income.

THE SENSES THAT SELL THE EMOTIONS

How many senses do you have?

Sight. Hearing. Touch. Taste. Smell. Intuition. Champions do their best to get as many of their senses involved as possible. Now, if you're the kind of person who's just talk, talk, talk, *talk*, how many senses are you involving?

One only—hearing, plus a little bit of sight. But after a while even your most interested potential clients get sick of looking at you. That's why the Champion operates on this theory, and it's one you should highlight:

The more senses you involve, the better your odds of making the sale.

Throughout this book, you'll find techniques to help you involve more of your prospects' senses in the service or product that you're offering. In this connection, let me tell you about one of the Champions I've had the privilege of training. This young man quickly became number one in residential resales in his state.

You're familiar with the real estate open house—flags and arrow signs on strategic corners to guide people to a house that's for sale. And, of course, a salesperson is there to help people get happily involved in that or another housing unit in the area.

As soon as he had committed himself to pushing his volume far above average performance, this young man decided to review his entire selling sequence, starting from the basics. So he asked himself, *What is the most powerful common factor that's been present in every sale I've made so far?*

After quite a bit of analysis and thought, he realized it was that the prospects became excited about the home emotionally, and then they worked out the necessary details—in their heads and on paper—so that they could own it.

Once he began looking for it, he soon learned to recognize the emotional involvement even with people who habitually concealed their feelings.

So he set about determining how to reach their emotions sooner and better. When people in light summer clothing walked into his open houses and found a small fire merrily blazing, a look of amazement would appear on their faces. That's when he'd warmly smile as if to agree with them and say, "Are you wondering why I have a fire going in this weather?"

Aren't the odds good that they'll answer and break the ice?

Then he's say, "Let me explain. I want to do my best to help everyone coming in here experience the emotions of all four seasons. My wife and I really enjoy a crackling warm fire in the fireplace on a cold winter night, don't you?"

Is that involvement? Will they remember that home? Will they remember him?

Yes on all three.

Of course, he didn't charge into his open house an hour late carrying an armload of wet stinkwood and a quart of diesel sludge to make it burn. With a little research in his fireplace at home, he learned how to build small fires that keep burning the whole afternoon with little attention and give off delightful woodsy aromas the entire time.

But he didn't stop there in his campaign to happily involve all of his prospects' senses. After selecting a few tapes of mood music, he acquired a portable player he could take to open houses. In their kitchens, he always pulled the old vanilla trick (baked a few drops in the oven) to fill that part of the house with a pleasant scent that evokes images of warmth, shelter, and good home cooking. He paid attention to how each room could best be lighted. In every house he looked for unique ways to appeal to prospective buyers through all their senses.

What did he achieve by bringing that high level of personal involvement to his selling opportunities?

He immediately began connecting with a higher percentage of the people who came through his open houses because they saw that he was different, bright, and concerned. He didn't have to tell them that; they saw it for themselves. Outstanding performance during open houses brought him the surge of referral business that vaulted him to the top in his state in prestige, earning power, and personal satisfaction.

He did it by using all his clients' senses to eliminate that powerful emotion called fear, and to create instead a galaxy of positive emotions that would draw them into happy involvement through him rather than through another agent. What he did—and does—is the very essence of what the Champion salesperson does: He makes use of every constructive and warm feeling that he can to bring his clients along with him emotionally until they say, "I want it, I want it, *I want it.*"

5. Why Don't I Do What I Know I Should Do?

Why don't I do what I know I should do? Ask this question of yourself. Ask seriously because the answer controls your future. Until you start doing what you know you should do, you're living under a law against success that you've imposed on yourself.

Behind that question stands this challenge: *How can I cause myself to do what I know I should do?* I'll soon tell you how, but first take time to understand the why.

You've frequently asked yourself questions like the above two. Everyone in sales has, except the top producers (who are doing what they know they should do) and the defeated (who've trained themselves not to ask anymore). You're not a member of that last group for many important reasons I can't know about, and for one that I do: You're reading these words. This means that you've opened your mind to new and possibly disturbing ideas, that you're willing to change your way of doing things whenever you discover a change that'll help.

When you began your new selling career, what did you have a big supply of?

Enthusiasm.

Do you remember? Burning desire. Excitement. The feeling of *Watch out, world, here I come. Now that I've got this terrific opportunity in sales, there's no limit to what I can do.*

Yes, you had enthusiasm and desire then. Yes, you were eager and excited about what you were going to do. No problem getting out of bed in the morning: You were raring to go. You had every-thing necessary for success except one item: knowledge. You sim-ply didn't know what you were doing. But that was okay; your enthusiasm made up for it.

Then what happened?

Some months passed. You learned your product, your way around the territory, how accounts are found, what the challenges are. But while you gathered that knowledge, what happened to your enthusiasm?

It dwindled a bit, didn't it? But your product is still as fresh to new customers today as it was the day you started—it's just not fresh to you anymore. You've had time not only to see the negatives that every industry, company, and product has, you've also had time to dwell on them, time to let these negatives influence your actions.

Your gain of knowledge merely matched your loss of enthusiasm, and balanced your performance out to about average—far below your potential. Make no mistake about it: Under your skin a Cham-pion is struggling to get out. A front-runner. A big earner. A high flier.

So now you know what to do, but you aren't doing it. Why? In most organizations, lack of the specific product knowledge required for that sales position isn't the main issue among the salespeople who've been there for several months. It probably isn't for you, ei-ther. Motivating yourself to do what you already know you should do is the main challenge.

Why is this true?

Because what you should do is not what you want to do. If it were, you'd be doing it.

Now we've come to the cutting edge:

Why don't you want to do what you know you should do?

The reason you don't is that you're in conflict with yourself. This conflict comes about because the push forward of your wants and needs can't overcome the push backward of your fears and anxieties.

A bit later, we're going to study these wants and needs of yours in detail. Wants and needs are motivators, and everyone feels them. We're also going to take a close look at the demotivators that everyone also feels. When you feel a demotivator, you feel fear or anxiety—which is why demotivators are so powerful. They can dry your mouth, make your knees bang together like loose shutters in the wind, and light a fire in your stomach—or they can work in soft and subtle ways to kill your action. They're powerful, all right. That's why we're going to study them.

Almost all success-seeking people have been torn by this conflict at some point in their careers, and most of us live with it all our active lives. Perhaps we can't eliminate this ongoing battle. But we can decide whether we'll lose every day, lose usually, win usually, or win every time. We can't, of course, win every sale. Forces beyond our control will cost us a sale now and then. That's okay. What isn't okay is to constantly lose out to our same old unresolved fears and anxieties.

Think about that. In the privacy of your own thoughts, consider whether this conflict isn't the chief obstacle to your being an outstanding success. Not lack of ability, not lack of product knowledge, but simply nonperformance of what you know you should do because of conflict.

Resolving these fears and anxieties is surprisingly easy when you know how to do it. The first requirement is to admit that you're like everyone else—you have them. They may not show on the outside. But the people around you have them, and you have them. Recognizing this fact is the first gate you have to go through. The next one is to decide that you're not going to let those beatable fears and anxieties stand between you and what you want in life.

When you've made that decision, read on. Explore how you get depressed. Study this enemy and find the weak point you'll strike at to eliminate it. Learn about the motivators and how to use them; about the demotivators and how to defeat them. Then you'll start doing what you know you should do. You'll do that naturally and without great strain because you want to.

HOW YOU GET DEPRESSED

Do you ever get down? Do you ever have times when you just can't get up and make yourself do what you know you should do? Days when you'd just as soon drive right by the office, not call in, and hide? Ever have that feeling? Let me show you how you got that feeling.

It's a safe bet that you wouldn't be in the profession of selling if you weren't interested in making money. And it's an equally safe bet that you'll agree with this statement: *I don't make as much money when I'm depressed as I do when I'm enthusiastic.*

If you accept that, I think you'll go along with this idea: *If I can decrease the time I'm depressed, and increase the time I'm enthusiastic, I'll make more money.*

Notice that I haven't said "Increase your enthusiasm and you'll automatically decrease your depression." Thousands of sales meetings every month prove that the pep imparted from the stage is lost before the depressed salespeople in the group get out the door. On the rust of conflict-caused depression, you can spray any amount of enthusiasm—and it always flakes off. But enthusiasm does stick to alertness, knowledge, and purpose. That's why I make this assertion in complete confidence: "Decrease your depression and you'll automatically increase your enthusiasm." Compare the two quotation-marked sentences in this paragraph. The difference between these deceptively similar statements is enormous: The second one works, the first doesn't. Following the first statement produces the slim pickings of failure; following the second produces the riches and satisfactions of success.

Certainly, build your enthusiasm by every reasonable means. But before you throw yourself into that useful activity, make sure your enthusiasm will have a clean surface to stick to. Sandblast the rust of depression off your brain first.

To do that, you need to know exactly how you get depressed.

Let's take a close look at the conflict that starts a frustration that grows until it depresses you. I call this whole process "forging the chain of depression" because it is a series of events. As with any chain, to destroy its holding power you need break only one link.

Here is the process by which you've been forging the chain of depression within yourself—the steps to getting down:

1. Conscious of your wants and needs, you motivate yourself—and move forward. Imagine yourself starting the engine of a high-powered sports car.
2. Conscious of your fears and anxieties, you demotivate yourself—and are stopped. Your sports car is sitting in mud up to its hubcaps; the drive wheels are spinning but you aren't going anywhere.
3. Some of the salespeople around you are moving ahead—but you aren't, and your frustration mounts rapidly. You see what they are doing, you know what you should do, but the more you want to, the harder it is to make yourself do it. In the sports car, you gun the engine and throw lots of mud. But you don't move. Instead, you dig yourself in deeper. Your frustration runs into the red, and you pound the wheel angrily.
4. Because you aren't able to close sales and move forward to satisfy your wants and needs, you lose faith in your product and company or—what's much worse—in yourself. When any of these things happen, the frustration eating at you turns into depression. It's as though you give up trying to gun your sports car out of the mud, shut off the engine, and step out into the muck to go it on foot.
5. Now you're too depressed to take any effective course of action on your own, and you'll remain in that immobile state until some outside force moves you out of it.

A sports car driver, confronted by the simple mechanical problem described, would immediately squish off through the mud in search of a tow. But we're slower to go looking for help when confounded by depression in sales work because the solution to our situation isn't obvious. In fact, we might not even recognize that we have a common challenge, one that can readily be resolved.

If you're depressed now about your sales performance, ever

have been in the past, or think it's possible that you could be in the future, you need to review the sources of motivation.

THE MOTIVATORS

The first motivator of the great salesperson is money. Why is money a motivator? It allows you to get the things you want and need. Money is good. Repeat that out loud.

Money is good.
Money Is Good.
MONEY IS GOOD.

Money is good so long as what you earn is in direct proportion to the service you give. It's good, but money by itself won't make you happy. All that money can do is give you opportunities to explore what will make you happy. And while you're searching, you'll be a lot happier with money than without it, don't you agree?

The way to get more money is to change the *s* in the word *Service* into a dollar sign: $ervice. This is because the amount of money you earn is totally dictated by the amount and level of service you provide to others. Money is what I call a scoreboard reflection of the service you give. If you aren't making enough money, you aren't giving enough service.

The second motivator is security. Maslow's Hierarchy of Needs is the foundation of most motivational courses. This theory teaches that the average human being strives daily to supply physical needs—that is, to obtain security. In a primitive society, security might be a flock of goats and a weatherproof cave or tent; in our society, security is something bought with money. Without money, you can't buy clothes. If you ran around naked, would you agree that you'd feel somewhat insecure? If you aren't wearing the right quality and style of clothes for a given occasion, you also feel insecure. Money buys a wide variety of possessions that to some degree provide us with a feeling of security. So money is a tremendous motivator, both as a direct measure of success and as a provider of a sense of security.

Achievement is the third motivator. Almost everyone wants to achieve, but almost no one wants to do what's necessary to achieve. I believe that people everywhere are broken into two groups: achievers and nonachievers.

Achievers make up only 5 percent of the world, and nonachievers account for the other 95 percent. This is explained by the fact that a nonachiever is achieving nonachievement, which is an achievement for the nonachiever. So nonachievers find it all too easy to accept their failure to achieve anything of real worth and meaning. People who have nothing are usually achieving what they think they deserve: nothing.

Many of us were raised in environments where our loved ones, mothers, fathers, brothers, sisters, were wonderful and upstanding people. They also might be nonachievers.

If so, that's okay—for them.

We're achievement-oriented, but maybe we've learned from nonachievers in our own families, and adopted the characteristics of nonachievement. Let's not concern ourselves here with trying to rescue any of your loved ones who might be nonachievers—because it can't be done. The will to achieve is not something that can be imposed on anyone from the outside; that drive must come from within. You have that drive or you wouldn't be reading these words. Your example may inspire your loved ones. Your success may make it possible for you to open doors to knowledge and opportunity for them. But you can't force the will to achieve on them. You can't achieve anything of lasting worth by pushing a nonachiever through doors of knowledge and opportunity if that person isn't eager to stride through.

Are you ready to throw off being a nonachiever? Are you ready to join that elite 5 percent of the population who earn the right to enjoy the delicacies of society?

Look at this from another perspective as well. Everyone you know also wants achievement. If what you offer, through your products and services, helps them achieve what they're after, they'll in turn help you with what you wish to achieve.

Through seminars, audio programs, videos, and this book, I've been fortunate enough to train people who are tired of being average, people who are ready and willing to join the elite, people who want to reach out for more, people who are ready to make the investment in personal change and effort. I hope you've decided that it's time to quit messing around being average, time to stop wallowing in the quagmire of mediocrity, time to reach out for the greatness that's inherent in all human beings.

The fourth motivator is recognition. This is an interesting motivator, one I often think is the most important to our breed of sales folks. People will do more for recognition than for anything else. Everyone needs recognition: husbands, wives, children—even your boss. We all do. When you were young, why did you do cartwheels out in the backyard? What did you want to get?

Recognition. "Hey, Mommy and Daddy, look at me. I'm doing great!"

In our search for recognition as adults, we play far more complex games. The cars we drive, the clothes we wear, the restaurants we dine in, the places we travel to, and a host of other things along those lines are all devices that we use to seek recognition.

We can argue that most of these things are necessities. Perhaps. We can claim to enjoy these things for themselves. Certainly. But without the need for recognition, would we be so obsessed with style and personalization?

We all crave and require recognition. That's why this motivator has such awesome power when it's used at full throttle. Many sales managers boost their sales force's performance more with recognition than with any other motivator. Even more managers get scant benefit from it because they give too little too late and too carelessly. To be effective on a sales force, recognition must be real. It must be prompt. It must be given with sincerity and without favoritism. Its quality or value must be in line with what was achieved.

Acceptance by others is motivator number five, and this is a dangerous one.

Do you know how many people strive every day to be accepted by everyone else? With many people, including many in sales, that's their greatest motivation—and their greatest weakness. But we all want to be liked, don't we?

Now, here's an interesting thing that happens to every new salesperson regardless of the product or service. When you're brand-new to your company (and maybe you're also new to the profession of selling) and first go into your new sales job all loaded with enthusiasm, who's sitting there waiting to accept or reject you?

Is it the achievers or the nonachievers who're parked there? Is it the Five Percent or the Ninety-Five Percent?

Which group lives in the office? Which group is out running for more business?

The chances are good that someone will say, "Now, let me tell you how things really stand around here." When that happens, you'd think there's one chance in twenty of that someone being an achiever, but in fact you may not even see the achievers for weeks. They're busy doing the things that make them great. When you're finally introduced to one of the Five Percent, they'll say something like this and not much more: "Glad to have you with us. This is a terrific company, and you're going to do great here. Nice meeting you. See you later."

Some people in your company will tell you that my training won't help you. Without giving these concepts and techniques a fair trial, they'll say that. After merely skimming these pages, looking for something to ridicule, some of them will say that. Without even cracking this book open, a few will say that. These people are the losers, and they want you to join them. The last thing they want you to do is join the winners. To show why this is so important to them, let's get on the case of Jack Bumyears.

Jack's been in the sales department of your new firm for almost eleven years now—and he hasn't learned a new sales technique in 120 months. When you start, everyone from the company president on down wants you to succeed—except Jack and his friends. Every time someone new comes whistling in from nowhere and makes good, Jack is faced with a hard question: *This new jerk did it. Why can't I?*

Bumyears knows the answer to that question as well as anyone does: Jack is a nonachiever because Jack refuses to be effective. But that's the one answer Jack can't accept. To do so would be admitting to himself that his work habits and methods must be drastically changed before he can succeed. Too painful, too frightening to think about. Far easier to blame the newcomer's success on favoritism, pure dumb luck, a lack of ethics—anything that will steer the guilt away from Jack's shoulders.

But no matter how ingenious Jack's been about excuses, no matter how much time and effort he puts into keeping those excuses tight, the truth is always in there, gnawing to be free.

After this happens a time or two, Jack automatically develops anxiety whenever a newcomer shows promise. Alert, hardworking, eager-to-learn people have a nasty habit of succeeding quickly, Jack learns, and that always forces him into another agonizing search for an acceptable explanation. The pain reaches down into Jack's subconscious mind and demands relief. Then Jack begins to act on a sad and false belief: That the best way to cope with other people's success is not to have any of it around. Soon he's attained a high level of nonachievement by becoming skilled at stifling ambition among his peers. When a new person says, "Well, I'd better get going. I have a bunch of calls to make," old Jack will reply with, "At this time of day? You'll never find anyone in."

Every weakness detected in an eager person is deftly exploited. "You having a problem with your paperwork? The company has made it too hard to get it right. You'll always have problems with it."

Peer pressure is subtly guided toward containing anyone who shows signs of drive. If these tactics seem to be failing, Bumyears and friends will suddenly turn cold and reject the budding winner whenever they can, turning their backs when the new person enters the office, avoiding eye contact, and possibly not sharing information that should be shared. This is where the ambitious salesperson who has a strong need to be accepted by peers runs into danger, because the price of peer acceptance is to accept being average. Only the strong can resist this pressure; only the strong can pay this additional price of success.

Our profession of sales is one of the few that people can retire inside of. You can get by in this business doing very little, but as I mentioned in chapter 1, it'll be the lowest-paid easy work you'll find. If you discover folks who attack the usefulness of this book, find out their income. If they're not making what you want to make, you've found a Jack Bumyears and will know to avoid him or take whatever he says with a grain of salt.

Surround yourself with people most like the person you want to become. Whether you realize it or not, what happens is that you become more like the people you associate with, and less like the people you don't associate with. You unconsciously pick up little and large ways of achieving—or not achieving—from the people you rub elbows with every day. Unconsciously, you gather attitudes and ideas, absorbing everything from petty details to major concepts that'll spur you on to greater achievement—or sink you deeper into nonachievement.

Don't hang around with people whose financial and emotional thinking is on a lower level than yours. You need to grow. They don't. So they won't help you expand your horizons, and they can't inspire you. Choosing the right associates calls for hard decisions. But we have to drift away from people more messed up than ourselves, or we'll continue to soak up their influence, advice, and failings. Family responsibilities are one thing; your choice of friends is another. Mix with people who are pluses. It's hard enough keeping yourself up so you can climb higher. Don't make it tougher on yourself—possibly too tough—by trying to drag a bunch of losers up with you.

Are you trying to get everyone to like you?

Are you holding back a little on your push for success because you don't want to anger certain people who've let you know they don't care for hard drivers?

Why? You can't afford to be popular with the losers.

Write down the names of the people you spend most of your time with. Go over this list carefully, and think about whether each person on it is an emotional plus for you. Put everyone who isn't a positive force in your life on a second list, and then consider finding new people to be around instead of the nonplusers on your second list. If you decide to replace any of your present associates who are negative with enthusiastic new friends, you'll be pleased at how effortless this process will be if you do it gradually. No open breaks. No frank discussions. Simply make yourself less available to the minus people, and fill the time saved with activities that'll bring you into contact with positive new people. Some of them will become your friends.

The sixth motivator is self-acceptance. I hope you get this one because you can't realize your fullest potential without this achievement.

We all hunger for it. Self-acceptance is calcium for the bones of our personalities. Many of us keep those bones weak by making our self-acceptance dependent on the approval of others. Weak bones make for a hard life. Confusing self-acceptance with acceptance by others makes for a hard life.

You may have trouble thinking about self-acceptance in any way that doesn't involve acceptance by others. Many of us simply aren't in the business of accepting ourselves, although few of us ever get out of the business of rejecting ourselves. Positive input depends on others; negative input, we provide ourselves. This is a no-win system.

The harder we work at trying to succeed this way, the more vulnerable we make ourselves. People sense our need, play our weakness to their own advantage, and decide for themselves whether we fail or succeed. Watch carefully where you seek approval. If you drift into seeking it from someone who'd be threatened by your success, you're in big trouble.

Self-acceptance is the state of being your own person. You have arrived. Not where somebody else sent you, you have arrived exactly where you want to be. Self-acceptance marks the day when the opinions of other people don't control you anymore. It's the day you start making yourself heard when you don't agree. It's the night you suddenly jump a jet to Europe for a vacation; it's the morning you stay in bed because you want to. It's the hour when you're all through with the games you don't want to play, through with the roles you don't want to live. It's the minute you finally unlock your potential, become you, know that you've become you, and know that you are completely and gloriously your own person. Doesn't that sound exciting?

Very few people get there.

Why do so many of us fail to attain self-acceptance?

Because we don't limit the number of people we must have approval from.

Because we demand more approval from the world than the world is willing to give us—and weaken our action in a vain attempt to get it.

Because we don't grasp how important it is to truly accept ourselves. Some of us dimly see what's lacking, and try to force self-acceptance on ourselves.

But those little voices inside our heads keep on cutting us down to size no matter how loud and aggressive and stubborn we act.

Yes, it is difficult to become yourself until you've learned to be comfortable with an attainable amount of acceptance from other people. Until you can stop worrying about this, you can't become you.

And you'll never reach self-acceptance, the state where you can function best and be happiest, until you get some recognition and enhance your self-image. You won't get recognition until you have some achievement. You'll never have achievement until you develop a feeling of security. And you won't have a feeling of security until you start making some money.

You can get money, security, achievement, recognition, acceptance of others—and still not have self-acceptance. You probably know successful people who have all these things except self-acceptance.

We've all read about entertainers who reach stardom and then commit suicide. They had money; they had security; stardom is defined as recognition and acceptance by others—but they failed to achieve self-acceptance. Everybody liked them. That is, everybody liked each of them except one person. That one person hated what they'd become to get what they thought they wanted. The most sincere form of self-criticism is suicide.

The next most sincere form is the living suicide that so many people inflict on themselves when their cravings for the satisfactions of the six motivators far outrun what they can attain. Those who feel they're entitled to these things as gifts react the same way when the world refuses to hand them all they desire. They retreat into destructive habits and attitudes, and rob their lives of productivity, joy, and meaning. Don't defeat yourself before you begin to fight: Don't demand immediate satisfactions far greater than those you can immediately obtain.

There's one more motivator I teach. It's nearly as powerful as self-acceptance, though it doesn't appear on Maslow's original list. I've added this one after both my personal experiences and seeing those of others. **The seventh motivator is love of family.** It is tied in with all of the other motivators. You can work hard to achieve, earn money, be recognized, attain security, have others accept you, and accept yourself, but if you don't give your loved ones a high level of "service"—being involved in their lives, showing them recognition, providing them security, and so on—you'll find yourself successful by most people's terms, but alone. Don't lose sight of what's truly important in your personal life while attaining success in your business life. I know of too many top sales professionals who appeared to have it all yet destroyed their relationships with those who should have been most important in their lives. Having your family's love and admiration makes everything else you achieve ten times better.

Those are the seven basic motivators—powerful, gut-level emotions that drive us all. Untamed, they drown us; harnessed, they supply unlimited energy. Study them.

They affect you in many ways: on the surface, in the shallows, and in the depths of your ego. You can't learn too much about them and about how you can control their enormous forces.

As a starting point, look at your past. Feel your past. Your past has determined where you are at this moment; your immediate future will soon be the past that will determine your more distant future. As you get farther into these pages, please realize that I'm writing to you about your life. Time passes at the same speed for everyone—it just seems to pass more slowly in slums than in Monte Carlo. Where will you be in five years? Develop a plan, and then activate that plan to put yourself where you want to be in five years. And be sure to update your five-year plan at least annually.

THE DEMOTIVATORS

Now we're going to talk about why people don't get all the things they're motivated to seek. Open your mind up now, because the first demotivator is common to many of us. Do you know how many people are so afraid of losing the security they have that they won't give it up to get the greater security they crave?

But what exactly is security? Is it really possible to have it?

I believe that there is no such thing as security other than the security you build within yourself; that you are secure only to the extent of your ability to cope with the challenge called living; that you cannot be more secure than your capabilities for handling insecurity allow you to be.

This means that you have to give up what you've got to get what you want. Hanging on to everything you've got often means that that's all you're going to get. This applies to business matters and to personal matters: to possessions, responsibilities, opportunities, and relationships.

It means that you'll spend money to make money. This is true for all businesses. You may be a sales representative for a large firm, but you are in essence building your own clientele, your own business. And a professional knows, a Champion knows, that an investment is required—not only of time, but also of money. In a later chapter, I'll discuss some of the methods of spending money to make more money: mailing pieces, for example. Few beginning salespeople use the mails as effectively as they could and should. Why don't they? Primarily because they're unwilling to give up part of what they have to get what they want. They want to achieve the outstanding sales record that breeds a large income along with security, recognition, and acceptance. But they don't want to give up anything they have now to get what they want from the future.

Isn't that strange? It's as though they don't believe that the future will ever get here. Or that it doesn't need any room in their lives. If your future is to be better than your present, your future must have space. Your future must be built. And your future must be paid for. You may not need a mail campaign. But you do need to invest in your credibility, as expressed by your grooming and clothing. You do need to invest in building your sales knowledge and skills. Success looks the part. Success knows how to do the job. When you have all that going for you, is there any doubt that you'll do the job?

So the first demotivator is fear of losing security, fear of losing what you already have.

To help combat this fear, give thought to the fact that all relationships, skills, and possessions require some degree of attention—or you lose them. Think clearly in this area. If you refuse to give up anything that you now have, where will the space, time, money, and energy come from for new achievements?

The second demotivator is fear of failure. Most people have a challenge with this one. I did, early in my career.

Would you like to learn a method to guarantee that you'll never fail to make the appointment, never fail to make a strong presentation, never fail to close the sale? I can teach you that very quickly.

Here it is: Never pick up the phone, never make a presentation, never try for a close.

You can avoid ever failing by just never trying. How many people in the profession of selling are hiding every day from the chance that they might fail?

Let me give you a personal example of this. The first time I ever stood in front of an audience was in a second-grade school play. I'd been asked to play Prince Charming. I got to prance around, wave a rubber sword, and kiss the princess. Now, this is exciting in the second grade. My mom and dad were there. My relatives and all my friends were there. I was excited to be the star. In the wings the night of the play, standing behind the curtains dressed in my purple pants and my purple cape, in my turned-up silver shoes and my plastic-jeweled sword, I was ready for my performance. Keep in mind that I had never seen an audience's eyeballs.

Suddenly my cue line came. I walked out on stage.

I froze.

I could not move.

Finally, they came out and just led me off. Now, you know that experience was traumatic. From that moment on, I had a phobia about getting in front of a group. I simply would not do it.

Then, many years later, after achieving a high degree of success, I was invited by a major firm to speak. They'd heard about my sales volume and wrote, "Will you come here and teach your methods to our sales staff?"

I shot a letter right back. "Pass. I don't talk to anyone."

Then a man very dear to my heart said, "Tommy, do what you fear most and you control fear."

Think about that. (I'm not talking here about defying physical danger, or hazardous thrill-seeking.) Think of something you should do professionally, something that you aren't doing because of fear. Then picture yourself doing that feared thing with ease and skill and success. If you can make yourself believe that you're actually going to do that thing soon, you'll experience some symptoms of fear.

Or you may not be able to take all this very seriously—because your fear of actually doing what you fear may be too great. Sometimes we have to let ideas cook in our brains until we're ready to serve them up. But don't let this idea get lost. Write these words down and put them with your business cards:

Do what you fear most and you control fear.

Read those words every chance you get. One day, when you're ready to act and eager to conquer your fear, those words will suddenly grab you. Then you'll be done with this sad truth: If you don't control fear, fear controls you. Then you'll prepare carefully, challenge your fear, and conquer that fear for all time. And every time you conquer one fear, you'll find it easier to take on and beat your next fear. But you don't always win the first time out. Be prepared for that. The important thing is to jump on that fear for the first time. After that, it's not an uphill road anymore.

But you have to get past that first time. After I thought about controlling fear by doing what I feared most, I had to agree that I was allowing a fear to control my life. So I called the company that had invited me to speak. I said I'd do it.

That was about a month before the date of my speech. I served those thirty days like an inmate on death row, wishing every hour that I hadn't done it. The nearer the time for my speech came, the more panicky I got. *What am I going to say?* I kept asking myself. *Why did I do this to myself?*

At night, after writing out what I was going to say, I'd read what I'd written out loud. Then I'd tear it up and start over. Finally someone told me to put it all on three-by-five cards. So I wrote it all out on three-by-five cards.

The night before my first speech, I didn't sleep at all. The next morning I walked into a huge auditorium. Three thousand people were seated there. I stood off in the wings as they started my introduction. They introduced me. I walked out—By the way, if you're not a professional speaker, have them provide a podium. That gives you something to hang on to. And the audience can't see your knees banging together.

Well, I looked down at my notes and just let 'er rip. I never looked at the audience, I just kept on talking. I was scheduled to speak for forty-five minutes. In eight minutes I'd covered every point.

That first time was awful. The second time was terrible. The third time was yuk. The fourth time they clapped a little. The fifth time they stayed. Now, after speaking day after day after day with the finest group I know, salespeople, I wake in the morning with anticipation. Excitement. All this for overcoming the fear of failure in the beginning.

How many people do you know who won't try because they're afraid they may fail? Isn't it sad how many of us consign ourselves to the junkyard of mediocrity rather than accept the momentary rejections that success demands? If you take just one idea from this book, make this one yours and it'll repay your reading cost ten-thousand-fold:

I'm too proud of my future to beat myself out of it.

The third demotivator is self-doubt. This one holds special interest for all of us in sales. Before you entered this field, you probably mentioned that you might to your friends and relatives. Then what did you hear?

"Selling? You're thinking about selling? For a living? Know what that means? Feast or famine. Chicken dinner one night, feathers the next. What are you, crazy?"

Listening to that refrain a few times can plant the seeds of self-doubt in your brain, and stain your enthusiasm with fear before you begin. That fear can spur you to greater effort—or it can cause you to look for a soft spot to fall. "Okay, I'll just give selling a try," you tell your friends and relatives. "I'll give it a chance. If I like it, fine. If not, no big deal—I'll give something else a shot."

The trouble is, you hear your own words when you hedge your commitment to sales that way. Elsewhere in this book, an effective method of convincing people is stated in these words: "If they say it, it's true." That method also works for us—for us or against us. You can't go into sales with a give-it-a-whack, see-how-it-goes attitude without weakening your resolve to do the difficult things (like facing rejection) that must be done if you are to succeed.

Tell people you've decided on a career in sales. No ifs, ands, or buts. Commit yourself to success in sales. Don't brag about all you're going to do, but don't excuse yourself from all-out effort, either. Don't predict your own failure and then float out to prove how good you are at making predictions.

And don't set your sights on being average. If you do, that's what you'll be. When you're new, with few or no sales yet, being average might seem like a safe and successful place to be. It isn't. Here's why: In most companies, one-third of the salespeople do two-thirds of the business. (Obviously, the exact figures will vary from year to year and from firm to firm—though not by much.) That's neat for the top third, but the bottom two-thirds of every sales force must live on the income generated by one-third of that company's sales.

That's twice the people splitting half the money. Every time a bottom-grouper gets one dollar, a top-grouper gets four dollars. Unless you're on the right end of this split, it's tempting to blame company policy for this huge difference. Resist that temptation. Yielding to it blinds you to three truths that all great salespeople know:

1. Management hates depending on so few of its salespeople for so much of its sales.
2. Management can't put you into the top group; only you can put yourself into the top group.

3. If you're only average, you're only making a fourth of what the top-groupers have proved can be earned in your job.

You stop being average the day you decide to become a Champion, because the average person won't make that decision. You stop being average the day you commit to an all-out effort to win the level of success you want, because the average person never makes that commitment. After you've made that decision and that commitment, you'll start handling rejection differently. When you fail to get the appointment, you don't ask what the average salesperson asks: "What did I do wrong?"

When people come into your showroom or display area and then walk out without your product or service, you don't ask, "What did I do *wrong*?"

When you demonstrate or present with eloquence and verve until the prospect warmly and with love asks you to leave, you don't ask yourself, "*What did I do wrong?*"

You don't ask that because doing so reinforces self-doubt. With enough reinforcement, self-doubt becomes negative conviction.

When you're gripped by negative conviction, you believe that everything you do will be wrong; being wrong, everything you do will fail; therefore, you will fail. That's negative conviction, and every sales position provides ample opportunities to catch it if you expose yourself to the virus. Negative conviction is especially dangerous to new people in sales. If they take every opportunity to ask themselves what they did wrong, they'll repeat that question an enormous number of times during their first few months.

What do Champions ask whenever they fail?

"What did I do *right*?"

Champions keep on doing what they did right, keep their up-attitude, overcome the rejection, keep on trying, and start to win. The wins pile up until they smother any sneaky self-doubt under a pyramid of positive conviction. Most people don't move because they are demotivated by their self-doubts, which they turn into negative convictions. From here on out, ask not, "What did I do wrong?" Dwell on "What did I do *right*?"

"Wait a minute," you say. "I'm standing by the showroom window, getting a face-tan and feeling good, when this nonbuyer comes in, proceeds to give me a hard time, and then walks out. Until he came in, I was feeling good. Now I'm feeling rotten. Naturally I'm going to ask, 'What did I do wrong?' Any fool can see that."

Any fool can ask that question, but Champions, the top-groupers, don't leave their self-esteem and up-attitude lying around where any stray hard nose can stomp on them.

What you did right was to get to work on time, groomed appropriately and with a positive belief in your product or service. What you did right was to be accessible to your potential clients. What you did right was to offer your finest service to them. If they chose not to own it, you can analyze what you might do differently the next time, but by all means don't discredit everything that you did correctly.

The fourth demotivator is the pain of change. This is the toughest and most challenging demotivator for my seminar groups to learn how to cope with. It's also one of the most harmful demotivators. I hope you'll make a special effort to conquer it.

Why does change always seem to involve pain? We resist change because it means that part of our old self must die, and that an unknown new self will be born. We grieve the loss of the familiar as we labor through the painful birth of the strange. It's all very primitive.

Some of us resist change because we've suffered sudden, painful events in the past, perhaps in childhood. In adulthood, this finds its echo in statements such as *I don't like surprises*, and the tendency to defend against disaster by striking at change.

Individuals aren't the only ones to fight change. Companies do it; nations do it. But the world changes anyway.

We've all heard this dull-witted comment many times: "That's how it is"; this pointless reason: "We've always done it that way"; this pure unreason: "I'm not changing." Meanwhile, the inevitable forces of change are modifying how it is by making that way unprofitable and phasing out the person who's not changing. We can fight the forces of change and win some temporary victories against it—but we can't win the war. In the end, we change or we lose.

So don't fight change, make it work for you. That's easier said than done because we all tend to fight change with strong emotions, and to use change for less potent intellectual reasons. Here's how to break that pattern. Here's how to make change a powerful and positive force in your upward drive:

- Face the issue squarely by thinking through your emotional fear of change. Then consciously separate your feelings about intensifying your work methods from your feelings about losing the familiar, about the passing years, and about coping with the strange and new.
- Keep the best of the old in your life so that you'll have a strong emotional foundation on which to build helpful change.
- Make a habit of trying new things when you don't have to.
- Every day, tell someone that you're quick to adopt new ideas, that you like sampling new things, that you're always learning, changing, and growing. Keep saying this and you'll believe it, act on it, and make it true.
- While there's an element of pain in all changes, those that are thrust on you by other people hurt far more than changes you put in motion yourself. Instead of sitting back and limply waiting for the next ax of change to fall on your life, be the cutting edge of positive change and improve your life.

My purpose isn't to ask you to change, it's to show you how to be happy. If you're unhappy, put up with the temporary pain that's involved in changing. If you won't put up with the necessary pain of change, however, then just be happy where you are. If you can't do that because your happiness is slipping away from you, recognize that you're starting to feel the pain of changes thrust on you by others. That situation is all too common in life. The best—and perhaps the only—way to beat it is to take command of your future and start changing things yourself.

There's going to be some pain involved in putting the ideas in these pages to work for you. Face it.

We all have certain ideas and values. We are us, and we're not going to change. Let me give you an example. Hypothetically, let's say that for health reasons it's a wise decision for you to lose weight at this time. Let's suppose that you're fifty pounds overweight. If you're happy being fifty pounds overweight, then you should just stay that way and never think about dieting. If you're unhappy with the extra weight, however, then you'd be wise to do something about it, don't you agree?

The day you commit to a diet, you're going to go through some pain. You're going to feel pain until you lose those fifty pounds. Then, as you slither down the street and everyone asks how you did it, you'll smile and say, "Nothing to it."

Stop reading this book right now and copy on whatever notepad is handy:

The pain of every change is forgotten when the benefits of that change are realized.

This is true of all changes. Once you've done it, the pain is forgotten. A perfect example is the young woman giving birth for the first time. Quite often, while that's happening, she's making a firm commitment: *Never again.* And then the beautiful baby, who is the creation of her and her husband's love, is brought to the new mother. She holds it and nurses it. Sure enough, in two years she's back in that same delivery room. It's the same with all positive changes.

I remember when I was prospecting day and night. I didn't like prospecting any better than the next salesperson does—until after I'd done it and the money started pouring in.

The pain of change is forgotten once you do what you commit to do. And besides that, there's such an excitement to taking command of your life in positive and effective ways. But now, watch this ever so carefully. Look how we begin our conflict. We all want the motivators, but we can't overcome the demotivators.

"I want to make a lot of money so that I can have security, acquire a feeling of achievement, collect some recognition, and be accepted by the people I come in contact with. And when I have all that, I know I'll accept and feel good about myself. But I'm not giving up the security I have now. I don't feel good—but I'm not miserable. So I'm not going to call those people back—

- "If they don't want our entertainment system in their home, that's tough."
- "If they can't see that our cars are the best on the road, that's their problem."
- "If they're incapable of grasping that our telephone system will be more convenient and save them money, that's just too bad. They've got the problem, not me."
- "And if I don't call them back, they can't bang a no on my head."

So it's easier not to pick up the phone than to put up with the fear of failure, the fear of taking a no on the chin.

When the next opportunity to follow up with a prospect comes along, this whole song is sung again. It always ends with "So I won't call them back just this one time."

And who loses?

I do. Because of my inability to handle the pain that change involves, I lost not only this one order but a host of similar orders by cutting a pattern of self-imposed defeat. Every time I scratch myself from a race instead of running and risking that I won't win, I cut this defeat pattern deeper. When the opposition between the motivators and the demotivators becomes a conflict in your mind, the result is the transitional stage called frustration.

"I'm so frustrated. I want to make more money, but I'm not leaving this place for anything."

"I'm so frustrated, but I'm not going through the files again. If they don't call me, oh, well."

Once you get frustrated, the next stage is the interesting one called anxiety. That's a fancy name for emotional pain. Some people voice their anxiety with such words as "I just can't stand this pressure anymore." Others silently let the pain boil inside them.

The next stage you reach is your danger zone. Many of us go in and out of our danger zones every day.

When in your entire life were you the most comfortable?

In the womb.

Now, that's security. Your own pool, all the food you could possibly want, and no taxes. Then all of a sudden comes the day when you enter this world. What are you greeted with after you come through the door? A nice slap—your first rejection.

Then they cut your umbilical cord.

Do you know how many people are walking around looking for a place to plug it back in? Think about that. If you can't handle the fear of insecurity by giving security up, if you can't overcome the possibility that they might reject you when you go for a close, if you can't cope with the fact that you have some of these doubts, if you won't change and develop your technique, then the chances are that you won't stay in your comfort zone very consistently. Let me give you an example.

I'm your sales manager. You and the rest of the sales staff at our branch are here for that always exciting extravaganza, our weekly meeting. I can handle pain and anxiety up to 700. On that scale, my P and A reading is 50 as I take a shower and think, *I'm all set to give those people a great meeting this morning. I'm really going to motivate 'em. Production isn't good—no one's making much money, but they're a really good group.*

At the breakfast table, I decide to check on my first flier in the stock market. After being a little leery at first, I finally decided to give it a go. In the morning paper, I locate the stock my broker assured me would keep my family cruising in the Caribbean for the rest of our lives. It's just dropped 50 percent. Suddenly my Pain and Anxiety meter is at 150. My wife figures that something's down, looks over my shoulder at the paper, and sees the report. She proceeds to advise me in graphic terms as to just how good my stock-selecting ability is, and that my brains are composed of a single ingredient that has a short name. My P and A meter hits 300.

When I jump into the car, I know I'm running late. Heavy on the gas. A policeman pulls me over. I'm so uptight that I don't use an assumptive close on him. (The next time a policeman pulls you over, before he says a word look him right in the eye with a big smile and say, "Officer, please forgive me for bothering you just for a warning.") But I'm too far gone even for that. So the traffic ticket pushes my P and A level to 500. When I finally walk into that meeting twenty minutes late, you're sitting there. The phone rings. You pick it up and tell me, "Tom, it's for you."

"I'll take it in my office and be right back." It's the regional manager calling to tell me how our office is doing and to give me a little motivational inspiration. It goes like this:

"Hopkins, are you aware that your office's performance is the lowest in our entire chain? Your people aren't working, your advertising budget's out of whack, and in general you look incompetent. If you don't get those people of yours moving fast, plan on looking for another job."

I hang up. Through the glass wall of my office I see the sales staff waiting for me to start our weekly meeting. I walk out there with my Pain and Anxiety meter at 750, well into my danger zone. There's so much adrenaline pounding through my head now that I'm down to just two options: the ancient ones of fight or flight. Since we usually don't literally do either in business anymore, that leaves the modern equivalents: withdraw or get hostile. I'm not leaving, so the meeting will now be different from the one I planned this morning. It goes something like this:

"Good morning. Are you people aware that your production stinks? We're the lowest in the chain. I warn every one of you—I talked to the regional manager—hear me, and hear me good—if I'm bumped out, I'm taking all of you with me."

Suddenly, I feel great. I've knocked my P and A reading down to 50 by using hostility to get rid of my excess pain and anxiety. I got rid of mine. Who'd I give it to? You and the other people on the sales staff. I've driven all of you up to 750 and put all of you in your danger zones.

It's vital that you learn how to handle a situation like this. Make no mistake. In every type of selling, you're going to have a load of pain dumped on you every day, and you're going to have another load marked anxiety dumped on you, too. Every day.

The key to meeting and conquering this situation is to realize that all you have to do is overcome the pain and the anxiety. Do that and you'll stay in your comfort zone. Why? Because there really are only two zones: danger and comfort. You have to be in one or the other. Pain and anxiety aren't real until you make them hurt inside your head. If you refuse to do that, they can't hurt you. Realize that every day there will be painful experiences. These experiences will all have the potential to create anxiety in your mind—if you decide to do that to yourself by concentrating on feeling pain and anxiety and avoiding any further risk of failure. If you decide to concentrate on doing creative things that'll turn your opportunities into reality, you'll stay in your comfort zone because your mind is fixed on doing, not on suffering.

You've had people upset at you. You've had unhappy clients. Every active salesperson has experienced this many times. Let's not blink at the facts. As long as you stay in sales, you'll frequently have people get upset with you. No one who sails the seas of success can avoid this. It occurs outside of you and often is beyond your control. Anxiety occurs only within your own skin, and anxieties of this sort are within your control.

You've had customers that you've given your heart and soul to and they still aren't happy. They tell you about it bluntly, perhaps rudely. They may go beyond that with a nasty phone call or letter to your boss. That puts you in your danger zone, and many salespeople in this situation start withdrawing or become hostile.

In the next chapter, you'll find a step-by-step formula. Use it every time people cancel an appointment, won't take a delivery date, say they wouldn't have your product around; every time they tell you no. Apply this formula to every rejection you get and you'll start looking forward to rejection instead of hiding from it. That sounds hard to believe, doesn't it? Turn to the next chapter and see for yourself.

6. Learn to Love No

What was the first word your mother and father taught you? The word *no*, wasn't it?

And how did they teach you the meaning of no? By inflicting pain on your bottom. Why did our parents do that to us? Was it because they didn't like us, or because they loved us?

They loved us, of course. And they knew that we'd hurt ourselves unless we were taught to avoid certain things. So, for our own good, they imprinted the meaning of no on our minds the only way they could—by making us fear no.

Today, what's the only thing that stands between you and everything you want from your selling career?

The word *no*.

The challenge afflicting most of us here is fundamental: We have the wrong attitude toward that most basic word. This attitude, held since earliest childhood, has long outlived its usefulness in our lives—especially since we're now in the profession of selling where the word *no* keeps us from serving others and achieving our goals.

When prospects or clients blow up over trivial matters or give you a rough time for no apparent reason, these people have been pushed into their danger zones—but not by you. They need someone to stand in for the bad guy who isn't there.

Turn down the bad-guy role, and grab the good-guy role instead. You can win being a good guy. I'll tell you how in a moment.

Confronted by a prospect who has suddenly turned hostile, average salespeople get anxious about their own dignity. If it requires shouting before withdrawal, they shout; if their dignity allows a silent stomp out, they silently stomp out—to oblivion with that particular prospect in either case.

Champions see the situation in an entirely different light. They know at once that their prospect is in pain—that countering the prospect's hostility with more hostility is nonproductive, and that their own dignity is beside the point. As human beings, they want to help relieve the prospect's pain; as businesspeople, they want to move that pain aside so they can get on with business.

Here's how Champions win by casting themselves as the good guy: They keep calm, listen carefully, and speak to the heart of the matter at the first opportunity.

"Mr. Prospect, I'm getting the feeling that you're really more troubled by something that has nothing to do with me or my company than you are about what we've been discussing. [Don't pause.] I understand how these things work. Why don't you lay a little of that burden on my shoulders? I think that'll make it easier for both of us. Getting things like that off your chest is something you just have to do, and talking to someone not directly involved can be a great way to clarify your thinking about a challenge. Would you like to tell me about it?"

Speak clearly as you say these words, and don't hurry them. The hostile prospect usually waffles at first—denies that he has a problem or pretends to ignore your statement. But then, if you've demonstrated genuine empathy, chances are that he'll drift into talking about what's bothering him. Once he gets started, he'll probably use up the available time telling you all about it. Don't worry. He'll invite you back, or he'll say something like, "Enough of my personal problems. What're you here to sell me?"

You tell him.

"What would my cost be?"

You tell him.

"Let's skip the usual blarney. You know what our needs are. Can your machine handle them?"

You tell him it can. That's true, of course, or you wouldn't be there.

"All right, I'll give you a purchase order for it. Stop in and see me the next time you're out this way—I might have a lead for you."

Champions know when the most effective presentation is not to give one.

HOW TO REJECT THE NEGATIVE EFFECTS OF REJECTION

No one in sales will dispute that being able to overcome the ill effects of rejection is vital to success in our chosen field. What's needed is a system that'll allow us to do that all the time. Here it is. I call it the Champion Formula for Rejecting Rejection.

If you'll concentrate on this formula when you get rejected, you'll feel good instead of feeling bad. Don't fight it, use it. And use it wholeheartedly—it will ignite a rocket under your sales performance if you do.

Step one. As the first step to using this formula, you determine the cash value of each rejection that you receive. I can't give you that value because this book is written for all kinds of selling, and values change over time. But to illustrate how it's done, let's just say that on the average you're paid $100 for every sale you close.

1 SALE = $100

Step two. Champions operate on ratios. As a sales professional, you know your contacts-to-closings ratio—that is, you know how many people you have to contact in order to close one sale. Keeping track of this ratio takes hardly any effort and yields valuable information. For example, a drop in the ratio alerts you to the fact that there are challenges with what you're doing before they get serious. I'll go into this further in a later chapter. For now, let's assume that you contact ten people to make one sale. This means that your contacts-to-closings ratio is ten to one.

All Champions strive to improve their personal contacts-to-closings ratio, of course, but the 10:1 ratio I'm using in this example is a reasonable average in many types of selling. Let's go with that. Here's how it works out:

$$1 \text{ sale} = \$100$$
$$10 \text{ contacts} = 1 \text{ sale}$$
$$\text{Therefore, } 1 \text{ contact} = \$10$$

You are not paid by the sale, you are paid by the contact.

This isn't a weird, twisted, nonsensical way of looking at sales activity—it's reality. You have to make ten contacts to close one sale. No contacts means no sales, which means no earnings. Earnings are not started by sales, they are started by contacts. This being true, why should you convince yourself that you're paid a hundred dollars for a sale but nothing for a contact? Not only is that self-defeating, it's untrue as well. But don't quibble. The difference between a Champion and the average salesperson lies in how they look at things like this.

So do as the Champions do: Psych yourself up with winning ideas. Use the above formula. Perhaps you average twelve contacts and $240 per sale: If so, for every genuine contact rejection that you get, you make $20. Find your own cash value and use that to psych yourself up before each contact call, and after each contact rejection. The payoff is built into this fact: You'll make more contact calls because you'll suffer less pain doing so, and you'll make better calls because you're more relaxed. Then, a little later, you'll realize that you're enjoying it. Now you're really rolling. You're banging out five, ten, or twenty calls in the time you used to spend staring at the wall trying to think of reasons not to make calls. Your sales are booming. And you're having fun, because winning is fun.

Isn't this exciting?

Every time you hear no, you've earned a specific amount of money: the cash value to you of one rejection. This is when you realize that no is good, that no is where the money's at.

That's right, no is good. It's not a hard slap on baby's behind that carries over as a hard jerk on an adult's anxieties. Hearing lots of no means you're in orbit, you're making money, you're streaking for your goals. There'll come a time when you'll hear sweet music in the words of no.

Concentrate on the cash value of rejection and you'll start looking forward to being rejected. As I've said, Champions and average salespeople differ primarily in how they react to basic things such as rejection. If you'll look at every rejection as ten dollars and handle it, some clients will give you two or three hundred dollars for just standing there. So what am I saying?

Start your climb to success by changing your attitude toward rejection. Now, I know that some of us, because of our upbringing, are petrified of being rejected. What's the answer?

Do what you fear most and you control fear.

If you make yourself handle rejection—if you let yourself feel the rejection and then overcome it once, overcome it twice, overcome it three times—you'll begin to realize that it isn't so terrible after all. Keep going; you're developing the ability to cope with it. Then, suddenly, you'll find yourself handling rejection without pain—and you'll wonder why you ever allowed the fear of rejection to block you from your goals.

THE FIVE ATTITUDES TOWARD REJECTION

From all over Canada and the United States, Champions who've attended my sales seminars have written to me about these five attitudes. Their letters repeat this story over and over:

"I took your advice and memorized the five attitudes toward rejection. Because of them, I've been able to handle more personal pain, more business pain, more emotional strife, more challenges, more pressure—and still keep moving forward."

These attitudes will do the same for you if you'll absorb these concepts. Giving them a quick read and then hurrying on won't have the slightest effect on you. To absorb these concepts, you must have the words in your mind. Then, when you need them— and when you're willing to use them—these concepts will be there, ready to revolutionize your attitudes toward rejection, able to plant the seeds of success in every pot of failure you can find.

Copy them on cards. Read them aloud. Commit them to memory.

The five attitudes toward rejection must be learned word for word. To make it more emotional and powerful, I've given you three alternatives for each attitude. Select the version (A, B, or C) that you're most comfortable with. Then memorize your five custom-fitted new attitudes toward all results that are less than success. (Substitute *rejection* for *failure* whenever that word more closely expresses how you feel.)

First attitude toward rejection:

(A) I never see failure as failure, but only as a learning experience.
(B) I never see failure in nonsuccess; I see a learning experience.
(C) I always see nonsuccess as a learning experience.

Second attitude toward rejection:

(A) I never see failure as failure, but only as the negative feedback I need to change course in my direction.
(B) I never see failure in nonsuccess, I see instructions for reaching my goals.
(C) I find course-correcting data in every nonsuccess.

Third attitude toward rejection:

(A) I never see failure as failure, but only as the opportunity to develop my sense of humor.
(B) I never see failure in nonsuccess; I see the opportunity to develop my sense of humor.
(C) I'm always quick to see the humor in my nonsuccesses.

Fourth attitude toward rejection:

(A) I never see failure as failure, but only as an opportunity to practice my techniques and perfect my performance.
(B) I never see failure in nonsuccess, I see an opportunity to practice my techniques and perfect my performance.

(C) I value the opportunity to practice my techniques and perfect my performance that every nonsuccess gives me.

Fifth attitude toward rejection:

(A) I never see failure as failure, but only as the game I must play to win.
(B) I never see failure in nonsuccess; I see the game that I must play to win.
(C) I always see nonsuccess as a necessary part of the game I'm playing to win.

Now let's take a hard look at these five attitudes toward rejection so that we can maximize our ability to reject failure.

1. The learning experience. When you go out prospecting and get rejected, when you present or demonstrate without making a sale, when you've already made the sale and then some small thing causes your order to be canceled in a corporate decision, what have you been offered?

Something of great value: a lesson in practical salesmanship that's specific to when, where, and what you sell—that is, to this month's competitive and economic conditions, to your territory, and to your product or service. Don't refuse the lesson; you've already paid for it with the loss of a sale.

Sometimes you'll have to do some research to learn the lesson, and sometimes it'll be obvious. But you'll always have to think it through. In any case, spend your time and energy analyzing the facts and studying the lesson you paid a sale to learn, not on wringing your hands and crying, "What did I do wrong? Why did I lose that sale?"

The lightbulb took a tremendous amount of mental and physical effort to invent. The main difficulty was to devise a filament that would burn for a reasonable period of time. Before he overcame this challenge, Thomas Edison conducted and wrote detailed notes on more than a thousand experiments that didn't produce a practical lightbulb. He kept on trying. Finally, Edison developed a filament that produced light for an hour, then a day, a week, and we were given the invention that has done more to improve our lives than any other.

People asked Edison, "How did you feel when you failed more than a thousand times?"

Here's what this man retorted: "I did not fail a thousand times; I learned a thousand ways that it wouldn't work." Isn't that amazing? It's all in the way you look at things. I find that our great Champions, the ones who earn huge incomes for themselves and their families, are people who have changed their attitudes and learned how to handle the same pressures and anxieties that defeat most people.

Every time you're rejected in any way, tell yourself:

I never see failure as failure, but only as a learning experience.

2. The course correction. If you're off course, it takes negative feedback to get you back on course.

We've all had clients who fall in love with everything we show them: "Oh, I like this one. And that's sensational. Look over here. Fantastic." They never give you any objections or negative feedback, and it's almost impossible to close them. You think they're going to buy everything on the floor until they walk out empty-handed.

Every morning we make a decision about our attitudes toward rejection. We can take it personally and have it destroy our day, or we can slough it off and keep going. You and I decide this every day.

In my sales seminars, I use an analogy that I believe really drives this point home. It's based on the modern-day target-seeking missiles. When the missile is fired, a device inside it homes in on the target and guides the missile through whatever zigs and zags it must make to hit that target.

Let's suppose that I'm the missile. There is the target. I've just been launched in the general direction of the target. Right away, I'm getting off course. The target seeker kicks in and gives me a "No, thank you."

I turn back toward the direction of the target, but turn a little too much and head off course again. The device gives me another "No, thank you." I turn again and again as I'm being rejected and then, there it is: the target. I've reached my goal. Ka-blam. Terrific explosion. Good-bye, target.

What would happen if the missile took rejection personally? What would it do?

Go home.

Here's how that'll work. A missile is fired.

"You're off course, missile."

"I can't take it," says the missile. "I'm going back home."

Somebody at the launch site yells, "Oh, fudge. Here comes one that couldn't handle it." Ka-blam. Terrific explosion. Good-bye, launch site.

Studies of sales behavior have found many consistent patterns. One of them crops up when outside salespeople get into their danger zones because they can't handle the rejection that's part of their work. Where do they start spending more and more time?

At home.

Too many salespeople hide at home. Or go home early. Or take that three-hour lunch hiding from the pain of rejection.

What else might the missile do if it couldn't handle the rejection?

It might explode at the launch site. People do that in sales. They can't stand it anymore. So they blow up in their office or showroom. Ka-blam. Terrific explosion. Good-bye, job.

The missile might just decide to go in circles. Salespeople do that in every industry. "I think I'll just kind of walk around today and settle my nerves. I'm not going to talk to anybody, though. Uh-oh. Here comes that hard-nosed guy who's hot for our model 360. Ah, what luck, he's looking the other way. I can duck into the restroom before he sees me."

Why would anyone in sales ever do a thing like that? Because the possibility of having to take another rejection is more than that person can handle at that time.

Faced with the same client who emotionally destroys the average salesperson, the Champion becomes creative and takes this attitude: "Okay, Mr. Hardnose, have at it. Sling your slop. That's nothing to me. I'm going to use your negative stimulus to find a positive way to overcome your objections, and I will close."

Doesn't it make sense to react this way rather than crawl into a hole and hide? Why let rejection shatter you? Why block out the negative feedback? Be thankful for negative feedback. Take it, change course, and hit that target—or a different one. It's fun.

It really is exciting when you know you won't let yourself be denied, when you know you've taken charge of your career, when you know you'll come up smiling after catching nine rejections in a row, saying:

> **I never see failure as failure, but only as the negative feedback I need to change course in my direction.**

3. Humor. This one is my favorite attitude toward rejection, and I think I've used it more than any other. Have you ever had a traumatic experience with clients that absolutely wiped you out? After it happened, you felt so bad you simply couldn't call them back. You were done. You didn't want to ever hear the names of those people mentioned again.

But what are you doing three weeks later?

Getting laughs with your wipeout. You're telling people, "You should've seen it. What a high dive into an empty pool. I went to see these clients, and . . ."

Three weeks later it's hilarious. All the hurt vanishes the first time you tell the story and laugh about your disaster. Unfortunately, until you can do that, you're a disaster yourself: reliving the pain, enthusiasm gone, ability to handle your daily ration of rejection down to nil. The weeks between disaster and laughter are wasted.

Life doesn't have to be that way. Laugh sooner. That's the key. Laughter softens anxiety's pain. Any humor helps, but the fun you poke at your own bloopers, faults, and misadventures does the most marvelous job of melting anxiety away.

All the great people I've met have a wonderful sense of humor. They delight in looking at the world's reality, and they see an uncommon amount of humor in it. Laughing is good. Laugh more. But don't laugh too soon.

If you take a call from someone who's just bought from you and the client says, "We're thinking of backing out," that's not the time to hoot and holler and tell more funnies. First, you do everything possible to hold that sale together. If it fractures anyway, *then* you look at the lighter side.

If you're new to the profession of selling and laugh every time something goes wrong, you're going to have a rollicking good time. As long as the laughs are directly related to the job and you're working effectively between them, why not? You'll be keeping your attitude up and learning fast. You see, it's once the lesson is recognized and learned that it's easy to laugh at what happened. In the beginning, you'll have to make an effort to laugh when you'd rather cry. But this, too, is a habit that's based on the attitude you've chosen. If you're willing to take charge of your life, you can develop the habits you want to live by. When success eludes you, always look for the lighter side by telling yourself:

I never see failure as failure, but only as an opportunity to develop my sense of humor.

4. Practice. Every time you demonstrate or present to clients but they don't buy, what have they given you instead of an order?

A chance to practice. Many of us don't realize the importance of this. People whose sales are below their potential have a tendency to sneer at practice, and that's one reason for their low sales. If their performance was perfect, could their sales be anything short of sensational?

A perfect performance is far more than a memorized sales spiel. No demonstration or presentation can be more than mediocre without including heavy participation by the clients, participation that's smoothly handled and guided by the salesperson. This demands practice and thorough knowledge of what you're selling. Whether you work with possible buyers in your showroom, their home, your display area, their office, or some other location, every time you're with a client who says no, you've at least had a chance to walk out and say,

**I never see failure as failure, but only as
the opportunity to practice my techniques
and perfect my performance.**

After every rejection, dismiss the negatives, focus your thoughts on positive aspects, and move forward. Do that immediately, automatically, and firmly. This is one of the precious few habits that make success certain. It's a learnable habit. Make it yours.

5. The game. Selling is a percentage game, a matter of numbers. Over the years, I've discovered that a single rule dominates every sales organization: Those who risk more failure by working with more people make more money; those who risk less failure make less.

If you risk failure frequently, you'll fail frequently. That's inevitable. It's built into the system. Also built in is the percentage effect: From a certain number of tries, you get success. That being true, all you have to do is accept the fact that success demands its percentage of failure and work the numbers. So when your efforts are crowned with nonsuccess, tell yourself:

**I never see failure as failure, but only
as the game I must play to win.**

If you know baseball, you know about Ty Cobb. During his best year he stole 94 bases in 144 attempts. Think about that. Two out of three times he was successful; 66 percent of the time he made it. On such records his enduring legend is built. On 66 percent.

Let's talk about another ballplayer. Max Carey was successful more than 90 percent of the time; during his best year he stole fifty-one bases in fifty-four attempts. What a percentage. But today Max Carey is forgotten. In life, it's not the number of times you fail that counts, it's the number of times you keep on trying. Had old Max pushed his ego out of the way and tried more, he would have been number one.

THE CREED OF THE CHAMPION

Here is our basic philosophy at Tom Hopkins International. This is what we live by. It makes Champions of us; it makes Champions of the salespeople we're privileged to train.

I am not judged by the number of times I fail, but by the number of times I succeed, and the number of times I succeed is in direct proportion to the number of times I can fail and keep trying.

Do more than just read the creed. Study it. Let it sink in. Let it change the way you look at any result that's not a success. I'd love for you to learn the creed word for word. Please set this book down, copy the creed on any handy piece of paper, and put it in your purse or wallet. Work with the creed and the five attitudes toward rejection; burn them deep into your mind and your performance and income will leap forward. From the bottom of my heart, I believe that Champions are Champions because they've learned to fuel their drive by overcoming more failure.

Review the five attitudes toward rejection and failure now, and use them every time you take a risk or make a move that results in less than a win.

1. I never see failure as failure (rejection as rejection), but only as a learning experience.
2. I never see failure as failure, but only as the negative feedback I need to change course in my direction.
3. I never see failure as failure (rejection as rejection), but only as an opportunity to develop my sense of humor.
4. I never see failure as failure, but only as the opportunity to practice my techniques and perfect my performance.
5. I never see failure as failure, but only as the game I must play to win.

7. Finding the People to Sell

You've been hired by a good company to represent a product you believe in. They have offered you product knowledge training and some company-generated leads. You've been in the early phase of sales training for the last six chapters, getting an idea of what you're facing. Where do you begin to make money in this business? It's by finding the people who need what you have to offer. This area, called prospecting, is often the biggest maker or breaker of sales careers.

Take a look around your company. How many salespeople are lying around the office like beached whales? I'm talking about the ones who say things like:

"I don't have anyone to call today."

"Oh, I hope some hot buyers walk in soon."

"I wish the company would give me more leads."

"Our advertising is a joke. How am I supposed to meet people if we don't do good advertising? Nobody calls us from our ads."

"I'm waiting for an important call and want to be available so I'm not doing anything else right now."

Those are the people whose careers will be broken by not mastering the art of prospecting. Those who excel at prospecting never have nothing to do.

It's sad, but the average salesperson doesn't really believe that getting to know people is the key to every door in selling. They'll say "It's all in who you know" without understanding that most people are knowable—if they'll just take the initiative to contact them.

As the last of the audience was leaving the auditorium at the end of one of my three-day, high-intensity seminars, a gentleman in his midsixties came up and said that he'd been in sales nearly forty years. I had noticed him taking copious notes during the lecture, and I was impressed that anyone with his extensive background would be eager enough to learn new things by attending the training.

"I enjoyed your seminar very much, Mr. Hopkins. However, you could have shortened it."

"Was it too long?"

"Not at all. I learned a lot. But in two minutes flat, you can give your next audience a secret that'll guarantee their success."

He spread his arms wide. "After pouring forty years into this business, I know the secret of selling success."

"Just a minute," I said. "You know the secret? My life is devoted to helping salespeople. Please—share this secret with me."

After looking at me for a moment, he said, "Tom, that's exactly what I'm going to do."

There was a charge of expectancy in the air—maybe even of reverence—when this great master of selling walked over to the board, picked up a felt pen, and drew this figure:

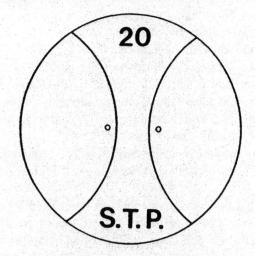

"There it is, Tom."

As I stared at his drawing, the charge of reverence leaked out of the room. Then I looked around, hoping I wasn't alone with this man. I was. Putting on a friendly smile, I said, "So that's the big secret, eh?"

"Exactly. Every month you talk to thousands of individuals who are struggling to make good in sales, don't you?"

"Yes, but a large percentage are already doing anywhere from good to great. They come to my seminars because they want to become even greater."

"Right—I'm in that category, and you've got a truckload of splendid techniques to help us. But the thing is, techniques count for nothing if they're not used. Tom, if you can get this one point across, you'll achieve your goal of helping everyone who hears you become successful in sales."

"Yes, but—"

He lifted a finger. "Tom, if you can motivate everyone to use my secret, they'll overcome every obstacle to earning big money." His hands flourished. "And the secret is: 'See Twenty People belly-to-belly every day.'"

Suddenly the air was charged again. He clapped his hands together and went on, "Get them to do that and they can't fail."

He was right. All my years in selling convince me of it. Never have I heard a formula for success that beats his for truth, simplicity, and practicality. Put your belly button near twenty others each day and you'll soon be living on top of the hill. The key to making more money is to see more people.

Now, I know not everyone reading this book will be in a type of selling that's done face-to-face (or belly-to-belly). You might be in telemarketing. You might conduct sales over the Internet, relying on e-mail and videoconferencing. That's okay. The premise still stands. If you'll meet twenty people every day, you can't help but succeed in sales. Even if they don't need your services, they'll likely know someone who does. It's all in who you get to know.

While the ink is still drying on your new business cards, you should be preparing a list of everyone you know in the contact management program in your computer. Start with Mom and Dad, brothers and sisters, aunts, uncles, and cousins. Don't forget Grandma and Gramps, either. Then move on to your best friends and neighbors. Use your address book. Use your Christmas card list, if you have one.

You might be thinking I'm crazy here. You might be selling highly sophisticated equipment that Grandma wouldn't understand if you spent a week showing it to her. Why would you want her on your business contact list? Because Grandma knows a lot of other people. She loves you and wants you to succeed. She'll be bragging about you at church, at the senior center, at the doctor's office— everywhere grandmas go. And you know what? Someone will hear or overhear her mention that dear little Johnny or Jean is helping people with fancy computer equipment and doing quite well. And guess what happens next? Someone asks her about you, gets your contact information, and good old Grandma has just sent you a lead. Be sure to thank her.

Once you have your list complete, draft a short and to-the-point letter about your new position. Be sure to explain the benefits your product offers—not the features, not the technical details. Don't tell too much, just enough so people get the gist of what you're doing. End by asking them to keep you in mind when the subject of whatever it is you're selling comes up and offer to serve them, their relatives, friends, or clients most professionally. Send that letter to everyone on your list.

Here's a sample you might consider:

Dear John and Mary,
Something exciting has happened in my life. I have recently been hired as an associate [salesperson, consultant] with [name of company]. This company is one of the largest [best, fastest-growing] in its field. I have learned a great deal about their products and services and feel confident in representing them.
It is my responsibility with this company to offer my friends [relatives, clients] the latest and most innovative ways to [state a benefit of the product or service]. There's too much

to tell you in a letter so I'll be contacting you for a time when we can visit. I would so appreciate the opportunity to share with you ideas on what benefits this product might have for you. I thank you in advance for your time.

Sincerely,

Follow this up with phone calls to the top ten or twenty people on your list who would be most likely to help you. It might be people you know in business. It might be Grandpa with all his connections at the country club—or even the barbershop. Elaborate on the services you offer. Exude professionalism. Ask if there's anything you can do for them in return for any help they give you.

To keep your list—and your business—growing, add everyone you talk with every day. Besides your company-generated leads, this might include your local dry cleaner, folks at the restaurant where you have lunch, people you strike up conversations with at the car wash. You might wonder how you get contact information from people during these brief encounters. It's simple and I'll show you exactly what to do and say. I call it the thank-you-on-the-business-card strategy.

Once the ink is dry on your cards, take a pen and, by hand, write the words THANK YOU on them. When you meet new people, hand them your card and say these words: "May I give you my card?" As you hand it to them, they'll reach out. They always do. Next, say, "You might notice I wrote THANK YOU on it and I guess I'm thanking you in advance for, hopefully, the opportunity to someday serve your [name of your industry] needs. May I have your card as well?"

Those words are totally nonthreatening. I designed them that way. You're polite. You're offering service someday—not being pushy at all. Asking for a card in return is only courteous. If the other person doesn't have one, simply say, "That's fine. May I have your permission to keep in touch here at the dry cleaners?" Most people will say sure, because they don't think you'll really do it. Little do they know you're being trained by me! Get the correct spelling of their name, say your thanks, and take your leave. Follow up by sending them a thank-you note. I'll cover thank-you notes in depth in chapter 18.

This whole technique takes less than three minutes to complete. How many three-minute segments do you have in a day? Do you see now how you can reach that goal of meeting twenty people every day? And that's just for those you meet in person.

It's a curious fact that, though few salespeople will disagree with anything I've written in the previous section, many salespeople won't act on it. They know that they have to meet new people to be successful, and they want to be successful, but they don't get out and meet the people. Why not? It's the old fear of rejection that I talked about in the last chapter. By now, I'm sure that you've changed your attitude. Now you know that every time you get rejected, you've actually made money. So you're ready to go out and meet some of those good folks who need your product or service.

Selling is finding people to sell, and selling the people you find. In the beginning, you'll try nearly anything. As you grow in your skills, you'll see what works and doesn't work. You'll constantly tweak what you say, how you present yourself, the material you'll send people, the number of times and ways you keep in touch. The only way to know what's working best is to keep track of the results. That's where ratios come into play.

KNOW YOUR RATIOS, AND STRIVE TO IMPROVE THEM

All successful businesses use ratios. Your sales activity is a business. Therefore, you must use ratios to be successful. If all this gives you a pain in the inferiority complex you got by flunking math in high school, relax. Whether you can precisely define the word or not, you're already making frequent use of ratios. But you'll use them more effectively if you understand them better. Let me explain.

A ratio is just a fraction that measures something against something else. Let's suppose that you have two savings accounts. One of them pays 6 percent interest. This means that the interest your money earns has the same relationship to the total amount of money in your account that 6 has to 100. This relationship is a ratio. It can be written in several different ways without changing the relationship between the two numbers:

6:100
6/100
$^6\!/_{100}$
6 percent
6%
.06
.060

Business ratios are frequently expressed in percent because percentages are easy to understand and compare. Let's do it on both of your savings accounts:

Bank	Amount on Deposit	Interest Earned
A	$8,979.80	$448.99
B	$ 332.00	$ 19.92

Few people can look at the figures above and immediately know which bank is paying the higher rate of interest. But if we compare two ratios, the answer is instantly obvious:

Bank	Interest Rate
A	5 percent
B	6 percent

Ratios that will help you manage your selling business are serious stuff. Here are some that you should be keeping track of—and striving to improve:

• Prospecting calls/hours spent.
• Prospecting calls/appointments made.

- Appointments/sales.
- Hours worked/money earned.
- Prospecting calls made last month/income this month.

Let's talk about each of these basic ratios in turn. When you're well into managing your selling business with this method, you may find other ratios that are more crucial to your particular operation than these. If so, great. Run with them. The point is this: Your activities can be expressed as ratios that, when studied, will show you how to best spend your time. If you're not keeping track, you're not steering your ship.

Prospecting calls/hours spent. We can be astonishingly ingenious at finding ways not to prospect when we sit down to prospect by phone—or have the time blocked out to go out and do it. If you really want to succeed, you'll discipline yourself. This means you set reasonable performance levels and make yourself meet them.

Prospecting calls/appointments made. As a very rough starting figure, the ratio for all kinds of selling is about 10:1. That is, make 10 prospecting calls: get one appointment. Don't ask about the ratio for your business around the office. The losers don't prospect because they're losers, and the winners don't prospect anymore because they're too busy with the referral business they built up through prospecting. Compile your own batting average. Start off with the assumption that ten good prospecting calls will get you one good appointment, and take it from there.

Appointments/sales. Again, 10:1 is a rough average, but this ratio varies wildly from business to business. Salespeople working a route of established accounts may go for days getting an order at every stop; salespeople working airlines for aircraft manufacturers may go for years between sales. Most of us operate well away from routine order taking at one extreme and salaried team selling at the other extreme. Once you've determined your own ratio for this activity, study it together with the previous ratio. If you're getting lots of appointments but making few sales, you may be losing out before you walk in the door through poor qualifying. You can't make money trying to sell the wrong people. Or, if they are qualified, it could be that you're not hitting their hot buttons during your presentation—

not lowering their sales resistance enough to take a serious look at owning your product.

Hours worked/money earned. At least twice a year, you should run a check on exactly how much time you actually spend working, and compare that to how much you're making. It'll take a tight log to ferret out the facts, and no one can do it but you. If you're serious about making more money, take a cold reading on how much time you're productive compared with how much time goes into looking busy. How you use your time determines how much you pay yourself. Take a hard look twice a year. You may want to make changes.

Prospecting calls made last month/income this month. The idea here is to emphasize the direct bearing that the number of prospecting calls you make now has on how much you take home tomorrow. Using the right time lag is vital. Decide on how long it takes to work the typical interested prospect all the way from initial contact to money in your pocket. This time delay may be three months or longer. Some salespeople fail because they don't gear their thinking to the time lag that's involved in their business.

Champions develop simple methods for keeping track of their personal performance ratios such as those given above, but they don't do it out of idle curiosity. They gather the necessary information for hardheaded reasons—so they can recognize opportunities while they're fresh, and correct potential challenges before they get out of hand.

Let's look at how this works. Suppose you're fairly new in the business but you've acquired some skill at prospecting, qualifying, demonstrating, and closing. You're consistently making one sale for every ten prospects you meet. We're talking here about the people you find, not those who wander in off the street.

By making about one call a day, you're meeting about thirty people a month, so you're closing three sales a month. Now what's going to happen if you decide to make two calls a day?

Your sales go up to six a month, and your income doubles.

Suppose you elevate your performance level again, and start making four calls a day?

Your sales go to twelve a month and your income again doubles.

So if you were making a thousand dollars a month off three sales before, now you're making four thousand a month off twelve sales—and feeling very good about yourself.

When I drop these figures on people in my seminars, I can read messages like these on lots of faces:

"I can't make four calls a day."

"In my business, two calls a day is tops."

If you think that, I disagree with you. Every potential Champion has to fight that kind of negative thinking in the beginning. Here's how you do it. Sit down and work out a schedule that will allow you to double your sales. Next, throw that schedule away and work out one that adds one more call a day. Then work out the time planning and organizing that will allow you to meet this second schedule. You can do it. All it takes is desire, discipline, and determination.

You will close a certain percentage of the people you meet. Your goal should be to up that percentage. But let's be realistic. I'll tell you very honestly that I can't show you how to close 100 percent of the people you meet. In a free economy, it's impossible to close ten out of ten. So there does come a time when trying to raise the percentage of people you close is more frustrating than realistic, a time when you should be putting your effort into acquiring more prospects to apply that percentage to.

My goal as a trainer isn't to have you close 99 percent. You can't. I want to raise your percentages and increase your income—and you'll do that by making more calls.

Why not fewer and better calls?

Because more is better—especially when you're new. If professional athletes only practiced twenty minutes a day, how long would their careers last?

There's another point I want you to remember—and act on. A Champion always makes one successful call after a rejection.

Why? Think about it. If you stop on rejection, what do you carry with you the rest of the day?

Rejection.

Champions are determined to keep their winning attitude. If they hang up on a negative note, their winning attitude is damaged for the rest of the day.

You're saying, "I might have to call four people or even more to get a positive response."

Then call them. That's what Champions do. That's what the Five Percenters, the great ones, the achievers do.

There's another time when you must call until you get a live prospect. Every time you make a sale to one of your existing customers or prospects, what do you have to do?

You have to replace that satisfied client with a new potential client.

After completing a sale, Champions say, "I must find two more good potential future clients to fill the space left by the person I just got happily involved in our wonderful opportunity."

One of the best things about selling, especially in the beginning, is that being busy at first leads to business. In other words, activity breeds productivity. Understanding this early in my sales career, I started charting everything I did each day. Then I would track my activities over a ninety-day period and compare them to my income during that time. It never failed. The more active I was, the more money I earned. Now, you have to be active at the right things, and I had quite a list I used in the real estate business. I'll cover those that apply to nearly every sales industry here:

- Keeping up with industry news. This can be done by reading articles or news posted in your office; on Web sites that contain industry news; or through industry-specific publications.
- Meeting new people. I set a goal to meet twenty people every day. In my business, that meant knocking on doors of homes. In business-to-business sales, it might mean walking from one company to another, asking the receptionist what type of business it is so you can determine if your product or service might suit their needs. Another method might be phone canvassing. This is meeting people on the telephone. In consumer sales, be certain to check the Do Not Call Registry before contacting anyone at home. With businesses, call as many as you can handle.

- Setting appointments. Since few sales are made on initial contact, getting confirmation of a meeting to discuss or present your product is critical. You should know from your ratios how many appointments you need to set each month in order to achieve your income goal and go for it.
- Making presentations. Again, refer to the number you need to meet your goals.
- Getting referrals. This is nothing more than getting leads from satisfied clients.
- Sending thank-you notes.
- Sending mailouts, brochures, e-mails, newsletters—whatever—to generate leads for yourself rather than waiting for company-generated leads.

Each of these seven areas is a productivity-generating activity. Include some of them in each and every business day until you begin reaching your income goals. Then start fine-tuning what works most effectively for you. You might be able to back off on the number of people you meet face-to-face when you perfect your phone presentation. You might be able to reduce the number of presentations you require of yourself if your closing ratio improves. The key is to just stay busy at the business of selling. Success will follow.

FOUR WAYS TO HOVER UNTIL YOU'RE READY TO FLY

Let's suppose that, for whatever reason, you're not ready and willing to put on a strong prospecting drive of any kind right now. If you're in a situation where no business at all is coming at you, you're dead. You either have to change your attitude or change your job, because you're not going to make a dime at what you're doing.

But you may be in a situation or a territory where there's a flow of business that comes at you without any prospecting on your part: company-supplied leads, repeat business from established customers, things of that sort. The following methods will allow you to hold that business, and even build it up, while you're also building confidence and learning your product or service.

Here's how to hold things together until you're ready to make your drive for the big money:

1. **Handle problems fast.** If someone has a challenge with your product or service, take care of it right now.
2. **Call people back immediately.** One of the biggest challenges most salespeople have is that they don't want to pick up messages and call people back. Return calls now. It's the only way you can build up a happy clientele.
3. **Keep every promise made.** To make the sale, some salespeople will promise everything.

   "Oh, yes, I'll take care of that adjustment."

   "I'll make sure that item is included."

   "You can count on me."

   And then they don't do one thing they promised to do if they can avoid it. You'll never get a referral that way.
4. **Keep in touch.** Call or see your clients regularly. Letters and mailing pieces can't carry the full load because there's no feedback from the disgruntled, or from those being wooed by a competitor. Phone them. Listen for their itch cycles.

Most of my top Champions send out some kind of mailing piece at least once every ninety days. Many top producers in the automobile business have a new company brochure going out in the mail to their list of clients and prospects between four and eight times a year. Almost every large company regularly produces literature that's designed to be mailed out by their salespeople.

Divide any sales force into low, average, and high producers. If you study what they really do with that mail, you'll discover that only the high producers actually get the mailers to their clients. All the others run out of gas before the mailers reach the post office. There's just too much detail for these unbusy people to handle.

One of the top insurance salespeople I've trained—and I've trained thousands—sends out a newsletter every month. He writes it himself. The newsletter is aimed right at his clientele, and it's strictly business. He doesn't draw cartoons. Instead, he gives them a little review of insurance basics in each issue and a lot of new tax ideas and advantages that he's turned up from his own ongoing research. (He's a professional, so he makes sure that he knows more about his service than his customers do.) And he tells them about the latest developments in retirement plans. If you're in this field, you know how important retirement plans are to insurance sales. This man gets a steady flow of referrals, as well as new business from old clients, while his newsletter is keeping his name before those of his clients who aren't thinking of making changes in their insurance and retirement arrangements now.

The monthly newsletter is backed up by a phone call every six months and a visit once a year. That's the program until he sniffs change, and then he swings into action. His clients are loyal, and their numbers are growing rapidly. That's keeping in touch. Without the newsletter, he'd have to increase his phone calls and visits to inactive clients—at an enormous cost in time, which is money.

There are only three ways you can keep in touch: send them things, phone them, see them. The best mix of these operations depends on your circumstances, but it's a rare sales situation that won't benefit from a combination of all three approaches.

Your company may provide you with fancy new four-color brochures once or several times a year. Several outside firms will supply you with printed newsletters or magazines that can be imprinted with your name and mailed out. Many of these firms will even do the mailing for you. But these prepared mailers are often too slick, too institutionalized, too impersonal, and too general to be used alone. What you need is a steady mail program that zeros in on your customers and the opportunities and challenges that are special to your trading area. Bridge the gap between your company's special concerns with a newsletter that you write yourself. Or you can write one letter that tells about a new technical advance every ninety days and personalize it to your entire list.

This doesn't have to be one more thing you feel bad about not doing because you don't have both the time and the skill to create your own mailers. Instead of ignoring the situation, solve it. Organize a group of salespeople in your office—or in noncompeting firms—to share the benefits and expense of having one newsletter written for all of you, a newsletter that's personalized to your general geographic area and to the general level of your several clienteles. The cost to you will be a fraction of the income you're missing by not using the mails effectively. Many authorities, experts, and Web sites offer free articles for reprint (including mine). You'll be amazed at what you will find by doing a little research in your field of interest. In most cases, all you need to do is contact the source by phone or e-mail and request that they grant permission to reprint their information. Most will want recognition as the author and will ask for their contact information to be included with the article in exchange for that permission.

If your clients have e-mail addresses, consider sending them information—including newsletters—that way. Encourage them to keep conversation open between you and them via the personalization of e-mail.

All of these mail systems can pay large rewards for small efforts. But they don't take the place of keeping in touch by phone and visit. Use mail to maintain contact and keep your image fresh with them; use the phone and visits to get the vital feedback you must have to keep their business.

If I were marketing corporate jets, here's how I'd operate. Every time I got a line on folks moving in the same circles as one of our owners, I'd go into orbit. I guarantee that I'd be in touch with these people. They'd get the brochure—but that would only be the beginning. I'd fly them somewhere exotic for lunch. I'd flatter their egos. I'd let them know how much they crave the prestige of owning a personal or corporate jet.

The thing is, these people just don't realize that they need it—that their position demands it. So I'm going to make sure they know. That's my job.

The same procedure holds true for a great variety of products and services. The time and money you spend, of course, will have to be in line with the return you can expect from closing the sale.

I hope you feel the intensity that I'm trying to project into prospecting, because it's the lifeblood of sales. You have people in your sales force who've never generated a single lead on their own. You have people there who won't pick up a phone to prospect. You have people who won't leave the office to prospect—they simply won't leave the place unless someone calls them out. They're hoping the company will somehow do it all for them.

"Gimme more leads."

"Gimme more."

"Gimme."

When you're in sales, you must see yourself as being in business for yourself. That's the only way you'll take the initiative you need to build a successful career. You'll build it on happy clients, service calls, and, most of all, by fulfilling your responsibilities to your clients so well that you richly deserve referrals and the success that attends them.

Relying on yourself instead of relying on the company is the only realistic way of building your own personal stature. In the next chapter, I'll review specific prospecting strategies to lead you to the success level of your dreams.

8. Nonreferral Prospecting Methods

These are the leads you generate where there's no referral involved. Keep this in mind: They're not prequalified, so you'll only be closing 10 percent of them. Therefore, you need to learn not only how to find new leads, but also how to prequalify them. Let's make sure we understand each other here. Please highlight what it means to prequalify the person or persons we call a lead:

A lead is prequalified when you know that the emotional and logical requirements for benefiting from your product or service are all present.

I've said it before: The sale depends on emotion backed by logic. The emotion comes first, and the logic follows. It does not happen the other way around. You prequalify people by finding out whether the emotion that's necessary to carry the sale to completion exists or can be created. And you also have to find out whether the logic—which includes but is not limited to the ability to pay—exists or can be created.

Finding these things out is like catching a bird. If you go thrashing and pounding in a wild charge, the bird will fly away long before you can get anywhere near it. But if you softly work your way in close and then gently cast your net, you'll catch a lot of birds.

Here are a few things to talk about with consumer prospects that are important qualification factors in selling many kinds of services and products:

- Employment.
- Marital status.
- Number of children.
- Product or service they now have.

If you know what they've got now, in most cases that means you know what they'll get later—don't you agree?

In business sales, you'll want to know how long the company has been in business; how long the purchasing agent or representative has held the position; whether or not the company is growing; and what prompted them to meet with you.

Each general type of product or service has its own set of vital qualification factors. You probably know those that are important in selecting the people most likely to buy what you're selling. If you don't have a clear idea of who buys what you sell, one of your top priorities should be to research this question. A careful study at your company's files of completed sales should quickly tell you all you need to know on this score.

TECHNIQUE NUMBER ONE: THE ITCH CYCLE

This is an exciting technique for prospecting, not a skin disease. It's a splendid way to acquire prequalified leads.

In real estate, the average turnover is three to five years; that is, the average family moves every three to five years. So we can say that the average person gets an itch to move every five years. If you're in automobile sales, you know that people get the itch to buy a new car about every thirty months. Office equipment salespeople know that their customers cycle their machines about every three years. These are the times when the itch is itchiest for most people. But can some people itch sooner?

Certainly. That's why a Champion keeps in touch with all her past buyers. These buyers are an important group among the select few in the world who have favored her with their trust, and the Champion knows that she has a special bond with them. So she makes certain that she's there to scratch when the itch strikes her special people.

When should you start helping your past buyers get the itch to buy again?

Start your campaign to update your old buyers sixty days before the itchiest time.

If it's a home or something else on the five-year itch cycle, you really move in on them after four years and ten months; if it's an automobile, you really start driving to get that itch going after two years and four months; if your product is any kind of office equipment, you really start sitting on them after thirty-four months.

As an alternative, or for longer itch cycles, try whetting their appetites after 95 percent of the itch cycle on their old item has run out. For example, you've determined that your average itch cycle is six years. Kick off your itch campaign after five years and eight or nine months. The longer the itch cycle, the greater the variation. This means the longer itch cycles require a greater margin of safety to make sure that you're there before they start looking elsewhere.

And, of course, a Champion never kisses his buyers good-bye by letting years pass without renewing his acquaintance with them. Visits, phone calls, mail, lunches—these are some of the methods the Champion uses to maintain his contact with his clientele. If you don't maintain contact, you don't have a clientele; your ex-buyers are abandoned souls looking for a new home.

When I suggest letting 95 percent of the longer itch cycles go by, I'm merely suggesting a starting point. There's an ideal time to recontact previous buyers of your offering that will give you the best chance to capture their replacement business. The exact ideal time—for your offering, area, and personality—can only be discovered by trial and error.

If what you sell involves weeks or months for design, custom manufacturing, recruitment, or whatever, you'll want to allow for that period; if your offering is a readily available shelf item, you may find that it's more effective to work closer to the itchiest time.

Be aware that the itch cycle for products differs from the itch cycle for services, and that all itch cycles vary from place to place for the same item. Many things influence this interval: seasonal factors, general economic conditions, the income level of the people you're working with, and especially the personalities of the individual buyers. But it's really quite easy to overcome these complexities if you go about it right. Here's the process:

First. Determine the basic itch cycle for your product with your customers in your area. I'll tell you how to do that soon, but for the moment, assume that you've discovered the basic itch cycle that you'll be working with.

Second. Consider the calendar factors. Some sales are affected by tax dates: year end, April 15, local date for assessing inventory tax. The sales of most products and services are affected anywhere from slightly to greatly by the changing seasons. And of course, Christmas exerts a tremendous influence over discretionary buying, generally delaying every decision it doesn't accelerate. You simply look at each of these questions and then adjust your action accordingly. That is, you decide whether to speed up or slow down your re-contacting schedule to cope with these factors.

Suppose you have a basic itch cycle of thirty months and, on a particular group of buyers, you see that if you recontact them to get the itch going after twenty-eight months, you'll come banging in during the holiday season. Since yours is not a Christmas gift item, you have a choice. (You should make this choice several months in advance.) Either you recontact your soon-to-itch buyers after twenty-six months, in September or October, or you wait until January. What to do?

The answer is simple. If you wait until January, some of your former buyers will already be committed elsewhere. Make sure you're there, ready to scratch, when they start to itch: Recontact early, and then give them another contact in January.

Third. Every time you complete a sale, consider that buyer's personality in relation to your basic itch cycle. Impatient types (and people whose careers are moving rapidly upward) tend to itch sooner than average; low-key types (and people whose careers are on a fixed course) tend to itch later than average. Here's how you turn this awareness to your advantage:

At the time you close the first sale, decide whether that particular buyer is impatient, average, or conservative. (Put all doubtful cases in the average group.) When you tune your thinking on this wavelength, you'll find that about 10 to 20 percent of your buyers will strike you as being jumpy types. Schedule them for early recontact. About an equal number of your buyers will seem like noticeably steady people. Schedule them for late recontact. (Classify your buyers in relation to each other, not to what you think is normal for the general population of the country.) The remaining 60 to 80 percent of your buyers are the average group that you should schedule for recontact two months before your basic itch cycle has run its course.

Sounds great, you may be thinking, *but how do I find out what the itch cycle is on my product? Nobody around my office has ever mentioned it.*

HOW TO DETERMINE THE ITCH CYCLE FOR YOUR PRODUCT OR SERVICE

It'll take one full day. But while you're determining your product or service's itch cycle, you'll be picking up some tremendous qualified leads, too.

Let's suppose that I just started at Champion Marine Sales. My product is boats. Since I'm new, one of the first things I want to discover is the itch cycle that I'll be working with at this boat dealership. You can do it for your product or service the same way that I use here.

Start by getting to the company files. Most companies today keep records on all their clients. Find out where the files are, sit down, and start making calls. I'll show you the method by giving the dialogue for one call.

If you'll spend just one day going at it as I do below, and call all the clients you can in that time, you not only will establish your product's itch cycle, but will also strike some more exciting things that I'll tell you about. So come with me now as we go through the old buyer files at Champion Marine.

The first file looks interesting. It tells me that a gentleman named

Max Polk bought a Spee-D-Ski boat eighteen months ago. Without wasting time, I call him.

> TOM: "Good morning, Mr. Polk. My name is Tom Hopkins, and I'm with Champion Marine Sales. You've owned one of our Spee-D-Ski boats for approximately eighteen months now, and I wanted to call up and make sure that you're happy with it."
>
> MR. POLK: "Hey, that Spee-D-Ski is the best ski boat my family's ever had."
>
> TOM: (warmly) "I'm happy to hear that. I'm in the process of conducting a little market survey to establish projections for the upcoming year. Would you be kind enough to help me by answering just a few questions?"
>
> MR. POLK: "I wouldn't mind. Go ahead."
>
> TOM: "Prior to purchasing the Spee-D-Ski, did you have another boat?"
>
> MR. POLK: "I sure did—a Fastwater-16."
>
> TOM: "Oh, really? How long have you been a boating enthusiast?"
>
> MR. POLK: "Well, Mr. Hopkins, ever since we moved into this area, about fifteen years ago."
>
> TOM: "How many boats have you owned in the last fifteen years, Mr. Polk?"
>
> MR. POLK: "Let's see—well, about five, I guess, counting the Spee-D-Ski."
>
> TOM: "About five boats. I also wanted to ask, are you familiar with Spee-D-Ski's new line?"
>
> MR. POLK: "They've already brought out a new line? What's wrong with the model I've got? It has everything anyone could possibly want."
>
> TOM: "That's what we thought until we saw the Spee-D-Ski II. It's the work of the same design and engineering team, and they just aren't the kind of people who rest on their laurels."
>
> MR. POLK: "You mean they've changed the styling a little."
>
> TOM: "It's true that there's a wider choice of style features now, but the important changes aren't so obvious. They're

in things like hull refinements that give you a smoother and safer high-speed turn in rough water. In fact, they've made a number of technical advances that only someone like you, who really knows the old Spee-D-Ski, can fully appreciate. And there are several exciting new options that we didn't have before. Would you mind if I send you a brochure?"

MR. POLK: "No, I wouldn't mind at all. I'd like to see the new models."

TOM: "Fine. Let's see—you're still on Slalom Way?"

MR. POLK: "That's right, at 1218."

TOM: "That's what I have here, 1218 Slalom Way runs into Flying Bridge Road, doesn't it?"

MR. POLK: "Sure does."

TOM: "I'm going out to Flying Bridge this afternoon. Would you mind, while I'm in the neighborhood, if I stop by with the brochure and just take a minute to say hello? I'll be servicing your account from now on."

MR. POLK: "That's okay, but it'll have to be fast—I'm getting ready for a trip. But I would like to see your brochure on the new models."

TOM: "Wonderful. I'll drop by around two, or would three o'clock be more convenient?"

MR. POLK: "Anytime before four."

TOM: "I'm looking forward to meeting you, Mr. Polk. And thanks for all the help on my survey."

MR. POLK: "That's okay, Mr. Hopkins. I'm looking forward to seeing you, too."

What is his itch cycle?

To get it, simply divide the time period involved (in Mr. Polk's case, fifteen years) by the number of times (five) that he bought the item in question. The answer is Mr. Polk's itch cycle—expressed in years—for that kind of boat.

What you're looking for is the same thing the Champion is looking for: the average itch cycle for a specific product when bought by a definable group of people. I'll explain what a definable group of people is in a moment, but first, let's discuss what you should count in the average that establishes the itch cycle you're looking for.

Suppose the first three people tell you that a Spee-D-Ski is the first boat they've ever bought. Not only that, but they don't know when—if ever—they'll buy another one. How do you figure them in the average?

You don't. Leave them out. During the day you spend establishing itch cycles, you should talk to at least twenty people—and they'll all give you different answers. Do like the Champion does. Throw out all the offbeat answers and zero in on the average itch cycle for the involved, on-the-track owner of your product or service.

As you work through the day, you'll be learning what's important to your owners. And you may establish more than one average itch cycle. For example, perhaps the owners of Spee-D-Ski boats can be divided into two easily defined groups: active competitors (in boat racing and waterskiing) and noncompetitors. The competitors might trade boats every two years, or even every season, while the noncompetitors keep their boats for three years. Now that you've separated your owners into definable groups with different itch cycles, you know where to concentrate your efforts, don't you?

Mr. Polk is the perfect example of the itch cycle at work. Over a lengthy period, he's proven that he can't go more than about three years before the itch to have a newer and snazzier boat drives him down to the dock, checkbook in hand.

Did you notice the steps that I followed to acquire this vital information?

The first thing I told him was that I knew how long he'd had the product or service that prompted my call.

The second thing I told him was that I was calling to make sure he was happy with the product or service.

After those preliminaries, I moved in to qualify what product he had owned before his present one, and how many of them he had owned over a specific period of time.

Now you know how to establish the itch cycle for your offering. Before you set out to do that, let's cover the next technique.

TECHNIQUE NUMBER TWO: ORPHAN ADOPTION

Orphan adoption? Before you decide that this heading got mixed in here from another book, let me assure you that the technique is a gold mine if you're willing and able to use it. Every company has turnover in its sales force. When salespeople leave an organization, what do they leave behind?

Their clientele.

Now, we know that many people fail in sales because they don't follow up. But the salespeople who failed in your company did make some sales, and their abandoned clientele can become your gold mine. Of course, if your company assigns specific territories, you'll have to be guided by that circumstance. If not, you'll find a lot of people in the files who need someone to serve them. Be sure to check with your manager to see if the company has a system in place for reassigning orphans. Few do. If yours does, ask for them. If they don't have a method of handling those orphans, offer to do the research to locate them in the files if you can have the accounts.

I've received letters from all over the country that tell me things like this: "Tom, as soon as I started going through the files of the salespeople who've left this firm, my income took off. I called these abandoned customers, reestablished rapport, picked up prequalified leads, and closed a high percentage of them."

Why are these leads prequalified? Because you represent the product or service they're already happily involved with, and the files you have in your hands are jammed with details about them. You're in a perfect position to handle any little challenges they might have; you're in a perfect position to advise them on maintenance; you have perfect reasons for contacting them.

But the exact way that you handle the contact is critical. Let me clarify that statement. If you're in commercial, industrial, or any other type of sales that involves big-ticket items or large-scale transactions, you're working with busy people. Every day you talk to corporate executives, professional people, or independent businessmen who aren't careless with their time. The people sitting on the park bench watching the world go by generally aren't the sort of folks who make the decisions about purchasing office supplies, installing new computers, or replacing corporate jets, are they?

Will you agree that the kind of person who buys what you sell gets a large amount of mail? What does the corporate executive—the busy doctor, engineer, or investor, the harried businessman—do with a letter from someone who's just writing to introduce himself as the new representative of a company that person has bought from in the past?

Zip into file thirteen. About 99.9 percent of the time, that piece of paper is on its way to oblivion as soon as the receiver recognizes what it is. The easiest thing to get rid of is a letter. The people you're selling have to get rid of a mass of paper every day or they'll be buried in it.

And what do these busy people say when the new representative calls them during their hectic work hours?

"Thanksforcallingoodbye." Click.

That happens 80 percent of the time when the new representative has nothing more in mind than to report his existence to the previous buyer. Why? Because the second easiest thing to get rid of is a phone call.

What's the hardest thing to get rid of?

A body.

That's why you should contact these former clients of former salespeople in person. These busy people—unlike any other group of prospects you're likely to encounter—have already proven that they need, want, benefit from, and can afford your offering. And if you pick the ones who've reached the right stage on the cycle, you know that most of them are starting to itch to do it all over again. So go see these orphans in person.

If necessary, phone the executive's secretary—for a meeting—but be sure that you have a strong answer ready for the secretary's inevitable question: "What is this concerning?" Because if you say "I just want to introduce myself," you're not going to get in, and that executive's secretary isn't going to let you at the boss to ask market-survey questions, either.

That's why the Champion goes to see them. A surprisingly large percentage of people are more easily seen simply by going to where they are rather than by going through the routine of lining up an appointment. But first, you have to sift through the files.

Let's suppose that your company is fairly typical in this regard. You've determined that the itch cycle is three years; the files hold a large number of orphans; you can readily pull them out by the date they bought your product or service. Not only that, but you're embarrassed by riches: The files are bulging with records of buyers who haven't been contacted for up to ten years. Where to start? Hadn't you better start working on those old files of people who bought nine years ago before any more time passes?

Forget them. They aren't orphans any longer. If your offering really has a three-year itch cycle, those people have long ago made a connection to satisfy their urge to update your product or service with your competition.

Start right on the three-year mark, and work forward through the people who are just starting to itch until you've seen every orphan who bought up to two years and ten months ago. Only then should you start on the buyers who bought more than three years ago. Start with the buyers from thirty-seven months ago and work back until the returns no longer justify the effort. With most products, this won't take long if you've accurately determined the itch cycle.

In order to speed up the process of seeing the orphans who are itching to reorder your product or service because they bought it two years and ten months ago—and they're tickled pink with it—make discreet phone calls to determine whether they're still breathing and blinking at the same old stand. Some of them will have moved on.

In personal sales, that's usually a dead end. In commercial and industrial sales, it simply means that Mrs. Newhouse is now making the decisions that Mrs. Oldbarn used to make. When the old copier Mrs. Oldbarn bought from your company starts to creak, Mrs. Newhouse will start itching to get the latest model on the same schedule that would have ruled Mrs. Oldbarn had she not retired.

Perhaps you're wondering, "Suppose they don't get the itch?"

The Champion believes that it's her obligation to help busy people become aware that they have a bad case of the itch. The Champion starts seeing them and calling them and doing all sorts of things to excite their interest and make them realize why they should cure that itch by reordering or replacing the product or service.

To be a Champion, you must know—and passionately believe in—compelling reasons why they should:

- Replace those old welding machines with the latest models that run beads 20 percent faster and save X dollars of labor cost.
- Trade in their old motor home for a new one that delivers more mileage and greater comfort.
- Get rid of the outdated system that, though it was a marvel three years ago, simply can't match the system you're able to help them enjoy today.

Find the reasons that make the product or service you're offering today so much better than the best available three long years ago. Make the effort and you'll find the reasons. Three years ago, they bought the best—but what's best today is the latest. You want them to have the best, don't you? Then do your job. Show these people—who've already demonstrated their faith in your company by owning part of its output for three years—that your brand-new state-of-the-art performance leader will deliver greater benefits to them than their old model does. You can do that, can't you?

Certainly you can—because you're a professional. The next time you walk into your office, go straight to the records and start looking for people who bought your offering from salespeople no longer with your company. Adopt those people. Make them your clients. Make them wish they'd bought from you. Then get them happily involved in a repeat performance with your offering.

TECHNIQUE NUMBER THREE: TECHNICAL ADVANCEMENT

Of course you use the lure of technical advancement when you're talking to people who've made their itch cycle's full circle. But I'm talking now about technical advancement as a specific prospecting technique in its own right.

Do you know that almost every product is already obsolete in the minds of its creators the moment it's scheduled for production?

Already they're looking to the future. They're asking, "How can we make it better?" They know that if they don't, someone else will. And of course, all those engineers, designers, and inventors aren't ready to fold their tents and silently steal away. They want to hang in there and keep on inventing, designing, and engineering tomorrow's surprises.

Many finished products quickly become obsolete, and few last long before they're outdated. Rarely do finished products wear out to the point where they can't be kept in service. Far more often, their original owners are used to the best, and they dispose of the product when it starts requiring frequent service, or when something better comes along. This applies to all finished products, from calculators to supertankers. The people who could afford the best when the previous model of your product came out can still afford the best. In fact, very often they can't afford anything but the best. Sometimes this means that a blue-collar worker drives an old car so he can afford the latest dirt bike because racing them is his hobby. He can't afford to have anything but the best dirt bike for exactly the same reason the major airlines can't afford to have anything but the latest jet aircraft—they're both competing.

In this country—in fact, in the entire free world—we all want the best, latest, shiniest, newest, fastest, highest-performance products and services.

When you have a new product—or an old product in a new style or with a new feature—call everyone who already has your product. Of course, use some discretion. If you used to sell them in packages of twelve, and now you have them in packages of a dozen, don't call everyone and tell them you have a fantastic development.

And use some flair. When you work with people, take a few minutes to find out a little about their interests and values. Save that information. Then when the exciting new development comes out next year—the one you haven't even thought about now—you can go through your files, calling people to say, "I know where you're going to be in three weeks—and wait till you hear about the exciting development I'm calling you about."

Of course, you call your own old customers first. Then sit yourself down and figure out a way to reach people you've never spoken to with that fantastic new innovation. Had I been a TV salesman when HDTV came out, I would have called every doctor, lawyer, and dentist in my area along with every other person I thought could afford it.

But it's late if you wait until the new innovation is in your showroom before you start to think about how to exploit it. If you sell for a company that's coming up with new developments all the time, start now on compiling a list of people to call when you have an especially important breakthrough to share with them.

Technical advancement. What an exciting and profitable way to collar new business.

TECHNIQUE NUMBER FOUR:
YOUR LOCAL NEWSPAPERS

Champions do not dwell on the doom, destruction, and despair that crowd the front page. Champions read their local newspaper to generate business with pen in hand because dozens of people are advertising a message of great importance in every edition. That message is, *I need help.* But of course, it's never written in those exact words.

Let me give you an example. Newspapers carry lots of little items about people who have been promoted because that's one of the ways newspapers build their own clientele. You can count on a steady flow of these notices. Skim these articles and send the people who were promoted a short note of congratulations. Do you think they'll appreciate that?

They'll not only appreciate the note, they'll probably be very receptive if you pick up the phone a day after you know they've received it and call to see how you can help them.

A story I heard from J. Douglas Edwards shows how this approach can be turned into substantial earnings by salespeople for a wide variety of products and services. One of Doug's close friends was a professional baseball player who received one of the largest salaries ever paid a ballplayer for going to a new club. In the city he was going to, the newspapers ran half-page articles telling about his coming, and that he was going to establish a second home for his family there.

Now, what did that well-paid professional athlete need in the new city?

A home. If you're in real estate, here's a live one for the best neighborhood you serve.

If you're selling an interior designer's services, furniture, carpeting, or any of a host of things for the home, here's a hot lead.

What about the grounds? A tennis court, a swimming pool, patios, landscaping—this man needs all sorts of products and services for his new home.

What else does he need? Money always burns holes in our pockets, and this man has a bundle of bonus money. He isn't going to be without wheels either in his new city or at the house he's keeping in his old hometown. So he needs a car. And since athletes like to watch themselves on TV, he's going to need video-recording equipment. Of course, he doesn't want to miss detail, so he's a prime candidate for a big-screen TV.

With a new home and car, what's he going to need in the way of services? Not only the landscaping and interior design that I've already mentioned, but also insurance for the house and car and his possessions, and for the liability risks he'll be exposed to in the new city. And he's moved up several brackets on the income scale. Now he's batting in a new league of tax and investment opportunities—so he might need new tax and investment counselors. And his wife needs accounts at the finest stores, along with a number of other products and services to go along with her new station in life.

You know, we Champions could help him spend all his bonus money, couldn't we? And while we're doing that, we'll be making sure that he and his family get the maximum benefit from it, won't we?

Here's the clincher. The ballplayer moved into that new city several weeks after the story ran in all the local papers. Later, Doug asked if a swarm of salespeople had overwhelmed him with attention. The ballplayer said, as far as he could tell, not one salesperson had contacted him as a result of the newspaper stories. He and his wife arrived in that new city and set about satisfying their needs exactly like anyone else might: by asking people they knew for recommendations, by driving around and spotting things, and by checking the yellow pages.

Where were all of us when they came to town?

Just sitting in our showrooms, waiting for somebody—anybody—to wander in.

Very often, the publications that have the most leads for the alert salesperson are the small, local ones, such as your local business journal. Champions aren't looking for news about the latest catastrophe in Kabul, Karachi, and Kimpo when skimming through these papers. Champions are looking for news about their sales territory. Who's been transferred in, who's been promoted, who's won an award, who's developing a new project? That's what the Champions want to know.

Another section of the papers to watch if you sell to consumers is the personal announcements. Engagements, marriages, births, and deaths all generate needs for new products and services by those people.

Check out the little local papers that you've been finding on your doorstep and throwing away without looking at. Some of these papers are bulging with local news. Also check out the specialized business newspapers that cover certain industries or certain areas. These can be rich sources of leads. Obviously, if you're active in the yacht business, you'll already be reading the local boating newspaper—but what if you're selling insurance, fine furniture, art, luxury automobiles? People who can afford yachts don't buy their clothes at the Goodwill, and the dentist who's winning all the yacht races around there is almost certainly a heavy consumer in other areas of life. The chances are that he needs your product or service—and he'll appreciate a note of congratulations on his latest victory.

But what about the people who came in second, third—or just entered the race? They're heavy hitters, too, and they'll be even more appreciative that someone noticed they competed.

More leads than you can possibly handle are being printed every day in your area—and your best source for them may be in publications that you've never thought of reading. If you're in any form of personal sales, expand your thinking. Search out new printed sources of leads.

TECHNIQUE NUMBER FIVE: CLAIM-STAKING

After reading the story about Doug's ball-playing friend, you may be saying, "If I wait until someone new arrives at a club [or any local organization], it'll be harder to make a connection there in time to get the business. Maybe I should start working some clubs right now—before the new people who'll get publicity arrive. Then, when they show up, I'll be an insider and get first crack at them."

That's what the claim-staking technique is all about. You make yourself known, learn the ropes, get acquainted with carefully selected organizations where you feel comfortable and are meeting people who are prequalified—by income and interests—for owning your offering. This is one of the best techniques I've ever encountered because you can stake out as many claims as you can handle. Every one of them will be a gold mine of contacts and solid prequalified leads. Yes, there's no limit to how many organizations you can claim-stake, but don't be like some of the old-time prospectors who wandered the canyons with a donkey and a pickax. Don't stake out more claims than you can work properly and lose out on all of them.

Bear in mind that with this technique, it usually takes a little time before you can start bringing the ore out of the ground. So start work right away. Put a few hours each week into developing this approach. Invest enough time to keep your presence and influence growing in the clubs or organizations you've selected for this technique, but don't allow this medium-term project to prevent you from working your ready-to-buy-now prospects for all they're worth.

How many organizations should you claim-stake? And how do you work them?

Check out as many organizations as you can before deciding on your answers. Keep looking until you find an organization that offers you both encouragement and opportunity. Having one without the other is useless. When you locate such a group, the best way to work with it will suggest itself to you. Be as active as possible. If it's a country or social club, join it and volunteer for committee work—there's no better way to make your presence felt. If it's an organization that you can't or don't want to join, start taking to lunch the people who are active in it, write thank-you notes, do favors, run errands, make yourself useful. If you're right for that group, you'll know the right song to sing there. If you don't, move on to another organization. One club may offer more contacts than you can possibly work with, or you may enjoy and profit from working with several. If you decide to claim-stake companies—by getting acquainted with their personnel directors, for example—you may find that you can effectively work with twenty or thirty. The only rule about how many to claim-stake is to do what's most effective for you.

What kind of organization is best for claim-staking?

That depends on your offering, your preferences, your personality. The range of organizations that you can effectively bore into is almost limitless: private companies, business associations, charities, church groups, country and social clubs, amateur and professional sports organizations, special-interest groups, service clubs, political parties, hobby clubs, and cultural societies. To determine the best group for you, compare the time, money, and energy cost of establishing yourself in any organization that interests you with the benefits that you can expect in the way of contacts and leads from doing so. Your analysis will develop the right answer.

TECHNIQUE NUMBER SIX:
SWAP MEET OR LEADS CLUBS

Do you know that you can easily create a source for some of your best leads by setting up your own swap meet or leads club? You do it on a small scale; it costs you nothing beyond a little effort.

The idea is to meet regularly to swap leads with carefully selected salespeople who sell in noncompeting fields. Four to six people is the ideal number; more than that gets out of hand.

Here's how to organize this fantastic fountain of new business:

Think about some fields of sales or service that complement yours. For example, if you sell real estate, you'll want to work with an insurance person, a mortgage broker, a landscaper, home repair service . . . You get the idea. Select one strong salesperson in each field to join your swap meet, and agree with them on a time and place. That's all there is to it.

SELECTING STRONG SALESPEOPLE FOR YOUR SWAP MEET

Here's the technique for picking the people you'll really enjoy and profit from. Suppose that most of my customers are executives who generally drive luxury cars, although that's not my product. I can assume that many of these executives lease their cars for tax and other reasons. So one of the people I'd want in my swap meet would be a top producer in the luxury car leasing field. Why? Because I can help her—and if I can help her, I know she can help me.

Call the sales managers of leasing companies until you hit pay dirt. The chances are that you'll do so with the first call you make. Tell the sales manager what you want to do, and ask him who you should get to go to your swap meet from his company. That sales manager is going to put you in touch with someone he knows will follow up on leads from your swap meet—which means you're going to get a top producer.

For top recommendations for your swap meet, go to the top. If you've called a sales manager worthy of the title, that person is going to be excited by the fact that you're creative enough to start a swap meet, and he'll want his firm to benefit from it by having a strong person there.

How the swap meet works:

- Meet every week. Unless you do, it won't become habit.
- Meet at the same time and place. Otherwise the time consumed by making arrangements will kill the whole thing.
- Meet first thing in the morning. You'll never be able to get together on a consistent basis at any other time. Drop anybody who can't get up in time. Your swap meet is for people who mean business only.

- Meeting for breakfast at a centrally located coffee shop is the most convenient plan for sales leads swap meets. Don't burn anyone with the entire check—all participants pay their own way.
- Don't dawdle. This is not an excuse for killing time. Unless your swap meet is brief, upbeat, and useful, it'll wither away.
- Everyone who attends commits to the goal of bringing two good leads to each swap meet. But sometimes people won't have two. Agree that they are welcome anyway; it's better to come with one lead than not to come at all. That person should then feel an obligation to bring three leads to one of the next swap meets.
- At the meet, the leads are exchanged. As a group, you try to make sure that the person who can help any given lead soonest is the one to work on it first. That same lead might be good for several people. However, the intial contact person will need to qualify him to determine which other service he needs first.
- The strongest commitment must be made by all to follow up promptly and thoroughly with every lead they take. The swap meet won't last unless its members get solid benefits from it.
- Nothing destroys a swap meet faster than letting it divide into takers and givers. If you see that start to happen, talk to the takers privately. Persuade them to change their ways or eliminate them from the group.
- And no swap meet can survive being the dump for the group's gloom. Don't tolerate pessimism and put-downs. Make it clear that the swap meet is to be the springboard for a day of effective selling and moneymaking, and that no one who's forgotten to bring enthusiasm is welcome.

I've been in swap meets as a salesperson and know I've been a lead at someone else's swap meet. Of course, I didn't figure that out until much later. So from both ends, I know they work.

The swap meet is exciting. It's fun. And it's a business boomer. After you get your first swap meet running smoothly and making money for you every Monday morning—who knows? Maybe you'll want to start a second swap meet on Thursday mornings.

TECHNIQUE NUMBER SEVEN: SERVICE YOUR SERVICE DEPARTMENT

If you sell any kind of mechanical or electronic product, your company probably has a service department. This means that the owners of your product call them when the old model they've got starts creaking and groaning. Now, what happens when a machine's maintenance cost goes up? Its productivity goes down— and its owner starts to itch for a new one.

Check with the service department and find out who's calling in to get their existing equipment worked on. Service calls give you the perfect opportunity to go over and get these people happily involved in the new model that'll do a better job for them with no downtime.

This can be a tremendous source of business for the alert salesperson.

If you have a service department, service it every day and it'll service your bank account for you.

TECHNIQUE NUMBER EIGHT: COMMUNITY INVOLVEMENT

If you work in real estate sales or another area in which you want to reach people living in a certain geographic area, consider getting involved in local community events. This will allow you the opportunity to meet others while doing good. This is a wise move for many reasons. One is that you will feel great about helping out. Another is that you'll meet people you might otherwise have had to work hard to meet. A third reason is that you'll become known as someone who cares.

If appropriate consider some of the following possibilities:

- Volunteer at your local library, senior center, or hospital.
- Assist with food drives and with fund-raisers for youth sports teams, schools, and churches.
- Attend city council meetings. Be fully aware of what's going on in your community so you can tell those you want to serve. Let them rely on you for the latest information (not gossip) and as an expert.

When the need for your type of service comes to mind, the people you are involved with in your community will remember you, come to you for service, and refer others.

These eight strategies work—if you work them. Select the one that sounds most interesting and begin there. Once it's generating a good flow of leads for you, consider adding a second strategy. Don't try all eight at once or you'll either drown yourself in leads you don't have time to handle or manage the strategy ineffectively and not reap the rewards that concentrated effort brings.

9. Referral Prospecting, or The Art of Getting Quality Introductions

Ask yourself this question: Of these groups, which is the easiest to close?

- The people who just walked in off the street.
- The ones who called in from an ad.
- The leads on little slips of paper that your company hands to you and says, "Go get 'em, Tiger."
- Or is it the people referred to you by someone who knows them and is happy with your product or service?

The referred lead is the easiest to close. In fact, you'll spend half the time selling the referred, prequalified lead as you will selling the company-generated, nonqualified lead. Champions close referrals twice as fast as they close nonreferred prospects.

Even more exciting is the fact that Champions will close 40 to 60 percent of their qualified referrals. Compare this with the results they get working with their nonreferred and unqualified leads. The success rate with referrals is 400 to 600 percent of what it is with nonreferrals. That being the case, is it any wonder that Champions are champions at getting referrals?

The fact that you're reading this book is a strong indication that one of your immediate goals is to double your income—or multiply it by an even greater factor. If you're going to make that happen, referrals will have to play a large part in your future.

Let's get to work and learn how to create a rich flow of these neat moneymakers. Have you ever asked your buyers something like this after you've closed them: "Do you know who might be interested in [what they just bought]?"

You've done that, I'm sure. How many of them said yes?

Not too many, right? Most of them probably answered vaguely along these lines: "I can't think of anybody right now."

They are telling you the absolute truth. But if you believe the old saying that birds of a feather flock together, you know they know people who have the same needs they do. They just "can't think of anybody right now."

Why can't they? Because you've given them the entire world to look at with your question. No wonder they can't say, "Oh, yeah, Zack was telling me he wanted—" Most people have their mind's eye fixed on other things right after buying something, and their excitement crowds out any possibility that they'll remember what Zack wanted.

When about the fifth person says no, you come to a conclusion: "That doesn't work." So pretty soon you stop asking.

Let me show you what Champions do. This is the backbone of their prospecting system. When you master this technique, you're going to walk out with qualified, referred leads after every sale. But you have to follow every step very carefully. There's another requirement: You have to use this technique in a casual, unthreatening manner or you'll tighten your buyers up and they won't be willing or able to help you.

The process of getting referrals—or what I like to call "quality introductions"—begins the moment you meet people. When you first meet potential clients, you work on building their trust. People won't buy from you if they don't trust you. During your initial rapport-building chat, you must be like a detective and look for clues as to the small groups of people they know. You also set up the right to ask for introductions in the beginning. You might say, "John and Mary, you haven't seen a tremendous amount of television advertising about our company, have you? [Only say this if it's true.] The reason we don't spend millions of dollars in advertising is we have chosen to build our business on word-of-mouth recommendations.

When we have satisfied your needs with our product, done the job, and you are totally thrilled with what our company has done for you, would you have any challenges with me asking for an introduction to a few other people I might serve?"

If you are meeting with these people because of a referral from another satisfied client, mention that as well: "It's how I got to meet you fine folks . . . an introduction by your friends Jill and Wayne."

When you say it warm and nice like that, they'll agree. It's early in your relationship. They're being nice. They haven't been asked to own anything yet. You just set the stage.

After the sale is made and they're excited about the wonderful benefits they'll derive, it's time to remind them about their agreement. "John and Mary, do you remember when we first talked, I asked if you'd mind giving me the names of a few other people to serve—that is, once you were satisfied that we could help you? Well, you have decided to enjoy the fine benefits of our product now and I can see how excited you are. Let's see if we can come up with anyone else you know who might be just as happy once I bring this opportunity to them."

CARD REFERRAL SYSTEM

All you need is a few three-by-five-inch cards of the kind sold in all office supply and most drug and grocery stores. These cards allow you to get all the information you need to build a clientele. I'll give you the steps first, and then show you how to use them.

1. Isolate faces for them to see. Bring up small groups of people that they know. They may have mentioned that they bowl, golf, or participate in another sport. They may be involved with clubs or community activities, church, or school programs with their children.
2. Get the full names of the people they mention. Ask for the correct spelling if the names are unusual.
3. Ask qualifying questions. "John, what did Tim say or do that brought him to your mind just now?" Get as much information as possible.

4. Ask for the contact information. "What's the best way for me to reach Tim?" If they don't have addresses or phone numbers, get as much information as possible so you can find it yourself. Or have them get the phone book so you can look it up together.

5. Ask them to call. If the referral is a family member or very close friend, people will often be willing to do this. If it's a business associate or acquaintance, they won't, and that's okay.

6. If they show nervousness or refuse to call, get permission to use their names when you call the referral. When they grant permission, say, "John and Mary, because you have asked, I promise I will contact these people and give them the highest-quality service possible." That statement is designed to allay any fears they may have about how you'll use their good name with others.

The role play that follows shows how the system functions. In it, John and Mary Harrison have just bought a new automobile from good old Tom. The Harrisons are ecstatic about their new car. They worked the figures out with me, of course, and they were shrewd and good. Believe me, I had to know my product and how to close. But it came out well. The Harrisons got the colors and options they were looking for; I got them emotionally involved, and I helped them rationalize the wisdom of their decision to own what they wanted. So they're happy.

Normally, the first time you can get a referral is right after you've completed the sale. That's also the best time in many cases. But some Champions sell something that has a lengthy design, installation, or servicing period, and they prefer to work on referrals throughout that period. Different Champions select different times to gather referrals. Since this will be the key element in your expanding success, the vital thing is to have some specific event in the selling sequence that always triggers your drive for referrals. Never forget that every person who owns your product or service knows someone else who can own it, too. All you need to get at that sale is the referral.

Read this role play and you'll see how it all happens.

The Harrisons are sitting across a table from me and my three-by-five cards and my ballpoint pen as I wrap up the sale of their new car.

TOM: "Well, John and Mary, I'm really happy for you both. I can really see your excitement with your new car. John, you mentioned that you play softball.

"Tell me, when you were playing last week, was there anyone on your team who either mentioned an interest in a car like your new one, or who you feel might be as excited with a new car as you and Mary seem to be?"

JOHN: "Well, I know one guy who needs a new car."

TOM: "Oh, do you?"

JOHN: "He might be interested, yeah. George Zack."

TOM: "George Zack. What did he say that brought him to mind just now?"

JOHN: "He had just gotten his car out of the shop again. It's broken down three times in the last three months. I have to believe it's getting pretty expensive to keep it up."

TOM: "It sure sounds like driving something more reliable would be a good idea for George. [Now I'm going for the referral from the wife.] "Mary, you volunteer with your daughter's Girl Scout troop, don't you?"

MARY: "Yes, I do."

TOM: "Well, when you were at the last meeting, did any of your girls or their parents mention, or give you any hint, that they might be as delighted with a new car as you are?"

MARY: "One of the girls' parents was late picking her up because of car trouble. It was Karie's mom. Her name is Lorna."

TOM: "Do you know the last name?"

JOHN: "It's Cabbot."

TOM: "Lorna Cabbot. [Here's a nonthreatening question that'll help establish how well Mr. Harrison knows George Zack and also tell me a lot about Zack.] "Going back to George for a moment. John, how many children does he have?"

JOHN: "Three. A couple of boys and a girl. They're all still pretty young."

TOM: "Then he has a medium-size car now, doesn't he?"

JOHN: "Yeah, and he probably needs at least that, or maybe a van next time."

TOM: "The youngest child's how old, do you think?"

JOHN: "Oh, about seven, I'd guess."

TOM: "He might enjoy something bigger, then. Where does he work, do you know?"

JOHN: "He's a soil engineer at Femmes and Loess."

TOM: "Great. Mary, tell me more about Mrs. Cabbot. Do you know much about their family? How many children do they have?"

MARY: "She has Karie, and one on the way."

TOM: "Oh, one on the way. They'll want a vehicle that works well with toddlers, won't they? I think I know what she'll love. Do you know what I'd like you to do for me, John? Do you have some idea of the Zacks' address?"

JOHN: "They live on Mainsail, I'm not sure of the number."

TOM: "That's M-A-I-N-S-A-I-L, isn't it? All right. And where does Lorna live?"

MARY: "They live over by Roosevelt High on Margrave."

TOM: "Okay. Would you like a soda or a nice fresh cup of coffee? Do you take it black or with cream and sugar?"

JOHN: "Black coffee for both of us."

MARY: "That would be great."

TOM: "OK. Why don't we do this? [I reach for the phone book.] I'm going to ask you a favor. While I'm getting all of us a cup of coffee, will you look up their addresses for me? Would you mind?"

MARY: "Not at all."

TOM: "Here's one card to write it on. [I hand it to Mrs. Harrison.] I use cards for this information so I'll always have it handy. There's the second card. [I give it to Mr. Harrison.] Now, I'm going to get the coffee. Be right back."

A few moments pass.

TOM: "Okay, here's your coffee. Ah, you've got their addresses. Good, good. When I have new owners who are happy with their new car call one of their friends and tell them about it, that friend often wants me to show them a car like it. Would you mind giving them a call?"

If your new client makes the call on your behalf and gets the permission for you to contact the referral, you have just avoided the potential challenge of the referral's being in the Do Not Call Registry. So, it's very important that you at least give it a try.

JOHN: "Okay."

TOM: "Wonderful. There's a phone on the desk over there. Why don't you give George a quick call while Mary and I just chat? Then we'll let Mary call Lorna. I'd really appreciate that."

Right here I'm going to change gears because you won't often hear good news like this. Instead of that ready agreement to make the calls, suppose the Harrisons look at each other and start backing off. They don't want to call. Let's pick it up from where I ask them to call.

TOM: "—I'd really love for you to give George a quick call and let him know I'll be contacting him."

JOHN: "Well, uh—That would be a little uncomfortable."

TOM: "I understand entirely. [Notice that I get off this fast, and don't press them at all once they've indicated reluctance to call. By moving past the rejection fast, I'm very likely to get their approval of the next best thing. In actual speech, there'd be no pause between "I understand entirely" and what now follows.] May I ask you this? Would you mind if I just used your name?"

JOHN: "That's okay."

TOM: "You don't mind at all? That's great. I'll contact him. In fact, I promise you that I will. And I promise you, too, Mary,

that I won't forget Lorna. I'll let her know that I promised
you I'd contact her and offer the highest-quality service possible. May I?"

MARY: "Certainly."

TOM: "Well, again, I thank you so much, and I wish you many
happy days with your new car."

Realize that you must go through all six of the steps if you're going to be successful with the card referral system. And it only works
if your buyers have a reasonable level of satisfaction with your product or service. Of course, it works best with buyers who are ecstatic,
but some people aren't capable of ecstasy. Maybe they're simply satisfied, or just so darn glad to have the product that if you handle your
referral request like this, they'll just get going with you.

As you read that role play, how did it feel? Do you think the Harrisons wanted to help me? I believe that most people on this continent, if you ask them properly, will help you do anything within
reason. Do you agree? If you stop while you're out driving and ask
people for directions, what'll they do? They'll start pointing. Many
of them will come out to your car and, while you're trying to drive
away, they'll hold on just trying to tell you. Millions of people will
do that for strangers.

The people you know in selling situations will help you even
more—if they like and trust you, if your product or service is what
they're looking for—and if you'll let them.

Would you be afraid to do what I did in the role play? I've done it
hundreds of times in real selling situations, but I remember the first
few times because I was fearful of trying the system, too. It's natural to be afraid of what you've never done before, but it's not wise
to let that stop you. Read the role play aloud until you've memorized the entire pattern and can carry it off with the confident ease
that people can't resist.

Prepare in depth and your success ratio with this powerful system will do wonders for your sales and income. A thorough understanding of your objectives in this interview and how you should go
about achieving them is vital to make this system work. Note how I
jumped on every opportunity to make a small joke or go off on a

brief tangent in order to avoid building tension. Note that my attitude was nonthreatening throughout the interview, and yet I still maintained control of it. In this situation, a straight line is not the shortest route to where you want to go. There were jokes and asides, but we never strayed for long from the path I wanted to take.

Get the feel of the role play in your bones, and then write a script for a referral-gathering interview based on your own product or service. Decide what you'll say first, imagine what responses your customers might give, and write down the effective replies that you could then make to keep them moving toward your goal of collecting solid referrals.

I'll say it again: Prepare in depth for the referral-gathering interview. It looks easy, but don't let that lull you into complacency. Time enough for that after you've mastered the technique and have all the referrals you can handle.

As you study the role play, notice how warmly I isolated a dozen faces for the Harrisons by pleasantly probing into the areas that would bring friends and referrals into their minds. How many names did John have to run through to cover his entire softball team? And how many girls does Mary have in her troop? In both cases, we're talking about very small numbers of people compared with all the folks that John and Mary know. And don't people frequently talk about automobiles at social gatherings? But that's just an example. Forget autos and think about your own product or service.

Let's suppose that you sell to company executives. Do you think that the executive who just purchased a new computer system has lunch with executives from other companies?

Of course he does. And what does he do when he's having lunch right after approving the computer purchase?

He brags a little.

"I okayed the computer agreement this morning. It's knocking us back a quarter of a million, but it'll do a lot for us."

"Which one did you go for?"

"The Bytebarfer 2500. It's got some fantastic features."

"You know, we've got to get moving on a new computer system, too."

We choose our friends from among those who share our status, preferences, and needs. When we like someone's product or service, we're likely to brag about it. Our friends will be interested because they have the same interests that we do. And no one has the time to become expert at everything. So we have to rely on the people we know for much of the information that leads to our buying decisions.

This knowledge of the characteristics of buyers can easily be turned to great advantage in referral gathering:

- If your procedure requires after-sale visits (so you can make the delivery or give training, for example), ask the buyer which of her friends or associates she's told about the purchase.
- If your procedure doesn't require after-sale visits, ask the buyer which of his friends or associates he intends to tell about his purchase. (That is, *brag* about the purchase—but of course you never use the word *brag* to a buyer.)

In either case, the idea is to focus buyers on those among their friends, loved ones, or business associates who are the best candidates for owning what the buyers just bought from you. Once those faces are in their minds, you'll find that it isn't difficult to pull the information from them that you need for a solid referral.

What results can you expect from the card referral system?

The answer depends more on the level of competence in sales that you aspire to—and are willing to plan, practice, and work for—than on anything else. A single success with the card referral technique marks you as a comer who can go as far as you wish in sales. When you're averaging one referral per sale, you've edged into the top half of the selling community. When you're averaging two referrals per sale, you're in the top 20 percent. When you're averaging three referrals per sale, you're in the top 10 percent. Four referrals per sale puts you into the charmed circle where the Five Percent make the really big money. Anything over that—five referrals or more per sale—proclaims that you're one of the great ones.

We've agreed that of course the referral is the finest type of prospect to work with. Referrals are people who have already accepted you. Now all you must do is get them involved with your product or service—something you know they need and can afford.

But you may be sitting there thinking, *I couldn't do the card referral thing. I just can't see myself pulling that off.*

Now, before you give in to that emotion, examine your feelings carefully. See whether you really want to pay between twenty-five and a hundred thousand dollars a year for catering to that kind of whim. Make no mistake about it—you can't pass up a powerful, basic technique like card referral gathering without paying a heavy penalty. I'm not stating this fact to make you feel bad—nor am I concealing it so you can feel good. You should know that accepting a lower level of competence in your chosen profession than you can achieve will cost you an enormous amount of money.

10. How to Find Fortune and Felicity with the Phone

I t's amazing how few people in any sales office really understand the function of the telephone. Once they get the hang of dialing—usually at the age of about three—they turn off their brains and just let their mouths run on automatic when they pick up this incredible instrument.

You'll really need to open your mind in this chapter because it's impossible for me to take all the phone techniques I have for you and tailor them to your product or service. You'll have to stretch and twist and hammer them to fit your needs. All I can do is give you the basic concepts, and pass on an increased understanding of how you can present yourself more professionally and effectively over this potent audio medium that we all have literally at our fingertips.

The telephone is your second most important selling tool—the first being your mouth. Yet, for reasons that escape me, few salespeople really study the techniques of the telephone. Only the extra-ambitious—the potential Champions—do so. The average salesperson, who desperately needs greater skill with the telephone, won't bother studying such a fundamental thing. However, more than knowledge of technique is needed. To use the telephone with greatest effect, you must also have a keen understanding of its limitations. The worst misconception the average salesperson has about the telephone is the idea that a telephone call can substitute for a face-to-face meeting with the prospect. In some areas of sales, such as telemarketing, it can. In most, it does not. The Champion is convinced that no strange voice coming over a wire can ever match in-the-flesh presence for effectiveness. Here's the first of several ideas that I'll isolate so you can highlight them:

I must meet all qualified, interested callers in person.

That must be your goal in every conversation with people calling in who show interest in your offering and give an indication that they are qualified to own it.

INCOMING CALLS

Companies invest huge sums in programs aimed at creating calls: mass media and directory advertising, publicity, signs, direct mail, trade shows, and other promotions. All that money is wasted, and all those ads aimed at making the telephone ring are for nothing, if when the telephone does ring and you answer it, you fail to arrange a meeting with the caller.

More and more, ads are written to generate calls for more information as a first step to purchase. If you know how to handle the phone, such calls can easily become sales for you.

Let's take the process from the beginning.

1. What is the right time to answer the phone? You may laugh, but there is a correct time to answer the phone. If you snatch it up before the first ring is fully rung, you'll startle some people and make others think you're too anxious. If you let it ring six to sixteen times, they'll decide you aren't attending to business. The perfect time, the professional time, to answer the phone is on the third ring. It gives the right impression.

2. What kind of image does your voice create? When you answer the phone with a tone and manner that suggest you're suffering from a terminal illness, or that they're bothering you, they won't want to meet you. This is why Champions answer the phone with some excitement, some happy notes in their voices, some enthusiasm. No matter what catastrophes you're involved with at the moment, every time you pick up the phone at the office you may be talking with someone who wants to be helped by your offering. If you're mature, if you're controlled, if you're competent, you'll be able to put your immediate concerns to one side while you speak cheerfully with the caller.

That's one of the reasons why you answer on the third ring. With the first ring, stop what you're doing, clear your mind, and pump yourself up. It's a simple trick. All it takes is a little practice and knowledge. Select a mental image that pleases you—a happy hope, a specific goal, a solid achievement you're proud of—or even just a good feeling that you can vividly recall. Make your choice and then, whenever you hear the phone ring, block out what you're doing at the moment and flash that mental image across your mind for an instant. Use it to shift gears so you can speak with a fresh and alert tone that tells the caller that you handle the finest product or service available and you're eager to meet anyone who's interested.

3. Acknowledge the other person's interest. Let your callers tell you why they're calling. They may refer to an ad or ask about some specific item. You might respond along these lines:

"Yes sir, we've had a lot of calls about our new Whippledipper. We're really excited about it."

Then you continue on to the next step.

4. Put them on hold so you can obtain information for them. Say, "May I place you on hold for a moment while I access that information?" But do this only if you can fit it in smoothly. The professional looks for an opportunity to put them on hold so he can gather his thoughts, as though saying to himself, *All right, I've got a live one on the line—now, what's my best strategy?*

So you put them on hold once, if you can, early in the conversation. Be sure to take careful note of this: Never keep them on hold longer than seventeen seconds.

What happens when you leave them on hold for a minute or longer? When you come back on the line, they simply aren't the same human beings who called in. If they're still on the line, they don't even sound the same. The roar of rage you hear isn't the opening movement of a beautiful symphony of sales achievement. Long holds equal lost sales.

5. Close for the name. Champions do their best to get the name of the person calling for several reasons, one of which is that it's very helpful in creating rapport with callers if you can address them by name. The best way to get the name is simple, and the exact words are important. Here they are:

When you come off hold, say, "Thank you for waiting." Always acknowledge their courtesy with courtesy.

Then say, "This is _____," giving your name. (Of course, you wouldn't do that if they asked for you by name when first calling.) "May I ask who's calling, please?"

You'll almost always get the name this way if they're really interested in considering you and your firm for the purchase in question—provided that you've been cordial.

6. Answer most questions with questions and lead them to the confirmation of a meeting. This is where many average salespeople lose calls. They act and speak as if they're trying to close the sale over the phone. Unless you're in telemarketing, this is very unlikely to succeed. Your goal with incoming calls is to close for an appointment, not the sale. The meeting or visit you seek might require you to go to their home, if it's a personal or family sale; it might mean that they'll come in to your showroom or display area to see what your company has advertised; it may involve your going to the caller's office if it's a corporate situation. You might even meet in a public place. Whatever the case, you must always be moving for the appointment. Now, answering questions with a question means that you use what technique?

The porcupine.

For example, when someone calls and says, "Do you still have the special price on that copying equipment?—Is it still available?"

Champions would not answer yes or no to that question. Instead, they'd say, "Is that copying equipment the type you were hoping to find?"

"Yes, it is."

"Fine. I'd be available today or tomorrow to talk further with you. Would you like to come to our display room, or shall I come to you?"

That's a porcupine, but it's also an alternate of choice, isn't it? That's double power.

7. When making the appointment, reconfirm all details. I have to warn you about something. Studies have proven that only a small percentage of people will follow a set of instructions if they're only given to them once. Would you agree? When you set appointments, what happens many times? They either forget the whole thing, or they may not realize exactly where your location is. They may forget the time of the appointment; they may not remember your name. That's why a professional reconfirms everything. Make a note to ask them to write down the pertinent details.

Here's what Champions say:

"Do you have a pencil handy? I'd like you to write down some pertinent details."

Guess what the pertinent details are? They include your name, office location, the address, the time, and anything the caller needs to get back in touch with you.

8. Champions drop a second anchor after the meeting is set and confirmed. This final step is especially important if you're going to be waiting for them in your showroom or in a mutually convenient coffee shop. Another 10 percent of people will keep the appointment if they know you can call them up if they don't show. And of course, it's always possible that something could happen that would make it impossible for you to keep the appointment. So, after confirming all details, you say:

"If something very unusual happens and I have to ask you to change the time of our appointment, at what number should I call you?"

OUTGOING CALLS

Whether you market a product or a service, there's at least a fifty–fifty chance that you'll have to call out to get leads. In fact, true Champions, regardless of what they sell, know that the telephone can enormously increase their sales volume. Thus they're on the phone every moment they can squeeze from other needs, calling new people.

So let's discuss that kind of call.

Almost everyone will answer the phone when it rings. Even

salespeople afraid to make outgoing calls will take incoming ones. In fact, they're often so eager for someone to call that it's pathetic.

Why will salespeople cringe at the thought of prospecting by phone, but jump at the chance to talk with the same sort of person when they're receiving instead of initiating the call? When you stop to think about it, there's something really strange going on here. That something gets even more strange the more you dig into it.

After all, these salespeople are there to make money. They know they'll make money by finding more buyers. They also know that they'll find more buyers by using the phone to hunt them down. Prospecting is simply this: You get on the phone and call possible buyers until you locate some who are worth seeing in person. Then you go see those people and arrange for them to pay your company money in exchange for the benefits your product or service offers. A portion of that money is then paid to you. That's the essence of sales work. It all starts with prospecting.

Yet there are salespeople who don't want to prospect. They can't be afraid of the telephone because they grew up with one, and another sits within arm's length on their desk. Most people these days also have one in their pocket or purse. They've gotten used to it. They know it won't bite, explode, or cause a bad smell. However, calling out is thought of as being difficult. No sense pretending that it isn't, if that's your attitude about it. In the first place, you are the intruder when you make the call, not the intrudee. You may think that's the reason you're not prospecting by phone. It isn't. Oh, sure, there's that vague unease we all feel about telephone prospecting at first. It's uphill work, not a downhill slide; a movement out, not a withdrawal in. But that's the way mountains are climbed and fortunes are made.

Don't beat yourself with nightmares about not having the thick-skinned aggressiveness necessary to prospect by phone. That isn't what you lack, and it really doesn't take much in the way of courage and aggressiveness to be an outstandingly effective telephone prospector. It takes knowledge. If you're afraid to prospect, it's because you don't know *how* to prospect.

The first thing to remember is this: You can always say, "I'm sorry I disturbed you. Good-bye." Make sure that ends the matter in your own mind. After all, you've just called them; you haven't ruined their life.

The second thing to remember is that you must always have a success goal, not a performance goal, when you prospect. Let me explain. If you write down this as a goal: "I will make fifteen prospecting calls starting at nine tomorrow morning," you can make all fifteen of those calls and have nothing.

Set success goals: "Tomorrow at nine I will start telephone prospecting, and I will continue prospecting until I have three confirmed meetings to demonstrate my product to people I believe can and should own it." Set a reasonable success goal and then do it. Stop for meals, go home nights, but keep prospecting until you achieve your success goal.

The third thing to remember is that, before you start calling, you must have an effective call formula and a good list of names and phone numbers. Your chances of success are no better than your formula and your list. If you're not getting encouragement after ten calls, pause, look at your list and formula, and consider making changes. By *encouragement*, I mean getting confirmed meetings or visits, being asked to call back later, or being given names of people to call who might be interested. Don't let a few profitless calls discourage you. That is, don't let a few strangers—grouches you don't even want to know—cause you to walk away from success. Accept that you'll reach a few people who'll be less than delighted to hear from you. Be professional when you prospect—which means that you (a) have a legitimate offer that you're knowledgeable about, (b) call only those numbers that are not on the Do Not Call Registry, (c) call during reasonable hours, (d) are unfailingly polite, (e) bring any unfavorable call to a quick and courteous close, and (f) put any unproductive conversation out of your mind and immediately make another call.

The last point is vital. In organizing your prospecting routine, set yourself up to chop off the negatives fast. Don't allow time for them to nag your enthusiasm away. Instead of singing sad songs for a spell after a washout call, give your head just one quick shake and immediately dial another potential client's number. Do that and you'll be delighted at how easily and effectively you'll prospect, and at how fast your prospecting sessions will go.

THE PHONE SURVEY

I have a little challenge for you here that's really exciting. You get to write your own market survey. Don't fear. I'd never make you do it alone. I'll provide the starting information and guidance. Perhaps it'll go faster, and you'll wind up with a better survey, if you team up with two or three like-minded people in your sales organization and write a market survey together that you'll all use as a prospecting formula. Start with the basic format that follows and tailor it to fit your product or service, your trading area, and your company's strengths and selling methods. As you develop your survey, give careful thought to the order in which you'll ask the questions. After the third step, some other sequence may suit your offering better than the one I've given here.

1. Use people's names immediately. This is crucial. Using their name soon and often causes them to listen more closely to your message.

"Good morning. Is Mr. Hammersmith there?"

2. Introduce yourself and your company. As soon as you have the right person on the line, identify yourself in warm and friendly tones.

"This is Tom Hopkins with Champions Unlimited."

Then move immediately into your market-survey approach.

3. State your purpose and ask the first survey question. Do this without pause between purpose and question. Use a pleasant tone that invites a conversational reply. Your first survey question should get right at whether or not they're interested in what you're marketing.

"I'm conducting a market survey—it'll only take a moment. Do you mind telling me whether you presently own a boat?"

4. If they say no . . . With many products and services, getting a no at this point is great; with others, it means that you should pleasantly end the call and go on to the next one. If you're looking for a no here, carefully rehearse how you'll handle it. Frame your next questions to invite conversational replies that give you critical information and help to establish rapport.

"Would you like to own a boat sometime in the future, and if so, would you prefer a powerboat or a sailboat?"

Anytime you have a friendly conversation with folks who turn out not to be emotional and logical candidates for your offering, ask them for a referral. If you're working a good list, they're very likely to have a friend or two who is precisely the kind of prospect you're looking for. Use the card referral system's principle of helping people isolate a few faces from the multitude they're familiar with. For example, if the list you're prospecting from is a club roster, ask them if any of their friends at the club might be interested in having a brochure mailed to them on whatever you're marketing.

5. If they say yes . . . "Yes, we own a boat."

"Oh, fine. May I ask what type and make it is?"

After this step, your prospecting call can go off in any of several different directions, and how our boat salesman would handle them all need not concern us here. What's important is to outline the answers you're likely to get, and rehearse how you'll handle each one of them. Organize your response to each answer so you continue to work toward a time to meet the people, toward getting permission to send them a brochure, or to the realization they aren't a good candidate for your offering, so you should say a cordial good-bye.

6. Ask how long they've owned (used) it. Find out where they are on the average itch cycle. The importance of this step speaks for itself.

7. Discover what they like about their present one. Here are some of the questions you might ask if they own a product or use a service similar to what you're selling:

"Are you happy with the accuracy and promptness of your payroll computing service?"

"Is your telephone system doing everything you want it to?"

"What do you like most about your present deburring machine?"

Find out how people feel about what they presently own—what they like, and what they'd like to change. When you know that, you know how good your chances are of happily involving them in your company's latest version of that necessity. And you can see exactly how to go about involving them because you know what's important to them. It's important to ask the question in positive terms: "What do you like most about. . . ."

Why is it important to be positive here? For three reasons: (a) People feel less threatened when you ask what they like, as opposed to asking what they don't like; (b) they're more likely to tell you what they don't like if you don't ask them directly; and (c) you must be very careful about exciting their brand loyalty—unless, of course, you're selling the brand they're loyal to. More about this later.

You're looking for qualities and standards at which your product or service can outperform whatever they have now. If they like speed and your latest model is faster than the old one they own, you've found a strong emotional urge toward buying. When you strike one of these urges in a prospecting call, go for an appointment to demonstrate. Don't talk to them about buying it, talk to them about experiencing its speed—or whatever their urge is. You want them to see, feel, touch, and operate it. That's all you want at this point. Not until they've sniffed the leather and heard the engine purr can you safely mention owning it.

8. Carefully uncover their negative feelings. Unless they have some, you're running into heavy brand loyalty that requires careful handling. Never work yourself into a situation where you're knocking what they presently own, because that's knocking their judgment. There's no quicker way to chill your chances than to let your prospects know you think they're dummies for owning the product, or using the service, that they've already invested in. Ask for the vital negative information in a positive way that relieves prospects of any need to defend their previous decisions:

"What would you like to see changed in your company's health insurance program?"

"Are there any features your present conveyor system doesn't have that would be helpful to you?"

"What improvements would make your present machine more efficient in your operation?"

With the market survey, you're searching for unsatisfied needs. You're trying to find something about their present product or service that your item can do better. They have to want more where you can give them more, of course.

If you can give them more of what they want, this ability of your product is (a) something added or improved since they bought their present product, or (b) something in which your product or service was superior to what they bought all along. They just didn't know about it, or they didn't value that factor highly enough when making the decision to buy from the competition.

In the first case—something added or improved—you're bringing them good news. You can now resolve a challenge for them that you couldn't solve when they acquired their present item. You can praise what they have now as being an excellent choice for its time—which has now passed.

In the second case—your product or service was better all along—you have to cope with a situation that at best is delicate and at worst is explosive. There's no place for smugness or careless comment here. Every year, thousands of these situations blow up in the faces of overconfident salespeople who have logic on their side, so they forget emotion. Then they can't close. Usually they don't know why. The reason is simple: The prospect won't accept the emotional distress involved in admitting a mistake. People can be extraordinarily sensitive on this subject—and equally obstinate. In many cases, the only way to replace the competitive product or service with your own is to make a convincing statement along these lines: You think the prospects made a wise decision when they invested in what they now have. Given all the circumstances in force at the time, they did the right thing then, but in the changed circumstances that now prevail, the right thing today is to upgrade to your offering.

Surprisingly, there are many salespeople who prefer losing sales to helping their prospects save face. But it's more fun to concede the point and win the sale.

9. Introduce the strong points of your offering. We all love to sell a basic competitive advantage—if we have one—but some of the most challenging and rewarding sales positions involve products or services that don't have any simple and easily described superiority over their competition. If you do have a basic competitive advantage, drop it on the prospect at about this point in your survey:

"Do your delivery trucks get thirty-five miles to the gallon?"

"Is your present supplier giving you next-morning delivery?"

10. Closing for the opportunity to meet them. As you conclude the telephone market survey with a prospect, thank them for their help. Then ask, "Could I mail you a brochure on our latest model?" If they say yes, they of course have to give you their address, if you don't have it, or confirm that the address you do have is their current one. With the qualifying you've already done, you may decide that this contact is too good to let its momentum be lost in the mail shuffle. Use fast delivery of the brochure as your entrée to meeting the prospect.

"After talking with you, Mr. Hammersmith, I feel that you have a desire to know more about this new development. With your permission, rather than wait for the mail, I'll drop the brochure by this afternoon so you can take a quick look at it and—because I know your time is valuable—if you have any questions, I'll be right there to answer them. Would around two—or three o'clock—be the best time for you?"

When you meet him, you may be able to go right into your standard presentation or demonstration and lead him emotionally to the close.

FINDING GOOD LISTS

Where do you get good lists of people to prospect with? Let me list a few of the sources:

1. Reverse directories. Also called the by-street or crisscross directory, this publication lists telephones by street and house number, and then gives you the name and phone number. This allows you to direct your prospecting efforts into the specific neighborhoods you believe will be most productive for you.

2. Club and company rosters. Some of the best will be the hardest to get. With a little persistence and ingenuity, you can be the proud possessor of the list you want. Many of these groups will sell a onetime use of their lists. Some keep their rosters confidential—or only make them available to members. If your product provides you with a strong enough fee, it might be worth the investment of joining the club in order to gain access to the other members in an ethical manner. Of course, you'll have to be prepared to be contacted by them as candidates for their offerings as well.

3. Libraries. There are an astonishing number of directories published on this continent today. They cover every important industry and activity. Find a public library that has an outstanding business section. People with unlisted numbers in the local telephone book are often listed in the national directory that covers their specialty. Since most of these directories are organized by state and city, you can go through quite a few of them in a single evening at your library.

4. Mailing list houses or the Internet. Hundreds of companies are involved in selling mailing lists. If you can't find the list you want in a published directory, research the direct mail industry at your library. Some mail houses will develop special lists for you, but use this approach as a last resort because you'll probably have to look up the telephone numbers yourself.

Go online and look for list providers. Check out their reliability before renting any list. If you plan to prospect via e-mail, use only those lists that were acquired by opt-in feature. That means the people on the list said they'd be willing to accept solicitations by companies other than the one they first became listed with. If you're calling consumers, once again cross-reference any phone numbers you plan to use with the National Do Not Call Registry.

TELEPHONE SCORING SYSTEMS

Let me give you some basic tips on using the telephone to generate money, not trouble.

1. Always be courteous. No matter how you feel, you owe it to your sense of dignity and self-respect, and you owe it to your company, to be courteous. You also owe that to the rest of us in the profession of selling—we all owe it to each other not to mess up our profession's reputation.

If you make people angry with you, they're angry at your organization, too. Your employers not only have the right to your loyalty, but also have the right to have you enhance, not damage, the company's image. Treat clients with respect. That's an important way of treating yourself with respect as well. Never lose your temper—that's what losers do. Champions refuse to let someone else control their temper.

2. Do anything to meet them. Some people call in and don't want to give you any information; all they want are answers. They can get pretty tough about it, but if you give them all the answers over the phone, why do they need to meet you? If you don't meet them, you won't sell them. It's that simple. I know it can be frustrating talking to people who want all the facts and figures although their attitude is, *Keep away from me, salesperson.*

But you know something? The people who try the hardest to keep from meeting you often are the easiest ones to close. That's why your goal has to be to meet face-to-face with callers.

When I was just getting up to cruise speed in my real estate sales career, we had a contest for a prize and a huge trophy. It was a large company situation with plenty of competition. Coming down to the wire, I was within striking distance of winning—but I needed one more transaction.

I took a call. The man wouldn't give me a name or number. I was getting desperate. "Please," I said, "can't I come by for a few minutes and just meet you?"

"No way."

"Can I call you back, sir?"

He said, "What for? I'm in a phone booth."

"Oh, sir, I'm sorry. I didn't realize that. Do you have the streets where your phone booth is?" I was grabbing at anything.

"Let's see, I guess I'm at the corner of Chance and Main, yeah, that's where I am."

I said, "Would you hold one moment, please?"

Chance and Main was only two blocks from our office. I ran out, jumped in my car, zoomed over there, screeched to a halt by the phone booth, and there he stood, waiting patiently. I walked up, knocked on the glass, and pantomimed, "It's me."

He walked out of that booth and said, "I don't believe you."

But he soon started believing me because I knew what I was doing. So I got him happily involved in the magnificent opportunity called owning your own home in time to win the contest. Do anything that's fair and legitimate to meet anyone calling to inquire about your service or product. They've already decided that they want and need what you're offering. If you can meet them, you can sell them.

3. Handle all leads or client calls immediately. Don't risk having them lose their impetus to learn more or make a buying decision. Any delay in getting in touch with leads or clients will allow them time to second-guess, change their minds, or move on to the competition. Never, never take that risk.

11. A Spectator Sport, Buying Is Not

Operating their mouths at high speed, some salespeople put on amazing demonstrations. They flip levers, punch buttons, zip stuff around. And out of the machines they're demonstrating come a flood of perfect parts, data, copies, or whatever. But they don't sell much with these superb performances.

Why not?

Because apathy rushes in where involvement fails to tread. Buying is action. It can't take place unless there are decisions, and decisions require a switched-on mind. Watching instead of doing is a switch-off. The longer your prospects are switched off, the harder it'll be to switch them back on again when you want the paperwork approved at the end of your demonstration.

The Champion avoids the long switch-off's low sales, and demonstrates by encouraging clients to enter the data, thread the needle, or feed the parts. Of course, clients won't do these things as well or as fast as a practiced salesperson can, but if they're doing them instead of watching, they're thinking about your product instead of letting their minds wander over a million other topics. In fact, they're doing more than merely thinking about your product— they're experiencing it. That means they're emotionally involved with what you're selling.

However great or small this emotional involvement may be, it's certainly going to be far greater than if your prospect just sits there while you sing your number. Owning is a very intimate form of involvement, don't you agree? Then doesn't it follow that the buying necessary for owning won't take place unless there's involvement?

If you accept that, you'll want to find as many reasonable and positive ways as you can to involve your prospects in your product. If you've been switching your prospects off with *I'm-the-star* performances, you'll need to completely overhaul your demonstration to successfully convert it—and yourself—to the client-participation method. And you'll find that giving up the *I'm-the-star* technique is like giving up smoking: You can't do it unless you really want to. Understand yourself here. Many of us—and I'm in this group—place a high value on applause, on appreciation, on being in the limelight. That's good—unless it leads you into making bad strategy decisions.

But the truth is that you're the star twice when you master the client-participation demonstration: first when you have your prospects happily involved in your demonstration and product, and second when you walk out with the endorsed file copies of an order.

The difference is small but vital. You win your oohs and ahs by showing your prospects how to do amazing things on your model, not by doing amazing things on it yourself. To fan their interest into a fire hot enough to melt their built-in sales resistance, you get them to chip rust, solve challenges, or boil water with your device. That's always more fun than watching you run the game. With good products, familiarity breeds confidence and scatters fear.

And fun sells better than frustration. Remember that your prospects aren't used to your machine's peculiarities; keep your steps simple and your attitude encouraging.

Here's how to develop the client-participation demonstration technique into a powerful selling tool:

1. List all the steps the uninitiated must go through to understand how badly they need your device's capabilities. Then

figure out as simple an exercise as you can to demonstrate each capability. Make each exercise distinctive, and give it a name that's easy to remember.

2. List every question and objection that you're likely to encounter during a demonstration.

3. Arrange the capability demonstration and the question/objection answering into a smooth-flowing sequence.

4. Practice your new technique on anyone you can. Check and recheck your lines: discard those that don't work well, and add new ones that do. The successful client-participation demonstration is organized so that each step is simple and leads smoothly to the next, yet the prospect feels a constant challenge and a growing sense of excitement. Keep the pace fast. Brush over minor details. And encourage, encourage, encourage:

"Terrific. You're catching on unusually fast."

"She's a whiz on this machine, Mrs. Lopez."

"It only seems tough because it's new, but you'll be delighted at how easy this machine is to operate when you know it."

"You're a quick learner, Miss Ellison—it must have taken me nine tries before I got that move down as well as you already have it."

"No—really—you're doing great. Everybody has a bit of a challenge here at first."

"Okay now—before you switch it on—I want you to promise to make lots of mistakes. If you don't, I'm going to feel very dumb because I sure goofed up a lot the first time I sat down with this machine."

Take the frustration and pressure out, put the fun and relaxation in, and you'll be successful with client-participation demonstration. When you're confident of your new technique, go out and happily involve two, three, or four times as many people in owning your product as you ever did before. Do that and two more benefits will automatically come your way:

- You'll spend less time making each sale because you will have solved the challenge of involving people in your offering.
- You'll get more referrals because you will be developing greater rapport with your clients.

But what if you don't have a product to demonstrate? Perhaps you sell something that's built to order, or a service. Can you still use this advanced demonstration technique? And will it increase your sales?

You can, and it will. In fact, the more intangible your offering is, the more you need your clients' actively participating in learning how it will benefit them—and the more you need your imagination working to make that happen.

Here's a golden opportunity for you people who sell things that can't be seen or touched. It poses a worthy challenge to your determination and willingness to grow. Overcome this challenge and you'll reap the rewards that go only to those who rise above the competition.

Of course, I can't tell you exactly how to do this with your offering because I don't have your expert knowledge of it. But the principle is simple and can readily be adapted to selling anything— services or products. One example will indicate the direction you should take.

Let's suppose that you sell insurance to self-employed people. When you call on a prospect, you could sit there and blow tax and insurance technicalities at him until his eyes glaze over and he's desperate to be rid of you. You could load his desk down with charts and visual selling aids that you flip, point at, and are generally active with while he sits there watching. You could show a spectacular minimovie on your laptop that includes moving illustrations and testimonials from satisfied clients. You could do any of these things, or you could show him how to calculate the advantages that you're offering. When he does that, he's actively learning why he should invest in your plan and your insurance. You'll lose control if you talk while he's supposed to work it all out on a blank pad of paper. (If you're working on large transactions, prepare a prospectus for each client that clarifies all the formulas and simplifies all questions.) In the repetitive sales situations that you work with, have a packet of forms ready. Keep them simple. Double-spaced. Wide margins all around.

Don't slow the process down with details. You can get things like Social Security numbers during the close or after the sale is made. For now, stick to the bare essentials, and urge the prospect to use the estimates and round numbers.

While your prospect is working his way through this benefit calculation folder of yours, have another copy in front of you so that you can guide him every inch of the way. Where do you wind up? At the close. And your prospect is ready to make a favorable decision because he understands what he'll be getting for his money, and he's grateful to you for making him feel smart.

Earlier in this chapter, I talked about salespeople who try to overwhelm their prospects with amazing demonstrations—and succeed only in boring them. You may not worry about that because you're troubled by the opposite situation: The prospects you demonstrate to aren't amazed at the show you put on, and they're too active, not too passive. They elbow you aside to get at the machine, pester you with questions, and demand instant answers. Your demonstrations remind you of a flock of seagulls scrapping over one fish. If you can maintain some sense of control, you can make enough sales to keep going.

If that's a rough description of your usual demonstration, rejoice: You're only a few easy jumps from perfecting a very successful mode of demonstrating. All you need do is organize the steps so that you keep control and they keep the product you're selling. In the next section, I'll tell you how to do that.

THREE FORMATS FOR SELLING INTERVIEWS

Selling is two-way communication. It's not a transmitter sending to a receiver, not a preacher exhorting the sinner, not a politician stumping for votes. Selling is a tennis match, with one of the players—the salesperson—trying to hit the ball to the other player—the buyer—instead of away from him. This viewpoint is lost in the first of the three most common formats for selling interviews that follow. As we discuss these methods, bear in mind that nearly everything I say about demonstrating a product applies equally well to presenting a service.

Monologue. The plan here is to dominate the prospect with fast talk. Back in the days of the traveling salesman, when city slickers rode the train from one hick town to another, fast monologue worked pretty well. It doesn't anymore.

Tangent chasing. This system is popularly called "playing it by ear." In reality, it's simply no preparation. You go in there with your ears open and a bright smile clamped on your face. The first thing you do is hand control to the prospect by making it clear that you have no plan for the interview. Whatever tangent she takes off on, you follow. If she talks about the dancing bear she saw on TV last night, you talk about the dancing bears you've seen.

If she's slow to get the point that she is in charge of making the interview work, let her know you haven't had time to familiarize yourself with your company's latest catalog, price list, or policy—the one issued five weeks ago. Of course, many of the salespeople who rely on tangent chasing know their product or service very well—but they don't know their customers well enough to lead them to the exact item they should own. Which is to say, their prospecting and qualifying techniques are a drag on their product knowledge that prevents them from using that knowledge as often and as effectively as they could—and must if they're going to earn high incomes.

Since it doesn't require planning, preparation, and thought, tangent chasing (playing it by ear) is a favorite with salespeople who intend to remain average. It's a method that sells no one and allows only the determined buyers to own, so it minimizes the potential of your territory, your offering, and your abilities—but it sure is easy. Now let's talk about the format that does require planning, preparation, and thought—and in return is a sensational selling technique.

The organized involvement interview. Begin with a brief statement along these lines:

"To get the most out of the time you can give me this morning,

I've planned my demonstration to answer the questions I'm most often asked about this machine in a natural sequence. If I don't cover something that interests you, chances are I'll get to it in a moment.

"I've found that if I give a quick overview of the complete process first, and then come back to the detailed questions later, a lot of my customers' valuable time is saved. Okay?—now, Mr. Marzano, if you'll be good enough to feed another blank in here like I'm doing—"

Involve them all the way. Show them how it's done, then have them do it. Do it with great tact and courtesy because they aren't familiar with your machine, so they may be a little awkward and unsure of themselves. Ever notice how you have to concentrate when you first get in to drive a make of automobile that's new to you? All the little things you do automatically in your own car take thought, and maybe you don't do them smoothly at first. But if you're a passenger in that same strange car, you just flop into the seat and think about something else while the driver is doing what has to be done to get moving. Let your prospects drive instead of making them be just passengers during your demonstration.

Your opening statement conveys the idea that you know what you're doing, and that your prospect's time is not going to be wasted. No sooner do you get that across than you have him plugging the machine in, turning dials—whatever—as long as it's necessary and useful physical action.

You're in effective selling control, leading your prospect smoothly through your planned sequence, not trying to dominate him.

You keep that control in a very simple way: by alternating selling statements and questions with involvement demonstration so your prospect is almost continuously busy with your product and with becoming its owner.

Of course, you watch very closely for signs of boredom if the tasks done on your machine are repetitious and the person making the purchase decision is a few rungs above those who'll operate it. Be on the alert for ways to keep your customers thinking and mentally active during your demonstration as well as physically involved. Use your ingenuity to devise involvement strategies to suit the varied personalities and positions of your clients.

For example: You're demonstrating a revolutionary new sand-blasting system to the owner-operator of a small rust-removing shop. Your involvement technique has him using the equipment himself on some of the jobs that are in his shop to be processed. But if you're demonstrating that same sandblasting system to an executive with a larger firm, your plan takes the difference into account. Hand the executive a stopwatch. Have him time his plant's regular sandblasting workers, and let him measure for himself how much faster your system is than his present method. This example is an extreme one. With your product, the gradations are probably more subtle—but they're still vital. The best involvement strategy in any given situation harmonizes the buyer's attitude and circumstance with the product's qualities.

The first step in preparing the organized involvement interview is to go over your present demonstration sequence and list everything that you can reasonably have clients do while it's going on. Remember that the more your prospective owners handle your product and the more things they do with it—that is, the more impact it has on their present consciousness—the more likely it is that your product will become part of their immediate future.

Next, list the questions you're usually asked in a sales interview.

Third, list all of your product's strong sales benefits.

Fourth, sit down with these three lists and outline a demonstration sequence that will cover all these points in a smooth flow from start to finish.

Fifth, go through that outline with this book in hand, and work in as many of the selling techniques given on these pages as possible. As you do this, keep in mind that your attitude must always be courteously flexible when you demonstrate. Prepare yourself to speed up for the impatient, to slow down for the detail-minded—and to cope with the flitter-brained—without losing control of your selling sequence or your positive attitude.

Sixth, practice your new selling sequence until you have a mental lock on it that can't be broken.

Seventh, go out and make a lot of money with it.

12. Put Champion Selling Power in Your Presentations and Demonstrations

Now we're getting into the area you probably enjoy most: working face-to-face with buyers. Unless I miss on two guesses, you're good at this—and you spend too much of your time doing it.

Let me explain. Research indicates that most salespeople put in 80 to 90 percent of their time presenting and demonstrating, leaving only 10 to 20 percent for other things. Champions, on the other hand, spend only 40 percent of their time presenting or demonstrating, and no more than 10 percent prospecting (some Champions spend no time at all prospecting because referrals keep them busy); about 50 percent of their time goes into the vital areas of qualifying and planning. These percentages apply to net selling time—that is, to the total amount of working time remaining after the trade shows and company meetings are attended, the routine paperwork is done, and the old accounts are serviced.

When we at Tom Hopkins International say that people are Champions, we mean that they are in the top 10 percent in their sales force in terms of income and production, and also that they've made our training and techniques an important part of their success.

Let's look at the figures given above one more time. The Champion spends half as much time demonstrating or presenting as the average salesperson does, yet the Champion still manages to turn in at least twice the volume. Actually, most Champions do far better than that: They bring in between four and ten times as much business as the average salesperson will. It's not uncommon for a single

Champion to outsell the entire bottom half of the sales force, and keep on doing it month after month, year after year. This drives sales managers crazy. If they could only get each of the people in the bottom half to sell a third of what the Champion does, their total volume would boom off the chart.

Obviously, Champions close a far higher percentage of the people they present to than the non-Champions are able to close.

No more than a fourth of this difference is accounted for by the Champion's greater skill and confidence in presenting or demonstrating. By far the greatest part of the difference between the Champion and the average salesperson lies in the Champion's attention to and ability at planning sales, at selecting and qualifying the right people to sell to, at overcoming objections and closing, and at deserving and obtaining referrals.

Techniques for becoming more effective in these areas are discussed in other chapters. All are vital—you must be competent in all major areas of selling before you can realize your full potential and become a Champion. So as I discuss the techniques of presenting and demonstrating in this chapter, keep in mind that, important as this part of selling is (and it's very important), if you do it with the wrong people because you didn't qualify properly, it's all for nothing. If you're working with the right people, but you let their objections beat you because you haven't prepared properly, it's all for nothing. And if you have no capability in closing, you're working for nothing. If you can't close, many sales you could and should make will go to the next competitor who comes along because you built the structure for the sale but couldn't close the door before she got there. Before discussing how a Champion presents or demonstrates, let me draw an analogy to illustrate the basic concept. If you want to make a half-hour speech, you really should write a ten-minute speech. Here's why. If you're going to get your points across to your audience, you have to follow these steps:

1. **Tell them what you're going to tell them.** This is your introduction.

2. **Tell them what you're there to tell them.** This is your presentation.
3. **Tell them what you just told them.** This is your summary.

That's the outline of all successful speeches, presentations, and demonstrations. In other words, we use repetition. We don't say exactly the same thing three times, of course. In the first ten minutes, we're introducing our new ideas. In the second ten minutes, we're covering our points in depth and relating them to our listeners' interests and needs. In the last ten minutes, we're drawing conclusions from our points and indicating the direction that things should take.

Repetition is the mother of learning, yet average salespeople don't like repetition. For one thing, they've used their material so many times that it's stale to them. In many cases, they've begun to think that anyone who doesn't get what they're saying the first time they say it is a lost cause. All too often, non-Champions have gone worse than stale on their presentation and feel it would be better off buried.

Champions, on the other hand, never tire of phrases that work, strategies that sell, and ideas that make sense to their buyers and money for them. Champions discard things in their presentations when they stop working, and not before. And Champions never forget that they're working with people who don't know their specialty as well as they do: They're always courteous and deferential about their superior knowledge in the narrow area of their expertise. So Champions work happily with lines they've said ten thousand times. They are forever finding slight variations on phrasing and timing that enhance their effectiveness. They revel in the fact that they know their lines so well, they don't have to think about them, but can concentrate wholly on their customers and the unique aspects of the situation they're working with at the moment. There's no question about it, one of the keys to the Champion's greater skill at presenting or demonstrating lies in the ability and willingness to use repetition effectively to reinforce every point. The Champion doesn't mind repeating the sales points because they lead to repeated sales to the same type of clientele.

So think in terms of tell, tell, tell.

When you prepare to make a presentation or give a demonstration, there's one point that should be foremost in your mind. I suggest that you highlight this concept:

The presentation (demonstration) is nothing more than the preparation for the close.

Giving a powerful presentation or a deft demonstration should never be your purpose in and of itself—you're not there to win an Academy Award, you're there to close the sale. The only purpose for presenting or demonstrating is to get the prospect ready to approve the purchase. Except for its value as a training exercise, there's absolutely no point in giving a splendid presentation unless it results in a sale.

There's no essential difference between a presentation and a demonstration. Both are processes by which you prove the reality of the benefits that the prospects are seeking. In the presentation, you do it with graphs, numbers, and words; in the demonstration, you do it with tests, samples, and performances. The result should be the same: the implanting in their minds of the conviction that you are their best source for the benefits they want.

Let's go through the tactics or methodology of presentation and demonstration:

1. You control them constantly with questions. I discussed these techniques in detail in chapter 3.

2. You don't lose to objections, you win by handling objections. For almost every product or service, any active salesperson will discover most of the built-in objections within the first month with a company. A built-in objection is one that the future client will give you nearly every time. After a few months in the business, the salesperson will say, "I always get hit with that objection."

If you think that, why not also say, "I'm lucky because I know in advance what objections I'm going to be hit with, so I can prepare to handle them before I go into my presentation."

One of our Champions told me a story that's a perfect example of what I'm talking about. The product was a fax machine—a good one. It was competitively priced and very popular. So popular, in fact, that my student's company was struggling to keep a large enough supply in inventory to meet the demand. People who decided they wanted her machine had to wait awhile to get it. There was a huge risk that they'd go to the competition in order to get a fax machine sooner. Rather than letting that known objection cost her sales, our Champion salesperson bragged about it early in her presentation. She would say something like this: "Mr. Jackson, once you see how the features and options on this machine will benefit your entire office, I'm certain you won't mind waiting for it."

When the client gave her a quizzical look, she continued, "You see, this machine is our most popular model. In fact, we're moving them so fast that our warehouse is in a back-order situation at the moment. There are plenty of machines on order and I'll be happy to set aside one in the next shipment for you. If you're in a hurry, you could talk with one of our competitors. They may have a machine in stock that might handle your basic needs. That would probably be because they're not selling all that well. The people we have served have been willing to wait a short time to get the better machine for their needs. Is that how you feel?"

Now, if Mr. Jackson truly had an immediate need, she would try to help him out with a loaner to ease the pain of waiting. However, knowing that everyone else was champing at the bit for that particular model helped many of her clients overcome the challenge of having to wait for it.

There isn't a product or a service on the market that doesn't have some built-in deficiencies and at least a few minor challenges. Brag about them. If you do that, you'll find that it's never as bad as it could be if your potential clients discover the difficulties themselves. I'm not suggesting that you should sit your potential clients down and, in an undertaker's voice, tell them, "This is why you're going to have big trouble with our product." Just be willing to point out the challenge, demonstrate that it isn't all that much of a problem—and then show that the advantage offered outweighs the disadvantage involved. Usually, if you plan how to bring up the major objection before your prospect hits you with it, you'll be able to settle it quickly.

3. You say it in words they want to hear. All of us come equipped with filtering devices—we all have the ability to filter out unwanted sound. This device is indispensable; it allows us to mull over our inner thoughts in peace whenever people are pounding our ears with anything less interesting than our own brain waves.

Everyone you'll ever try to sell has an effective filter of this kind that can be switched on instantaneously. You have to learn how to prevent the filter from being switched on. Otherwise, you'll make most of your terrific sales arguments to switched-off, unhearing minds behind deaf ears. Let's face it—you can't make any money talking to yourself.

The basic issue here is that most salespeople sound exactly alike. Same ideas. Even the same words. And they're all tired, overused, and boring words.

In this, as in all things relating to sales, Champions are different. They have a view of the world that's new with every dawn, and express their newly born ideas with phrases that have verve. They understand and respect the value of words, and are keenly aware of and interested in them. They constantly develop their ears for the beauty, power, and endless variety of the English language. They are forever trying new phrases, allusions, and words to expand the effective range of their vocabulary. They take delight in spoken wit and sensitive expression.

GLAMOUR WORDS

Champions see themselves as artists who cast exquisite crystals of thought from the common sand and lead of language. To do that, they avoid the worn-out words, the commonplace expressions, and the dull descriptions that afflict the average salesperson's presentation with the monotony of mediocrity. Instead, they enliven their speech with glamorous words that conjure up exciting new visions for their buyers. Potential clients can't help listening to them because they captivate their attention.

What makes a word glamorous? It has a freshness that sticks in the mind, yet it's common enough to be understood by your listeners. The last part is vital. If you dust off some of the fancy words that only the aficionados of esoteric utterances will understand, your listeners will switch their filtering devices on for sure.

Never forget that most people can look at you and nod at the right times and have their minds forty miles away. They're thinking about a problem totally unrelated to you, or about something they need to do after you leave. If you drone on and on, you're not going to sell them, you're going to separate from them—empty-handed, permanently, and soon.

Seek out the bright words that we all understand but rarely hear used. Champions do everything in their power to keep prospects and clients emotionally and physically involved and listening when they want to be persuasive.

What's glamorous in one situation could be inappropriate in another. Look for words that are charming, eloquent, picturesque, exciting, creative. Add sparkle to your speech by using common words in unexpected new ways. Here are some that my seminar attendees came up with:

Dynamic, unique, outstanding, innovative, state-of-the-art, exciting

Try inserting a few of these adjectives into your presentation and feel the difference they make.

WORDS TO REPLACE

From now on, when you have to listen to a tiresome speaker, listen attentively for the words, the phrases, and the manners of speaking that make him tiresome. Whenever you spot one, make a mental note to eliminate it from your vocabulary. But be aware that you have to replace it with another word that's more interesting. You may have to think a little to come up with one. If you've never deliberately worked on your vocabulary in this manner, it may seem difficult at first. But it won't when you get used to it. And there's a trick to this that takes all the strain out. Simply make a list of the words you want to get rid of on a piece of paper and go over it once a day. That will focus your mind on improving your vocabulary, and you'll find yourself spotting new words you want to use to brighten your speech as you read, listen to other people, and watch TV.

Slang is fresh and funny at first, but it usually wears out quickly. Most of us use it too long. Jargon can also be fresh and funny, but more often it's lost on the outsider. Cultivate an appreciation for the short, strong words that have come down to us from the Anglo-Saxon roots of our language. Use lots of short, punchy words in your speech. The more shorts you use, the more effect a few less common longs will have by contrast.

Be bold in your choice of language. Take risks with words. Say a few striking things that will seize your listeners' attention. You'll occasionally have to restate an idea in a different manner, but if they ask, they're listening. When they're doing that, you can win. When they're not listening, you can't win.

LEARN MANY DIFFERENT LINGOES

Do you know that the great Champions speak many different languages? I'm not referring to French, Spanish, and Navajo, but to the different languages of their clients. A Champion speaks to a plumber in plumbers' language and to a doctor in doctors' language. This doesn't require a tremendous training program. Your object isn't to make the plumber think you're a contractor and the doctor think you're a physician; your object is to make them both feel that you understand their challenges, viewpoints, and opportunities. Every job and hobby has its own jargon, its own special language.

The Champion learns to speak many languages because it's the most efficient way to establish rapport with different groups of people. We identify with people who share things with us; we instinctively feel less fear and more trust with them. You can't change the school you went to or the state you were born in to suit every client. But you can learn to understand and use some of your clients' jargon—if not of their specialty, at least of their general occupation. If you know a bit of construction jargon, you can talk more convincingly with carpenters, roofers, and craftsmen in a host of other specialties; if you understand an assembly-line worker's special phrases, you'll be able to talk more convincingly with any factory worker.

For this very reason, the winners among salespeople often choose a certain group of people to concentrate their sales efforts on, even though they sell something such as insurance that a wide variety of people buy. Since their chosen groups like and trust them—because they talk the same special language—they sell often and easily.

Many salespeople who never rise above the average spend an hour a day keeping up with sports, and justify it by claiming they need things to talk to their prospects about. Unless what they sell is tied directly to sports, this is a fallacy. Lengthy discussion of anything unrelated to the business at hand wastes time; rapport can be built without wasting time by talking the prospect's language during the presentation. And those special languages can be learned with the hours saved by skipping the sports page.

But how do you learn them?

Specialized magazines are one of the best sources for specialized language. Today there's a magazine devoted to almost every specialty you can imagine. Pay attention to editorials, letters to the editors, and such things because they'll give you authentic viewpoints held by people involved with that special interest. Read these trade magazines with a pad and pencil. Make notes of any new words and viewpoints that you don't grasp, and then ask someone who's active in that field to explain them to you.

The best way to learn any language is the way children do it—by trial and error and constant use. You'll enormously expand your knowledge of specialized languages simply by taking every opportunity to do so. When you have lunch, while you wait to have your car serviced—anywhere you can talk to people—find out what they do and explore their special words and viewpoints. Your business is people; jump at every chance you get to learn more about them.

KEEP CLIENTS MENTALLY AND PHYSICALLY INVOLVED

How? By asking involvement questions that will keep them thinking about how they'll use your offering once they own it. Pay attention to the answers; nothing destroys rapport like asking the same question twice.

Give them simple things to do. Let them figure something out or run the machine you're demonstrating. Have your clients take something from you. Don't ask, "Would you please hold this?" because the clients may say they don't want to. Say just one word: "Here." Clients' automatic reflex will cause them to take whatever you hand them, and then they're involved.

Once you gain confidence in this reflex, you can have a lot of fun with it while you're establishing control. Don't overdo it, of course, or they'll get irritated and balk at the worst time. But if you smile warmly and say that one word, it's amazing what they'll accept. Your order pad, for example. I've had people take it and approve the order because I picked the right moment to smile warmly and say, "Here."

Once they have it—the remote control for the machine you're demonstrating, a copy of your proposal, the owner's manual, whatever will help you most—the process of emotional involvement in your offering is well started.

HANDLE INTERRUPTIONS CALMLY

You can be sure that your finest presentations or demonstrations will be interrupted. The phone will ring. Some emergency will demand an executive's (or a parent's) attention. Doors will open unexpectedly, and unknown heads will stick in. Dogs will bark, sirens will screech, and kids will cry.

Sit through it all patiently. No matter how often you're interrupted, don't let any irritation show. Use the time to review where you've been and where you're headed, and make sure that you haven't overlooked any clue to closing that your questions may have uncovered.

If the interruption lasts more than a moment, do a brief benefit summary of the points your prospect has already accepted. This is urgent. Remember that any physical interruption causes a degree of emotional separation. That is, if someone else comes into the room, if your prospects leave the room or take a phone call, their emotions are changed. They don't have to get red in the face or yell at somebody; if interrupted, people's emotions change. So before proceeding, you must bring them back to the emotional and mental attitude they had before the interruption.

GIVE THE ENTIRE BODY OF YOUR PRESENTATION IN LESS THAN SEVENTEEN MINUTES

You may smile with disbelief, but hear me out. Suppose you're selling executive aircraft, and it takes your prospect an hour to get to the airfield. You've organized things carefully so that it only takes five minutes from the moment he arrives until you're ready to ask the tower for permission to move the aircraft, and another five minutes pass before you're in the air. None of this counts. Your prospect is excited: This time zips by for him.

But when you're back in his office two hours later presenting the case for him to own that beautiful airplane, keep it under seventeen minutes or the fine cutting edge of his decision-making ability will be dulled.

Regardless of what your product or service is, when you get to the nitty-gritty, cut through it in less than that limit. You can do it if you'll rigorously chop off unnecessary detail, if you'll streamline what you have to say, if you'll eliminate anything you're not positive is contributing to the close.

To become a Champion, you have to polish your performance and practice it against the clock until you can do an effective presentation or demonstration within the seventeen minute limit of maximum client concentration. It may be a stiff challenge, but meeting it will do wonders for your closing ability.

A CHAMPION PLANS EVERY PRESENTATION IN WRITING

You're backing off, aren't you? Saying, "Plan every presentation in writing? Tom is kidding. Nobody does that. I wouldn't know how to begin."

Don't worry—I'm going to show you how to plan every move and anticipate every challenge. Of course, it will take some time—more in the beginning while you're learning the technique. After it becomes second nature, you'll spend less time planning your presentations than the average wheel-spinning salesperson kills before going to see each prospect. You'll walk into every demonstration or presentation knowing exactly what prospects will listen to, what they'll say yes to, what they'll agree with, and what they need.

HOW TO PREPLAN YOUR PRESENTATION IN WRITING

First, let's talk about where you get the information necessary to preplan your presentation on paper.

Commercial and industrial sales. Published directories will give you an enormous amount of information. A few of these directories are available only on subscription, but many are in the reference section of public libraries or accessible online. You'll generally find the best libraries for your purpose in the more business-oriented and affluent communities. Check with a library before ruling out this source; some of them have surprisingly valuable material. The following is only a sample of the directories in the better public libraries:

- Dun & Bradstreet is a global provider of business information and company profiles for more than seventy-five million companies worldwide. You can check them out at http://www.dnb.com.
- The Thomas Register of American manufacturers publishes a directory of industrial products and services offered by US and Canadian companies in many different industries. http://www.thomasregister.com.
- Standard & Poor's is the world's foremost provider of independent credit ratings, indices, risk evaluation, investment research, data, and valuations. http://www.standardand poors.com.
- If you need the latest news on a company or product, search Google News (http://news.google.com). It includes headlines and a search engine for most major news publications.

These are just a few of the potential resources at your fingertips for gathering information on a company you hope to do business with. Once you find your way around them, you'll find other resources as well.

Gathering information in one directory and then researching that information further in another directory is often the most effective way to use them. For example, you discover how to apply your service to ball-bearing manufacturers. In Thomas, you find several such firms listed in the area you work; in Standard & Poor's, you then find the names of their corporate officers, together with some personal details about each of them. With this combined data in hand, you develop your marketing plan.

If you're working an established territory, or adopting orphans, your office's sales records will have detailed and valuable information. Few salespeople use Dun & Bradstreet as effectively as they could. While the D&B Directory gives only brief coded information and a credit rating, the full credit report for each company has a wealth of detail about the officers, operation, and history of the firm. These reports must be ordered separately for each company.

Governmental sales. Products and services designed for commercial and industrial use often have many applications in governmental activities. A large number of companies recognize this by assigning salespeople exclusively to governmental sales. Other companies leave this market to their local outlets and sales managers. The agencies most often overlooked are called "special districts." These bureaus cope with flood control, mosquito abatement, bridge operation, and a multitude of other issues that most of us rarely think about. All of them have offices and operations with needs. Where do you find the special districts? Ask at the information office of every county you serve. For starters, look on your property tax bill. In many states you'll find the local special districts listed there.

Educational sales. Schools and colleges invest in enormous amounts of equipment, supplies, and services. State and county school districts publish directories, as do some religious and private organizations. If you're unfamiliar with the school market but feel that you have opportunities there, call on a few schools and ask them what directories they're listed in. Also ask what conferences (these usually have trade shows) they attend. The educational field is well organized and easily reached.

Individual and family sales. If you're working with a referred lead, get all the information you can from the client giving you the referral. Your office's sales records may have valuable data if you're working with an orphaned client. If the people seem to be high achievers, they may be listed in a Who's Who publication. With most prospects in personal sales, the best source of information is the person involved. After you've confirmed the visit, lead into a few questions by saying, "So I can save your time during our meeting and serve you better, could I ask—"

After a few questions it helps to remark, "Please don't think I'm being nosy, but it really will save us both time if I have an approximate idea of your situation."

WORKING WITH THE PREPLANNING FORM

One version is designed for retail sales of products and services to individuals or families. The second version of the preplanner assists you in preparing for successful sales interviews with decision makers at all kinds of organizations: corporations and other companies in commerce and industry, governmental agencies, and the groups serving the religious, educational, and cultural needs of the nation.

Some salespeople climb the highest peaks exclusively with sales to individuals and families. Other salespeople stay in that field, or work only the mom-and-pop kind of business sales, because they're convinced that organizational selling is too big-time for them. Yet it's basically the same: You're still working with people.

I began my career selling shoes in a retail store at the age of sixteen. I soon went on to other things and other kinds of selling before I began marketing products and services to corporations. The basic principles are the same. You simply roll forward all your experience with people—and start doing more careful preparation and planning.

On both these forms, keep track of the sources from which you obtained your information. Knowing the source enables you to make a better guess as to its dependability, and it also helps you discard unreliable sources.

How you fill out most of the form is obvious. What they have now, and how long they've had it, tells you where they are on the itch cycle. What their choice was last time tells you much about what their next choice will be.

After listing the names of the family members, be sure to put an asterisk (*) after the person you think will be the decision maker. This is the person you must convince and close—without making the other family members fight you.

Find out where the husband and wife work, and what they do. If you know these facts, you know a great deal more about them, don't you? Will you agree that a presentation to someone who makes his living treating concrete with a jackhammer should be different from a presentation to someone who makes his living treating people with pills?

The purpose of getting all this information is to move you closer to what they want and can afford.

Benefits referrer accepted. This is important. You'll often find yourself going in for an appointment with potential clients without having heard from their own mouths what benefits they're really interested in. If you can get this information when you arrange the visit, fine. But never forget that many people won't tell you the truth about what they really want because they have a conflict. Someone in their family, or logic, or "what people will think" tells them to buy what they don't want. In other words, they can't square their wants with their needs. If you come in contact with them before they resolve this conflict, their problem becomes your problem—and your opportunity. Solve it and you sell them. Fail to solve it and you lose them. These opportunities arise constantly, whether you're prospecting on the phone or working with walk-ins.

PERSONAL SALES PRE-PLANNER

Name of individual/family _____

INFORMATION GAINED **Names Involved: (*Primary Decision Maker)**	**SOURCE**

If individual only: _____

If family:

Father _____

Mother _____

Children _____

_____

_____

Sources of income & amounts, approx.:

Man—employed by _____

Position _____

Income est. _____

Woman—employed by _____

Position _____

Income est. _____

Other _____

Type of comparable product or service they now have:

_____

How long? _____

Benefits referrer accepted: _____

_____

_____

_____

_____

Other benefits they may accept: _____

_____

_____

Other information—home, furnishings, car, hobbies,

group affiliations, etc. _____

_____

_____

_____

SEQUENCE PLAN

Benefits to be used to gain telephone appointment: _____
_____

Benefits to be used in qualification questions: _____
_____
_____

Benefits planned for presentation/demonstration: _____
_____
_____
_____
_____
_____

Anticipated primary objection: _____.

Planned comparative question to eliminate primary objection. Isn't it true that _____
_____

Demonstration and presentation equipment and materials to be used: _____
_____
_____
_____

Similar situation stories to be used (name of story only) if on cassette, indicate with *:
_____
_____
_____

Physical involvement to be created: _____
_____
_____
_____

The items regarding competitors—current market position to be referred to in order to underline need or desire: _____
_____
_____

CORPORATE SALES PRE-PLANNER

Name of company _____

Individual & title _____

Is this person decision maker? _____

If not, name individual who is, with title _____

Type of company _____

Product or service _____

Approximate gross sales _____

INFORMATION GAINED	SOURCE

Individuals involved, with titles _____

_____

_____

_____

_____

_____

Which one greatest problem? Why? _____

_____

_____

D & B or other financial ruling: _____

_____

Benefits referrer accepted: _____

_____

_____

_____

_____

Other benefits they may accept: _____

_____

_____

Other information—competitors, current market position,

organizations belonged to, etc. _____

_____

_____

_____

Ask Alvin Gotmorkids what he's looking for and he'll say, "I need a small, stripped-down station wagon that'll go a zillion miles on one drink of gas." But when Alvin looks at small, stripped-down station wagons in auto showrooms, he grunts and swallows and walks out without buying. Finally Alvin stumbles into Ron Realist. Ron listens to Alvin's words, and reads between the lines when he learns Alvin has looked at many small, stripped-down vehicles yet still doesn't own one. So Ron takes Alvin over to the latest low-slung, tiger-under-the-hood, loaded-with-options model.

Alvin gets pale. Objections pour out of him. But he doesn't walk away. Then Ron suggests a trial spin. They put the tiger through all five gears around tight curves. Then Ron explains how logical it is for Alvin to own that car before he gets any older, and shows him how he can own it. Alvin drives it home.

If Ron Realist had been guided by what Alvin said about small practical station wagons, he would have been another auto salesperson whom Alvin Gotmorkids did not buy from. Be careful about believing what prospects say they want.

With many prospects, the benefits that the referrer has already accepted and bought are a much firmer set of facts. They represent genuine emotions that were backed by action, not loose talk that may only express fashionable logic. People are heavily influenced by their friends, and they are much like their friends in the ways that are important to you. For these reasons, the benefits the referrer has invested in are often the most reliable guide to what the prospect will also want. If there's any way to get this information from the referrer—and this will often be no trouble at all—don't go into a presentation without it.

Benefits to be used to gain telephone appointment. What are you going to tell them on the phone to generate the emotions that will make them want to see you?

Remember that all you want at this point is a firm time and location where you'll see them. If you run off every bit of your good stuff to get the appointment, the actual face-to-face meeting may be an anticlimax. So use the lightest guns that'll get you the appointment, and save your heavy artillery for when you're with them going for the close.

Benefits to be used in the qualification questions. Use the qualifying steps given in chapter 14.

Benefits planned for presentation/demonstration. Note here all the benefits you believe they'll accept as having value to them. This is where you fire your big stuff. But never lose sight of the probability that what makes a heavy hit on some buyers will only be a light tap on others. And never assume that the feature you value most in your offering will be the feature your next prospect will value most.

Wouldn't you like to know what they're going to say before you push the copier in through their revolving door, before you fly in to detail a new production facility, before you walk in to present your custom-tailored service?

If you spend all your time making layouts in four colors to resolve prospects' challenges—giving no time to anticipating their concerns—you're going to lose a lot of sales you could otherwise make. Fitting your service to their situation, demonstrating how the machine whizzes the stuff out, or explaining how the cog fits the track are all necessary to logic. Objections have their logical base, too, but they are mainly emotion—which means that they control the purchase decision more than the logic of your presentation does. Make sure that you give adequate time and energy to anticipating objections and planning how to address them. One of the ways you do that is with:

Planned comparative questions to eliminate the primary objection. A comparative question melts the primary objection down by focusing the prospect's attention on answering a minor issue. I begin all my comparative questions with the words "Isn't it true that—"

An example from insurance sales will illustrate the concept of the comparative question:

The primary objection I anticipate here is money—the size of the premium. When it comes up, I say, "Isn't it true that the size of the premium is less important than being prepared to invest in your children's education should something unforeseen happen by the time they're ready for college?"

What are they going to say? One of the most important things to average people is the education and welfare of their children.

When the entire picture is considered, the primary objection that most people raise in most sales interviews is not, in reality, the point of primary importance to them. It's our business as salespeople to put that primary objection into proper perspective, smothering its negativity with positive emotions.

Demonstration and presentation equipment and materials to be used. Once you have the comparative questions written, list the tools you think will be most effective on that particular call. Most Champions don't take everything in to every prospect; they have a bigger bag of tools than they can get through the door with. And there are practical difficulties with time and space that must be considered. Again, speed is important. You want to make your basic presentation within seventeen minutes and then shift into your closing sequences. You may need to hand them a detailed prospectus, but limit your remarks to pounding the pith of the matter.

Similar-situation stories to be used. I go into this in detail in chapter 17. Being prepared to tell your prospects similar-situation stories is an effective presentation technique; putting written similar-situation stories in your presentation binder is a better technique; having the words and voices of happy clients recorded in audio or video format is the best.

The last two items on the personal sales sequence plan need little comment. Can you get them physically involved by having them use your calculator or run the machine you're demonstrating? Devise some form of physical involvement for every presentation or demonstration.

Every salesperson will understand the need to create common ground through some item of mutual interest. Still, what some of us do with this item is wing it—we don't think about it until we're walking into the person's office. But how do you plan something of mutual interest to talk about when you don't know the person?

If it's a referred lead, the referrer will usually be able to fill you in on the prospect's interests. If your prospects are corporate officers or directors, there's a good chance they'll be listed in Standard & Poor's or in Who's Who. If not, ask about their interests at the time you confirm your meeting.

THE CORPORATE SALES PREPLANNER

At the bottom of this form, you'll notice a change from the personal sales version as you raise the question of where the prospect's company stands in its own competitive race.

Here's how you use this information:

Let's suppose that you've just found a new market for your product or service by getting an air-conditioning contractor involved in your type of product for the first time. The person you helped claimed that his company is the largest of its kind in the city. Don't ask who number two is and upset him. Instead, go back to your office, pick up the yellow pages, and make a list of the air-conditioning contractors who have the largest ads. By checking that list against the Dun & Bradstreet Directory, you quickly rank them by size, and discover that your new client really is number one in the city.

Start calling those air-conditioning contractors. Number seven wants to move up to be number six, number six would like to move up to be number five, and so on. As their ultimate goal, most of them want to be number one. And in every one of those companies, there's a corporate eagle who's watching how his company is doing. He's also watching the competition because the last thing he wants to do is slip down a notch or two. You can bet that they'll all be interested in what number one is doing—which is using your product or service. They'll all be wondering: *Is what you've supplied number one giving that firm an edge?* If it's even remotely possible that it does, they'll want to talk to you. That's why the Champion wants to know where each prospect ranks competitively.

WHEN DO YOU PLAN?

The night before your meeting. Be sure to fill out the front of the form right after confirming the meeting. Then you won't have forgotten a lot of vital details when you sit down to review the form, write out your questions, and plan your selling sequence the night before your appointment. This, by the way, is the habit of the pro.

All the Champions I know plan everything they're going to do on their next day's appointments the night before. And they do it in writing because then they know they've done it; they know they've impressed it on their minds, and that they can give it a quick review before walking in for each appointment. Please, stop winging it. Please stop going to an appointment not knowing what you're going to say or do. If you walk in without having a plan laid out, you're going to cut your effectiveness in pieces—and you'll have to eat off the smallest piece.

As you get more into preplanning in writing, as you catch the excitement that the power of this method creates, you'll find yourself seeing with greater clarity the pitfalls and opportunities that wait for you in each presentation. You'll find yourself driven to prepare even more carefully so you can approach each presentation with even greater confidence—and your success ratio will soar.

Yes. Preplan in writing. The results will raise your sales performance to new heights.

VISUAL AIDS

If you sell for a large company, chances are good that (a) it supplies you with a variety of costly and colorful visual selling aids in various formats, and (b) you don't use those aids much.

Here again we find that the people who make the greatest use of company-supplied visual aids are the top producers. The ones who make the least use of them are the sellers in the cellar, those who never make a quota and change jobs most often.

If you're in the category that doesn't use visual aids and isn't ranked in the top third of your sales force, don't feel guilty. It's a common failing. But you're reading this book to stop being common, aren't you? Then start using the tools of success. Some of those tools are called visual aids.

The top Champions I've trained realize a basic truth: People just can't sit and look at your face and listen to your mouth all day. That's one reason why the top producers are always looking for new methods, and improving old methods, to involve more than their prospects' ears in their presentations.

Most top producers have only two basic tricks up their sleeves, and they're simple ones: (a) They use their time effectively, and (b) they concentrate on what has to be done and ignore the non-essentials.

Winging it is not effective. Sure, it can save an hour of preparation time on a call that takes you an hour to arrive at, an hour to present, and an hour to return from. Winging it without visual aids and without adequate preparation almost guarantees failure, however. You can't be effective if you waste three hours to avoid working one.

Here's another fact I've discovered: Visual aids cut down preparation time.

And one more: If you think of future applications as you plan each presentation, you'll find yourself spending less and less time preparing as the months go by, and you'll prepare better.

Two of the best examples of this are the prospectus type of presentation binder and PowerPoint presentations where you organize a mass of facts for your clients. The first time you do it, the task will seem overwhelming. But if you work with an eye to creating a format that you can use over and over, the second prospectus/presentation won't take half as long to prepare as the first, and each succeeding one will go faster.

Your contents page may not have to change at all. You'll find that many pages can be common to several presentations. Think ahead like the Champions do. Make everything standard that can be standard. Then concentrate on the pages presenting information that's unique to each presentation. If you're selling the same products or services over and over, so much the better. You can develop your skills to great heights by relying on visual aids and organized presentations that make use of reusable material.

SEVENTEEN MINUTES ARE ALL YOU'VE GOT

After seventeen minutes, people start to lose interest. Boredom sets in; they remember other things they could or should be doing;

they stop listening attentively. When you start losing their attention, you start losing your opportunity to make the sale.

The answer is to pack more punch into that seventeen-minute period when you have the best chance to score a knockout. How do you do that? Not by talking faster, but by presenting better. This means using the visual aids.

Why is it that visual aids are so important, and so widely ignored by the very people who can profit most from them? I think that ego comes into it. We like to talk, and we like to think that we're persuasive. So we talk ourselves into the idea that if we just go in there and wing it—*after all, we know our stuff*—they'll just sit there and listen while we tell them the entire story about our offering. We want to hear our own words, not use what someone else has created. That's how we feel if we're not Champions. Champions don't care who created it—if they can legitimately use it to make money, they do so. Champions take their pride in closed sales rather than in the knowledge that they can survive by winging it. Your company relied on a huge variety of talents to create the visual aids it has made available to you. Use what you're given. Exercise your creativity by finding new and more effective ways to make sales with your company's visual aids.

HOW TO MAKE VISUAL AIDS PAY OFF FOR YOU

Visual aids give you control and allow for speed. Without control, you can't achieve speed, and without speed, you can't maintain control. You can slow down or repeat if you're going too fast, but if you're too slow, there's no way you can speed up enough to catch prospects you've already lost to impatience.

If you aren't in control, you can't sell—you can only take orders from the very few who are determined to buy no matter what. Right at the beginning of meetings, many salespeople lose control—and from then on they never have a chance. How do they lose control? By not getting the seating right.

If you think that seating is too simple to bother about, compare it with putting gas into your car. That's simple, too. But if you don't do it, you stop moving. If you don't control the seating in sales, you also stop moving.

Take the sales situation where appointments are made to go into homes and give presentations or demonstrations. Every time you sit on a chair in the living room, that sale will die. That position forces you to swivel back and forth between the two potential clients while talking and trying to make notes. The process is painfully slow. Before long, the couple is exchanging those eloquent glances that married couples develop. Without a word being spoken between them about it, they agree to get rid of that salesperson as soon as possible.

Visual aids allow you to deliver more information in less time, but an even greater value lies in their ability to get you seated across from them at a table. Why is this so important? Because it allows you to put yourself in the position of power. This occurs when:

- You are able to maintain eye contact with both of them simply by shifting your gaze. This is vital because it's fast.
- You can see both of them at once.
- You can make notes while they're watching the visual aid. This is necessary since their attention will wander if they have to wait while you scribble.
- You can work quickly enough to complete your presentation within the first seventeen minutes.

You must know every page of your visual aid completely. But even though you know what's on the page by heart, you still have to look at it. Why? Because of a common response that we all have. If I look at you, you'll look back at me. If you look at the visual aid, so will they.

Don't set up your visual aid presentation so that they're supposed to be looking at it while they feel your eyes on them. If that happens, either they'll stop looking at the visual aid and stare back at you, or they'll feel threatened and have trouble concentrating on anything.

Eliminate this by arranging your presentation so that you look at the visual aid, make a point or two, and then look up to regain eye contact with them for an instant. As you repeat this process, pause slightly after finishing a point to signal that you're going to look at them. Unconsciously, they'll slip into a comfortable, reassuring rhythm of shifting their gaze from the visual aid to your eyes and back again.

Maybe you're wondering, "What if I can't remember everything?"

Write notes in pencil on the back of each page of your visual aid. A flip chart or binder type of visual aid makes it easy to give your presentation the most effective sequence. You start at (a); work your way steadily and smoothly through (b) and (c); and then go on to all the other steps. You cover everything in the sequence you find flows best. Nothing important is forgotten.

With a PowerPoint presentation, you should have a printout of the slides as Notes pages so you can write a few words to remind you of what to say with each slide. Set these pages behind your laptop where you can quickly glance if you have a momentary lapse in concentration.

Let me warn you about something. Some salespeople have beat-up old binders that they use for every presentation. Instead of working smoothly, they spend half their time flipping over pages and muttering things like:

- "You aren't interested in that."
- "We don't have that model anymore because it was a maintenance nightmare."
- "Doggone it, where's that side view I wanted to show you?"

Meanwhile, the prospects are getting more and more irritated. And they're losing faith in you and your company fast. What's in some of those pages you're flipping over so rapidly? Something they ought to know that might discourage them from buying what you're selling? At best, you look disorganized and inefficient; at worst, you look like a con artist.

You may say, "But I have so many products, I have to use the same binder for all of my presentations."

Baloney.

You can have a visual aid for each important product or service—

or you can pull just the pages you need for each presentation from a master file and put them in a separate binder.

If you're selling, as opposed to merely taking orders from a catalog you carry around, you can organize yourself to have a crisp presentation that you make from a binder that's free of dead pages. Look at the sales books or presentation binders the slowest-selling half of any sales force carries and you'll see binders that are bulging with outdated, dog-eared material that is anything but an invitation to own. This sorry stuff is only there because the salesman it belongs to would rather read the sports page than purge his binder when he stops for a cup of coffee he doesn't need.

One of the top insurance salespeople I've trained—a multimillion-dollar producer—has a visual aid presentation for term insurance, another for whole life, a third for income protection, another for IRA—you name it. If it's any form of life insurance, he has a visual aid presentation for it that covers every aspect of the subject without skipping pages or having to grumble about things left out.

With a reasonable amount of thought and planning, you can have a visual aid to cover every separate major line or item you sell. And you can also have a format for quickly developing the unique details that apply to—and will appeal most to—each individual you work with. For maximum impact in some types of selling, you have to develop the unique details before you meet with the people; in other kinds of selling, you have to develop those details from information you can only obtain during the presentation. In either case, what's essential is to have a highly organized, fast-moving method of covering all the points the prospects must know about before making their decision.

Good visual aids employ psychological methods to convince prospects on both the emotional and logical levels that they should buy from you and your company. They do this by working on three vital areas:

- Visual aids tell them who you and your company are. Many people feel that all companies are about the same. A strong visual aid gives you a chance to blow your company's horn without seeming to brag. You should be proud of your great company, and here's the time to let it show.

- Visual aids tell them what you've done. People often base their decisions about the future on what's happened in the past because that's where their comfort level is. If you— as a sales professional—haven't done much yet, tell them more about what your company has done.

- Visual aids tell them what you're going to do for them. The visual aid, specifically and graphically, shows them what benefits they'll receive after they own your product or service. A picture is worth a thousand words when it comes to conveying emotional impact.

TESTIMONIAL LETTERS

Letters from happy clients you've served are a powerful means of building trust in prospects. These letters take effort to acquire. First, you have to service your clients so well that they feel almost an obligation to give you something in return. Then you have to cope with the fact that not many people will sit down all by themselves and write a letter to you. They'll tell you on the phone how much they appreciate your extra efforts, how much they've profited from your expertise, but in the daily scramble they just won't get around to writing that enthusiastic letter.

Carl Slane sells high-technology machinery, and he's one of our top Champions. When Carl first started to do well in sales, he realized that testimonial letters would be a tremendous help to him but, although many of his clients said they were delighted with his product and service, he wasn't getting many letters. His clients were just too busy. Then Carl hit on a simple way to get those letters, and in a short time he built up a very impressive display of them. Here's how he did it:

When a happy client was on the phone, Carl would make notes of the conversation. As soon as it was over, he'd draft a letter to himself that related in the client's own words what the client had said. Carl was careful not to add comments or praise the client hadn't given, and he was equally careful to leave out any knocking of the competition that might not look wise on paper. He'd have the draft typed, and then he'd make a luncheon appointment with the client.

Before leaving with the client to have lunch, Carl would show him the draft and say, "I put what you were kind enough to tell me on the phone the other day in letter form. If you still feel that way, would you mind having your secretary print it on your company letterhead while we're at lunch? It would help me a lot." They always said yes. Clients are glad to help salespeople who've done an outstanding job for them.

HOW TO USE PRINTED LITERATURE

Use brochures and catalogs like you use visual aids. Hold the brochure in your hand, look at it as you talk, and frequently look up at your prospects to regain eye contact. Circle the important points that you talk about on the brochure; when you leave it with them, they'll review that brochure, and remember what you said.

MODELS

Models are powerful visual aids, especially the kind that have moving parts and aren't too costly to leave with likely buyers. Some of our Champions who sell expensive industrial equipment have found that when someone is really keen on the model, they almost always buy the real thing. The prospect will take the model home to show his wife and kids how it works. All the time he's doing that, he's getting more involved with the whole idea, and he's convincing himself emotionally that his company should own the full-size version.

VIDEO EQUIPMENT

If used right, film or video presentations can be very effective. Keep in mind that these are still visual aids, so the same rules apply. Set up the screen so you can exercise control. If it's a silent film, be careful not to jabber all the time. If there's a sound track, it's even more important that you keep quiet while it's on. It's annoying when a salesperson takes over a narration the client thinks is more interesting and informative. If you need to say something, stop the film—but not more than once or twice per presentation. The video was likely developed to carry certain points in a methodical manner. Your interruptions might create confusion in the mind of the viewer rather than adding to its impact.

Far better than talking is to sit where you can unobtrusively watch the prospects' reactions. From their facial expressions and movements, you'll discover what does and doesn't interest them. One spouse will nudge the other at significant times. A member of the committee will whisper agreement or disagreement. Everybody will make small but revealing comments in body language with such things as nods, shakes of their heads, notes taken, and grimaces. Make mental notes of these emotional markers and they'll guide you to the sale.

Pause the video sparingly and only when great interest is shown in a particular scene and there are details you can add or point out. Know how to replay segments that might bring about oohs and ahs from your potential clients.

Here are some simple but vital tips on working with video presentations:

- Bring a long extension cord so you can set up the equipment in the best location for selling, not the only location the cord will reach. If you're showing the video on your laptop, be certain the battery is fully charged before your presentation.
- Bring a heavy pad with you. Instead of plopping your equipment down on their beautiful coffee table or polished desk, protect it with a soft pad or tablecloth.
- Always get permission before setting up the equipment. You'll get it more readily if you bring in the protective pad first.
- Accept offers to help set up. Our Champions tell us that prospects who help organize the showing watch it with greater interest. Many salesmen make a mistake here that

few saleswomen do. Men often insist on doing all of the setup themselves, leaving the prospects sitting there fidgeting. Women welcome the help, start their presentations faster, and show them to prospects who are already involved because they helped plug it all in.

- *Never put your visual aids away until you've completed the entire presentation and tried all your closing sequences.*

This is vital. If you start folding your screen and rolling up your extension cord, the prospect is thinking, *Okay. That's over. On to other things. Let's see—who do I have to call?* You simply can't pack up and then sit down and go into your closing sequence. The whole mood has changed by that time; the impact has blown away. Even if your prospect takes a phone call, wait. You're not saving five minutes by packing up then; you're losing all the time it took to get there and play your whole number.

One last point: *Take care of your equipment and materials.* Use only clean, new-looking visual aids, brochures, and catalogs. If your visual aids are beat-up, dirty, wrinkled, and scratched, what will clients think? That if you're sloppy with your own materials, you'll be sloppy with how and what you supply them. Organize your car to protect your selling materials and visual aids, and once a month inspect all of it to make sure that everything is clean, crisp, and ready to go.

13. Finessing the First Meeting

Here's a scene that's repeated thousands of times every business day in the stores and showrooms of this country: A married couple goes in where merchandise is on display. Instantly, a salesperson takes off from his perch and swoops down on them like a vulture who's seen a rabbit go stiff.

"Hi folks, I'm Bob Bountiful at your service. Thanks for coming in—it's nice of you to stop by. I'm happy to tell you folks that you've come to the right place. We beat every price in town, and we've got specials and sales you won't believe."

"We're just looking," the wife says.

"Right, and I know what you're looking for—a good deal. Well, you've come to the right place and the right man. Old Bob Bountiful will make sure you're treated right."

"Let's get out of here," the husband says—and out they go. Good old Bob Bountiful just shrugs his shoulders and mutters something like, "Some people just don't want good service that saves them money. Oh well, there are more fish in the sea."

What happened? Why is old Bob standing there gasping for air? He didn't ignore the people. He came up, smiling, and introduced himself. He thanked them for coming in. He offered to be of help. He was so nice—and they practically ran out of the store. Why? Because he was practically shouting, *I'm going to sell you something.*

That jerked up a tremendous psychological wall between Bob Bountiful and his prospects. They knew right away that no matter how they handled it, he was going to be puffing in their ears and working up a sweat trying to sell, sell, sell—and they didn't want to be sold. But they did want to own something in that store or they wouldn't have gone in. The store never got a chance to take hold because good old Bob ran them off before they'd been inside ten seconds.

The first impression you make with potential clients will make or break your chances of serving them today and for many years down the road. That's why this chapter is devoted to clarifying how you should handle the original contact with any kind of possible buyer.

The first principle of approaching potential new clients is to come on softly so that you relax them enough to allow their emotion of desire for your product to overcome their emotion of fear of being sold or talked into something. You want them to be thinking about how much they want it, not thinking, *Watch out. This guy is really out to sell me.* So they say, "We're only looking." If you make them say it as a defense, you'll almost always cause them to make that statement true by walking out empty-handed.

This also happens with a meeting in their home or office. The only difference is that, when you do the vulture swoop on their turf, you encounter hostility instead of withdrawal. In both cases, they do the easiest thing: Smile politely as they brush you off and escort you to the door.

So how do we avoid making them fight or run? We understand and act on this idea:

Our main goal when first meeting people is to remove fear and allow them to relax.

If the dominant mood in their minds is fear—that you'll push them, that you'll try to sell them—they simply aren't capable of making the kind of positive decision you're looking for. They won't even agree to one of your minor closes when they're dominated by fear. So your first aim with a new person is to get that person to be comfortable with you and the situation.

At times my schedule keeps me flying so much I feel like I'm living on jets. There's a lot more to my job than talking on a stage;

I often have to work as I fly. I love people, of course, and I like to exchange stories and views when I have time. But if someone sitting next to me wants to chitchat when I need to work, I just wait. Pretty soon they ask, "What do you do for a living?"

Then I smile and say, "I sell for a living, and I can't thank you enough for sitting right here beside me."

Guess what happens next? They excuse themselves, go to the restroom, and never return.

Most people have developed a fear of being sold. This development likely occurred from a bad past experience or from being told by their parents and others they trust not to trust people in sales. This is why it's so important in the original contact to create confidence, not fear.

Let's analyze the steps involved in meeting a potential client correctly.

1. Smile. Some people have forgotten how to smile because they don't do it much. Salespeople should practice smiling. Exercise your smiling muscles every time you use the restroom. You have everything you need there: a mirror, privacy, and your face. I'm serious. A Champion leaves no stone unturned in developing skills. Certainly the ability to smile pleasantly—whether you really feel like it or not—is an important sales skill.

A smile radiates warmth. To come on warmly, smile with both your mouth and your eyes. Of course, it can be overdone in some situations, but a nice warm smile is almost always a necessary first step to a sale.

Some people have trouble putting on a smile when it's needed for another reason: They don't shut off old challenges and feelings before greeting new people. You can be sure of two things: Your future clients aren't responsible for or interested in your troubles; and you won't help your situation by driving them off with a sulky attitude. Resolve now to give your challenges and negative feelings an intermission every time you meet someone new. Then, if you have to, go back to your troubles later—after you've given yourself a boost by handling the person well.

2. Look into their eyes. Many salespeople destroy all chance of making the sale by avoiding eye contact when meeting someone new. They look down or past the other person. Both habits are un-nerving. If you won't look me in the eye, why should I trust you? Shifty-eyed people cause us to question whether they have both oars in the water and honesty in their hearts.

3. Greet them properly. Give some thought to your standard greeting. If you're using only one, the odds are that it only works well with a certain type of potential client. Don't offend or allow the others to dismiss you because your greeting doesn't strike a chord with them. Practice at least three different greetings. For starters, you may need a formal, respectful greeting; a friendly greeting; and a happy-go-lucky greeting. Later, you may want to work up even more variations. Study each person for an instant and then select the greeting you think best suits the personality. This is a great way to focus your attention on someone's individuality and get yourself thinking of the best way to work with that unique person.

4. To shake, or not to shake, that is the question. Many average salespeople can't wait to rush forward and shake everyone's hands. They have a subconscious conviction that if they can just get the other person to shake their hand, they'll make the sale. It's almost a superstition with these salespeople. The fallacy of this is that these salespeople are thinking of their own feelings, not about those of the potential client. Many people don't want to be touched by strangers. And what happens with typical salespeople? Because they are anxious to shake hands with prospects who don't want to, they get rejected frequently. Relating acceptance to shaking hands gets in the way, and the average salesperson doesn't even realize it. Rejection makes them even more anxious to shake hands. So they start getting more and more tense and possibly aggressive about shaking hands. The added tension is communicated to the pros-pects, who then become even more reluctant to shake hands with this overanxious, sweating salesperson. I'm not exaggerating. A friend of mine owns a chain of dry-cleaning establishments. He said, "Tom, I can always tell which of my customers are in sales. There's always this telltale mark on their clothing where they keep rubbing the perspiration off their palms before shaking hands."

For the average salesperson, that quick rub to get rid of the cold sweat becomes a fixed habit, along with "Hi, there. I'm—"

In today's competitive selling, we have one bedrock goal in meeting and working with people. Our main goal in meeting people is to have them like and trust us. That's why Champions think when they're meeting someone: *This person is going to like and trust me, because I'm a very likable and trustworthy individual.*

Isn't that a good thing to be telling yourself all the time? *They're going to like me.* Don't keep telling yourself, *I've got to make these people like and trust me or I'll lose out.* That's planting negative seeds and fear into your own mind. Every time you tell yourself, *I've got to do it,* you make yourself feel anxious, perhaps even a little desperate. If you're relaxed and confident, you communicate relaxation and confidence to the prospect; if you're tense and worried, you radiate fear, and the prospect will pick that up, too.

I have a very clear-cut way to help: If you're greeting a nonreferred prospect (usually this will be the person who walks into your office, store, or showroom), don't expect to shake hands. Of course, if the prospect puts out a hand, you'll take it, but this rarely happens. If it's a recontact or a referred lead, you may shake hands or you may not—simply let the prospects determine it. The important thing is to get rid of the idea that you have to touch them.

Don't allow the embarrassing situation where you reach out and they don't. Then they realize you wanted to shake hands. They reach out and you've put your hand down—all very awkward and unprofessional. When approaching someone new, cock your right arm at about halfway to a handshake. That way, if they reach out, you'll be ready. If they don't, you can lower your arm. Having your arm in this position is not weird. If you'll watch strong actors on television or in the movies, they never just stand. They pose. They gesture. They appear animated even when they're not speaking. That's because they keep their hands in the picture. You need to practice this drill and do the same. It'll save you many awkward moments with new clients.

Now let's go over the two basic meeting situations in detail.

THE REFERRED LEAD

Let's suppose that I'm meeting a married couple for the first time under circumstances where I know their names. We have a confirmed time to meet at my office and I see them coming in. As I walk toward them with my hand swinging easily at my side, I begin to smile because I'm genuinely looking forward to meeting them.

I'm going to introduce myself. This makes sense because they've never seen me before and I want to relax them by letting them know they're in the right place at the right time talking to the right person. So I say, "Good afternoon, Mr. and Mrs. Meisner. Tom Hopkins with Champions Unlimited." As I say *Mr. Meisner,* I look him in the eyes; then I flick my gaze to Mrs. Meisner's eyes as I say her name, returning to Mr. Meisner as I introduce myself. If I were a woman, I would probably be looking at the wife as I state my name.

It's important that I don't look down at their hands to see if one of them is moving toward me. I don't have to in order to see that movement because we're blessed with something called peripheral vision. This means that we can see things we're not looking directly at. Use your peripheral vision to catch a movement of shoulder or hand that shows the other person intends to shake hands with you.

Convince yourself that you don't need to touch your prospects. Then you'll stop wiping your right palm because you won't be sweating anymore. You'll be truly relaxed because you've taken the strain off the meeting situation, and more people will like and trust you because you're radiating warmth and confidence instead of tension.

As you walk up to Mr. and Mrs. Meisner, you are smiling easily and your right hand is swinging naturally at your side. If there's a movement and Mr. Meisner's hand comes out, you take it easily, give it a firm shake, disconnect promptly, and let your hand swing down as you turn slightly toward Mrs. Meisner. If you've shaken hands with the husband, there's more chance that the wife will make the same gesture. As you look into her eyes, be aware whether she's making any move to shake hands, too. If not, your slight turn toward her and the dropping of your hand can work smoothly into a slight bow or nod to her.

THE NONREFERRED SITUATION

A couple walks into your store or display area. You don't know their names. At this stage, it's just plain pushy to ask. All chance of building the necessary relaxed feeling is often lost in the first moments by overanxious salespeople who stick out their hands, introduce themselves, and ask people for their names. The prospects are startled and embarrassed because they weren't ready for that kind of attention.

Here's how to avoid the possibility of this happening. A couple walks in. You don't know their names and have no reason to believe they want to make your acquaintance. When you walk toward them, stop several feet away to avoid invading their space, and say something along these lines:

- "Hi. Nice of you to come in. Why don't you just make yourselves at home and look around. If you have any questions, let me know."
- "Hello. Thanks for coming in. Please feel free to look around all you want. If I can give you any information, please don't hesitate to ask."
- "Good afternoon, sir—madam. Welcome to [name of your store]. I hope you'll both enjoy our display. If you have any questions, I'm at your service."
- "Welcome to [name of your store]. What brought you in today?
- "Good morning. Thank you for coming by. My name is Tom. If you have any questions or need assistance, I'll be over here. Just ask."

When you've spoken your version of one of those greetings, turn and prepare to walk away.

That's right, walk away.

Don't whirl and run, of course. Turn away slowly. If they stop you by asking a question, you're there and ready to help. If they acknowledge you, then turn to move elsewhere in the store, you simply step aside but stay in the general vicinity so they'll know where to find you. If you're where you should be, they can easily ask you a question if they care to.

It's curious how many people will head for the door when you crowd them, but will ask for the product or service they came in for when you speak courteously to them and then start turning away. By showing that you respect their privacy, you assure them that they'll be safe in asking for what they want.

Often they won't say much—especially in places where big-ticket items are sold. Move off. You've done all you can do until those people make the next move.

Many of them will cruise around your showroom without stopping anywhere for more than a few seconds and then leave. These people almost always are killing time, are out of their price class, or really are just looking in advance of real need or willingness to buy. If so, you gain a great deal by letting them browse and go. They are far more likely to come back when they're ready to own if they haven't been pressured the first time they came in. And by letting them go, you haven't burned up your energy and enthusiasm on people who weren't qualified or ready to make a decision.

If they don't ask a question or leave, they'll do what you should be hoping they'll do.

5. Let them settle. If you leave them alone after greeting them, and if they have any genuine interest in your product or service and the ability to buy it, they'll home in on that item. All you have to do is let them settle.

If your product line is appliances and your store handles several types, including television sets, watch without staring. Using peripheral vision, you can be looking at something in the dishwasher section when they light on a particular TV set. If they stay there for a full minute, they've settled. Now it's time for you to stroll over and casually move into the next step.

6. Ask an opening involvement question. An involvement question, of course, is any positive question they'd ask themselves about the benefits of the product after they own it. You don't know their names yet, of course, and it's too soon to ask.

Walk up and say, "Would the television replace your old one, or is it going to be an additional set for your home?"

With slight changes in wording, you can adapt this opening involvement question to almost any product or service. Once you get them talking about why they want what you're selling, you know how to go into your qualification and minor closing sequences, how to eventually lead them into happy involvement with a purchase.

14. Qualification Is the Key to Quota Busting

Many salespeople never qualify before presenting or demonstrating. They simply never do it. As soon as they get near warm bodies, they put their heads down and plow right into excitedly telling them all about the product or service, whether they need it or not. Some of them do it because they don't know how to qualify, and others aren't organized well enough to tone down their excitement by learning more about who they're talking with and whether or not it would be wise to proceed. Whatever explanation there may be for failing to qualify prospects before giving a full presentation, the salespeople who don't do it are often depressed because they aren't making enough sales. They decide they couldn't close an Eskimo on a hot lunch when actually they are fairly good closers. Their problem is that they try to close the wrong people too often and too hard.

We evaluated the selling skills of more than two hundred thousand salespeople and found that the biggest difference in those making high incomes and others who are just getting by was their strength in the area of qualifying. Since it can be learned, done simply and professionally, why don't more salespeople build their skill in this area? Mainly because they don't even realize how much it's costing them.

It's often been said that sales work is largely a matter of using time effectively. For some reason, many average salespeople think that the only important thing is to demonstrate the product or present the service with a lot of slick phrases and gimmicks. If they do that, if they tell the prospects everything about it, they'll hear, "Yes, we'll take it."

Champions know better. They know that qualification is the key to high production. And since they understand the need for and the methods of qualifying, they also appreciate the value of prequalifying techniques that are a part of some of our prospecting strategies, specifically the referral system, swap meet or leads club, and orphan adoption.

If you use those techniques, your leads are prequalified before you meet them. You're assured that they have the needs and resources to own what you're selling—so you'll close 50 percent of them. You'll close one for every one that gets away. With unqualified leads, nine will get away while you're closing one. As a general rule, it takes as much time to see ten nonqualified leads as it does to see ten qualified leads. The primary difference is that your sales are 500 percent greater with qualified leads than they are with the nonqualified type. That's a figure that should give you pause if you aren't effectively qualifying your leads. Any system that can increase your sales fivefold fairly screams for your attention, doesn't it?

Will you also agree that no matter what it takes to develop this skill, you must do it if you possibly can? Certainly you must. Fortunately, the process isn't difficult. When you're through reading the next few paragraphs, you'll have a superb qualification strategy. This strategy allows you to qualify prospects as you meet them. In many cases, you'll be able to qualify over the phone before you meet them; if they don't qualify, you politely avoid wasting your time and theirs presenting a product they won't own.

How often have you committed an hour or half a day meeting with people, demonstrating and possibly coming back for a second visit, only to discover that they can't afford your offering, can't make the decision to own it, or can't use its features? The most valuable thing a salesperson has is time. Time wasted demonstrating to nonbuyers is time that could have been spent demonstrating to and closing buyers—or at the very least prospecting for them.

I call this my NEADS Qualification Sequence. If you can remember the word *NEADS*, you can remember and effectively work with this strategy. First of all, the word *needs* is really what you're after when qualifying. You must determine their needs before knowing how to proceed with potential clients. I just spelled it differently to match the sequence of questions you're going to ask.

THE SIX-STEP QUALIFICATION SEQUENCE

Here are the steps:

1. Find out what they have now. The *N* in *NEADS* stands for "now."

When I know how they are presently handling their need for the benefits that I can supply, I know the kind of people they've been. Knowing what they've been tells me a lot about what they want to become. When I know where they're headed, I know how to sell them what they need to get there. Sometimes people will be eager to tell you what they have now. With other products and services, they may be less than eager to give you this information. In that case, you'll need to develop indirect lines of questioning that are capable of digging out the facts you need. Give this much thought and practice. Qualifying is too important to allow some difficulty here to stop you.

2. Find out what they like most about the product or service they now have. The *E* in *NEADS* stands for "enjoy."

Knowing how they feel about what they have points you straight at how to make the sale—or, equally important, alerts you to the fact that you'll be wasting your time trying to sell these particular prospects. Every product and service has its limitations; trying to sell outside those limitations is unwise. If what you're offering doesn't come close to what they've previously enjoyed, you'll be wasting your time going farther. If your product or service has everything they enjoyed and more, you're on the right track with these clients.

Let's illustrate this point by going back to Champion Marine Sales. I'm on the phone with Mr. Ivey, who has the itch to replace the custom boat he's owned for three years.

"Tom, why don't you take a run out here and give me your opinion as to how much I could get for my boat on today's resale market."

"I'd like to do that, Mr. Ivey. Tell me, what do you enjoy most about your boat?"

"Well, I guess that would be its seaworthiness. It's kind of a slow old tub, but I wouldn't be afraid to ride out a storm in it."

"A fast boat can put you back in a snug harbor before the weather gets really bad."

"Yeah—if your engine doesn't quit. My boat's a motor sailer—it's got a steadying sail that could get me home in a blow if I were to have engine trouble."

Now I've found out what I wanted to know before making that trip. Champion Marine sells the finest high-speed boats made—and no other kind. In other words, the boats we market are precisely the type that Mr. Ivey would never own. After spending a few moments asking astute questions, I've eliminated Mr. Ivey as a prospect for me. He may be an avid yachtsman, he may be loaded with money, but Mr. Ivey isn't going to own one of my Spee-D-Ski boats.

"Mr. Ivey, I really appreciate your calling me, but we're not the right people to serve you. A good friend of mine is this area's leading expert on displacement boats. Let me give you his number."

All I need do now is place a quick call to somebody who sells the kind of boat Mr. Ivey likes so that person will feel obligated to send me people wanting what I have that he doesn't handle.

Notice that I don't ask Mr. Ivey to tell my friend that I sent him because there's not one chance in ten he'll remember to do that. Instead, I take it on myself to build my relationship with this noncompeting member of my industry. Sure, it takes three minutes—but those three minutes can return many qualified buyers.

With the time saved by not driving out to see Mr. Ivey's boat, I continue taking and making calls. An hour later, I'm talking to Max Schnell.

"What do you like most about your present boat, Mr. Schnell?"

"It's a goer, Tom. It gets me out to where the fish are fast."

"Your boat turns up about thirty knots, doesn't it?"

"Thirty knots? No way. But it's good for a solid twenty-two right through a three-foot chop."

"The Spee-D-Ski II will take you through that same chop at a solid thirty knots. And that's cruising speed—not flat-out."

"Wow. We've got to talk business, Tom. When can we do that?"

"At your convenience, Max. I'd like you to take a demonstration ride with me. Could you be here by three? Or would five be a better time for you today?"

"Hey, great. I'll see you at five."

If I'd rushed out to see Mr. Ivey's "slow old tub" I would've missed Mr. Schnell's call. Someone else around the office would have given him a trial run—and chalked up the sale. Don't waste your time working with people who want what you don't have. If you spend your time that way, you'll have the "bad luck" to be out every time the business comes in.

But if you follow these steps and concentrate on working with the people you can help enjoy the benefits they want, you'll be working with buyers who've precommitted themselves to what you have. They'll literally be sold before you even demonstrate. Your demonstration will, in fact, simply be a confirmation that they've got to have it. Can you feel how excited and fulfilled you'll be closing in these kinds of situations? The right way to sell is not only the moneymaking way but also the easy way once you learn how to organize yourself to do it.

3. "What would you like to see altered or improved in your new [name the product or service]?" The *A* in *NEADS* stands for "altered."

Champions use the answers to this question to find which qualities they must emphasize in order to close the sale.

Now I'm selling factory machinery. Paul Flinn answers this question by saying: "I'd like to see some method of cutting down the setup time. The production rate is okay on our present machine, but we lose too much time changing over from job to job on it. You don't get many long runs in this business."

I'm going to file that vital bit of information in the front of my brain. When I'm doing my demonstration a few days later, I'm going to say something like this:

"Mr. Flinn, one thing we're very conscious of at Champion Machinery is the high cost of setup time. Not only is setup labor very expensive, but slow setup time eats profits by keeping the equipment out of production longer. So our company has invested huge sums in engineering faster takedown and setup times. Here's what we've done to keep our new machine pumping out parts—"

Build your demonstration or presentation around the things that prospects want altered or changed in what they have now. Feed back what they've told you they want, and they have to agree that you're making sense.

4. "Who in addition to yourself will make the final decision?" The *D* in *NEADS* is to remind you to be certain you're talking with the real decision maker.

It's understandable why people who can't make decisions want to give the impression that they can until the last minute—it makes them feel important. So you have to handle this carefully. Again, you'll have to structure your response to this problem around your own offering. The more time-consuming your demonstration or presentation is, the more important it is to have all the decision makers present. There's nothing more discouraging than putting on a demolition derby for folks and then having them tell you, "That was great. But I really can't give you the go-ahead until I talk to Mr. Snodgrass. Gee, you sure went to a lot of trouble. I wish he'd seen it. Can you come back next week and do it again?" In many cases, however, the person will answer, "I'm the final decision maker on this project," and you'll know you're one step closer to giving the right person the best presentation you can.

5. "If we were fortunate enough today to find the right solution for your needs, would you be in a position to proceed?" The *S* in *NEADS* stands for "solution."

You must earn the right to ask for the sale by proving that you have the right solution for them. If you can find out how soon they'll make a decision before giving your presentation, you're batting a thousand in your qualification sequence.

I didn't blurt out, "Look, I'm not about to sweat through the whole demonstration unless I know you're really going to buy if it does the job for you."

When you say, "If we're fortunate enough today," shrug as though that's not very likely. This reduces the pressure on them because you've indicated that you don't think you're going to hit the right note today anyway—so they're more likely to own up to the truth about whether they can or can't go ahead today.

"Oh, no. Before we go any farther, our board of directors has to meet and approve it."

I didn't really want to hear that, of course, but I know that negative reality doesn't self-destruct merely because it's ignored. I've discovered that going into the full closing sequence is useless until I get in front of the right people, so now I know how to move this particular sale forward.

At this point, you might also hear them say, "Well, I don't know. We're just getting started on looking at what's out there." In other words, they're shopping around. You can work with this answer, and I'll show you how in chapter 17; don't let it stop you from moving to the next area. Just know that in your presentation, you're going to have to be able to address the strengths and weaknesses of the competition. Do this properly and you'll show them that you've just saved them a ton of time doing the checking themselves. Just be certain your information about the competitor's models is current.

FOCUSING THEM IN WITH THE TRIPLICATE OF CHOICE

The next two techniques are delightful to work with, and they're highly effective.

6. Give them a triplicate of choice for product. Complete knowledge of your product line is the first essential. Let's say that your line includes eight different copying machines. Instead of trying to go from eight possibilities to the one machine that given prospects will buy, frame them in to the most likely three first, and then in a second step isolate the one that's best for their particular application.

"Mary, we have three basic functions with our copiers: copying, separating, and collating. Of these three, which is the most important to you?"

"Collating. We've got to have that feature on our next machine."

Because I know my product line, I instantly know that we've eliminated three machines. That leaves five for Mary to choose from.

Color and size often are important purchase considerations.

What I must now determine is whether she's prepared to devote as much office space to copying as our largest, fastest, and most versatile machine requires. If not, we have two smaller machines. I explain the options in terms of size and ask her which best suits her needs.

"The medium size," Mary says. I'm not surprised. Most of the time, they go for the medium choice.

"Our machines come in three colors: light beige, which would go nicely with your paneling. We also have a glossy black that looks very distinguished, and this unique shade of red. Which of these do you think will provide the right touch?"

"Definitely the beige," Mary tells me.

We're down to a medium-size machine, beige in color, that copies, separates, and collates. Now the challenge is not selecting the machine, it's determining if Mary's company is prepared to invest what that machine costs. My next step is designed to maximize the chances that she'll decide it is.

7. Triplicate of choice for money. This is a beautiful strategy for overcoming what in many cases is the trickiest question of all. Average salespeople baldly state the price, frequently in a manner that shows they think it's outrageously high—in effect, daring the client to come up with the cash. That's not the way to close.

Stick as close to the exact wording as you can when adapting this technique to your offering—all the elements are important. Here's how it works:

"Most people interested in acquiring this machine with all its features are prepared to invest twelve thousand dollars. A fortunate few can invest between fifteen and twenty thousand. And then there are those on a limited or fixed budget who—with the high cost of everything today—can't go higher than ten. May I ask, which of these categories does your company fit into most comfortably, Mary?"

"We were thinking of spending about twelve thousand."

Why did she say that? In actual fact, Mary possibly didn't have an exact amount in mind. She doesn't want to be in the bottom category, though, so Mary opted for the middle figure.

I've structured the figures to allow me to say at this point, "What

I'm excited about is this: The machine that meets all your requirements involves an investment of only ten thousand dollars—substantially less than the amount you're prepared to spend." Where can Mary go now except to her desk for a purchase order?

I'd still be okay if Mary had assigned her company to the lowest category. You see how it works. Structure this technique so that you come up a winner no matter what figure they pick. This is the best single strategy for eliminating the money as a potential objection later in the process. In fact, many sales are made at this point; it's just a matter of demonstrating the one product that's best for them and wrapping up the paperwork. You may not even have to concern yourself with objections or closes that are typical of most selling situations.

Here's the formula, the triplicate of choice technique that allows you to bracket up for money:

1. Begin by stating a figure that is 20 percent above your investment. ("Most people . . . are prepared to invest twelve thousand dollars. . . .")
2. Continue by giving a range from 50 to 100 percent above your amount. ("A fortunate few can invest between fifteen and twenty thousand. . . .")
3. Give the actual amount as your last figure. ("And then there are those on a limited or fixed budget . . . who can't go over ten.")
4. Then ask, "Which of these categories do you [does your company, family, organization] fit into most comfortably?"
5. Whichever category they pick, your response is, "What I'm really excited about is this: The model that meets all your needs [that's exactly what you want] only requires an investment of—"

If they pick the bottom category, finish with, "—which is exactly what you planned to spend."

If they put themselves in the middle, finish with, "—which is substantially less than what you're prepared to spend."

Before you go on your next presentation with the intention of putting the triplicate of choice for money to work for you, face the fact that it won't work (and you won't even try to use it) unless you have all your figures down pat. If you try to wing this and get your figures mixed up, you'll botch it. Remember this:

To use the triplicate of choice for money, you must practice the figures until you know them perfectly.

You can only use this technique once in each presentation, of course.

Often it's the monthly investment, not the total investment, that's the key money element. If that's how you sell, you can easily adapt the triplicate of choice for money to your selling sequence by saying, "Many people interested in this service are prepared to invest $120 a month to enjoy its benefits. We have a fortunate few willing to invest between $150 and $200 each month. And then we have those few on a limited or fixed budget who feel they can't go higher than a hundred-dollar monthly investment. Which of these categories do you feel most comfortable with?"

Monthly investment buyers, like cash buyers, usually jump on the middle figure. After they do that, give them the good news: In order to own exactly what they want, they don't have to invest what they expected to invest. The amount of money that's involved is much smaller than that. At this point I've often had clients ask me, "Tom, what can I say?"

I smile and tell them, "I know. Isn't it nice when a good decision is so easy? Now all you need to do is okay it right here on the paperwork."

THE UH-PRICE NONTECHNIQUE

Some of us go shuffling into a meeting dreading the moment when we have to get down to the hard facts of money. So we uh-price them.

"What's it cost?" the customer asks.

"Well, that one is—uh—it's about—let's see, with tax and freight and the small installation charge we have to make—uh—it's going to run you right at—well, maybe just a shade under, tuhthzzert. Um, yeah, that's about it."

"What? I didn't catch the price you're quoting me."

"Ten thousand."

"Dollars?"

"Yes, ten thousand dollars, more or less."

"Well, which is it, more—or less? It better be a lot less if you expect me to buy it."

"Uh—let me double-check my figures."

While the hapless salesman frantically adds and subtracts, the buyer sits back and calmly plans her next move to keep him off balance and drive a better bargain. Or her next phone call—to the competition.

Never uh-price a possible client. Control the money issue by facing it squarely and boldly. The triplicate of choice for money allows you to win every money vote that can be won. Use it. This technique is a reliable workhorse—if you know your figures, adapt the phrases to your offering, and practice them carefully.

15. The Objection Connection

Most new or average salespeople have a dream. In the dream, they meet smiling, happy people. They build rapport, qualify, and give a dynamic presentation. At the end of the presentation, the smiling folks can't wait to own the product. They clap their hands. They whip out their checkbooks or credit cards, sign on the dotted line, and shake hands profusely with the salesperson for showing them the greatest thing since sliced bread. Yep, that's a dream, all right.

Let me give you a short lesson that will take you far in sales. If the people you're talking with don't object to anything during your time together, they're either not listening or not qualified. In other words, they won't buy!

Objections (concerns) are nothing more than ways for your potential client to slow things down—to keep themselves from making a rash decision—from feeling as if they're being "sold." Objections are a common aspect of every sale you'll attempt to make. Accept this fact and you'll open your mind to the ways to handle, address, and overcome objections that I'll cover in this chapter.

Until you learn how to handle objections, you're not going to approach your potential in sales. Champions have an affection for even the peskiest objection because it's something concrete. They know they've reached the Klondike and are digging for gold when they start hearing objections.

MAKE THE HANDLING OF OBJECTIONS AN INTEGRAL AND EXPECTED PART OF YOUR SELLING SEQUENCE

I hope that you'll highlight this achievement-oriented statement:

Objections are the rungs of the ladder to sales success.

When you climb to the top of that ladder, they own what you're selling. There just isn't any other way to where you want to climb except by grasping and overcoming the most common concerns. If you decide to overcome objections by learning the material in this book, you'll learn to love objections as much as I do—because they announce buying intention and point the way to closing the sale.

WHAT IS AN OBJECTION?

An objection is a statement by potential clients that they want to know more. Of course, objections don't usually come out sounding like a polite request for additional information. People aren't trying to make it quite that easy for you. They usually are sincerely objecting—they don't realize they're just asking for more information. It's your job to know that, and to know what to do about it.

There are two kinds of objections, minor and major. Please keep this in mind at all times:

Minor objections are defense mechanisms.

People use them to slow things down. They don't mean that they don't want to buy; they just want to mull things over before committing themselves. Maybe they need clarification on something. Perhaps they've thought of a need they forgot to tell you about. It doesn't matter the reason. It's always a good sign when someone gives you a concern. And you don't necessarily have to address all of them. Trust me, there are people who look at selling situations as opportunities to debate. They'll toss objections at you all day long if you'll allow it.

If you sell frequently to couples, you'll have one of them start to go along with your demonstration and then the other one suddenly starts objecting and fighting you. Sometimes the other spouse, the one who's going along, is more surprised than you are. The fighting spouse may only want to catch his or her breath, or make sure that you can answer minor objections eloquently before things get any thicker.

Of course, not all concerns should be overcome. You'll often encounter conditions that prevent the purchase.

Major concerns are things such as: The new SUV doesn't fit in the garage. Your product doesn't come in a color that complements the decorating style of the potential client. In other words, your product has limitations that simply don't fill enough of the needs of the client.

WHAT IS A CONDITION?

A condition is a valid reason for not going ahead. It's not an objection to overcome; it's a total block to the sale that you must accept and walk away from. Champions are quick to recognize conditions. The major aim of qualifying is to determine whether there are any conditions that make the sale impossible, and further attempts to sell pointless. So Champions, being expert qualifiers, never destroy their enthusiasm by trying to overcome conditions that can't be overcome.

One of the most common conditions for large purchases, of course, is that the prospects don't have the money and can't qualify for a loan.

Even skilled qualifiers may occasionally be well into their selling sequence and then encounter what appears to be a condition. When this happens, treat it like an objection. That is, try to break it down. If it doesn't break down, it's a condition, and you'll need to develop the ability to swallow hard and then quickly and courteously disconnect from the prospects who, you've just discovered, can't own.

Some of us have a severe challenge here. If we spend time with people and get into our selling sequence with them, we get emotionally involved to the point where we lose our ability to see the difference between an objection that can be overcome and a condition that can't.

In this, sales is like poker. Professional poker players are quick to throw in a losing hand, no matter how much they've already bet on it. Average poker players stay in the game and keep on calling bets with hands they know have little chance to win. Instead of accepting a small loss and getting out, they stay in and take a greater loss.

As Reinhold Niebuhr said, "Give us serenity to accept what cannot be changed, courage to change what should be changed, and wisdom to distinguish the one from the other." Have the wisdom—and sometimes it also takes courage—to pleasantly and quickly withdraw from losing situations.

You'll appear more professional for doing so and, hopefully, when conditions change in the future for these people, they *can* become clients of yours. If nothing else, by being extremely professional you will earn the right to ask them for qualified referrals to friends, associates, or relatives who might not have the same conditions. So all is not lost. It's just different.

Now let me repeat what an objection is. An objection is a request for more information. Believe me, 1 won't waste my time objecting to small things unless I'm really considering taking the product or service—I'm the same as most buyers on that point. But understand this: Potential buyers who object really can't see how your offering will suit their needs. Your job is to use your superior knowledge of what you're selling to show them how it can satisfy their needs.

Take a bright highlighting pen and make this point stand out:

If no conditions exist and they don't buy, it's my fault.

It's important to understand and agree with that concept. You represent a fine-quality product, or a service that's conducted with skill and integrity. When people own it, they benefit. Let them. Do your job. Help those people enjoy the benefits that only you can bring them.

Do you realize how many salespeople won't let their prospects benefit from their offering? These salespeople won't do what has to be done in the way of practice, planning, and performance to permit their prospects to benefit from owning what they sell.

I love the profession of selling. It's been my entire life. I know what a leading part it plays in maintaining our national prosperity and way of life. What I think is sad is the large number of salespeople who damage our profession because they buckle when they hear an objection. These klutzes don't realize that by failing to overcome objections, they not only fail themselves and their families, but also fail their companies, the public, and our nation's future. Prospects came to you in need of the product or service—or you found them in need of it—and if they don't get it, they lose. Everyone else loses, too.

As I fly around the country, I talk to people who aren't in the selling profession. When I say that I train salespeople, some of them look at me as if I'm doing something wrong. I don't accept any shade of that idea. We have the most honorable profession there is. Selling means helping people benefit and grow. Yet average salespeople sit and wait. When they finally meet a prospect, the slightest breeze of objection blows them away—and that prospect walks off without the benefits.

I hope you'll decide right now that you'll no longer buckle under and then blow away. Make today the day you take the material in this book (or in my audio and video programs) and start working with all your energy to learn and then shape it to serve your unique requirements. When you've made it yours, you'll love objections like I do because you'll know in your bones that finding and overcoming them is the only way you'll ever get the yes you're looking for. You'll learn to go in hoping to hear the nos you've got to hear before you use your skills and get the yes.

TWO DON'TS AND ONE DO THAT EVERY CHAMPION LIVES BY

Here are two things that no Champion ever does, and one thing that all Champions constantly do. Please highlight these three precepts so you can review them quickly and often.

1. Don't argue. Do you know how many salespeople argue with potential buyers? Prospects voice a concern—meaning that they show a need for more information—and what do they get? An argument. With anger or sarcasm, or other forms of sales-killing heat and pressure, the salesperson tries to beat the prospect down. Quite often, the salesperson succeeds in winning the argument—and thereby loses all chance of making the sale. Why? Because then the only way the prospects can get even for the way they've been treated is to buy from someone else.

2. Don't attack them when you overcome their objections. Put space between your prospects and their objections. By this I mean that you must be careful to separate your people from their objections. You need to be sure that when you fire at the objection, you don't hit the potential clients in a vital spot. Develop sensitivity to how your prospects feel when they voice their objections. You can't reject their objections as being anything less than intelligent and reasonable without striking at their self-esteem. Show concern for their saving face, not determination to prove them wrong.

Never allow a potential client to feel that he's in danger of being proven wrong. If you start fighting their feelings, their negative emotions will always take over. You can't make sales by winning logical battles at the cost of losing emotional ones. Objections tell you where their interests lie; this being the case, objections tell you what must be emphasized, eliminated, or changed before they'll own.

3. Do lead them to answer their own objections. A Champion always tries to help them to answer their own objections.

Here's another point to highlight: When I say it, they tend to doubt it. When they say it, it's true.

Anything and everything said by a salesperson is likely to be met with skepticism by potential owners. After all, what you say influences their decision and, unfortunately, due to the lack of professionalism of some in this industry, salespeople's words aren't often trusted. So they'll tend to doubt what you say until and unless you back it up with facts or through hands-on demonstration. When they make a statement, they believe it to be true. People won't normally tell themselves untruths when in purchasing situations. Your goal is to get them to state the answer to their objection.

The average salesperson doesn't suspect that this can be done and never tries to do it; the Champion knows that it usually can be done and develops great skill at doing it. Do you know that most prospects will answer their own objections if you'll just work at it, give them time, and lead them to it? After all, deep down they want to go ahead—if you'll just show them how, and guide their faltering footsteps. They wouldn't keep on talking to you if they didn't want what you sell.

Most buyers have certain reflexes they aren't even conscious of that come out as objections. When the secretary says, "We only see vendors on Thursday," or someone coming into a store says, "We're only looking," you're hearing reflex objections. Here's how to overcome these and other types.

THE OBJECTION-HANDLING SYSTEM

1. Hear them out. Far too many salespeople leap on an objection before the other person has a chance to finish saying it. The prospect barely gets five words out—and already the salesperson is yammering away as though the evil thing will multiply unless it's stomped out immediately. *I gotta make him wrong quick, or he won't take the product*, seems to be their panicky reaction to the first hint of any objection.

Not only does the prospect feel irritated to be interrupted, but he also feels pushed. And uneasy. *Why's the salesperson jumping on that so fast and so hard?* your prospect will ask himself. *I smell a rat.*

And suppose you answer the wrong objection? Maybe even raise one he hadn't thought of? How embarrassing.

2. Feed the objection back. This is one of the best techniques for getting them to answer their own objection. It works especially well with husband-and-wife buyers. I've often fed an objection back to the husband, and then sat back while the wife hopped on it and closed him for me. To feed a concern back to potential clients, all you need to do is repeat it back to them with a sincere questioning tone in your voice.

3. Question the concern. Ask them to elaborate on or clarify their concern. Do it seriously. Avoid any hint of sarcasm, impatience, or contempt. If you really get into the detail of their objection, they'll feel a strong pull toward removing it themselves. Even if that doesn't happen, while the prospects are expounding further on their objection, you have more time to decide what course will best overcome it. "Mary, you think this table is too large for your dining room? Could you elaborate on that for me?"

4. Answer the objection. You might think, *Well, that lets me out.* Don't worry—I'm going to show you how. Have you ever stared at the ceiling in the dark of night thinking about all the objections that prospects could hit you with? Sometimes it seems like they have their own training program to learn every negative that can possibly be raised. Some salespeople strike one objection they can't seem to overcome, and it gives them nightmares. It works on their minds so much that soon they're expecting to hear the objection they dread most from everyone they meet.

Guess what? Pretty soon that's the one they always get.

Here's how it works. That cruncher objection is on their mind when they go in for every meeting, or walk up to every potential client. They don't know when, or even if, that wipeout objection will strike—but they can't get it out of their thoughts. So the tension builds until it's too great. Without realizing it, they start dropping little hints that cause the prospect to bring up the concern they dread most.

Is there a single product or service that doesn't have a few soft spots, a few places where it isn't quite as good as something else?

If there is, I've never encountered it.

I feel very confident in telling you that throughout your career, everything you sell will have a few features or weaknesses you wish it didn't have. There'll always be something that can turn into a cruncher of an objection if you let it prey on your mind.

Champions study the weak points their offering has, and they learn how to handle the situation. They often do this by admitting the disadvantage and immediately comparing it with an advantage. "Yes, our matrix platform adjusts only forty degrees horizontally, but it provides 50 percent more vertical adjustment than any other machine. That's because our engineering studies prove that . . ."

5. Confirm the answer. Don't reply to the objection and then leave it hanging in the air. They may not have understood you. Or maybe they stopped listening before you finally covered the point because they thought of something else. Always allow for the possibility that people who are close to a decision may get a little strange. After you've answered the objection in a way you feel should overcome it, confirm that you have. Ask things like:

- "That clarifies this point, don't you agree?"
- "That's the answer you're looking for, isn't it?"
- "With that question out of the way, we can go ahead, don't you think?"
- "Do you agree with me that we've covered the question you raised, and given you a way to handle it?"
- "Now that settles that, doesn't it?"

6. Change gears, and immediately go to the next step in your selling sequence or on to the next objection or concern they raise. You may end up repeating these six steps two or three times if you're working with someone who likes to object. Once you're good at this job, you'll eliminate many objections in advance with your qualification sequence and preplanned presentations— designed to do just that.

Once you've confirmed that you've overcome an objection, move on briskly.

To signal that the last step is over, and that you're all now going on to the next step, use body language as you speak. That is, make an appropriate gesture, look or step in a new direction, turn the page of your proposal, shift in your chair—make some physical move. As you do that, introduce the next step with a phrase such as, "By the way . . ."

Let's review the six steps to handling objections: (1) Hear it out, (2) feed it back, (3) question it, (4) answer it, (5) confirm that the answer was accepted, and (6) move on with a gesture and a "By the way."

Make this your standard method for addressing every concern. Learn this material and it'll be better for your energy than any sleeping pills you can buy—no prescription, all the side effects are wonderful, and you'll sleep soundly because you won't fear what bedevils the nights of the average salesperson.

That's the method. Now here are four techniques to break through specific barriers. Incorporate them into your arsenal of objection-busting weapons by writing questions and answers that fit your own situation.

FOUR SHOCK TREATMENTS FOR CONCERNS

1. **Put the shoe on the prospect's foot.** Use this technique to overcome a direct challenge arising from the prospect's previous experience with your company. Here's how it works. For our example, let's assume that you represent the Dimm Company, which markets a high-quality line of office copiers. You've just walked in to see Jack Rinehart, a referral from your swap meet. Right away you run into trouble when Mr. Rinehart says, "We had a Dimm Copier two years ago and we had to get rid of it. Too slow. We lost a lot of valuable employee time with your machine."

In this situation, the average salesperson often gets into an argument about whether the Dimm Copier is now as fast as the competition. Such arguments rarely go well. Mr. Rinehart soon says, "Yeah, I hear what you're saying, but I don't want another Dimm around here. Thanks for coming in. Good-bye."

The Champion puts the shoe on the prospect's foot by saying, "Mr. Rinehart, would you for a moment pretend that you're the president of Dimm Copiers, and you've just found out about the challenge we had with the reproduction speed of our copiers. What would you do?"

Mr. Rinehart will say something like, "I'd get my engineering department cracking on it, and make them solve the problem in a hurry." By putting him in the shoes of your company's president, you've asked him a question with an obvious answer that strokes his ego, haven't you?

Then you warmly smile and say, "That's exactly what the Dimm Copiers did." What can Mr. Rinehart do now but listen to the rest of your presentation?

A common experience in sales, especially when starting a new job, is to take over an established territory. Let's suppose you're doing that.

It doesn't take you long to find out that the person you replaced wasn't promoted for doing a great job. In fact, the opposite happened—your predecessor tore the territory down. Now you're picking up the pieces.

As you get around your new area to meet clients, you start running across a lot of unhappy people. Most of them are now buying your product or service from the competition. When you go in to introduce yourself and say that you're going to be servicing their company from now on, they tell you something like this:

"Listen, we aren't going to do business with your company anymore. That last guy was a real loser. Made all kinds of promises he couldn't deliver on, and then he'd never call us back. I've had it. Any company that would put a man like him on the road for them is off our list."

Smile and say, "Ma'am, please forgive me for what happened in the past before I joined the company."

"Nothing personal, but we've had enough."

"I understand what you're saying. But may I ask you to pretend something with me for just a moment? If you were the president of our company and it came to your attention that one of your salespeople was giving your clients the kind of service he gave you, what would you do?"

"I'd fire him."

Then you smile again and say, "That's what we did—and here I am to provide you with the level of service you should expect from our company."

But what if the last representative is now your manager, your boss, or is still with the company in some other capacity?

You smile and say, ". . . If you were the president of our company, and it came to your attention that one of your salespeople was terrible at follow-up even on very important business, but you also knew that this person had some great talents in areas where you badly needed help, how would you handle it?"

You're practically spelling out the answer for her, aren't you?

So she's going to give you a response along these lines: "Well, if he really had talents I needed, I suppose I'd try to put those talents to work where we could keep an eye on him."

Whatever your prospects say about the person in question, you reply, "That's what we did." Don't get into a long explanation. Stop the discussion of the old disasters right there and go with your presentation about the new and exciting things your company now has to offer.

2. Change their base. Ask a question that highlights major benefits while it dwarfs minor objections.

Here's an example from real estate sales: You've shown the entire home, and they like it. But as you're walking with them down the hall after seeing the three bedrooms in the house, the husband suddenly starts fighting you.

"That last bedroom is too small," he says.

As you feed it back, intensify it to see whether it's more like a condition than an objection. "The third bedroom is too small? How did you plan to use it?"

"It would probably be the guest room. But it's sure small."

If the wife doesn't jump in and overcome the objection for you, change his base. "Tell me, Mr. Bjornstad—and this is an important question, sir, because your answer can eliminate this house from consideration—what will you base your decision on, the warmth and livability of the entire home, or a few inches in the guest room?"

Of course, he's going to pick the warmth and livability of the entire home. If he doesn't, you'd better forget that house and find one they will own.

You're with a prospect who is considering your medical insurance. She says, "Mr. Hopkins, one of my major concerns is that I'd really like to have the insurance company pay the doctor and hospital direct and save me all that hassle."

Your company doesn't handle things that way. So you ask in a cordial way, "Mrs. Wimmer, what will you base your decisions on—the method of payment or the quality of coverage for you and your family?"

She'll say, "The quality of coverage."

Then you eliminate the objection by saying, "Let's discuss the quality of the coverage for your family first, shall we?"

3. Question down. People walk into your retail store and settle by one of your entertainment systems. When they ask questions, you give your demonstration and learn two things. They are Mr. and Mrs. Tellgren, and they want that system. You go through a few closes with no success, and then Mr. Tellgren says, "Thanks for your time. We'll think about it and let you know."

What does *I'll let you know* really mean in cases like this?

It means, "Now that I've found what I want, I'm going to shop around and see if I can buy it any cheaper."

Remember the rule. Always lead them toward answering their own objections.

"We'll look around and get back to you."

"Fine. That's a wise decision. Mr. Tellgren, I'd like to ask you a couple of questions before you go. Were you impressed with the quality of the sound on this model?"

"Oh yes."

"Is the cabinet the size you're looking for?"

"Well, yeah, it's about right."

"And I think you mentioned that you wanted adequate controls, but not something too elaborate. Does that model fit your needs on this?"

I gently list all the things they were pleased with. As I do this, I work in—very briefly—all the positive things I can: We service everything we sell, we have free delivery and installation, we offer liberal credit terms, whatever. In a few cases, you'll be able to close them by striking a responsive chord with some of the services that you can offer. If not, you'll be able to get down to the final objection—which, nine times out of ten, is money. When you get them to agree that the reason they won't buy right now is money, you've isolated your challenge. The techniques for coping with this problem are given in chapters 14 and 16.

4. Review their history. This technique is especially effective if your product or service is something that's purchased on a regular basis by organizations. You might be selling industrial raw materials, processing services, supply items, generic merchandise. The buying of these products and services often becomes a matter of habit: It's easier to keep on buying the same thing from the same source than it is to cope with change. Many suppliers don't really keep on their toes with their established accounts. Usually they put more value on acquiring new accounts than on keeping old ones, even though the cost of acquiring new accounts almost always far exceeds the cost of keeping old ones. And of course, many successful suppliers become overly satisfied with their positions and get careless. When they stop bringing fresh ideas to their established accounts and stop keeping in close personal touch, a gap starts opening up between the best and what they're giving. This means that the supplier isn't helping the customer keep up with change anymore. The customer is falling behind and losing profits. The wider the gap grows, the more likely it becomes that someone in the competition will discover it, charge in through that gap, and capture the customer's business.

If you have established accounts, keep in close personal touch with them, make sure you keep them posted on all new developments in your industry, and stay alert to their best interests. If you're on the prowl to take over some of the competition's accounts, here's an effective way to continue when you hit their resistance to change.

You're selling service, FM radio advertising spots to be exact. Your station is K-WHEE. Red Eye Soap, a major radio advertiser in your market, plays all its spots on K-TOO, a competing station. You're going for the business in a meeting with Jane Mota, Red Eye's advertising manager. (With many products and services, you'd have to ask what they're using now. In this case, you know because you listen to the competitive stations to see who's advertising on them.)

"Are you satisfied with K-TOO, Mrs. Mota?"

"Oh yes. They do a wonderful job for us."

She wants to discourage you so you'll be easier to get rid of. But you have a plan and press on.

"How long have you been using K-TOO?"

"About three years."

"And before K-TOO, did your firm do any radio advertising?"

"Red Eye started on K-ONE in the late 1990s, I understand."

"May I ask how long you've been Red Eye's advertising manager, Mrs. Mota?"

"I've been here five years."

"Then I'd probably be safe in thinking that you had a great deal to do with the switch from K-ONE to K-TOO."

"Yes, you would."

"And you recommended, or made, that switch based on quite a bit of research and analysis, didn't you?"

"Yes, on a tremendous amount of research. We made a detailed market analysis of ten stations. Our studies convinced us that our FM budget would influence more potential buyers on K-TOO than on any other station."

"You were looking for sales potential when you did your study three years ago, weren't you?"

"Certainly."

"And the results have lived up to your expectations?"

"Yes, they have. We're very satisfied."

"Tell me, since you received greater performance by considering, and then making, a change three years ago, why should you deny yourself the opportunity to repeat the process? Your research back then led to greater profits for Red Eye and greater professional prestige for you personally. You did it once, so the possibility must exist that you can do it again, don't you agree?"

"Yes, I have to agree with that; it's a possibility."

"Wonderful. It will just take me a few moments to explore that possibility with you—"

She's given you the right to make your entire presentation. The last change worked out well, and she wants to look good to management. So now she has logical and emotional reasons to consider another change.

Isn't that a beautiful technique? What you have to do is adapt it to your offering, and then rehearse a number of variations so that you'll roll it off smoothly no matter what they say. Instead of going back to your manager and saying, "Red Eye's happy with K-TOO and they wouldn't talk to me," you'll deliver.

Learn the pattern, write out your approach, and practice it. Then the next time someone says to you, "We're happy with what we're buying now," you'll think to yourself, *You may be using them now, but within the hour you're going to start getting happily involved with me.*

The job of Champions is to realize that they represent the finest product or service available, and then to make sure that everyone who can benefit from it owns it. After you get Mrs. Mota and Red Eye switched to K-WHEE, after you do your thorough job of follow-up and service, they'll all be delighted that they made the change. And you did it. It never would have happened unless you had adapted and learned the four shock treatments: Put the shoe on their foot, question down, change their base, and review their history. Adapt, learn, and use all these techniques and you'll be well on your way to becoming the number one salesperson in your organization. Now, that's exciting, isn't it?

16. Closing Is Sweet Success

I t's the winning score, the bottom line, the name of the game, the cutting edge, the point of it all. I've given you lots of techniques for prospecting, meeting people, building a flow of referrals, qualifying, presenting, demonstrating, and overcoming objections—and they're all important. But unless you can close, you're like a football team that can't sustain a drive long enough to score. It's no good if you play your whole game in your own territory and never get across their goal line.

So welcome to the delightful world of closing. If you don't love it now, start falling in love, because this is where the money is. Make no mistake about it: The money isn't anywhere else. When you learn how to close, you'll be delighted with the results. You'll be able to get far more people happily involved in your offering than you ever were before.

Champions begin closing the moment they meet someone new. They constantly try test closes, and go into the final closing sequence anytime they sniff the sweet smell of success. Many salespeople get so wrapped up in their selling sequences that if prospects want it before they're through, they won't let them have it.

Some people get sold fast. If you keep talking instead of closing them, you'll unsell them just as fast. After all, they can only buy it once today, so don't risk having to sell them twice. I've seen it happen. Some salespeople get so excited that they can't stop talking when buyers give a sign that they're ready. Curb your urge to tell all. Don't be one of those who keep on plowing when it's time to harvest. I've watched salespeople literally grit their teeth as though to say, *You haven't heard it all yet, and you're gonna hear it all before I'll take your order.*

More talk just triggers more opportunities to raise concerns. When the clients are ready to run with it, shut up and start filling out the form.

Later I'll give you three test closes and sixteen major closes. But first, let's study some specific closing tips:

1. Always have your closing materials with you. Be ready to close anytime and anywhere. Everyone has heard about all the sales that are made on golf courses. Business is also done on tennis courts, in spas and on boats, on jogging trails and at the track— anywhere, in fact, that people play, work, exercise, or relax. Yes, a lot of business is done outside offices and showrooms, and a lot of it soon falls apart. Why? Because salespeople take half a week to get their closing materials and the clients together after the okay over the long lunch. By that time a different wind is blowing and the clients have other things on their minds. In a word, the sale is unclosed. The salespeople have to do it all over again—if they can. The second time around, the emotional odds are against them.

When I say *Have your closing materials with you at all times*, I don't mean in your hip pocket on the ninth hole. Doing business on golf courses and in elegant eateries demands discretion. People hate it if their salad fork loses its chill because you pushed papers at them to approve. It's just not classy, not professional. When you're selling in social circumstances, it can be tricky to find the right moment, so be ready to make that moment count. A supply of closing materials should take up permanent residence in your attaché case, club locker, overnight bag, car—and let's not overlook your office desk. Keep a cache of closing forms and materials in every place you frequent.

2. When do you flash the form? Give careful thought to how and when you'll produce your closing materials. If you go into your full presentation and closing sequence and then reach into your briefcase to pull out the sales agreement or order pad, the prospect sees you do it, sucks in air, and tightens up. While you're flipping forms, he's thinking, *What have I done?* He's looking for ways to escape. Since you must get the forms out of your briefcase before you can write on them, and since doing this at a critical stage of the closing is likely to be unhelpful to the emotional climate, get them out sooner. You don't have to wave them in the air and sing out, "Watch out, folks—this is my order pad." You don't need the whole pad. All you need is one form handy in your presentation binder.

If you take orders on a laptop, have the order information window in the background while giving your presentation. That way, it's only a click away.

3. Work clean. Use crisp new forms, not the ones you spilled your coffee on. If you pull out a form that looks like a baby's used bib, your prospect will think you haven't made a sale in six months—and she won't want to break your streak.

4. Find figures with finesse. Champions do their selling arithmetic with a pocket calculator, not a pencil. Why? Because buyers believe calculators; they think their numbers must be right. If you're still penciling up the numbers in front of possible owners of your product, it's time to change. Sure, it feels more down-to-earth and human to scratch away with a pencil stub, but your clients are going to think that you can easily make a very human mistake.

5. Make your proof letters talk. Earlier, I discussed the value of getting proof or testimonial letters. These are powerful tools to help other people get involved. The important thing to remember here is that the most powerful letters are those from people known to your prospects. The next most powerful are those from people who live nearby and are, therefore, easy for the prospect to check with.

When you have a proof letter from a local happy customer, you have a chance to create an even more powerful closing tool—a taped message that you can play at strategic moments. This can be either in audio or video format and stored on your laptop. If the best message for a particular client to hear is audio only, try to get a visual image of either the logo of the company that the person speaking represents, or a photo of the person speaking. This is where your digital camera or video recorder comes into play. You can take a quick photo, let them see it, give approval, and record a message in less than five minutes.

Let's say that you sell life insurance. One of your best clients is Dave Barkdale, who owns his own company. Dave has been an officer in local service clubs; he's served on civic committees; he's well thought of in the community.

You get on well with him and he was happy to write a proof letter. As you service his account, talk to some of the executives covered by Dave's insurance plan. After you introduce them on the tape, ask questions to get their feelings about having the additional life insurance for their families that the plan includes. After gathering some of this material, meet with Dave and tell him about the enthusiasm they expressed to you.

"Dave, it's obvious that your insurance program has generated a lot of company spirit among the people it covers. Do you believe these feelings will have any effect on profits?"

"I think we've already seen results. Of course profits depend on many factors, but there's definitely an improved climate here that I trace directly to the implementation of this insurance program."

"I'd like to ask you a favor, Dave. Many companies aren't taking advantage of insurance the way your firm is, and I really feel that there's a great need for improvement in this area of management. What I'd like to do is ask you some questions about your experience with our insurance and the service I've given your company, and record your feelings. But before asking you to do that, I want to make you some promises."

You've got to make some promises. Usually, what follows will about cover it.

"First of all, I promise that this material will be in my possession only, and it won't be reproduced. Second, I'll only play it for executives with companies that have attained a stature similar to yours. That I promise you."

With his agreement, start your recording, ask your questions, and let him talk. You might first say, "I'll just play Jay Leno for a few minutes."

What does this remark trigger in his mind?

That he's in a relaxed, warm, and personal kind of interview situation. Your recorder should have a PAUSE button so that you can omit silences and interruptions. And if it doesn't quite go the way you want it to, just press the PAUSE button and tell him, "Beautiful. That's just beautiful. But let me just try a new slant on it." Always encourage him. Keep it light. When you get him moving, you'll be amazed at what a forceful interview he'll give you.

Here's a vital point: End your interview with a strong close. "By the way, what you said about the special service I've given your company puts me on the spot.

"It means that I have to continue giving you and your company— and all my clients—very special service. But that's fine. That's my philosophy for doing business. Thanks, Dave, for your time."

What's exciting is the snowballing effect of these interviews. When you work with another executive who's having trouble making the decision, say to her, "Do you know Dave Barkdale? His situation was similar to yours, and I'd like you to hear what he said about our solution."

Then you play the audio. Your happy client tells what a great job you've done, how happy he is, how he's benefited and increased profits.

And what will your new client want to do after she's happily involved with your product or service?

She'll want to make a recording for you, too. It's an ego trip. And she'll want hers to be better than your first one, so she'll work at it harder and maybe make several until she gets it perfect. It snowballs. By the time you're working with your fourth client, you'll have testimonials of epic quality and sales effectiveness.

Some salespeople fight the idea of using this technique because they're afraid to ask—but some of your clients are hams who'll love the idea. Write notes for questions that will start your client interviews off strongly. Don't press anyone who's self-conscious. You'll find that many of your clients will be delighted to cooperate with someone who's been a good supplier and a faithful server of their needs.

TEST CLOSES

Test closes are special questions. When answered, they show that potential clients have reached a high level of interest, and that they're happy, excited, and ready to go farther. When you ask a test question, you're looking for an answer that gives you positive stimuli. Here are three test closes:

1. The alternate advance test close.

"Mr. Shealy, which delivery date would be best for you, the first or the fifteenth?"

When he says, "I'd need to have it in my shop by the first," what's happened? He's virtually bought it. Keep on with your closing sequence and you're in.

2. The erroneous conclusion test close.

A Champion listens all the way through his presentation for anything they say that he can use later for an erroneous conclusion test close. For example, you're in a home selling some kind of furnishings. During your demonstration, the wife tells her husband, "Honey, your mother's coming on the tenth. If we find what we want today, we ought to get it before then."

Many salespeople would ignore that remark, or regard it as an interruption. But the Champion hears it, and he remembers it.

Later, he might smile at the wife and say, "I can see that you're kind of excited about this design. Now, your mother-in-law's coming in on the fifth, is she?"

She'll say, "No, on the tenth."

"So about August 8 would be the best delivery date?"

"Yes."

"Let me make a note of that." Zap it on the order form.

You can use the erroneous conclusion test close on color, size—on almost anything. She might say, "Well, against our walnut paneling, I think the ebony would look best."

Later, you use that. "Let's see. You liked the bronze against the walnut paneling."

When she says, "No, I liked the ebony," you respond with, "Let me just make a note of that." Fill in the information on your order pad. If you make a mistake and they correct you, write it down and they own it. It's fun—and there's nothing to it. Just be careful not to use it more than once or they'll think you're not paying attention to what they're saying.

3. The porcupine test close.

Here's another technique you already know from previous chapters. It's a terrific test close.

The prospect says, "Does that system come with the multiplex unit on the side?"

Your answer: "Do you want your system to have the multiplex unit on the side?"

When they say yes, they've bought.

Automobiles again. She's walking through your lot looking at colors. All of a sudden, the lady stops and points at a car. "The four-on-the-floor I think I'm interested in, do you have it in that shade of blue?"

This situation occurs thousands of times a day. The average knight of the car lot says, "If we don't have it in Morning-Surf Blue, I can sure call around and get one for you in a big hurry." And what does he have? Zilch.

But you answer, "Bernice, do you want it in Morning-Surf Blue?"

What's she going to say? Bernice has already told you that she's interested in the four-on-the-floor, and she likes that color.

When she says yes, go get her the keys.

HOW TO STEER SAFELY THROUGH THE MOST DANGEROUS CLOSING TIME

What's the most dangerous time in the closing sequence?

It's when you're busy doing any kind of calculating or writing, and the silence brings on the buyers' anxieties. While you're concentrating on your scribbling, the buyers don't have anything to occupy their minds except fear. This is why Champions know their forms so well that they can flash through them while talking casually to clients and keeping them interested. You must have your paperwork down to a reflex action that won't soak up all your attention.

Most new salespeople lose their first two or three sales for just one reason: They lack the knowledge and practice to fill out their order form or sales agreement quickly. I discovered this when I was promoted to sales management. Upon realizing it, I required all new people to spend a whole afternoon just filling out forms. Then they could do it almost without thinking—certainly without concentrating fully on it and letting their prospects get cold feet.

THE CRASH-AND-BURN CLOSE

Keep the same emotional tone when you adapt all the material in this book to your own product or service. Let me illustrate what I mean with an example based on the porcupine close used as an alternate advance. Here's the sales master's version of the close:

PROSPECT: "Do you have it in blue?"
CHAMPION: "Would blue best suit your color scheme?"
PROSPECT: "Yes."
CHAMPION: "Let me make a note of that." (And he writes the information on the order form.)

When Mr. Average Salesloser adapts this close to his own product or service, here's what comes out:

PROSPECT: "Do you have it in blue?"
SALESLOSER: "If I can get it for you in blue, will you buy it?"
Not wanting to make the commitment after such an abrupt question, the prospect bows out and tries to move on to something else—like going home.
PROSPECT: "No, I don't think so. Say, uh, I didn't realize how late it's getting. Just leave your brochure and I'll call you when I have more time. Thanks for coming in."

Salesloser adapted this close like a wrecking ball adapts a brick building. The sentence "If I can get it for you in blue, will you buy it," is a say-no question that reverses a powerful positive thrust. What results is another version of the sorry old crash-and-burn. That close will put you on the street quicker than chewing gum with your mouth open.

MOVING TO THE MAJOR CLOSE

When a test close works, move softly but immediately to a major close. Most people, when they finally make up their minds, want the product now. Talking about alternatives after they've zeroed in on one thing is playing with dynamite. Don't do it or a lot of sure sales will blow up in your face.

WHAT THE ACTUAL CLOSE IS

Large numbers of people now at work in our profession (but not necessarily for much longer) don't know what a close is. Even more of our colleagues only have about two anyway. The first goes like this:

"Well, what do you think?"

If that powerhouse doesn't charge prospects with buying fever, they wait until the right opportunity comes along to jolt them with this one:

"Well, can I put you down for one?"

Now I ask you, is that closing? More like slamming the door, isn't it?

The definition of *closing* is this: professionally using people's desire to own the benefits of your product. Then blending your sincere desire to serve in helping them make decisions that are truly good for them. The key is the last three words. It must be a decision that's good for them. If it's good for them, it'll be good for you. If it's not good for them and you persuade them into it, it will be bad for you in the long run.

Having the ability to close strongly is, of course, a very good thing for you and your family because it enables you to earn a large income. There's another benefit of equal importance—closers are always in demand.

CLOSE WITH EMPATHY

When I say you must close with empathy, I don't mean that you have any difficulty closing when it's to the prospect's benefit to be closed. Because unless you have the ability to call for, and frequently get, a positive decision, everybody loses. Your family loses. Your company loses. The national economy loses. But the biggest loser is the client, who didn't get the benefits because you couldn't close.

If you don't develop this skill of calling for and getting a favorable decision that we call closing, it will probably force you out of the profession of selling. At best, you'll be able to stay in it only as an order taker. That means, of course, that you'll only earn order taker's wages. If you want to earn a professional selling income, make a commitment now to learn how to get favorable decisions.

Except for the regular purchases of everyday life, the average person can't make decisions about investing in anything without help. The reason so many people need help in making decisions is that they're afraid of making bad ones. Indecision is one of the great destroyers. It drives a few people crazy, and saps the energy out of most of us.

The one quality I find in all great human beings is their ability to make decisions. I've seen another quality in all the great people I've known: They don't have to be right all the time. They know that if they're right a good percentage of the time—and are quick to cut their losses when they're wrong—they'll prosper.

Insecurity causes procrastination, and that leads to indecision. Procrastination is the art of living in your yesterdays, avoiding your todays, and ruining your tomorrows.

Rather than involving people in insecurity, help them find their way to ownership. People love to buy after they own.

They only have challenges with indecision, insecurity, and procrastination before they own. That's why the Champion becomes skilled at making people feel that they already own their product as quickly as possible.

LIKES AND DISLIKES

Many salespeople have a challenge with their own likes and dislikes. They only sell what they like to the people they like, and make only a fraction of the best income they could achieve. Cater to your own preferences on your own time. During business hours, enthusiastically sell what the customer likes, not what you like; enthusiastically work with all types of people qualified to buy your product or service. To reach your full potential, you must expand your comfortable working zone until you can effectively help people with backgrounds and lifestyles that greatly differ from your own. If you can't work with someone because your mental outlook is too narrow, you lose. Prospects don't. They'll find someone else to supply their needs and make the money.

CLOSE THROUGH THEIR EYES

Several years ago, I attended a huge banquet for real estate agents. Before I gave my talk, the speaker introduced someone in the audience and said, "This man earned twice the national average in residential real estate sales last year—"

The speaker's manner suggested that it was quite an achievement. But it wasn't all that impressive, so everyone craned their necks and looked at the man in puzzlement.

"—and he's totally blind." There was a burst of applause. When that quieted, the speaker said, "I'm sure that many of us are wondering how you got into the top third in sales achievement with that handicap."

"Wait a minute," the blind man replied over a portable microphone, "I don't have a handicap. I have an advantage over every other salesperson in this area. I've never seen a property I've sold, so I have to close my buyers through their eyes. What I'm forced to do, all you sighted people could do—and you'd serve your clients better and make more money if you did."

It was quiet in the hall for a moment while everyone thought that over, and then there was another spontaneous round of applause for this courageous man who could hold his own selling blind, and still offer sage advice to the rest of us.

The point is, you must see the benefits, features, and limitations of your product or service from potential buyers' viewpoints; you must weigh them on the buyers' scale of values, not your own; you must close on the benefits that are of value to them.

And you must radiate the conviction that you can satisfy their needs. After you've qualified them and discovered their true motives, you must start radiating confidence that you know how to cope with their requirements. If, instead of that, you radiate a profound doubt about your ability to fill their wants, why do they need you? Buyers need to have a feeling of confidence before they can rationalize the decision they really want to make.

The last time you bought an automobile—did you spend more than you wanted to? If it was a new car, did you go into the showroom with the firm intention of not buying any extras—and drive out loaded with options? If so, you met a professional salesperson who helped you rationalize the decision you really wanted to make.

Aren't you glad when you tilt the seat back, adjust the right-hand mirror from the inside, listen to stereophonic sound, and relax in cool air when it's sweltering outside? Of course you are—and the small additional amount on your monthly investment is forgotten.

WHEN DO YOU CLOSE?

There's a certain electricity in the air when they're ready to go ahead. You will want to watch for the signs. Start your closing sequence:

- When they've been coming along at a certain pace, and suddenly they slow that pace down.
- Or when they suddenly speed that pace up.
- When they've mostly been listening, and suddenly they start asking lots of questions.
- When they give you positive stimuli at the right time. Some people come in and immediately start asking questions about delivery and initial investments before they've settled on a particular model. They know they're safe because you can't close them on the whole store. But if they ask these same questions after you know exactly what they want, it's a positive stimulus. So are questions about guarantees and

cancellation options. Use a test close after getting positive stimuli.
- When they favor your test close.

WHERE DO YOU CLOSE?

When you know they're ready, don't stand on ceremony. Close anywhere. You may think you've got to haul them up the stairs and down the hall to your office. You don't. Highlight this so you'll remember to make it part of your creed:

I am always ready to close anywhere, anytime.

Most sales are made on the hoods of cars, in restaurants, on the customer's desk, on kitchen tables, standing in display rooms, and in countless other places that are not designed primarily for closing business. For many people, there's a special excitement about executing a decision right now. Most of us feel joy at having the mental strain behind us; we see only the pleasures of ownership ahead. Don't spoil it for your people—and risk having them cool off about buying—by insisting on squishing down in your favorite swivel chair before writing up the sales agreement.

But keep in tune with their feelings. Some people can't handle the idea of approving the paperwork on the run—and if you press them to, they'll pull back, fearful that there are sinister reasons behind your haste. So close where they want to be closed, not where you want to go for that purpose.

THE ANATOMY OF THE CLOSE

Let's cut the close into pieces and see how it goes together.

1. Understand what they want and need.

- Qualify them thoroughly. Determine their emotional wants and ability to make the investment.

- Understand buyers' motives. If buyers tell you, "I just hate that," explore their feelings. Don't simply say, "I don't like it much myself," and go on talking. Find out why they hate that feature so you'll understand their motives in wanting one thing and rejecting another.

2. Recognize buying signs. People often tell you they want what you're selling by giving you signs instead of saying so. There are two kinds of signs the Champion watches for:

- Verbal. They ask more questions. They develop a need for more technical data. They talk about things that would happen if they owned your offering. Sometimes, they'll simply start making agreeable sounds all of a sudden.
- Visual. A smile can be an important buying sign. Their eyes may light up or start twinkling. If your buyers are husband and wife, they may show more affection and consideration for each other after they find the right home, car, appliance, insurance policy, or whatever. Wanting to see it demonstrated again is one of the strongest buying signs. When they say, "Will you go over that one more time," they've almost always bought it.

3. Make the decision. Decide that the best thing for them to do is to own it. Then lead them through that decision by working on things they like and feel are important. What appeals to you about your offering has no place in the picture—only what's important to them about the purchase does.

4. Close the sale with casual confidence. You've asked questions and led them to the close. Now casually start writing the order. You'll be amazed at how often that's all it takes. Unless they stop you, they've bought. If your tactics are sound and your timing is right, they won't stop you.

5. Don't change when you start closing. Speak warmly and use glamour words as you close. But don't change your tone, manner, or the pace at which you speak when you go into the closing sequence. Be very careful about this. Many salespeople do great until they see that their buyers are ready. Then they suddenly change. The warm, friendly style the buyers have become used to vanishes, and a tense, more aggressive manner takes its place.

Every time a prospect freezes up because of this sudden change and walks out without buying, that salesperson is more likely to repeat the same mistake in the next closing situation. Remember this:

If you tense up and change your manner when starting to close, the clients will know what's happening and they'll bite you. Your closes must be so thoroughly learned that you use them with relaxed alertness.

6. Use the planned pause. Champions use a very simple technique: When they want clients to really listen, they pause and look intently at the other people until they get their full attention.

THE FOURTEEN MOST IMPORTANT WORDS IN THE ART OF CLOSING

Next I'm going to give you a priceless dozen plus two. This is the most powerful pair of sentences that have ever been spoken about the complex, demanding, and enormously well-paid art of closing. Please lock these words in your memory and never forget them. If you've skimmed through this book so far and haven't marked anything yet, get your highlighter out now. Here they are:

**Whenever you ask a closing question, shut up.
The first person to speak loses.**

The paramount phrase is *shut up*. That's why J. Douglas Edwards shouted it at his audiences. I was sitting in the front row the first time I heard the fourteen words, all jumpy from the excitement of his seminar, the sleepless nights of studying it, the gallons of coffee I'd put away. When Doug shouted *Shut up*, I dove for cover. My papers flew in every direction. The moment is carved in my memory— along with the words. Those fourteen words have been the most important single element in turning my disastrous sales experience up to that time into the success it became.

Ask your closing question—then shut up. It sounds simple.

Believe me, it isn't. I know. At the time, I had a real challenge with that area—and the worst part was that I didn't have a clue as to what I was doing wrong until the moment I heard J. Douglas Edwards say those fabulous fourteen words.

The first time I tried asking a closing question and then shutting up, I was prepared for the other people's reaction. I expected them to keep silent. What I hadn't prepared for was the intensity of my own reaction: The silence hit me like a ton of wet sand. Doug Edwards said I would feel the pressure of that silence keenly, but I didn't really think it would affect me much. It did. I sat there that first time with my insides churning, biting the inside of my lip. Finally, the husband said something. They went on to own—and I never again had as much trouble sweating out the awful silence after asking a closing question.

Why is it so important to shut up and not say a word? Because if you say anything, you relieve the pressure on prospects to speak first, answer the close, and commit themselves. When you ask the closing question at anywhere near the right time, prospects have to go ahead.

Here's how it goes. You've been working with Maggie Thrush, the purchasing agent for a medium-size company, and you feel that she's ready for the close. So you say, "Mrs. Thrush, we've just about covered everything. Which would be more convenient, delivery on the first or the fifteenth of next month?"

The average salesperson can't wait more than ten seconds after asking a closing question like that. If Mrs. Thrush hasn't answered by then, he'll say something like, "Well, we can talk about that later," and go on talking, unaware that he's just destroyed the closing situation.

And it's not just that one close he's destroyed. All succeeding closing situations—if any more do come up—are doomed to failure. Mrs. Thrush can't be closed because now she knows how to escape this salesperson's closes. She merely has to keep quiet for a few seconds and he'll crack under the pressure. Mrs. Thrush can always keep quiet for a few seconds—almost all undecided buyers can. If you're Champion material, you can sit there with your mouth shut all afternoon if you have to. You'll rarely need to hold on more than thirty seconds. This is something to practice. It takes concentration because if you say anything, or even make much of a gesture, you'll relieve the pressure and blow your chances of closing.

Although having the skill, the courage, and the concentration to sit still and be silent for half a minute is the most vital single skill there is in selling—and despite the fact that this is the easiest thing there is to practice—very few people have done just that. It isn't something you can practice driving down the street, though. For it to work, you have to sit in a place you might very well be closing in and concentrate on doing nothing and saying nothing for thirty seconds. I'm very serious when I say practice this when you're alone. Then it won't be so nerve-racking when big money rides on how calm and silent you can be in a real closing situation.

YOU WEAR THE SUIT OF LIGHTS

I once watched a bullfight on TV. About three minutes into it, I began to see parallels between the broad aspects of bullfighting and selling. So come with me to the arena, where thousands of people are watching—like all the people you know are watching the progress of your sales career.

A roar goes up as a ton of live beef charges onto the sand. The bull—the client—has entered the arena.

Then the matador comes out in his "suit of lights" and all of a sudden it gets quieter—like when you go in to make your presentation. Who has the advantage now?

The bull outweighs a dozen matadors and is armed with animal fury and sharp horns. The matador at this point is armed only with a cloth cape and courageous skill. Isn't that the usual sales situation? The client has the absolute power to buy or not buy from you, and you have only your technique and courage.

You can't overpower your client for the same reason the matador can't overpower his—the strength is all on the other side. Like the matador, you must have superior skill to win against the odds you face every time you step out onto the hot sand of the sales arena.

The first thing the matador uses is the cape—to lead the bull. This is what I'm advocating that you do with your prospects. Lead them with questions. Develop a sense in them of your expertise on your offering.

When your prospect snorts, stamps the ground, and then charges at you, do you meet that charge head-on? Not unless you want to be carried out on a stretcher. Of course, your wounds won't be visible. You'll walk out on your own two feet. But you'll be hurt in your pocketbook, confidence, and pride.

No, you don't clash heads when your prospect charges into you. Instead, you step aside like a matador and let the prospect run. You listen to his grunts and stompings and watch which way he hooks with his horns. And then you work with him, getting closer all the time, leading with questions and more questions.

Tell me more, he says. *Tell me more*, you think. You ask and you answer. You use your cape with exquisite technique and finesse, and in a predetermined sequence gain control of your more powerful opponent.

To hold the crowd's admiration and end the match cleanly, the matador must go in over the bull's horns at exactly the right time and put the tip of his sword through a point the size of a quarter. That's a good description of what the skillful closing of a large and difficult sale is. Both in bullfighting and in sales, the time of greatest danger comes at the close of the performance, and the matador's final thrust is much like your final close. For the unskilled, the unpracticed, the unprepared, the close in selling is like the matador's estocada over the horns of a fighting bull. In both cases, it's all or nothing—the only things that count are knowledge, technique, and courage.

One question I've asked many times: "How many closes do you try before you succeed?"

Among the great ones, it averages out at about five closes. That is, the great ones usually close after their fifth attempt. You can immediately see from this extremely important bit of information that if the great ones have to use five closes to succeed, you're not going to get very far in sales if you only know two closes—or none. If they have more reasons for not going ahead than you have techniques for helping them go ahead, they aren't going ahead. It's that simple.

Learn these closes conceptually. Then learn them word for word.

Adapt them to your needs. Then learn your adaptations word for word. You're probably fighting the idea of doing all this work. I know. I fought it, too, at first. But just remember that there's an alternative to learning and growing and paying the full price of switching to success—you can try to stay just as you are. Good luck—the world is rapidly changing all around you.

17. Sixteen Power Closes for Aspiring Champions

I prefer short chapters in my books. However, this won't be one of them. It will be one of the longest chapters in the book. That's because I'm going to give you a bunch of closes to use as needed in your selling situations. Make a mental note that chapter 17 has all the closes you'll need for quite some time. They'll all be right here. Every time you master one of these closes and use it, you'll increase your sales by at least 10 percent. It's possible that you may double your sales with each close that you master. You may even do better than that. Some have.

Some of these techniques may not apply to your particular field of sales. Most of them will. I've tried to include the closes that apply to the widest range of products and services here. I'd have to write another whole book on closing to give you all of my forty-two closes. Adapt every one that you possibly can, and then practice your adaptations until you can use them with conviction, warmth, and flair while planning your next move.

Suppose you can only use ten of these closes, and each one of them, on the average, increases your sales by only 10 percent. That means you've doubled your sales volume. So let's get to them!

POWER CLOSE NUMBER ONE:
THE BASIC ORAL CLOSE

This is used primarily for industrial, commercial, and governmental sales. When you've defined the needs you can fill, ask this question:

"By the way, what purchase order number will be assigned to this requisition?"

When they tell you they don't know, smile and say, "Why don't we find out?"

In most of these situations—industrial, commercial, and governmental sales—you haven't made the sale until you get "the PO number." So start hunting for that number at the first reasonable moment.

POWER CLOSE NUMBER TWO:
THE BASIC WRITTEN CLOSE, AKA THE
"LET ME MAKE A NOTE OF THAT" CLOSE

This is an effective close if you use an order form. Walk in with a leather binder for a letter- or legal-size ruled pad. Have an order form there under a cardboard separator to protect it. This allows you to flip to it instantly when the time is right. My favorite way to work with this close is to answer a question of theirs with one of my own.

PROSPECT: "Does it come in walnut?"

CHAMPION: "Is that the wood grain that you'd like?"

PROSPECT: "Yes, that's the color I'd prefer."

CHAMPION: "Let me make a note of that." Then write that bit of information on your order form.

PROSPECT: "What are you doing? I'm not ready to give you an order."

CHAMPION: "Mrs. Palmer, I organize my thoughts and keep everything in the proper perspective. I do that on the paperwork so I don't forget anything." (If it suits your product or service, add: "particularly anything that could cost you time or money.")

Then roll on to the next close. Go into every closing sequence by asking a reflex question. A reflex question, you'll remember, is any question they can answer without thinking.

CHAMPION: "Mary, do you have a middle initial?"
PROSPECT: "It's H."

For corporate executives, a good reflex question is to ask for their company's complete name and correct address. If they hand you their card and let you copy that information on your order form, they've bought what you're selling.

Let's run this close through an industrial situation. You sell machinery, and Mr. Zale is your prospect.

MR. ZALE: "Yes, we'd need the heavy-duty gearbox."
CHAMPION: "Let me make a note of that."
MR. ZALE: "Are you putting that on your order form? You're getting ahead of yourself. I haven't decided to buy it yet."
CHAMPION: "Mr. Zale, I organize my thoughts to keep everything in proper perspective. I do that on the paperwork so I don't forget anything."
MR. ZALE: "You're probably wasting your time. At this point, the odds are against me buying from your company."
CHAMPION: "Oh, I know that. But I just don't like to risk forgetting anything—particularly anything that might cost you time or money."
MR. ZALE: "Well, I guess I can't quarrel with that."

Perhaps you think you'd be better off making your notes on the legal pad so you could save yourself the hassle. If you decide to do that, you've also decided to demote yourself from salesperson to order taker. Let them stop you. It helps, not hurts, to have them understand that you're a strong seller who's there to do a job, not a pencil nibbler who doesn't know how to make things move.

Keep filling out that order form. By the time you've gone through your entire presentation, it's going to be almost entirely filled out. In many cases, the forward momentum you've developed by completing your order form will be enough to get it approved. It becomes the easiest thing for the prospect to do. Once your pen touches your order form, your run for home begins. The problem with most salespeople is that they won't start writing during the sales interview.

POWER CLOSE NUMBER THREE:
THE BENJAMIN FRANKLIN BALANCE SHEET CLOSE

When I was involved in the high-intensity five-day seminar with J. Douglas Edwards, we had a contest in the form of an examination on the last day. I wanted to win that contest. So I sat up, studied late, and got by on about two hours of sleep a night. The item that won the contest for me was the Ben Franklin balance sheet close.

Salespeople frequently tell me that they've heard of this close. Some think it's old hat. When they say that, I ask, "Do you use it?"

Almost always, they say no. This never ceases to amaze me because this is the close that made the biggest difference in my own real estate sales career. Maybe I shouldn't be amazed, because I fought it at first—but I did try it. Not only did I try it, I made it work and I still use it. Always remember this: If you've qualified them, if they need your offering, if you know what you're selling and if you're strong in your tactics, they can fight you, but they can't win. You'll win—because it's the right decision for them.

By the way, I really do depend on this technique for arriving at many decisions in my private and business life. Here's the Ben Franklin balance sheet close:

1. Validate it with good old Ben. If you went to elementary school in the United States, you'll remember studying Benjamin Franklin's life and epic achievements. On his way to eternal fame, he made thousands of wise decisions. This close is based on the actual way he arrived at decisions, and much of its persuasiveness comes from our respect for his name. That's why you'll introduce it by invoking his name.

2. Learn the exact words. Do that first, and then let your adaptation come naturally. Here are the words:

"As you know, Mary, we Americans have long considered Benjamin Franklin one of our wisest men. Whenever old Ben found himself in a situation such as you're in today, he felt pretty much as you do about it. If it was the right thing, he wanted to be sure and do it. If it was the wrong thing, he wanted to be sure and avoid it. Isn't that about the way you feel, too?

"Here's what old Ben used to do. He'd take a sheet of plain paper and draw a line down the middle. On this side he wrote yes, and under that he'd list all the reasons favoring the decision. Then, under no, he'd list all the reasons against the decision. When he was through, he simply counted the columns and his decision was made for him.

"Why don't we try it and see what happens? Let's see how many reasons we can think of that favor your decision today."

Take a piece of paper and start listing all the benefits you've discovered that appeal to your prospect—that is, all the selling points that you and she have agreed on. When the two of you have written down all the yeses, here's what you say:

"Now let's see how many reasons you can think of against it." And you let the prospect handle this part of it on her own. It's no part of your business to help her list negatives. When that's completed, move forward with:

"Now let's count them." (Do it out loud.) "One, two, three . . . twelve. That's twelve on the yes side. And on the no side we have, one, two, three, four, five. Twelve yeses and five nos. Well, the wise decision is pretty obvious, isn't it?"

Don't hesitate more than a split second here. Go right into a reflexive closing question:

"By the way, what is your full name?"

If she gives it to you now, she owns your product or service.

Here's the Ben Franklin close as done in a corporation executive's office:

". . . so you can see that adding the JLG Lift to your facility might be a wise decision, can't you?"

Frank replies, "Well, Tom, this is a pretty expensive investment here. I don't know—it's not that I have any trouble making decisions—"

"I'm sure not. You make decisions on this level all day long, of course."

Frank mutters absently, "Yeah."

I can see that he really doesn't want to bite the bullet. He's impressed with the JLG Lift. He needs it. The numbers work out. He knows his company will profit greatly by having this lift—but he's hoping for a way out of committing himself. In other words, he's behaving like a typical buyer. So I call on old Ben:

"Could it possibly be, Frank, that one of the problems is that you haven't had a chance to weigh the facts involved?"

"Yes," Frank says. "I think that I haven't really gotten down to the nub of this thing yet."

"Well, a decision is only as good as the facts, isn't that right?"

"I believe that's true," Frank says.

"You know, it's interesting—a while back I was reminded of someone we Americans have long considered one of our wisest men—Benjamin Franklin."

"Oh, Tom—you're not going to pull the old Ben Franklin close on me, are you?" Frank laughs out loud. "I used to be in insurance. I heard about that one in a seminar a long time ago."

That doesn't bother me because I know it's likely to happen once in a while. I go along with it. "You know what's amazing?"

"What's that?" Frank says, still chuckling.

"When I first heard about the technique, I wasn't sure about it, either. Let me ask you this, did you try it? Did you use it selling insurance?"

"Oh, no," Frank says. "I never used it." (It actually doesn't matter much whether he did or not. My purpose here is to relieve tension and then lead him on through the close. If he has experiences with this technique to relate, fine. If not, it's still fine. In either case, I'm going to move ahead.)

"It's a funny thing," I tell Frank. "I decided to try Ben's system not only in my business life, but on personal questions, too—and pretty soon I had my whole family using it to make all sorts of decisions. It's amazing how it simplifies and clarifies decisions. We started making some excellent ones. Do you remember how it goes?"

"I remember—you draw a line and you put the yeses on one side, and the nos on the other."

"Right. On this side you list all the reasons favoring the decision, and on the other side, all those that weigh against the decision."

"Yeah, right," Frank says.

The important thing here is to keep going with the flow of the conversation, rather than to try to stick rigidly with a set of words you've learned. When you've mastered the material, you can wander on both sides of the path and still get where you're going.

I continue with, "Ben Franklin said if it's the right thing to do, he wanted to be sure he knew about it so he could go ahead. And if it was the wrong thing, he wanted to be sure to avoid it. Isn't that more or less what you're going to do now? Analyze the decision and get down to the nub of it, as you put it?"

Frank shrugs. "Yeah, that's what it boils down to."

"So you're going to list all the reasons favoring the decision on one side, and all those against the decision on the other side. Then you'd do as old Ben would do: Add up the columns and the decision is made for you."

"Well, I'd like to think my method of analysis is a bit more sophisticated than that."

"I'm sure it is. But if the reasons for and against are sound, a count of them would certainly point the way toward the right decision, wouldn't it?"

"Well, I suppose so."

"We both know the Ben Franklin method. It's logical. It's simple. Emotionally, at this point, I think we ought to try it. May we?"

"Well—" Frank lets it hang.

"We've got the time, haven't we? A couple of minutes—"

"Yeah, okay."

"Let's start it off here. Let's think of the reasons favoring the decision," I say. "We agreed originally that if one person in the basket could operate the whole vehicle and eliminate the need for the second operator, you'd realize a large savings in labor cost. Isn't that right?"

"Yes, it is," Frank says.

"And I sent a man out for one purpose only, you'll remember, to measure all your doors. So we know that the JLG can get to every part of your facility."

"Right—it fits through all our doors," Frank says.

"I made sure of every one of them."

"All right—that's an important point."

"The biggest challenge that a lot of hydraulic equipment has—I know you're aware of this—is in the seals. The hydraulic seals. That's why the JLG has the finest heavy-duty seals that are available."

"No leaking?" Frank asks.

"No, none."

"All right."

"The JLG is far more agile. It can go into smaller spaces and get the work done."

"Okay."

"And it's got a smaller turning radius."

"Yeah, that's a factor. We've got some narrow squeezes at the end of aisles."

"Multiple uses in maintenance" is my next yes point. "For maintaining your facility—how many uses do you have for that lift? The eighty-foot boom if you wanted it, the twenty-foot—the JLG has outstanding versatility, don't you agree?"

"All right. Put it down."

"Local servicing is available. Now, that'll cut out a lot of downtime, and you know how much it costs to have a machine sitting waiting for any type of maintenance or repair."

"Yeah, that's true," Frank says.

"We were looking at the tax benefits. We felt that a lease might be better than purchase because of the tax savings, and of course keeping the cash flow—"

"Okay."

"If you decide to build the warehouse, Frank, you won't have to worry about not having the finest crane equipment. We've got them. It's not like we give you the lift and say good-bye. No way. We stick with you. Let me think, can you come up with any others, Frank?"

"Well, your lift has higher maximum load capabilities than the others."

"Okay, we'll put that down. Now, Frank, how many reasons can you now come up with on the negative side?"

Frank thinks for a moment and then says, "Well, okay, number one, this is not planned in our current budget. And what about our present equipment? I'd want to do something with it because I know how the guys in the plant are—if the JLG was busy, they'd just wait for it instead of using the old klunker we've got now. So I'd have to get rid of it—sell it or trade it in."

"Those are both valid points, Frank. Okay. Any others?"

After a pause, it's apparent that Frank isn't coming up with any more objections. As you can see, both his points are really money issues. I don't want to get into that right at this moment, so I say, "Why don't we just add them up?"

I count out loud and announce the results: nine yeses and two nos. "Frank, don't you really think that the answer is rather obvious?"

I expect to wait through a long silence now. The key thought here is to shut my mouth. Frank doesn't disappoint me. There isn't a sound in the room for some time while Frank thinks this over. At last he speaks, "I'll tell you something, Tom. I'm the kind of guy who just has to think it over."

Could you pick up off this cold printed page how nicely and warmly this technique was delivered? That's how techniques should all be handled: in a relaxed and alert, friendly and respect- ful, confident and competent manner. Now, you know he sees that the JLG Lift would be great for his company. He's just stalling the decision by wanting to "think it over." That stall is one of the most common concerns you'll hear in your career. Don't ever let it bring your sales process to a screaming halt. It's too vague. You need something specific that's holding him back. You need the "I want to think it over" close.

POWER CLOSE NUMBER FOUR:
THE "I WANT TO THINK IT OVER" CLOSE

Nearly all of your potential clients will try to slow things down by making one of the following statements:

"I'll think it over."

"We want to sleep on it."

"We don't jump into things."

"Let us mull this thing over."

"Leave your information and we'll consider it."

"Why don't you come back tomorrow [next week, after the holidays] and we'll let you know."

When you hear any of those lines after you've learned this close, you'll think, *I own this one.* They expect you to say okay and leave, because that's what the average salesperson does. If you do that, will they think it over? In a word, no. As soon as you leave, new things will come up. The prospect will forget about your proposition.

Then suddenly it's tomorrow, next week, or after the holidays. You come back and ask, "Did you run my proposal through your think machine like you said you would?"

They don't want to tell you the truth because they would have to say something like, "No, we haven't had time to give it a second thought. We're exactly where we were when you were here last." If they say that, they sound inefficient. So what do they say?

"Yes, we gave your proposal very careful consideration, and I'm sorry but we're not going on it now. We'll keep your proposal on file, and if anything changes, I'll call you."

What can you do? Nothing. You're dead—because you allowed the momentum of the sale to die.

Here's what the Champion does when they play the old "I want to think it over" number:

1. Agree with them.

"That's fine, Harry. Obviously, you wouldn't take your time thinking this thing over unless you were seriously interested, would you?"

What will they say? "Oh, we're interested. You bet. We're going to think it over."

It helps to give them a brave little smile and act defeated as you ask the question.

2. Confirm the fact that they're going to think it over.

"Since you're this interested, may I assume that you'll give it very careful consideration?" Speak the last three words slowly, with just a touch of emphasis.

What will they say? Because you're acting like you're leaving, you're letting go, they'll say yes.

3. Clarify and twist harder.

"Just to clarify my thinking, what is it that you wanted to think over is it the integrity of my company?" Notice how I ran those two separate sentences together. More about this later.

What'll they say?

"No, your company is great."

"Is it the level of service I'll provide?"

"Oh, no, we think you're the greatest," Harry says.

"Is it the lift's capability to handle your loads?"

"No, no. We agreed on that. It'll handle it."

"Is it the agility of the lift?"

"No, that's fine, too."

Every time they say no, they're in essence saying yes, aren't they? This technique allows you to summarize the benefits that you're offering them, and to do it with subtlety and finesse. Don't argue. Don't tell them. Ask.

What do you ask them about?

You ask them about every benefit or feature your prospect wants that you can supply.

"Is it the speed of the lift?" you ask.

"No. As a matter of fact, I think the speed of your lift is a real plus."

Ask questions that'll cause them to tell you how good your product or service is. There's no better way to convince them of its merits.

What will people do when you've learned this technique and are working it effectively on them? They'll say to themselves, *I know what he's doing.* So what will they grab?

One of the objections. Once they grab one, what do you have?

The final objection.

Now, if they were going along with you at all, what should you normally come up on last?

The money.

"Is it the investment that's involved in purchasing the JLG Lift?"

What'll they usually say? "Well, we don't put out that kind of money without really doing a lot of considering."

"So the challenge really is money, isn't that right?"

"Yeah, that's it."

So what have I accomplished? Quite a lot. I've broken through the think-it-over-and-forget-it routine. Now I'm down to the real objection, which is money.

That's nothing new, is it? Money is the major objection we have to face on every, or nearly every, sale, unless we eliminated it during the qualification sequence.

The problem with *think-it-over* is that it's too big an objection. It's a whole colony of ghosts, and there's nothing to grab on to. Smoke those ghosts out as we've done above, get down to the final objection, and then you'll be able to use the six steps for closing on a final objection from chapter 14.

But please, be careful when they give you the old *think-it-over* routine. Don't say to yourself, *Okay, it's really the dollars*, and put all your money on one roll of the dice by going straight for, "Is it the money?"

Why not?

If you ask them that first, they'll say, "No, it's not the money; we just want to think about the whole proposition."

Since you're almost certain that money really is their final objection, all you can do now is go away—or stay awhile and chase yourself around in circles with pointless "Is it—?" questions. Your only hope is to eventually lead them back to the money, and then close on that final objection. In this situation, it almost takes a miracle for that to happen.

This close, like the others, works only if you follow the steps and use it right. Shortcuts cut your throat.

There's a critical instant in this close that comes when you say, "Just to clarify my thinking, what is it that you wanted to think over

is it my company's integrity?" Remember that a pause between
over and *is* will often be pure disaster. Don't turn this most important element of the close into two sentences: ". . . what is it that you
wanted to think over? Is it my company's integrity?" Don't pause or
even raise your tone to indicate a question after the word *over*.

Why is this important? Because if you pause, they'll say, "I want
to think over the whole proposition." And you have nothing to grab
on to.

4. Confirm that it's the money. You've got to make sure that
you're not dancing with phantoms anymore. There's no point in
trying to close on the money problem if they aren't sure they'd buy
it even if it's a wise money decision for them. What do they care
what it costs if they don't want it?

When it seems to be down to money, you're very near pay dirt if
you handle it right—so handle it right. Ask them if there's anything
else they're unsure of except the money. Confirm that you're at the
final barrier before busting through it with our next close.

POWER CLOSE NUMBER FIVE:
THE REDUCTION-TO-THE-RIDICULOUS CLOSE

Have you ever heard, "It's higher than we wanted to go"? I have—
hundreds of times. And I never sold much until I learned how to turn
this stall into a close.

We salespeople tend to look at the total investment when we're
hit with the *it-costs-too-much* concern. That's big trouble. Go for
the difference instead. For example, you're selling high-speed office copiers. The total investment required is ten thousand dollars.

The first step is to find out how much too much it is. When they
express the idea that it costs too much, say in a warm and pleasant
way, "Today, it seems most things do. Can you tell me about how
much too much you feel it is?"

Let's suppose that the prospects say they've only budgeted
eight thousand dollars for the copier. The money challenge isn't
ten thousand dollars, is it? They never expected to get your product or service for nothing. No, the challenge in this case is only
two thousand. That's what you focus on—the difference—the

smaller amount. Once you determine what the difference is, stop talking about total investment.

Let's work through our example on high-speed copiers. Your prospect is Ruby Wellman. She's interested in the model that involves a total investment of ten thousand dollars. Ruby budgeted only eight thousand. Here we go.

"So really, we're talking about two thousand dollars, aren't we, Ruby?"

"Yes, it's two thousand dollars too high."

"All right. My thought here is that we should be careful to put this into proper perspective. Here."

Hand her your calculator. "Let's just say that, hypothetically, you own the SuperPow copier. Do you think you'd keep it for five years?"

"That's about right," Ruby says.

"Okay, divide two thousand dollars by five years and we get four hundred dollars a year, don't we? Now, your company would use the SuperPow all the time, right? Assuming your office is closed for most national holidays, you would use the copier for fifty weeks a year, right? If you'll take four hundred dollars and divide it by fifty—we get eight dollars, don't we?"

Of course, the figures you'll actually be working with won't round out so neatly—that's why you ask the prospect to figure them on your calculator. Bear in mind that having them use your calculator is physical involvement.

We continue: "I understand that there's a lot of weekend work in this office, a lot of overtime, so I think it might be reasonable to say that the copier would be in use six days a week. Okay? Would you please divide eight dollars by six? And we get—?"

Ruby says, "$1.33."

You smile and say, "Do you think we should let $1.33 a day stand between your company and the profits, the increased production, and the expanded capabilities that the SuperPow will bring you?"

"Well, I don't know."

"Ruby, may I ask what the lowest-paid entry-type job in this office is, and roughly how much it pays?"

"The clerks get about eight dollars per hour. That's about the bottom."

"About eight dollars. So the $1.33 a day that we're talking about will buy just over an hour of work from your lowest-paid helper."

"Well, if you put it that way, yes."

"Ruby, let me ask you one more thing. Won't this high-speed machine with all its sophisticated capabilities and timesaving features—all the benefits we talked about—won't this machine make more profit for your company in a whole day than a clerk can in twenty minutes?"

"Yes, I think it will."

"Then we've agreed, haven't we? By the way, which delivery date would best suit your time schedule—the first, or the fifteenth?"

Are you thinking something like, *Wow, I couldn't do that.*

Why couldn't you?

Money is an objection you're going to encounter frequently in sales. That being so, can you reach your full potential without learning how to cope with it? Of course not. So adapt this technique to your offering, work out the bugs with a friend, memorize every word, get the numbers down pat, and *use it.* Your sales results will show a startling difference.

If you really have a hang-up with any of these closes, decide that it's okay to fail with them while you're learning, but it's not okay to avoid learning and using them. Make it your goal to use each one ten times. If you try each close ten times, you'll have some success. Try each one ten more times and you'll have a lot of success. Try each one a third set of ten times and you'll be flying high, eating well, and ordering custom-made clothes.

If you've qualified potential clients and they need the benefits, you have the right to reduce their final objection to the ridiculous. Ignore the time periods that don't apply to what you're doing. When you walk into a presentation, you probably won't know what the difference is that you'll be reducing with that particular client—but you will know the time period, won't you? If you're selling office machines, you'll try for five years; if you're selling elevators to hotels, you'll go for forty years.

Make knowing the figures easy for yourself: Use one key number. If you represent SuperPow Copiers, all you need to remember is sixty-seven cents, because that's what a thousand dollars reduces to over a five-year period.

If they hit you with a difference of two thousand, you simply double sixty-seven cents in your head and come up with a dollar thirty-three. Before they can calculate the answer, you know what it should be, and if they've made a mistake, you can lead them through it again smoothly to eliminate the error instead of retreating in confusion.

Now let's suppose that you're selling elevators using the forty-year period. A thousand-dollar difference amounts to only seven cents a day if they're in use daily. What's exciting is that a million-dollar difference costs them less than seventy dollars a day on the forty-year line. (Just move the figure in the $10,000 column two decimal points to the right to get the rounded number for $1,000,000.) Know your figures. They're fantastic.

Let me give you a cautionary note on the reduction close: You must know the figures. With a calculator, you can easily work out a table like the one below for your product or service.

TABLE OF AMOUNTS
REDUCED TO THE RIDICULOUS
(COST PER DAY)
(Based on 50-week year, 7-day week.)

PERIOD	AMOUNT REDUCED		
	$100	$1,000	$10,000
3 years	10 cents	95 cents	$9.52
5 years	6 cents	57 cents	$5.71
10 years	3 cents	29 cents	$2.86
25 years	1 cent	11 cents	$1.14
40 years	—	7 cents	71 cents

POWER CLOSE NUMBER SIX:
THE SHARP-ANGLE CLOSE

The sharp-angle close carries the porcupine technique (discussed earlier) to a higher level of effectiveness. Instead of merely answering your prospect's question with a question, as in the standard porcupine, answer with one that, if they reply the way their original question hints they will, assumes they've bought it.

In this example of sharp-angling, you're leading Mr. Zale toward buying a batch mixer.

> MR. ZALE: "If we decided to go with your product, we'd have to take delivery by June 15. Could you handle that?" (Most salespeople would be tempted to jump in, say yes, and have nothing. Note how a professional takes advantage of this opportunity.)
>
> CHAMPION: "If I could guarantee delivery by June 15, are you prepared to approve the paperwork today?"

The Champion, of course, now remains silent until Mr. Zale answers.

In order to use the sharp-angle close, you first have to watch for them to make a demand or express a desire that you can meet. There are many demands or desires (that is, needs) that you can sharp-angle besides delivery. Getting an order in before a price increase takes effect is a powerful one. Credit terms, installation assistance, and color choice are others. Almost any benefit that people want can be sharp-angled.

Favorable delivery is the benefit that's easiest to sharp-angle in most sales organizations because it's the most predictable. And because it's a universal situation, the delivery question lends itself to further detailing of the sharp-angling idea. Bear in mind that the principles suggested are easily applied to whatever benefit you can most effectively sharp-angle to sell your product or service.

Sharp-angling involves two pivotal points:

1. You must know what benefits you can deliver.
2. You have to know how to pan the gold from that information.

I've already shown you how to handle 2. Now let's talk about 1. Using the information is the easy part; getting it is about 99 percent of the battle. I want to emphasize this point:

Champions develop superior sources for sharp-angling information because they understand what a powerful closing lever this information is.

I'm going to continue to talk about sharp-angling information as though it were the same thing as delivery, but again I remind you that other benefits may provide you with better sharp-angling tools than being able to offer favorable delivery.

POWER CLOSE NUMBER SEVEN: THE SECONDARY-QUESTION CLOSE

When used at the right moment with the right people, this close is excellent!

Here's the technique: Pose the major decision with a question, and without pausing add another question that is an alternate advance involvement question.

I'll give you an example that'll make it clear. You're walking around the plant with the head man at Frankly Better Products, a manufacturing operation. Frank is pondering whether to buy a JLG Lift from you. Sensing that the moment is right for the secondary-question close, you say,

"As I see it, Frank, the only decision we have to make today is how soon you'll start enjoying the increased efficiency the JLG Lift will create for you—by the way, are you going to use it in your main plant or your new warehouse?"

Let's try the secondary-question technique on a service you're selling.

"As I see it, Marilyn, the only decision we have to make today is how soon you'll start enjoying the increased profits that a happier staff will make for you—by the way, are you going to pipe the music into your offices and warehouse only, or to the entire plant?"

You can easily adapt this format to any product or service. The major decision is introduced with these words:

"As I see it, the only decision we have to make today is how soon . . ."

The major decision is then followed, without pause, by the secondary question that you introduce with these words:

"By the way . . ."

To use the secondary-question close successfully, you must:

1. State the major decision in terms of a benefit to the client.

"The only decision . . . is how soon you'll start enjoying [the benefit]." Never pose the major decision in negative terms: ". . . how soon you'll stop losing money . . ." Or, even worse yet, in aggressive terms that are thinly disguised by an attempt at humor: ". . . how soon you'll get on the ball and start saving money by ordering from me."

2. Avoid any pause between posing the major decision and asking the secondary question.

3. State the secondary question in terms of an alternate advance involvement question. Let's review that. An alternate advance is any question that indicates a choice of answers, all of which confirm that they're going ahead. An involvement question is one that requires them to make ownership decisions.

Now, you don't really care whether Frank uses your JLG Lift in the plant or the warehouse, do you? But when he thinks about where he'll use it, he's thinking about some of the choices he'll have after he owns your product. So that one sentence is both an alternate advance and an involvement question, isn't it? That gives it double-barreled sales power.

4. Prepare your complete close in advance. It may require some effort to create a secondary question for your offering that packs as much selling force into so few words as the example above does. That effort will be repaid many times over. I doubt that there is any other sales activity that can make you more money in less time than developing an effective secondary-question close. When you've worked out your complete close, memorize the words until you can roll them off effortlessly. Losers wing it; winners prepare.

5. Use the casual format given here. The introductory phrases not only keep this close organized in your mind, but also help you deliver the close properly. Delivery is so important that I'm going to emphasize it below:

6. Deliver the close in a relaxed and alert manner. Practice this close so that you can say it clearly and casually. Otherwise your art will be obvious—and unlikely to succeed.

The purpose of all this, of course, is to get Frank to answer something like, "Well, I guess we'd better assign it to the new warehouse because they'll use it all the time. We'll only be using it in the main plant once or twice a shift." When Frank says that, he's bought.

The casual approach is the cornerstone of sales success. By *casual*, I don't mean careless. You must cultivate an alert but nonchalant attitude that people feel comfortable with. Learn to be relaxed without seeming impertinent or inefficient; learn to be alert without seeming nosy or officious. In a word, be competent.

We ask questions not to threaten, but to get next-step information. We ask the questions in a warm and nice way. If we see that we're threatening the other person, that we're building tension, we back off. When the pressure is off, we try again.

You must learn many closes because you have to know more ways to get yes than they know ways to say no. If you don't outgun them here, you're dead. This book would be worth a million dollars to you if I could give you one close that would work every time. There'll never be one close that will work every time. If one close worked even a quarter of the time, so many people would jump on it that overuse would ruin it within days.

All Champions are multiclosers. This is just difficult enough to keep the uninspired majority from paying the price for this entrée to sales and financial success. But you don't need a towering intellect to become a multicloser; all you need is the determination to organize your time so that you learn several closes thoroughly. It's really that basic. I'm always amazed at how few salespeople will pay this price—a ridiculously low one in comparison with other professions—for becoming skilled enough to earn a professional's income in their chosen field. In sales, it's the sharp scissor of competition that cuts away the incompetent. Ours is a free field. This means that you're free to succeed, and you're free to fail. As you tell the world you're a professional salesperson, dedicate yourself to mastering your art: Invest the time and effort that's required to:

Learn multiple closes.

Let's say that I just used the Ben Franklin balance sheet close and the client hit me with, "I'll think it over."

If I can't handle that, I'm in trouble—I'm not going to make that sale that day. This means that I probably won't ever make it. Now is always more certain than later.

BRIDGING

How do you get across the creek that runs between a close that didn't work and the next one you want to try? You build a bridge. Here's how:

1. Apologize. Especially if you feel you've pressed a little too hard, back off with a quick apology. I used to say, "I'm sorry. I just got carried away. I didn't mean to move so rapidly." What you're really doing is apologizing to yourself for not making the close. Don't worry about it. All it means is you get a chance to practice another of your many closes.

In this situation, one of our Champions says, "I didn't mean to push you." He is sincere in apologizing because a Champion doesn't push--he pulls. That is, he pulls by leading with questions.

2. Summarize the benefits they've already agreed to, using tie-downs. Play it safe, and aim only for minor agreements right now.

- "I know there are still a lot of questions in your mind, but this model is the size you wanted, isn't it?"
- "You wouldn't let me in your office if you weren't interested, would you?"

- "So all I'm trying to say is that the JLG Lift seems to meet your needs, doesn't it?"

3. Ask a lead-in question. Complete your bridging to the next closing sequence by asking a lead-in question. I used to say it this way: "I know I went through that rather rapidly, but those are the things we've discussed thus far, and we've agreed on them, haven't we?"

Now you're set for your next close. If you keep using this technique to roll into your next close, eventually they will own what you're there to sell them. Why?

Because you know more closes than they know objections. Won't that be an exciting change?

It will if you've been losing because your prospects all just naturally react with more negatives than you have positives. But is it ever fun when you know more ways to get them to say yep than they know ways to say nix. That's when you're the champ.

POWER CLOSE NUMBER EIGHT: THE "MY-DEAR-OLD-MOTHER" CLOSE

This is a cute one. In the right situation, it'll really shake the apples out of the tree. To use it, you have to talk to someone's mother—your own, if possible; someone else's, if not.

You first ask Mother to repeat some advice she probably gave you years ago that you've forgotten. So ask her, "Mom, would you tell me, word for word, that silence means consent?" After she's told you that, mind your mother. (It's absolutely essential to go through these steps by talking to your mother—or someone's mother—before you use this technique. Unless you demand honesty of yourself, you can't project a convincing image of integrity.) Here's how you use Mother's advice:

Let's go back to J. Douglas Edwards's statement: "Whenever you ask a closing question, shut up. The first person who speaks, loses."

That's very sound advice. Between 90 and 95 percent of the time, if you go against it and speak first, you'll lose. So don't go against it until you've risen far above the average and can start going for that last 5 or 10 percent, until you've learned when the tension hurts the close instead of making it, until you've learned a way to break the tension and still close. That's where dear old Mother comes in.

This technique can be your salvation when you find yourself involved in a series of silences as you roll from close to close with the same prospect. If you have a clever way to break tension, pressure turns into humor. Lots of people can handle pressure, but laughter will pop them wide open.

So when the pressure of silence doesn't seem to be getting you anywhere, grin from ear to ear and say, "My dear old mother once said, 'Silence means consent.' Was she right?"

The potential clients will usually laugh, and laughing is just like talking—it means you've won, you're closing. It's a minor technique that's only for the special situations where your intuition tells you it's right. It breaks the tension and it works.

But don't use it until you've talked to Mother.

POWER CLOSE NUMBER NINE: THE PUPPY-DOG CLOSE

If you use this one, it'll send you cruising around the world in the best cabin on the ship. The puppy dog is something of a paradox because it's the most powerful closing sequence known for many products and services, yet in reality it eliminates the need to close. So it flies in the face of everything I've been telling you about closing. The buyers close themselves. All you have to do is be sure that you use it on the right people. And you have to be selling a top-quality product or service. If you've got that going for you, stand back and watch the money roll in.

Here's how this close works. You sell your product or service just like it was a puppy dog. How do you sell a cuddly little puppy?

You let them take it home with them.

Then what happens? That puppy puts its wet nose against their cheek. It stares at them with its big, soft eyes. It whimpers when they leave. The kids adore him—and suddenly there's no way they'll let you take their puppy away from them. It's really that simple.

POWER CLOSE NUMBER TEN: THE SIMILAR-SITUATION CLOSE

When you find yourself working with someone who has a concern similar to one you've already overcome, you can tell them about the previous situation. Champions take a few moments after making every sale to document what the situation was, what was said, and how it was resolved. They keep in touch with satisfied clients and know how well the product is performing for them and the benefits they have gained. Champions have the facts documented. When they pull a memo out of their briefcase that shows how another company solved the same challenge, the prospect is impressed—and convinced.

POWER CLOSE NUMBER ELEVEN: THE "IT ISN'T IN THE BUDGET" CLOSE

Here's one that must be in the repertoire of every salesperson calling on companies, institutions, or governmental agencies during times of tight money. It's designed to be used when you're working with the president or owner of a business, or with an upper-management executive (such as a CFO or COO) in a large company or institution.

When you're told that your product or service isn't in the budget, respond in a cordial manner with these words: "Of course it isn't. That's why I contacted you in the first place." Don't pause here. But how you proceed depends on whether you're selling to a profit-seeking company or a nonprofit organization. Let's look at the commercial and industrial application first.

Continuation for use with companies: "I'm fully aware that every well-managed business firm controls its money with a carefully planned budget. Am I also right in assuming that the chief executive of a productive, trendsetting company such as yours uses that budget as a guideline, not as an inflexible anchor?

"So you, as the chief executive, retain for yourself the right to flex that budget in the interest of your company's financial present and competitive future, isn't that right?

"What we have been discussing is a system that will give [name the buyer's company] an immediate and continuing competitive edge. Tell me, Mr. Chamberlain, under these conditions will your budget flex—or is it an anchor?"

Continuation for nonprofit institutions and governmental agencies: "I'm fully aware that every well-managed institution controls its money with a carefully planned budget. I'm also aware that your office [agency, institution, district] is very responsive to the public's rapidly changing needs. Isn't it true that you have this reputation?"

After the response, go on with, "This means that you, as the chief executive of such an effective organization, must be using the budget more as a guideline for expenditures than as an inflexible anchor. How else could your public be gaining the benefits of new developments and new technologies as quickly as they are gaining them through your facilities now?

"So you, as the chief executive, retain for yourself the right to flex the budget to allow your organization to carry out its responsibilities in the most efficient manner possible.

"What we have been discussing is a system that will give immediate and continuing cost savings [gains in attendance, increases in visitor security and comfort—whatever your benefits are]. Tell me, Mrs. Spencer, under these conditions, will your budget flex—or is it an anchor?"

POWER CLOSE NUMBER TWELVE:
THE ECONOMIC TRUTH CLOSE

Let's say you have a superior product and run up against a competitor with a lower investment yet, as you know, an inferior product. The potential client is only seeing the lower investment as the advantage and is ready to shut you down. Try these words:

"John, it's not always wise to guide our buying decisions by price alone. It's never recommended to invest too much for something. However, investing too little has its drawbacks as well. By spending too much, you lose a little money, but that's all. By spending too little, you risk more because the item you've purchased may not give you the satisfaction you were expecting.

"It's an economic truth that it's seldom possible to get the most by spending the least. In considering business with the least expensive supplier, it might be wise to add a little to your investment to cover the risk you're taking, wouldn't it?"

The logic here is that if they're willing to cover their risk, why not remove it entirely with a superior product? This close also sells with emotion—the emotion of not losing face by purchasing an inferior product that might prove disappointing.

POWER CLOSE NUMBER THIRTEEN: THE "I CAN GET IT CHEAPER" CLOSE

This close runs along the same lines as the one above, but with a slightly different take. It may be more effective with consumers, while the economic truth close works better for business-to-business sales.

When potential clients flat-out say, "I can get it cheaper somewhere else," agree with them. Then instill little doubts in their minds about just what they're getting for their money.

"That may very well be true, John. And, after all, in today's economy, we all want the most for our money. A truth that I have learned over the years is that the cheapest price is not always what we really want. Most people look for three things when making an investment: the finest quality, the best service, and the lowest price. I have never yet found a company that could provide the finest quality and the best service for the lowest price. I'm curious, John, for your long-term happiness, which of those three would you be most willing to give up? Quality? Service? Or low price?"

Few people will want to give up quality or service. These words are just a simple reminder that you get what you pay for.

POWER CLOSE NUMBER FOURTEEN:
THE COMPETITIVE-EDGE CLOSE

This is a great close for businesses that are in a very competitive market. And most businesses today are, aren't they?

"Kathy, please realize that many of your competitors are facing the same challenges today that you are. Isn't it interesting that when an entire industry is fighting the same forces, some companies do a better job of meeting those challenges than others? My entire objective here today has been to provide you with a method for gaining a competitive edge. And gaining edges—large or small—is how you can make this one of those few companies in your industry that is doing a better job."

POWER CLOSE NUMBER FIFTEEN:
THE HIGHER AUTHORITY CLOSE

This is wonderful—if you know it thoroughly and set it up right. I'm going to use an example to show in detail exactly how the technique works. You may be selling carpet-cleaning services to homemakers, group insurance to companies, or works of art to collectors. Whatever it is that you offer, the principles in this example apply. All you need do is adapt the wording to your own product or service.

The higher authority must be exactly that—a person respected by and known to prospects. The prospects don't have to know your higher authority personally; all that's necessary is that they know of the authority's existence and position. If you're selling agricultural machinery, you'll want a prominent farmer; if you're selling furnishings or home services, you'll want a civic or social leader in your community; if you're selling industrial equipment, you'll want to use a decision maker at a large and growing company as your higher authority. You should constantly be on the lookout for several higher authority figures. For now, let's work on the idea of using one.

Here are the steps for using this close successfully:

1. Select your higher authority figure. Let's assume that you're a salesperson for Brawnybead Welding Equipment Corporation. The number two steel fabricator in your area, Finekrax Inc., is a happy client of yours in the person of Mark Cade, its production manager. You've given first-class service, and, of course, your Brawnybead machines are doing a great job at Finekrax Inc. Mark Cade is an ideal higher authority figure for any of the smaller steel fabricators in your entire territory.

2. Recruit your higher authority figure. On one of your visits to Finekrax after it's had your Brawnybead machines long enough to be experienced with them, you ask Mark Cade if he'd be willing to share his knowledge of your machines with other steel fabricators. Now, it would have to be smaller companies—not Mark's direct competition. Mark agrees to do this for you because you've done a solid sales and service job for him with a good product, and you've assured him that you'll only call when you need help with prospects operating on his general level. In other words, you promise not to bother him if you're trying to sell one small welder to a fix-it shop.

3. Set up your higher authority figure for the specific sales situation. You're out to replace all the outdated welders at Slagfild Iron Works with your new high-speed Brawnybeads. Slagfild is number four in your territory, and Tony Alioto is the decision maker there. While planning your appointment with Tony, you decide that you'll need the higher authority figure close, so you call Mark Cade and determine that he'll be available to take a phone call while you're with Tony Alioto. With Mark set up, you complete your plans for a powerful presentation to Tony at Slagfild.

4. Set up your prospect for the higher authority figure close. You know that Tony will have the same concerns about the reliability of your Brawnybead welders that Mark Cade had: "Will the innovations that make the Brawnybead superior stand up under actual shop working conditions? Is your service department really as good as you say it is?"

In planning your presentation, you expect Tony to have specific technical questions. A simple demonstration is pointless; Tony knows your machine will make two pieces of metal stick together.

So you recognize that the primary purpose of your interview with Tony Alioto is to isolate the specific technical and other reservations that he has about your equipment and company. Once you've clarified these questions in his mind, you're ready to close. It's vital to make that list of reasons specific, and to get agreement that they are all the reservations Tony has. Write them out on a piece of paper. As soon as you come to this point, reach for the phone.

"You know Mark Cade, don't you?"

"Runs the shop at Finekrax, doesn't he?"

"That's right. He's one of our clients." Then make the call.

When Mark Cade is on the phone, tell him, "I'm here at Slagfild with Tony Alioto and he has some questions about the Brawnybead." Then hand Tony the phone and let him take it from there. He has the list of his questions in front of him, so nothing will be missed.

5. Close after the call. Once Mark Cade has discussed the technicalities and reassured Tony that the Brawnybead is performing well in his larger shop, Tony's objections aren't there anymore. When the phone conversation ends, you're in a position to ask, "By the way, what delivery date is most convenient, the first or the fifteenth?"

If something happens and Mark Cade isn't available even though you set it up with him—after all, his job comes first—you probably won't be able to close that day. Set yourself up for a recontact, and leave the higher authority's phone number with the prospect so that Tony can call Mark on his own. Take a copy of Tony's objections with you so that at the start of the recontact, you'll be able to get back quickly to where you left off.

Some salespeople turn away from the higher authority close because they feel competitors hate each other and won't cooperate. There are exceptions, but as a general rule the people in companies operating in the same field are friendly. They respect each other and have many reasons to cooperate, not the least of which is the possibility that they may be looking for a job at another company in their industry someday. If you do happen to run into one of the few cases of bad blood between competitors, simply back off—but never assume in advance that there's trouble. The truth is, most people in business are too busy to waste energy hating the competition. And it's a big ego boost to be a higher authority.

POWER CLOSE NUMBER SIXTEEN: THE LOST-SALE CLOSE

I've saved this for last because it should be used as a last resort. If you've done everything you can and you still feel your product or service is truly good for your client, give it one more shot with this close.

First, you begin packing up whatever papers, or things you've had out during your presentation. Shut down your laptop. Put everything back in your briefcase. In other words, you're preparing to leave. The mood shifts. Then you ask for clarification as to what you did wrong in order not to make the sale.

"Pardon me, Mr. and Mrs. Smith, before I leave, may I apologize for not doing my job today? You see, if I had not been inept, I would have said the things necessary to convince you of the value of my product. Because I didn't, you will not be enjoying the benefits of our product. And believe me, I am truly sorry. I believe in my product and I earn a living helping people own it. So that I don't make the same mistake again, will you please tell me what I did or what I said wrong? And please be very candid with me."

If you deliver those words with warmth and sincerity, the clients will usually give you something you can work with. They may bring up a concern that you hadn't heard from them yet. They may repeat something you thought you had overcome. It doesn't matter. If they give you anything, you try to bridge back into closing them one last time.

Get familiar with all sixteen of these closes. That way you'll recognize situations in which each would best apply. Get intimate with at least five. Remember, most Champions reach the final closing of the sale after five attempts. Once you master all sixteen closes, you should be closing enough sales to earn a Champion's income.

18. A Clutch of Moneygrabbers

The product or service that you help people acquire, and the location you work in, are less important than your techniques, planning, and determination to do the most productive thing possible at every given moment. If you make all the habits of the Champion your habits, you'll become a Champion. You'll have the prestige, the money, the recognition, and the self-acceptance that all Champions have.

I'm talking now about the great ones who earn in a good week what the average worker earns in a year. Now let's talk about eight systems that the great ones use to turn little dollars into big dollars.

TURN LITTLE DOLLARS INTO BIG DOLLARS

The Super-Champions, and most of the top producers, combine all the techniques given in this book to build a base of referrals into an ongoing operation that continues to generate its own momentum. The average salesperson has a hard time getting referrals from the people he sells; the Super-Champion often gets referrals after a short phone conversation with people he's never seen. The super-Champion paid the price to acquire his skills, and he has the confidence to use them to the fullest possible extent. "Nothing succeeds like success," Alexandre Dumas wrote more than a hundred years ago, and the words were never truer than they are today. To succeed, gather the skills and knowledge that are the tools of success. Then use them.

Having done that, you'll be ready for the systems to magnify the values you work with.

Multiplying money is money-clutching system 1. The people you involve in your product are surrounded by other people who have the same aspirations, interests, and financial capabilities. Each person you sell can be multiplied by the number of associates who are prospects for your offering.

The average family has two and a half automobiles, but the average automobile salesperson stops when he sells them one car. Why? Because she's organized to work only with the people who come into her showroom. The concept that every buyer is a referral base for more sales is foreign to her. Yet Champions work with their buyers and multiply the one sale by a factor of two—three—five—sometimes ten or more over a period of time.

Highlight this thought:

> ### If they'll take one, they or their friends
> ### will always take more.

You've got to do the job, of course. You have to work with them, make sure they're happy with the service, and handle any problems quickly. So highlight this idea also:

> ### Work with every buyer as though that person
> ### represents a thousand referrals.

Let's think about this for a moment. Suppose you make only one small sale this week. However, you give fine service and obtain four prequalified leads from that buyer.

On Week 2, you work with those four prequalified leads and sell the number you should sell, 50 percent. So you pick up two sales. You also get four leads from each of your new buyers. During Week 3, you work with your eight leads, sell half of them, and ring up four sales.

When all this happens, let's say that you're working in a home appliance store. A terrific new product has just come out, a kitchen blender priced at $79.95. You make ten percent—eight dollars—on each blender you sell. There's something about this blender that makes you decide to give it a good solid push.

Here's how your results look after three weeks:

WEEK	SALES	LEADS	EARNINGS
1	1	0	$ 8.00
2	2	4	16.00
3	4	8	32.00

Not very impressive, is it? You've pushed that dang blender hard for three weeks—and all you've made is a measly fifty-six bucks.

Now here's what I'd like you to do. Take your calculator and work out what would happen if you doubled the sales of the blender for ten weeks, getting four leads from each sale, two of which you sell the following week. In other words, extend the table above a full ten weeks. It'll only take you a minute.

Rather than give you all the answers here and spoil your fun, I'll just tell you one thing. If you could actually do that with the blender for ten weeks, and then hold your sales at that level for a full year, your income would be one-fifth of a million dollars—$200,704, to be exact, assuming that you take three weeks off.

Isn't that exciting?

Of course, it may not be realistic to plan on selling that many units of the same appliance out of one retail store. But you could have a good thing going on several different appliances, including some priced at ten times what our blender goes out the door for.

This example illustrates the enormous multiplying effect of the referral. Use this concept. Why be satisfied to let a buyer—and his thousand possible connections—walk out with only one of your products? Probe a little. Among his friends, relatives, and fellow workers, there are bound to be several people who need the benefits you're purveying.

During my last year in sales before I went into training, my business was 100 percent referrals. It wasn't just the service I gave—I used this concept. The only time I prospected, I was showing other salespeople how to do it. Now, what did the referral nature of my business allow me to do? Spend every bit of my selling time working with people who trusted me. About all I did was qualify and close.

If you're new, of course, you can't start right out working with referrals—you have to wait until you make your first sale. Most new salespeople are so concerned with making each sale that they don't open their minds to the tremendous number of opportunities that a single sale can create for them.

Add-on is system 2. The second system for expanding volume involves using your imagination. Keep thinking of ways to add on accessories and additional products, and of ways to find different uses for your product or service with the same client. Always keep this question in the front of your mind:

How can I add on to what my clientele already has?

If you're selling to companies and you get one of your products into the shipping department of a firm, are you satisfied? Or will you service that shipping department and work with them to give you a referral to their accounting department or production department? Of course, it depends on your product or service, but I keep hearing about salespeople who go in with a piece of equipment that many different departments of a company could use. They sell one department and forget about the rest of that firm.

Here's a fundamental rule for add-on sales that I recommend you highlight:

Never go for the add-on sale until you've completely closed the original sale.

If I walk into your appliance store looking for a vacuum cleaner, I don't want to discuss the fantastic new blender you're all excited about until I've satisfied my need to suck up dirt. Once that's off my mind, you have a chance to arouse my blending urges. But don't even mention blending until I own the best vacuum cleaner you can provide me.

J. Douglas Edwards and I were close friends and next-door neighbors in Scottsdale. We frequently swapped stories that people told us at our separate seminars. Doug came back from a speaking tour in Canada one day and told me, "A young man in Toronto said, 'I've become a multimillionaire since the last time I heard your program, and it's all because of one sentence in your speech.'"

Now, that's heady stuff to a speaker. It's the hope of hearing exciting success stories—though rarely as spectacular as this—that keeps professional speakers boarding planes. "From one sentence?" I asked, somewhat wistfully. "What was it?" His answer is the name of the next and my favorite system for turning small change into big money:

"Sell them in bunches, like bananas," is system 3. Here's what the young man, Ed Dardon, did with the concept he discovered in Toronto at Doug's seminar. A few weeks later, Ed went out to see a referral. The man had a challenge, of course. He was a member of a real estate syndicate that had built a magnificent apartment complex. The problem came when they completed the project and set their rents to earn a return on their investment. They had priced themselves out of the market; their project was just too magnificent. So it sat vacant. Taxes and expenses were mounting up, and nothing was coming in to service those costs and the mortgages.

So Ed Dardon opened his mind and came up with a plan. Then he met with the entire syndicate and outlined his program. Condominiums are very popular today, but at that time they weren't well known. Ed convinced the syndicate that the only profitable way out of their predicament was to convert the apartments to condominiums and sell out.

Speed was essential. Ed trained a small, capable sales force around the concept of selling the condominiums in bunches, like bananas. He packaged them by threes, fours, and fives—and often they sold two or three bunches to one investor. The people who bought weren't intent on getting immediate cash flow because of the tax advantages.

Along with his sales organization, Ed also set up a management company to handle the rental details for the new owners. Both companies were profitable and grew rapidly. Ed's success at turning a financial fiasco into a profitable venture for the original developers brought him a flood of new opportunities. Not only was the word out that Ed was someone special, but the trade magazines hailed his achievements throughout Canada. In less time than he'd spent in high school, Ed Dardon became a multimillionaire.

Keep looking for opportunities to sell them in bunches, like bananas. And keep this thought in the front of your mind:

Every time you hit pay dirt, dig all the way through the mountain. That's system 4. Sell one bank, and you know how to sell them all. If one boat catches more fish with your net, you can sell one to every tuna clipper in the harbor. Are you bothered about how you'll make doing an all-out job of preparing to sell one customer pay off? Stop worrying. Start planning how to use the new knowledge you'll gain. Sell everybody in that same business or interest group. In other words, look at each prospect as if he were a member of a specialized group that you're now going to learn how to sell—because that's exactly what he is.

Now, if you use the same plan to sell bunches of things to bunches of people, how are you going to spend all the money you'll earn?

Use your business cards to reach people you've never met. This money earner is system 5. When we're new in sales, many of us give out a thousand cards. Then we stop doing it because we've got enough business to get by on. We don't realize how much of that business came from the cards.

When I was in real estate sales, I sent one of my cards along every time I paid a bill. Someone had to be opening all those envelopes, I thought. One day a woman called me and said, "Mr. Hopkins, you don't know me, but my husband and I want to buy a bigger house, and we'd like to talk to you about it."

After telling her that I'd be delighted to work with them, I asked, "How did you get my name?"

"I handle your account at the gas company," she said, "and I've got about two dozen of your cards in my desk."

The fee I earned for satisfying that lady's real estate needs paid for more business cards than I could use in a hundred years—and that's only one instance. Unless you sell special things to limited groups, miss no opportunity to put your business card in the hands of anyone you come in contact with, however remotely or briefly.

Be a walking ad for yourself. Put system 6 to work for you whenever you go out in public during the workday. Do it with class—carry a plastic writing pad binder that's imprinted with an attention-catching message. The next time you're in a restaurant at lunch time waiting to be seated, look at the crowd waiting with you. How many of them need what you sell?

Rather than stand there fidgeting, relax, look friendly, and casually hold your binder where it can be seen. Have WE STRETCH DOLLARS or some other teaser slogan imprinted on it. Your company's name, if it's well known or tells what you sell, may be your most effective binder imprint.

Champions know that people will read their binder advertisement and start conversations. Often they'll say something like, "Oh, you're with _____," as they read the company's name.

Every time this happens, the Champion smiles and says, while handing them a card, "Yes, I am, and obviously you wouldn't have asked unless you had some needs." Another thing Champions know is that these chance encounters often lead to lucrative business they wouldn't otherwise get.

Learn how to recoup on the recontact route and take advantage of money-clutching system 7. Whether we like it or not, recontacts are an essential part of many selling sequences. The need for recontact arises when, after you've demonstrated your product or presented your service, prospects aren't ready to make the decision. In many cases, their reasons are valid and can't be overcome. They ask you to leave your figures and brochure, and say they'll look at them and let you know. In chapter 17's Power Close Number Four, I gave you a technique for overcoming many of these delaying causes, but you'll always encounter some situations that can only be won by recontact at a later date. If recontacts are a common occurrence with you, study how to raise your score on closing them. I've broken down the process into steps:

1. Prepare the way in the prior meeting. Don't hard-sell your-self out of any chance to work with the prospects again. And avoid committing yourself to phoning for an appointment for the second meeting; it's too easy for them to have a secretary tell you to call back next year. In most cases, you can simply go in and see the person on a recontact even though you had to make an appointment for the first meeting.

2. When you walk in on your recontact, smile, greet them, repeat your name and company if there's any possibility they don't remember it, and, again, unless they make the move, don't push for a handshake.

3. Begin with a summary of benefits. Average salespeople don't do this. Instead, they start off with a say-no question that immediately kills the sale. Then they spend the rest of their time with the client trying desperately to breathe life back into the corpse. How do they kill the sale?

By asking something like, "Well, did you decide?" Charging straight in for the decision, without first renewing the agreements reached during the last meeting, almost guarantees a turndown.

Professionals never ask a say-no question; they take another tack entirely. Let's suppose that a week ago I demonstrated a piano to Mrs. Kellens. Ordinarily, I'd want both husband and wife present at the demonstration, but in this case it was clear that Mr. Kellens wouldn't be available, so I went ahead with the wife only. Now I'm recontacting, and the first thing I do is get back to where we were.

"Mrs. Kellens, I thought I'd reiterate what we've already talked about. As we agreed, the piano you liked best, the Singsweet, would fit nicely in that corner, wouldn't it?

"And we also agreed that the tone and quality of the Singsweet, even though it's not our largest or most costly piano, is more than sufficient for your needs, didn't we?" Mrs. Kellens says yes to both these propositions because she already agreed to them in our previous meeting. I go on.

"And we agreed that one of the most exciting things about having this piano in your home is that your children would be better able to take advantage of the five years of piano lessons you and your husband have already invested in."

I give her a chance to say something positive about this and then continue: "And we also thought they would bring their friends home more often if you have a piano. You said you want to have your children home more often, didn't you?"

She has to agree with all this because it's what she told me herself. Of course, when she did so, I recognized the vital importance of these emotional buying triggers and tried to etch them in my brain. (Many Champions don't trust their memory here. If they need a recontact, they jot down all the prospect's reasons for buying as soon as they walk out of the first meeting. Then they can review them before the recontact and be sure not to overlook any.)

Not until I've reviewed all the benefits she expects from the purchase of the piano, not until I've brought all those emotions back into play, do I get to whatever held up the purchase at the last meeting. But I still don't ask for a decision. Instead, I focus on the emotional barrier.

"I really feel that the only thing we didn't adequately discuss and agree on was whether your husband would be as excited with the investment you want to make in your children as you are, isn't that right?"

What have I done? Brought her back to the emotional state she was in after the demonstration. When I walked in on the recontact, if they'd definitely decided to buy the piano, she would have interrupted to tell me so. Mrs. Kellens expected me to say something like, "Well, I'm back. Did you talk to Mr. Kellens? What did he say about buying the Singsweet?"

Then she planned to answer: "I'm afraid he said no. I'm sorry— I really tried—but I guess we'll have to wait another year."

She and the children want and need my Singsweet. They can afford it. It's my job to help her get that piano, not make it easy for her to get rid of me. So instead of leading her into saying "Sorry. Good-bye," I lead her through the emotional reasons why she wants the piano. If I can keep her talking and emoting about having the piano for her children and their friends, she's going to think of a way to get it. Tell yourself, *I'm not taking up space on this earth to be a sponge for negative feelings; my purpose is to help people own benefits.*

Here's a popular line with salespeople who enjoy no great success selling in the corporate situation: "Well, I'm back. Did you think about my proposition?" What answer do they almost always get to that brilliant query?

"Yes. No." ("Yes, we thought about it. No, we don't want it.") One chop and the salespeople are dead. But they asked for it.

In a business situation, as in a personal situation, you have to do a benefit summary of what you've already agreed to when you go back on a recontact. You have to restore the climate of benefit consciousness that you had at the last meeting. When recontacts are the rule rather than the exception, Champions play the game with an ace up their sleeves. They deliberately leave a benefit out of their original presentation so that when they come back for the recontact, they can say something like this after doing the benefit summary:

"Mr. Selvan, when we were together last, we discussed how your corporation would benefit from the higher rate of production our Chomp-slick will give you. I think I overlooked mentioning something during our last meeting that I believe is critical to your decision. I know that we're over the budget figure with our present proposal, but I'd like you to keep this in mind: With the Chomp-slick, you're not locked into its high production rate. We can supply a robot feed mechanism that will increase production up to 80 percent."

After dropping that gem, you go into your closing sequence.

Our last system works like wings, costs almost nothing, and isn't used much. Yet it's one of the greatest moneygrabbers around. System 8 is the most powerful method I know for obligating people to boost your sales potential. For some reason that I've never been able to understand, few salespeople use this technique. Maybe I shouldn't be surprised. After all, only about 5 percent of us are using all the techniques we could to make more money and do our jobs better. And only about 5 percent of salespeople are using this simple technique regularly. Maybe it's not direct enough—or maybe it just requires alertness and a little effort.

What are the two most important words in the English language for our profession of selling? Not *gimme, gimme.* The words are *thank you.* That's right, thank you. I found this out years ago when I started writing thank-you notes to everyone I could. The results were amazing. Let me give you one example. When I cashed my first sizable check in sales, I went right out and bought a suit because I needed clothes desperately. During the next few days, that suit got a lot of wear. Then it had a collision with a gob of oil. When I rushed my suit to the cleaners, the owner of the shop rushed it out in time for my next appointment. So I wrote him a thank-you note that he taped on the front of his cash register along with my business card. Three days later I got a call from another customer of his who'd seen my note. That call led to a large sale. Besides putting a chunk of money in my pocket, that incident taught me a lesson.

Thank people. Do it in writing. And do it right away.

Spoken thanks are nice. They're necessary to courtesy, and sometimes they're the only thanks you can give someone. But spoken thanks rarely bring in referrals. For that, you need to write a thank-you note.

Don't think that my note to the dry-cleaning establishment was the only time this technique has worked. I get letters all the time from Champions who have taken my advice and made thank-you notes part of their selling sequence.

One of our trainees wrote: "Tom, at the supermarket, the woman checking out my order said, 'Aren't you in real estate?' I said I was, we talked for a moment, and I gave her my card. Then I got to thinking about it, so I found out her address and sent her a thank-you note for taking my card. Two weeks later she called me up. Her brother-in-law and sister wanted a house. Because I sent her a thank-you note, I was able to get that couple happily involved in owning a home."

THE POWER OF THANK-YOU NOTES

If you're starting out and have no clientele, send a thank-you note to almost everyone you meet. Bear in mind that this is a broadcast technique. Send lots of messages and some of them will get through. Beam them in the right direction. If you sell insurance or real estate and almost everyone is a potential client for you, send thank-you notes to the manager of the neighborhood ice cream parlor and everybody else you get the slightest attention from. If your product is diesel trucks, be more selective.

No matter what you sell, always carry a set of three-by-five cards for the express purpose of fueling your thank-you note machine. Suppose you're out prospecting by cold calling on company offices. In one of them, while waiting to see someone, you happen to meet and have a brief but cordial chat with an executive from a company other than the one you're calling on.

When he goes back to his office, he won't remember much about meeting you, and in a few days he will have forgotten all about you. But what if you send him a thank-you note that very day? For what? For the pleasant chat you had with him. If you can learn his name and company affiliation during your chance meeting, you can look up the rest of the address later.

The next day, what will his secretary give him to read first? Your thank-you note. Do you realize how few he gets? She'll walk into his office and say, "We sure got a nice thank-you note this morning. Has he ever been here? I don't remember him."

"Oh, yeah, I remember this fellow. Nice guy. I just met him." How you work from this point depends on the situation. Even if the company this executive works for doesn't use your product or service, he very likely is acquainted with the executives of many companies that do. Selling is not an isolated function done in a vacuum—it's the thread our society's fabric is woven from. None of us can foresee or understand all the complex relationships within a community that influence who buys what from whom. But we can be sure that the more people who like and trust us, the more success we'll have in sales.

Here are some of the times you should send thank-you notes:

1. Contacts. Anytime you meet someone and there's any discussion of your product or service, send them a thank-you.

2. Recontacts. Mail them a thank-you note for seeing you after every visit.

3. Client after demonstration. Every time one of your established clients allows you to demonstrate something new, send a thank-you note.

4. Client after purchase. "Just a note to thank you again for . . . and to let you know that I'm available to help if there's any way I can be of service." Generally it's better to avoid suggesting that they may have challenges, but make it clear that you're available if needed. And then, of course, be fast and energetic in solving every challenge that does arise. Shortsighted salespeople make themselves scarce when their clients have challenges. These are the kind of people who keep moving from company to company because they never can build up a clientele. Champions have a completely different attitude toward product or service issues. They know that if everything goes with perfect smoothness, the client will have trouble remembering them. They're in, out, and that's the end of it. But if there's a challenge and it's handled promptly and well, that client remembers. The best source of referrals is the client you've solved challenges for.

5. Client after referral. Whether you make the sale or not, a written thank-you to the people who referred you is essential. You may want to take them to dinner—or send them out to dinner at your expense.

6. For efforts above and beyond the call of duty. Remember anyone in any industry who does something nice for you. For example, do you ever take clients out to lunch or dinner? Would you like the maître d' to treat you with special attention when you walk in with clients? Then send him a thank-you note. Tell him how happy you were with his service, and how you look forward to bringing anyone you can to his restaurant. You'll find that you get treated beautifully when you make reservations and return after he gets your note.

How would you like to be the only person who never has to wait for your car when it's in the shop for maintenance? The next time you take your car in, write a note to the service manager afterward: "Dear Chet, thank you for getting my car out so fast yesterday. I really appreciate it. I'm going to send you all the business I can. Sincerely." Send a copy to the owner of the business. If you know the name of the particular mechanic who worked on your vehicle, mention that name in your note to the owner. Word will trickle down to that mechanic—in the form of either praise or possibly a raise.

7. To people you don't sell. Why not send them a thank-you note? After all, they did give you the courtesy of hearing your presentation. What if they don't like what they bought, or if the competition hasn't done a good job on service and follow-up? They may regret their decision and tell their friends to check with you before buying. That's called a referral, and this is the best kind: from someone who owns your competition's latest model and now says your item is better.

Yes, send thank-you notes to the people who don't buy from you. And keep in touch with them. The odds are that the person who sold them won't—or they'll be orphaned by their salesperson and get lost in the shuffle at the competing company. Keep these foreign orphans posted on new developments and, when the itch cycle makes a full turn, you'll be in a perfect position to capture their business. By then, the price and feature factors that caused them to buy from the competition will probably have changed.

The thank-you note that kicks off this whole process runs something like this: "Thank you for letting me show you [whatever]. I enjoyed meeting you, and I appreciate being considered. We couldn't get together on your needs this time, but I hope that when you think of [your general line], you'll remember me.

"Please let me know if there's any way that I can be of service. Cordially."

I carry three-by-five cards with me even today, and I travel with my company's thank-you notes. I average between five and ten thank-you notes every single day to the Champions I meet, to the people who attend our seminars, to business owners who invest in our training systems, and to a variety of other people who serve my needs and the needs of our company.

Ten thank-you notes a day is 3,650 a year and 36,500 in a decade. Some Champions tell me they get ten sales from every hundred thank-you notes. You'll certainly get more than one from every hundred. Multiply your average income per sale by thirty-six to see the minimum extra income this one technique will generate for you in the next twelve months. I think you'll decide it's a winner.

All it takes for each note is three minutes and a stamp. Use the time you'd otherwise spend staring at the wall waiting to see someone. Start doing it today because the results don't reach you overnight. And as with all successful methods of coping with life's opportunities, consistency counts. Ten thank-you notes a day is three hundred a month. That's enough to give you a tremendous boost.

19. How to Perspire Less and Profit More from Paperwork

To most salespeople, paperwork is like oil to the Arabs—messy and troublesome stuff they have little use for, but unless they keep it moving there's no money. Ask any sales manager about paperwork. Although the top third of his sales force generates several times the volume that the bottom third does, he'll tell you that he has more trouble with the bottom third's paperwork. Why? Because the people in the top third are too busy to answer avoidable questions about their paperwork. So they do it right the first time.

No single quality separates Champions from the average performers more than doing things right the first time. As an exasperated sales manager once said, "Why is there always enough time for the typical salesperson to do it over, but never enough time to do it right in the first place?"

COMPANY PAPERWORK

In sales, as in every area of life, there's no such thing as useless time; there's only time that's used—and time that's wasted. And nothing wastes more of it faster than turning in orders your fulfillment people have to guess at.

The first rule for working fast with orders is to be clear. Learn to print fast and clearly, or learn to type. Champions don't risk enraging their customers with costly delays or mistakes caused by carelessly written orders; they double-check everything relating to orders for accuracy and clarity. If your business allows you to generate orders online or on company software, by all means do so. Before sending the order on to the next person, double-check the details and your spelling. With the power of computerized ordering, you may not have to worry about someone being able to read your handwriting. However, you do still need to verify your accuracy.

But once we step away from the actual processing of orders, we get into areas where a different set of imperatives apply. Now your company is using documentation to:

1. Control you.
2. Furnish information the government demands.
3. Gather information for production and marketing decisions.

Let's talk about these three classes of paperwork.

1. Information to control you with. Most of the salespeople in most sales forces are, by definition, average. This means that almost all sales departments set up their paperwork with average salespeople in mind. In other words, because average salespeople don't motivate themselves, the company is forced to motivate them.

Think about that. With rare exceptions, all managers find themselves faced with these two realities:

- Less than 20 percent of the salespeople form a group that produces more than 60 percent of the total volume—and this group requires little urging to do the job.
- More than 80 percent of the salespeople form another group that produces less than 40 percent of total volume—if the pressure is kept on. If the pressure slackens, this group's production falls even farther.

The more challenges companies have with proper documentation, the more of it they require. I know this doesn't sound right. But companies live and die by accurate records. If they're not getting accurate information from their people, they'll try to come up with more and better forms to get it.

2. Information required by the government. Champions get this kind of information recorded promptly. They know the company has to have it and they also know that it takes less time to get it over with than it does to cope with repeated reminders.

3. Information your company needs for marketing and production control. Here again, Champions cooperate with enthusiasm. They realize their company's future is no better than the marketing and production decisions that are made based on what is reported. Most companies look to their sales forces for two vital functions: sales and information gathering. Because of the crucial nature of both categories, no company is stronger than its sales force.

The road to ruin is paved with good intentions. In school, were you ever given thirty days to complete an assignment that you knew could be done in a few hours of sustained effort? Did you knock it right out and get it off your mind? No. If you thought about it at all after three days, the comforting knowledge that you still had twenty-seven days removed any possibility that you'd give it even an odd hour's effort yet. Then two weeks were suddenly gone, and you began to feel some twinges. You saw the big F looming up in front of you. Failure. More days slipped by. The F kept getting bigger in your mind. You suffered more pain and anxiety. Finally, two days before—or the night before—the due date, you sat down and whipped out the assignment. And then you felt a great sense of relief. You probably said, "Why didn't I save myself all that cold sweat and get it done a month ago?"

Champions prefer the hot sweat of work to the cold sweat of worry—so much so that before long, they have plenty of time to work up the best sweat of all, the one you get playing hard when you've got your life together, your work and goals on schedule, and your bank account in good shape.

Being on time is a habit. Being late is a habit. You can set your mental clock on time, or ten minutes late. You can set your paperwork clock on time, or three reminders late. And you can change any habit that you want to change. All you have to do is concentrate on your new habit instead of your old habit for twenty-one days.

This means that you do your new habit for twenty-one days

without missing a stroke. If you slide back once, start all over. If you really want the new habit—and aren't sabotaging your own efforts with little voices complaining inside your head—you can own any habit you choose in just three weeks.

Here are some rules for handling paperwork fast:

- If it's clear that it has to be done sometime, do it now. The quickest way you can handle any paper is to finalize it the first time you see it.
- If it doesn't have to be done, trash it now.
- Develop a double standard of accuracy for paperwork. If big bucks are involved, give it your best (order form and sales agreement) grade of accuracy. If big bucks are not involved, give it your fast estimate grade of attention.

FOLLOW-UP PAPERWORK

Champions realize that they must operate like an independent company. The nature of the sales profession is that you are really in business for yourself. In fact, many salespeople have more freedom than most small-business owners do. But because we in sales have so much latitude to do things when, where, and how we want to, many of us don't discipline ourselves. You can earn twice as much money in half the time if you'll just discipline yourself to charge into your job, get on top of it, and then stay on top. To do that, you have to tear into getting yourself organized—you can't play around with this.

Why is organization so important?

It saves time, and all we have is time. Organization prevents future problems. It is the basis for building referrals. If you're organized, you won't forget the small details you promised to handle for the client.

If you say, "Sure, Mr. Boehm, when we deliver, I'll be there to make certain that the installation goes right," you'd better be organized. Otherwise, you won't be there. Then Mr. Boehm will start looking for little things to give you trouble about, things you could have brushed over if you had done what you said you'd do. You made promises to get the order that you should have kept, but didn't. So he wants to get even. And now Mr. Boehm won't believe anything you tell him. Why should he? You've already demonstrated what your word is worth.

Your company may supply you with a highly organized follow-up system or contact management software. These are great because they're designed for what you're doing. But you have to pay the price for using them by doing the work that's required to keep them up working. There's rarely a better place for some of your nonprime selling time than keeping your follow-up files updated—and pulling out calls to make at the times your file tells you are most likely to develop sales.

I like to keep organizational tools simple. If your software allows it, classify your client list into three sections:

1. Hot. These are the people who have the need, are qualified to buy, and are sincerely interested in making a decision soon.

When buyers are truly interested, they'll make a decision within seven days. Now, that doesn't mean they'll purchase *your* product within seven days, but they'll purchase *a* product within seven days. A Champion tries to work with between three and five highly motivated buyers at all times. Some average salespeople have a large list of all their leads—and they call none of them. If that's you, what good is your list? It's worth nothing if not worked properly.

2. Medium. The second division in your client-buyer file is for the people who are apparently qualified, have the need, but are not yet highly motivated.

Perhaps they're waiting for some future event to heat their medium needs up. Think back to the itch cycle. If you're working with a thirty-month cycle, buyers are medium a year after purchase, medium-to-hot two years after purchase, and hot when their old item is two years and four months old.

3. Cold. The third level of your buyer-client file is for all the leads you get from any source that you don't immediately classify as hot or medium.

These are the people who were just looking, who walked in, or who called in from ads or signs and seem to have a mild or future need for what you sell.

Keep in mind that few people call on ads, or come in when they see a store or sign, unless they have a definite interest in the product or service that's offered. Very few people spend their days wandering around looking at products and discussing services they have no need for and couldn't buy if they did. The average salesperson is far too quick to dismiss lukewarm people as being unworthy of any effort at all.

Champions go through their client-buyer file every three days, spotting the best opportunities that day for adding heat. Every time one of the hot buyers approves the paperwork, they find a medium to put on the front burner.

And all year long, they keep in touch with everyone in the cold section. Depending on the itch cycle of what they're selling and the individuals involved, they're in touch once every ninety days, once a month, once a week—in any case, often enough to make sure that when their need deepens, they'll be there to satisfy it.

Most people want everything that's new—but the average salesperson isn't organized to take advantage of this fact. When the company comes up with something new, Champions know exactly what to do. They work through their medium files, telling everyone about the new product or concept, knowing that it will turn some of those mediums into hots. And then they work through their cold file and turn some of the colds into mediums.

Here are some more categories you might wish to install in your follow-up system:

1. Swap meet leads. Leads from this source should be in a separate category because they're likely to become hot at any moment. Also, you should coordinate your sales activity on them with other members of your swap meet, and report your progress on each lead to the swapper who gave it to you.

2. Itch cycle clients. Set up your software to trigger the names of all those who should be beginning to itch a few days before you should contact them. That will give you time to review their past history and prepare yourself to make the right moves to scratch that itch.

3. Referrals. Contact each of these people as quickly as you can and classify them as hot, medium, or cold prospects.

In addition to the files above, you need a simple system for maintaining records of income tax deductions and expenses. The government wants a diary or logbook type of record that you keep on a daily basis—so do it. It's merely a matter of habit, and it'll save an enormous amount of strain when the tax deadline arrives. It'll also save you money, because missing receipts and unrecorded expenses are money thrown away.

The average new salesperson thinks, *I don't have time to keep records now. I'll wait until I have some sales income and then I'll worry about deductions.* The next time you think about it, you get a very sick feeling because you've made lots of money, you've lost hundreds of dollars of receipts for deductible expenses—and Uncle Sam has his hand out. File your receipts and jot down your expenses as you go, and take advantage of all the legal tax breaks you can. Tax competence is part of sales competence. Operate like a business because you are a business unto yourself.

One last word about paperwork. If you want to grow with the company you're now working for, don't fight its paperwork. Go with its flow, or you'll stifle your chances there. Business lives and breathes with documentation; people who can't push their share of it along can't rise far.

I've often heard people say, "I should've had that promotion. I was next in line."

I ask them, "Have you been operating like a business? Do your superiors know you are? Have you shown them that your capabilities are growing larger than the job you now have?"

Seniority isn't given as much weight as you might think when promotions are handed out. Few business managers will hesitate to pick ability over seniority anytime they have a clear choice. And what is ability?

It's largely a matter of having your work and your resources organized so you can perform with maximum effectiveness. Doing this requires that you use your time to best advantage, which leads us to the subject of the next chapter.

20. Fortune Building Starts with Time Planning

S alespeople who turn in average performances rarely plan their time. All Champions and top producers plan their time carefully. Therefore, to increase your sales and your income, you must plan your time.

I think you'll agree with the statement above—but will you plan your time? The odds are that you won't, because you have the strange idea that time planning is a difficult and complex task. It isn't. In fact, it's one of the easiest things in the world, one that starts paying immediate dividends. To start, list the things you must do tomorrow on a piece of paper, and then mark them in order of importance. If you'll do that at the same stage of your routine every night between the time you get home and the time you go to bed, you'll increase your efficiency and your income by at least 20 percent. You may even double your efficiency by this simple means. Far too many of us spend our entire days dashing about doing the next thing that grabs our attention. We keep so busy, we overlook important moneymaking opportunities that we could just as well be working at instead.

If you've never planned your time, start with this simple but highly effective method. Make it your firm habit, every evening, to sit down for a few minutes at the same time and list all the things you must do tomorrow to make the most of that day. Then number them in order of importance. Many highly successful people use this, and only this, system for controlling their time. Rather than listing twenty-five or thirty things and allowing yourself to get overwhelmed, I've taught my students for many years to write down the six most important things they must do the next day in order of importance. Six is doable. It's a realistic assumption that you can accomplish six tasks in an average day.

Next, tear into getting yourself organized. Sit down and list all the things you can do and learn to make yourself more effective, and work out a schedule for getting these things done or learned in the shortest possible time. The sooner you clear this list, the sooner your income will start shooting up. So don't wait. Start tonight. Some things you might want to include on the list are learning to type faster and more accurately. That skill will save you time with your computer entry. Consider taking a beginner's computer class if you're uncomfortable with any aspect of yours. Take classes on specific software. They can be formal classes or informal lessons from someone else you know who excels with certain software. Learn to read faster and with better comprehension. Study your ratios and decide what skill area would give you the biggest boost in production—it could be building rapport, qualifying, or presenting. Those skills are taught in this book. Set a goal of mastering one of them before moving on to the next.

None of the top Champions, the ones earning tremendous incomes, will go to sleep before they've written down the most important things they must do tomorrow. No matter what's going on, they first jot down in their planning notebook what they've got to do the next day in order to keep their great incomes flowing. Let me tell you what will happen if and when you start writing down each night the most important things you must do tomorrow.

Your subconscious mind will work on your list all night, without disturbing your sleep, because it wants to help you resolve your challenges and achieve your goals. But your subconscious mind can't help unless you tune it in to what's going to happen next. That's what listing the things you have to do the next day does: It cocks the hammer on the power of your subconscious mind. The very best time to do this is shortly before you go to sleep. When morning comes, you'll find that your mind fired some accurate shots in the night, and now you have fresh ideas up front in your conscious mind about how to handle the things on your must-do list better.

Give this process several days to start flowing. Nothing helps it more than going over your list in a quiet room, seeing yourself involved with the most difficult part of each thing you have on it. Equally important—and be careful never to omit this phase—see yourself happily enjoying the fact that you've successfully accomplished each of your goals for tomorrow. Make these sessions brief and upbeat. Don't concentrate on fear and dread of what you have to do tomorrow. If you try that, your subconscious mind may solve these challenges by figuring out ways to make you forget or otherwise avoid meeting what it sees as potentially painful experiences. Turn the primitive, powerful, never-sleeping subconscious part of your brain on to helping you achieve your goals by visualizing yourself confidently brushing aside an occasional setback, but succeeding most of the time.

Establish a follow-up system. There are many excellent time planning systems on the market that take your yearly plan down to a monthly plan, then to a weekly plan, and finally to a daily plan. These devices can do much of the organizing work for you.

Here are some things that should appear on your daily work plan, your list of important things to do tomorrow:

1. Leave the office. How many games would a professional ball club win if they never left the locker room? There are an awful lot of salespeople who lose a lot of games (sales) because they don't leave the locker room (office) often enough. The business, in the form of people who buy, is in the larger world outside the walls of your office. Go. Go often. And go early.

2. Scheduled meetings or visits. At the time you make a commitment to meet someone, you probably think there's no possibility that you'll forget it. But as you start to get busy, you'll start missing important meetings unless you write them down or enter them—all of them—in the planning device that you keep with you.

3. Research. Ours is a changing world; yours is a changing business. Whenever there's a new product or development in your service, you must sit down and research it, analyze its effect, and regain your competence to explain your offering adequately to potential buyers.

4. Family. Many of us salespeople take care of everybody else, but the last people we plan for are the ones who are most important to us: our families. Don't lose what you've got while you climb the ladder of success. When you should do something with your family, enter that in your planner and put it on your list of important things you're going to do the next day.

5. Physical health. Champions keep themselves in shape for three reasons:

- They don't want to be the richest people in the hospital.
- They know they're more effective when they feel good.
- The point of the whole exercise is to get more out of life, and they can't do that, no matter how much money they make, if they lose their health in the process.

So schedule your exercise program along with your business appointments. This is definitely one of your most important daily (or thrice-weekly) activities. You don't have to become a fitness nut. But at the other extreme are unfit nuts whose neglected bodies destroy their energy, enthusiasm, and zest for living. Somewhere between these two extremes, according to your interests, is where you should aim to place yourself.

6. Emotional health. Schedule personal rewards, and when you've earned them, never miss taking them. Don't try to cheat yourself here. The concept of personal rewards is vital to maintaining a strong sense of purpose. Without a strong sense of purpose, you can't maintain a strong drive to succeed. Your personal rewards may take the form of recreational activities, high-quality possessions, upward social movement, or charitable or spiritual activity. Many varieties of acceptable personal rewards await you, and they can make all the effort worthwhile. Schedule frequent recreational activity to reward yourself. Don't give it up except for clear and compelling reasons and, if you do, compensate yourself. Unless you adequately reward yourself, the entire concept of personal reward will cease to have meaning for you—with a disastrous effect on your will to win.

And schedule some of your time, money, and effort into something larger than yourself to build your sense of strength and personal worth. Nothing clears our minds for greater achievement better than doing something to make the world a better place because we are here.

7. Prospecting. If you don't schedule prospecting, if you don't put down the exact hours and days that you'll do it, what's the last thing you'll do?

Prospect.

And what's the first thing that'll dump your sales volume into the cellar?

Avoiding prospecting.

Keep your income growing: Schedule a daily stint of prospecting. Here's an allocation of time for most effective sales work:

- **Preparing to prospect.** Spend only 5 percent of your time getting ready to prospect, and 95 percent of the time allocated for prospecting actually doing it. (Many beginners spend half their time getting ready; a few spend *all* their time getting ready!) Prepare and practice your lines the night before. Remember, there's no substitute for on-the-job training, and the only way you can get that in prospecting is by talking to a potential client.

- **Prospecting.** When you're new, if you'll spend 75 percent of your time prospecting, you'll soon be in the top group in your company's sales force.

- **Preparing for meetings or visits.** You should be so well organized that you need spend only 8 percent of your time getting ready to make top-quality presentations or demonstrations.

- **Presenting.** Between 5 and 10 percent of your time should be spent actually in front of potential clients. Don't hang around. Get in and get out. Your clients will have more respect for you if you move things along. As you get more organized and experienced, and are working more with referrals, you'll be able to spend more time actually selling. The elite of our profession have secretarial, clerical, and technical help for the express purpose of allowing them to spend nearly all their time planning and presenting.

- **Merchandising and servicing.** Five percent.

Keep in mind that these starting percentages will change as your sales operation matures. Your initial prospecting will develop leads, then sales, then referrals. You'll start making money—and you'll prospect less because you'll be working with referrals more.

On the first day of every month, sit down with your planning or appointment book and write down everything you want to do that month. Write down any family or social event that you're committed to. Note all the company meetings that you should attend. Be mature, responsible, and realistic. Unless you support your company, your company can't support you. Be part of the team. Be part of the solution, not part of the challenge; be on time for meetings. And use your time there to help the company build a greater future for itself—which means for you. Enter all the educational programs you're getting involved with.

Then pull that month's itchers from your itch cycle file, call all of them, and schedule time to get together. Next, go through your other files of leads and schedule more visits.

As soon as you complete this work, you can see how much time you have available for the month. Work out a schedule for prospecting that will develop as many more leads as you can handle, and go to it. Isn't that simple? Your whole month is planned out for maximum efficiency and sales performance just by following those few easy steps.

Never allow yourself to think that planning your hours, days, and months is a baffling, frustrating, and impossible task. Take it one step at a time and it will go beautifully.

Let me tell you why I'm so sure by relating an event that has had a tremendous impact on me ever since it happened quite a number of years ago. After I started doing well in sales, I had a thought. Why not get some ideas from people who are more successful than I am?

I began going to lots of seminars. At one, I heard a man whose introduction impressed me more than his speech did. He was earning four hundred thousand dollars a year as the president of a major conglomerate.

I decided that I could learn something of great value from this man, so I set out to meet him for lunch. That took two months. When I was finally sitting across from him, I said, "I'm here for a very sincere reason. I want you to tell me how you've become so successful." I was twenty-one years old then.

He chuckled and started talking. After about ten minutes, I think he realized that I really was sincere. I said, "Tell me what I have to do."

Here's how he answered me: "Tom, all my adult life I've lived by a saying, and it's made all the difference. If you live by this saying, too, I don't see how you can fail to be extremely successful."

That was a pretty heavy statement. I grabbed a napkin and got ready to write. (I said I was doing well. I hadn't yet achieved Champion status where I'd have had something better than a napkin to write on.)

He went on, "If I give it to you and you really live by it, there'll be days when you'll hate me."

"I don't care. Give it to me."

He did, and I wrote these words:

I must do the most productive thing possible at every given moment.

For years, those words hung by my desk. Today I can state that I, too, have spent all my mature years living by that saying, and it's made all the difference. And I can also tell you that if you will live by that saying, I don't see how you can fail to be extremely successful. Let me also add the same caution that the president of the conglomerate did all those years ago: "If you really live by this saying, there'll be days when you'll hate me." But I also know that there'll soon be stretches of time when you'll bless me for giving you that saying.

Is sitting in the office jawing with other salespeople productive? Of course not. If you'll start doing the most productive thing possible at every given moment, you'll not only become a Champion and enjoy a high income but also become a finer, happier person. Let's understand each other here. The most productive thing that you can do at every given moment is not always something aimed directly at making money. The most productive thing you can do during many given moments is to be with your family, relaxing, playing, and rewiring your dynamo. Rest and recreation are essential parts of the productive rhythm. It's not productive to run a machine until it overheats and breaks down; it's simply stupid. The same applies to your own brain, body, and set of drives. It's also stupid to rest from goofing off, or to take a vacation from doing nothing.

Planning your time with productive activities is a vital key to success in selling. In fact, activity breeds productivity—you just need to be active in the right areas.

21. How to Sell Your Way Out of a Slump

So now you've learned the techniques in the previous chapters, you've put them to work, you've made some money . . . but you find yourself in a slump.

What's the biggest obstacle to getting out of a slump?

Knowing why you're in it in the first place.

Where do you start looking for the knowledge?

By asking yourself this question:

Am I happy?

Any genuine response to the question, when reduced to the basics, will drop into one of these categories:

- "I'm miserable all the time."
- "I'm happy all the time."
- "I'm miserable some of the time, and happy some of the time."

A lot of people don't want to face this question. They'll try to avoid it by saying, "I'm not miserable, and I'm not what you'd call happy, either. I'm just so-so all the time."

I won't buy that. If that's your reaction, you're doing what most people do: faking yourself out, sticking to the mediocre center, avoiding reality. If you're not enjoying your life, if you're not pursuing your goals and opportunities with joy in your heart, if you're not reaching out for more of the good things you're capable of winning, you're not merely unhappy—you're miserable. The opposite of *happy* is *unhappy*, but I'm calling it *miserable* because the importance of this idea demands all the impact I can give it. People who can't say they're happy are missing one of the greatest things life has to offer and that, I'm convinced, is genuine misery.

You won't get over having sales slumps unless you get over your misery. Why? Because every time you get rolling, the miseries reach up and pull you off the wagon. That is, the miseries will do that until you learn how to conquer them.

More people are successful part of the time than are successful all of the time. Average performance is often made up of a good month offset by a bad month. If you're blaming this on how the marketplace acts, on how the planets line up, on how your luck breaks, or whatever, you're hiding from reality. If you're in a slump now, you have a better record that you've slumped from. This means you've proven you can sell well. In reality, doesn't this also mean that you've proven your slump is because of your attitude?

Say yes. Until you've admitted to yourself that your attitude is responsible for your slump, you're not ready to get well.

We're all part of the greater community of humankind, and we all need help constantly to achieve our full potentials. But there's one basic fact that you must accept and act on if outside help is to make any lasting difference in your life: You must internalize outside knowledge through determination and discipline, and then you must put your new skills and wisdom to work with your own energy, determination, and discipline. Whether you get that outside help from a book, a seminar, an audio or video program, a personal interview in a professional's office—it's all the same in this respect: Unless you make it work, it won't work.

Are you ready to make it work?

Great. Let's start by studying how you really feel about the question, *Am I happy?* We'll discuss each of these broad categories in turn.

1. "I'm miserable all the time." If this is your answer, I feel for you. I've been there. Twice. I know you need help, just as I did, before you can shake the miseries, get effective, and go on to greater things.

My first case of misery occurred years ago when I started in sales and was a washout because I didn't know anything about selling. The only cure for that kind of misery is to learn how to do what you have to do to be a success—and then to go out and do it. I did. My nonsuccess misery vanished. Then a new kind of mental anguish started developing in its place.

After I finished my first year of success, I thought I was more miserable than ever. This was my second bout with continuous misery. It was different, of course, from the empty-wallet kind of pain I'd felt before! Now my family had the things they needed. I had the money to buy things I needed. But money doesn't buy happiness—it can only give you the means to find it. My new misery was the high-pressure kind created by doing a large volume of business with the wrong attitude. After suffering with my new pains and anxieties for several months, I realized something that's had a profound influence on my life ever since:

Being miserable is a habit; being happy is a habit; and the choice is yours.

2. "I'm happy all the time." If you gave this second reply to the happiness question, here's a note of caution that's worthy of your most careful consideration.

Some people really are happy all the time: Nothing bothers them, not even the things that should bother them. Carried to the extreme, this makes for another kind of dangerous person. When tragedy strikes nearby, we should feel grief. Then we should express that grief so that we can come to terms with it and go on reaching for our full potential. Anyone who can't do that should get professional help.

There are other times when we should feel unhappy—for a few minutes. When chance deals a particularly bad card, when something you could have prevented shatters your hopes for a sale, when a well-laid plan fails for reasons beyond your control, you certainly shouldn't be happy when you discover the disaster. Neither should you be smashed. But this kind of thing can't bother you for more than a few minutes. You've made the Champion's five attitudes toward rejection and failure (remember these from chapter 6?) part of your personality. This is when you turn to them and use them to bring your attitude back around to focusing on what you *can* do rather than what you can't do or didn't do.

3. "I'm miserable some of the time and happy some of the time." This is the best of the three answers to the happiness question, but it still isn't good enough. A Champion says, "I know that some trouble and grief are part of life, so I'm miserable for brief periods when I should be, and I'm happy the rest of the time."

Understand and act on the knowledge that you must meet and overcome your challenges yourself—not necessarily alone, but by and within yourself. Get all the help you can so long as the help you accept brings you nearer your goals. Always be alert for any yearning on your part to form the habit of being miserable.

In other words, don't be a neggie.

What's that?

A neggie is a negative person who wins by losing. Neggies feed on trouble, illness, and fear. If nothing is happening at the moment to justify the misery they've trained themselves to need, they invent something—or replay some past misery.

What's the opposite of being a neggie?

Being a successful, happy, and growing person.

You can be the opposite of a neggie by making it your habit to be happy except when there's a clear and present need for you to be sad for a while. Then be sad. Wash away your sorrow. Don't be afraid to cry. If your inhibitions won't let you do it in public, cry in private. Express your sorrow and get rid of it. Whether it's deep grief at a personal tragedy or superficial but keenly felt remorse for a business matter not handled well, you must give vent to your feelings of grief or disappointment. Then turn resolutely back to your usual happy state. It's not a case of "getting over" misery. It's more a matter of "getting through" it and not dragging it with you for the rest of your life. You learn to live with whatever situation has caused you pain. The situation may never change. The way you handle it can.

This is one of the most valuable habits you can cultivate: Change what you want to change. Accept what you can't hope to change. Be stubbornly happy no matter what, once you've rid yourself of the latest negative feelings that have a necessary part to play in your life.

When I made my breakthrough and started handling a large volume of real estate sales, my challenges multiplied with frightening speed. To most people, buying or selling their latest house is the largest transaction they've ever had to cope with. This creates pressure. Any quirks they have are exaggerated. A touch of greediness can run wild and blind them to their own best interests. Since most real estate transactions take weeks or months to complete, there's plenty of time for lots of things to change or go wrong. With the volume I was handling, for weeks at a time complicated situations hit me every time I showed my face at the office. Many days I didn't want to go in; I wanted to drive past the office and hide. The top producers in most fields have similar experiences.

When the urge to escape came close to overwhelming me, I'd pull into a public park and spend a few minutes staring at the trees and grass. Then I'd have a calm talk with myself. Champions believe in talking to themselves. But they don't do it in bars, they do it in quiet places where they won't be distracted—or unhappily involved.

After getting my emotions under control, I'd drive to the office. Bear in mind that everyone there had been taking messages for me from people who were crackling with anger or anxiety. And since I frequently called in, they knew that I had already heard about most it.

When I walked through the office door, I'd start pumping out the good cheer. Strolling down the aisle between the desks, beaming smiles right and left, I'd say, "Good morning. How are you? Isn't this going to be a beautiful day for sales?"

The confirmed neggies would put their heads down and pretend they were too busy to notice me. The seminegative types would grimace trying to smile. I could almost hear them all thinking, *Here he is, up to his eyeballs in alligators—and he's got the gall to keep on grinning. I hate him!*

Do yourself a favor. When you have a personal or business challenge, when you have an ailment, when you've taken a jolt from the school of hard knocks: Don't tell anyone. Twenty percent don't care, and 80 percent are glad to hear about it.

Don't give them the satisfaction. The only pleasure trouble can give you is keeping it to yourself—at least you know something that no one else around the office knows. If any rumor about your situation leaks out, play it down. Then change the subject to something positive as fast as you can. Humor is always positive. Any business problem is fair game for humor. Drive misery away with a laugh. It works. Misery loves company, and losers love losers. When you're down, you don't need sympathy. You need success. You attract what you are in both people and events. Happiness loves company, too, and winners also love winners.

Another thing about losers: They love to talk about losing, about problems, about why it can't be done. The next time someone in your office has a disaster, notice how people react to it. The losers will hurry over to get the whole story in all its grimy detail. Then they'll tell a few sad tales of their own, and before you know it a royal banquet of bad news is in full swing.

Winners handle someone else's trouble differently. With silence. Or they may offer a few quick words of encouragement. There's none of the loving analysis of catastrophe that losers insist on.

When someone has a great success, the same split between winners and losers shows up. This time it's the winners who are crowding around to hear every detail, and perhaps share a success story or two of their own. Now it's the losers who are too busy to listen.

Have you ever gone into an emotional slump? A financial slump? A performance slump? Of course you have. Slumping is normal for anyone who hasn't been trained to prevent slumps. I spent three months studying how to cure slumping, and I'm convinced that there is only one way. It's an old idea that goes under many names. This is the one I like best.

THE GOYA FORMULA

Using this formula is very easy—it only seems hard at the time. Here it is in its entirety: GOYA.

Get Off Your Anatomy.

Get out into the field, and go to work.

That's really all there is to it, except for making yourself do it.

This can be hard when your chin is on the floor and you're ready to give up on the whole world. I've been there, too. But the amazing thing is, it's always easy to GOYA.

Do I really think it's easy?

Yes. All you have to do is start—take the first small step—and after that it's all downhill. If you can just get yourself to start, you'll be all right.

The last thing you want to do when you're down is the one thing that you have to do to get yourself up. GOYA. You get lucky when you go out and meet people.

When you get down, it's because you've drifted away from the basics. You've stopped doing what you know you should be doing. It's strange how quickly salespeople can retire to executive administration. One good month does it—until reality hits in the form of a slump in sales and a smaller paycheck. Then they start feeling guilty. That makes them tense. The tension causes them to get upset over things that have little or no real importance. The real problem is that they're coasting, not working. And of course, they don't want to face up to that fact.

When you want to pull yourself up, get off your backside, go back to the basics, and do what you know you should do. It works every time. As soon as you start doing that, you start winning again. You see the money coming in. And you start ignoring minor annoyances and feeling good about yourself once more.

However, no matter how good your attitude is, no matter how resolutely you confront your difficulties, there will be days when things do not go right. On these days, a second challenge will hit you before you can put the first one on the shelf, and then a third one will slam into you. And another. And then it seems like there's no end to them.

Expect to have a few rough days in your selling career and you won't be disappointed. Just don't forget, while you're having one of those days, if you'll keep on working, the tough period will pass and the good days will come back.

Are you a worry machine? Some people keep thinking, *Will I make it? Can I pay my bills?*

Stop worrying. Make up your mind that you won't worry anymore. Ninety percent of what we worry about never happens. So why waste the energy? When you've finished making your plans, think of something pleasant. Remember that planning creates success, but worry kills. Spend your worry time relaxing. If you can't relax, spend the time training yourself to be more competent. If you're tempted to worry during business hours, stop, get a grip on yourself, and decide what is the most productive thing that you can do at that moment. Then do it. If you'll do these things, you'll soon have no need to worry about money because you'll be making more than ever. Don't worry yourself out of sales; work yourself into a successful career instead.

"What if—?" When you're afraid that something terrible may happen, sit down and accept that it will happen. Then outline all the things you can do to prevent it from happening. List those things in order of importance, and get busy doing them. If you'll follow that practice, none of your favorite nightmare what-ifs will ever come to pass.

If you're new in sales, realize that your work will soon become fun. Whether you're a physician or a salesperson, using skills confidently is fun. That's why the first of the ten steps in the GOYA system for unslumping starts with this one.

1. Become highly skilled at what you do. If you haven't perfected your knowledge and skills to the highest level you're capable of, how can you say that you're slumping? You don't need to get out of a slump in this case, all you need do is practice, drill, and rehearse. Get out of the unskilled mass of salespeople and join the highly skilled elite who are impervious to slumps.

2. Bum the past daily. We're all tempted to dwell on the past, to make up lists of wilted hopes that all start with "If only—" Every time you feel this temptation, say to yourself, *That's dead and I've buried it. I can't change it, so now I'm going to think about something I can turn to my advantage.* If you'll make that a habit, you'll start molding your future, you'll start making progress toward your goals, and you'll feel the special joy that comes only from being in control of your life.

3. Live in this moment. You can't live in your tomorrows. You can't live in your yesterdays. If you try to do either, the only thing you'll succeed in doing is ruining all your todays. Never forget that life is always this minute's consciousness. Whether you're ten or a hundred years old, today could be the last day. So why be overly serious about the future? Enjoy this moment. You'll never have more than one moment at a time to enjoy. Plan as if you'll live to be a hundred. Live as if all you have is today.

4. Plan your future instead of worrying about it. Once you've made your plan, give it a solid shot all day every working day—and then enjoy your free time. If you don't want to plan for success and happiness, what right do you have to worry about nonsuccess and unhappiness? If you're not planning where you want to be, what reason or excuse do you have for worrying about being nowhere? The biggest wasters of their own resources are the people who don't know who they want to be or where they want to go. Study how you want to have your life evolve. Then plan how you'll make it all happen. Schedule the time you'll work at creating what's success for you, and schedule the time you'll devote to renewing your energy, rewarding yourself, and enriching your sense of self-worth. Then be sure you never allow worry to intrude on your moments of renewal, reward, and enrichment.

5. Don't demand fairness from life. "That's not fair" is one of the most idiotic statements in the English language.

"She's getting the best leads from the manager—that's not fair."

"They didn't call me back—that's not fair."

"He got the business because they went to college together—that's not fair."

Forget fair. Our world was not designed to be fair. If you demand it, and use that unanswered demand to excuse a lack of drive, you'll be miserable. You have to survive—if you're going to—in a world where there'll always be people above you and people below you in every facet of life you can name.

Once in a while we should stop and be thankful for what we don't have. Some people out there are doing great despite heavier burdens than you yourself carry. And of course, there are also people out there with lighter burdens than you carry, and some of them have turned their lives into one long whine. Those are the saddest stories of all. People are amazing. Most of us are convinced that our problems are greater than anyone else's. They aren't. So quit asking for fairness and stop letting your limitations depress you. Take what you've got and get what you want with it. If that means not paying the price for success, be happy with unsuccess. You were born to be happy, but no one else can make you happy for long. Only you can do that. Being happy is a personal responsibility; it's a duty you can't delegate. The only way you can keep happiness is to accept that reality.

6. Don't be guilty. If you're tempted to do something that will make you feel guilty, don't do it. However, if you decide to do it, also decide to enjoy it and forget the guilt. You need to be hard-nosed about this. Push all the people back who'd love to drop a load of guilt on you for doing the normal things you have every right to do if you so choose.

7. Commit to high performance, and accept the consequences of that commitment. You can't be everywhere at once, and you'll have to learn how to say no. The best way is to say it straight out in a kindly tone: "No, I'm sorry, I can't fit that in. But thanks, anyway."

When you commit to high performance, you will see clearly where it's best to invest your time and energy. We all have a tendency to keep on saying yes to our families, our customers, our bosses, our friends, our associates. This means that the only person we say no to is ourselves. When you wind up having zero time for yourself, you're on a collision course with a crisis of will. When the crunch comes, you'll find yourself overwhelmed by demands. You won't have the willpower to meet those demands because you've failed to make it worthwhile to yourself to put out the great effort that's required. Take care of number one or you'll wind up not taking care of anyone.

8. Work on procrastination. Notice that I said *work on it*. You'll never overcome procrastination entirely because it's part of human nature to let a few things slide once in a while. And sometimes, when it's used with care, procrastination is a useful tactic. Many things respond best to no treatment at all, and a lot of pesky challenges will disappear if we ignore them. Just know which are best to give your immediate attention to and which are best to let ride.

I suffer from procrastination occasionally. Sometimes I fly half the night to get to my next seminar, and then the next morning I don't want to study the program I must learn. But I live by three words: *Do it now.*

Try them for twenty-one days and you'll start a whole new power pattern that will open up new vistas of opportunity for your future.

9. Keep your sense of humor growing. Our world is a riot of laughs. You can make it a habit to spot them and squeeze chuckles out of every possible situation. Or you can make it your habit to grind your teeth all day long except when you're licking your chops over bad news. Quick-to-laugh people get there faster and they get there fresher because they get more help along the way.

Some people have difficulty building their sense of humor due to something held over in their personality from childhood. This is one of the easiest challenges to solve but, like any other, you have to work it to solve it. Make sure you see funny movies. Select TV programs for their humor. Read things that make you laugh. Bookstores and libraries have large volumes of jokes and funny stories. Read one every day. Make friends with people who like to laugh, listen to their stories, and tell a few of your own.

If you're Chief Iron Mouth, you can't change overnight—but you can make a start tonight. Every morning and every night, tell yourself that you have a great sense of humor and it's getting better all the time. Also tell yourself that you love to laugh. Try this for three weeks and you'll own a wonderful new habit that'll put you on the highway to financial success and greater happiness.

10. Learn to love growth, change, and life. The truly successful person knows that growth, change, and life are interwoven; they are inseparable; they are one. Reader, friend, Champion-to-be, the methods in this book make whatever future you're willing to order yours for the taking. With these ideas and techniques, you can write a check payable by your own effort for your chosen future—and be sure it will arrive. Accept this idea. Have complete faith in it. And, most important of all, act on it. You can have whatever future you're willing to GOYA for.

22. The Most Necessary Skill of All

For years I've been asked: "How did you get it all together and do all you've done?"

I don't believe people ask out of idle curiosity. I think they have the same reason that compelled me when I was twenty-one to ask much the same question of an extremely successful corporate executive: a sincere desire to learn how to make my dreams come true.

The average human being has the ability to achieve almost anything. Lack of basic capability is rarely the cause of underachievement—we all have great reserves of untapped power. The challenge is almost always in finding out what you want. Before we go any farther, let me define how I'm using the word *want* here. I'm not talking about mere wishes now. I'm talking about wants that gnaw at you.

Maybe you think you don't have any gnawing wants. If you think that, you're wrong. You have the wants. But they're bottled up somewhere. It's often the fear of failure that makes us bottle up our wants. But failure isn't the worst possible result. Not trying is. If you try, you can succeed; if you won't try, you have already failed. Do you suffer from this fear? Then decide in advance that you've failed—and after that go out and give it the best try you're capable of.

Lots of us are willing to risk failure, but we still don't exert ourselves. We don't see any reason to. Why? Because we wouldn't do anything very exciting or satisfying with success if we could win it. If that's your challenge, you need to give it a lot of attention. Finding the answer will take deep thinking. Widen your horizons, seek out new friends and activities, and search for unthought-of rewards that will make success worth its price to you. The pivot point here is finding what will motivate your unique personality. Many of us are so blinded by what society and other people think we should want that we can't hear our own cries for help. Getting in touch with your true self must be your first priority.

If you really want something, that want will make a difference in your life. You'll work to satisfy that want. You'll sacrifice pleasures for it. You'll even be willing to change and grow for it. In fact, you'll deliberately change yourself and grow so that you can have what you really want. But you won't do any of these things for mere wishes. That's why you must put what you think you want on paper. Then look at your goals, written there in black and white, and commit to them.

You're not done yet, though. It's no good to write pages of goals down somewhere and then go on about your old routine as though nothing had happened.

Every day, look at each goal. Think whether you're doing what has to be done, whether you're paying the price that has to be paid to achieve it. It doesn't matter at this point whether or not you already possess all the abilities and resources you must have if you're to achieve your goal. Those you can pick up along the way. But you won't start without having the desire. The first step is to commit to the goal in writing. The great majority of people will never take this simple first step on the journey to achievement. For that reason alone, they'll never take the last step that brings them what they wish for. Apathy stifles more careers than inability ever does.

Since you can't unleash your creativity or accelerate your growth until you commit yourself to a goal, any positive goal is better than no goal at all. You'll probably make many false starts before you discover the course that'll keep you happily involved for the rest of your life. That's wonderful. All the time that you're committed to written goals, you're growing rapidly. You're experiencing much. Striving on the field, you're learning a ton for every pound the apathetic person learns sitting in the bleachers of life. Every moment that you're playing the great game of living to the fullest, you're charging toward an understanding of your highest potential, of what your finest destiny is. Allowing ourselves to bury our lives in apathy is the greatest crime—and we commit it by not committing ourselves to goals that are real to us.

You can achieve almost any goal you have the courage to set—but sometimes it takes a painful experience to light the way.

That was so in my case. When I was seventeen years old, I broke my father's heart. He had saved enough from a very average income to send me to college to become an attorney; ninety days later, I was home telling him that I had quit college—and for the first time I saw him cry. With tears in his eyes he said, "Son, I'm always going to love you even though you'll never amount to anything."

That was my first motivational speech.

When I walked out of that room, I was burning with something not everyone has the chance to feel. I didn't just *want* to succeed—I *had* to succeed.

But I couldn't see how to do it. I became a bridge deck specialist and carried steel up construction ramps for eighteen months—and all the time my father's words were eating at me. I had an hourly-wage job that led nowhere except to old age.

I went into sales—and the wages stopped. I earned nothing because that's what I knew about my profession. Then, just as I was going under for the third time in sales, a man came by and got me involved with the Edwards training seminar. I learned the closes and techniques. I lost no time putting them to work. Soon after that, I started tasting the sweet fruits of success for the first time in my working life.

Some time later, I told the management of the company where I worked that my goal was to meet personally with Mr. Edwards. They helped me achieve that goal. When the day came, I told him, "Mr. Edwards, my goal is to someday take your place and be able to train people as well as you trained me."

That all came to pass because I set goals to make it happen. Committing to the goal was the essential element. You can't rise unless you set goals that make you stretch.

Start with short-term goals. My first goal in sales—beyond making enough to eat and cover my back—was to buy a new car. Vehicles make great starting goals but, unfortunately, they often become the end goal. There's more to life than rolling around town in an expensive car. A lot of average salespeople set average goals, achieve them, and then fade into a state of suspended animation. Like a bear in winter, they go to ground and live off their fat. The true Champions keep setting new goals whenever they achieve old ones. Achieved goals are like yesterday's newspapers: useful only for lining birdcages.

In this most necessary of all skills, effective goal setting, some rules must be followed if the system is to work. Here they are:

1. If it's not in writing, it's not a goal. An unwritten want is a wish, a dream, a never-happen. The day you put your goal in writing is the day it becomes a commitment that will change your life.

2. If it's not specific, it's not a goal. As I found out carrying steel on my shoulder, broad desires and lofty aims have no effect. Merely wanting to be somebody, or having the determination to make it big, isn't enough. Until you translate your vague wishes into concrete goals and plans, you aren't going to make much progress.

3. Goals must be believable. Now I'm quoting Doug Edwards on one of the most vital aspects of successful goal setting. If you don't believe that you can achieve a goal, you won't pay the price for it.

4. An effective goal is an exciting challenge. If your goal doesn't push you beyond where you've been before—if it doesn't demand your best and a bit more you didn't realize you had in you—it isn't going to change your ways and elevate your lifestyle.

5. Goals must be adjusted to new information. Set your goals quickly, and adjust them later if you've aimed too high or too low. Many of the goals that have the greatest positive influence on our lives are those we set in unfamiliar territory. As we learn more about the realities, we adjust our goals downward if they become unbelievable, or upward if they lose their challenge because they're too easy. In some cases, we decide the goal isn't something we really wanted anyway. But we don't put off setting goals until we know more.

6. Dynamic goals guide our choices. We live in a world that constantly threatens to overwhelm us with alternatives. If you want something badly enough, you'll turn off the TV to get it. If your goals are set up right, they'll instantly show you the right way to go on most decisions.

7. Don't set short-term goals for more than ninety days. After you've worked with short-term goals for half a year, you may find that a shorter or longer period works better for you. Ninety days is the period that works best for me. If I set a short-term goal that takes more than ninety days to achieve, I tend to lose interest in it.

8. Maintain a balance between long-term and short-term goals. Your wants for clothes, cars, savings accounts, vacations, and all sorts of material possessions make great short-term goals that put excitement and frequent gratification into your goals program. If your goals are all long-term, you'll have difficulty keeping your performance up because all your payoffs are hidden in the fog of the future.

9. Include your loved ones in your goals. You'll be amazed at how hard you can work when your kids know that they get a bite of the larger pie if you reach your goal. When their goals are intimately involved with your goals, they'll buck you up when you need encouragement.

10. Set goals in all areas of your life. They aren't just for making money. Set goals for health, for exercise, for sports, in your personal life, and in your family and spiritual life. This is a system that works with astonishing power if it's used. It's simply too valuable to reserve only for your career objectives.

11. Your goals must harmonize. If they fight each other, you lose. Whenever you detect a conflict, set priorities that will eliminate the conflict. Use your goals program to eliminate frustration, not to create it.

12. Review your goals regularly. Remember that your long-term goals can only be achieved if they are the culmination of your short-term goals, and that your new goals will rise out of the old ones you've realized. In the future, you'll set short-term aims that are far beyond your present capacity—and you'll achieve them with the skill, confidence, and resources you've won achieving your present goals.

13. Set vivid goals. Excitement is the basic ingredient of successful goal setting. You won't stretch for the ho-hums of life, will you? You must be able to see your goals clearly.

My first airplane flight was from California to Arizona to make one of my early speeches. Since then I've made thousands of flights I can't remember, but I'll never forget that one. Perhaps you can remember your first flight. Were you white-knuckled? I was.

Just before we took off, I looked out the window. Sitting on the runway nearby was a beautiful little plane. I asked the man sitting next to me about it.

"That's a corporate jet," he said.

"What a neat little number," I said, taking out my goals notebook. In it I wrote "Ten-year goal—jet."

It's surprising—no, it's amazing—how goals work if you put them in writing and concentrate on them for a few moments every morning or evening. I kept seeing my jet landing and rolling to a stop right in front of me. I'll never forget when the jet arrived—ten years later to the day. I had just completed a program with a large audience in Baton Rouge. As soon as I walked off the stage, I hurried out to the airfield in time to see a beautiful little plane come in and land.

The captain welcomed me aboard, and off we went. *This is it*, I thought, *ten years and I've arrived*. I was seeing, smelling, and feeling the reality of what I'd practiced when envisioning the goal all those years.

14. Don't chisel your goals in granite. A lot of people put off setting goals every time they think about it because they're afraid. Remember that you aren't swearing an oath that'll cause your ears to fall off if you decide to change a goal later. I'll never forget the first time we refueled the jet. The pilot came back and handed me a bill for $882.

I said, "This is for the month?"

It wasn't for the month.

That long-term goal turned out to be a thirty-thousand-dollar-a-month item, which is why we only had it sixty days. What had once been a vivid and compelling goal, on realization turned out to be just another toy—and a ridiculously expensive one, at that, for my kind of activity. It had no place in my new aspirations. There are times when we have to change goals to conform to our growing awareness of what's really important in our lives. Your goal-setting and goal-achieving program is a lifelong commitment to growth. That growth will take unexpected turns, and your future holds achievements that you haven't yet thought about.

15. Reach out into the future. The whole idea of setting goals is to plan your life rather than to go on bumbling along, muddling through, taking it as it comes. Begin by setting twenty-year goals.

First, list the personal achievements you want to accomplish. Who and what do you want to be in twenty years? What do you want to own? Where, and in what kind of housing, do you want to live? Again, you're working with goals that can be changed. What are the status symbols you've always dreamed of? What do you want for your family? If you don't know what you want, how can you get it?

Start thinking about the net worth you want to have twenty years down the road. Start watching your equity position now and get ready for the future. It only happens when you start writing down goals, working with them, and causing your mind to reach out. Take a hard look at the future and at yourself. Say, "That's the person I want to be in twenty years, and I'm willing and eager to pay the price to become that person."

Once you have your twenty-year goals sketched out, cut them in half and there are your ten-year goals.

Halve them again and you've got your five-year goals. Do it one more time and your thirty-month goals appear before your eyes.

Then set up your next-twelve-month goals. Work on this one carefully. Then break your one-year schedule of goals down to months, weeks, and finally to goals for tomorrow and for each day of the coming week. Imagine planning your time for today by what your twenty-year goals are! You'll be amazed at the progress you'll make toward achieving those goals one daily step at a time.

16. Have a set of goals for every day, and review results every night. You may be saying, "This will take a lot of time. Will it be worth it?"

Is making a success of your life worth a little trouble? Let's be honest—it's not the trouble that's bothering you, it's the idea of submitting to any form of discipline, even self-imposed discipline.

Think that through before you turn away from this idea, because if you're not willing to accept your own discipline, you're not going to accomplish 2 percent of what you could—and you're going to miss out on 98 percent of the good things you could have.

17. Train yourself to crave your goals. Spend time (odd moments when you're driving, waiting, and so on) visualizing yourself possessing what you've set your goals for. The more ardently you desire your goals, the more ready you'll be to pay the price you must pay to get them.

18. Set activity goals, not production goals. How many people will you see today? How many demonstrations will you give? How many rejections will you go looking for? If all your goals are production goals, you're setting yourself up for a slump. A few lost sales, a change in competitive conditions and you're hopelessly behind, you're feeling guilty, and you don't want to even think about the system. But if your daily and weekly goals are based on activity (the number of prospecting calls to be made, the number of presentations to be given, and so on), you'll keep on meeting your goals during challenging times. Because you're active, you'll adjust to the new conditions faster and sell yourself out of the slump before it can get you down.

19. Understand luck, and make it work for you. Do you know that the really successful people, the big winners, the ones who are achieving their goals, all believe that they understand luck? It's really very simple. You begin by always expecting good things to happen. You don't rely on having good luck, you expect it. This means that you prepare carefully, keep lots of things going, and stay alert for Lady Luck's whispers. You never expect trouble—you plan ways to prevent it. Do you know that some people have been proven to be accident-prone? And why are they? Because they spend so much time thinking about getting hurt that their subconscious minds get confused, acting as if that's what they *want* to have happen.

The winners understand that good luck is a manufactured article. So they think in terms of good things happening to them and make themselves good-luck-prone. Always make your subconscious mind work *for* you, not *against* you.

20. Start now. Give goal setting two hours of concentrated thought today. Then set aside ten minutes a day for the next twenty-one days to review and revise your goals. After that, two minutes a day, plus one hour a week, will keep you flying toward the immensely greater and richer future that the goal-setting system will deliver if you follow these rules. Go to it. You'll have a terrific year if you have 365 fulfilling days in which you achieve your daily goals. And on into the future, as one terrific year follows another. What an exciting prospect! And it'll all be yours if you'll just start setting your goals now.

23. How to Sell to the Most Important People You Know

Now that you're rapidly becoming a professional salesperson who's earning a professional's income, your inner private self is changing just as your outer public self is. Adjustments will be required in many areas of your life. As this happens, you may discover that the more you achieve outside your home, the less you achieve inside your family or within your circle of friends. If this seems to be happening, maybe it's because you haven't been making full use of your new sales skills. They aren't only for work. Don't turn them off when you head for home—keep them turned on.

At this point in your life, you may be single. You may be living where you have few relatives or friends. If you're not satisfied with your social situation, use salesmanship to improve it. With a little thought, a little ingenuity, most of the techniques in the previous chapters can be adapted to the after-hours scene. There they can do wonders in helping you achieve your private-life objectives.

In order to be a master of the art of selling, you must be able to sell effectively to the most important people in the world—your friends and loved ones.

Sell them what?

On whatever you believe is best for them. On achieving their own goals. On leading happy, fulfilled lives. On keeping pace with you—or on accepting and respecting themselves as they are.

You may think it's enough to bring home a professional's income—that your responsibilities are over when you've worked long and hard. If you have loved ones, this cannot be the case. You and your devoted concern are irreplaceable in your family. If your swiftly rising career allows you less time with your loved ones or friends than you'd like, make every minute you do have with them count. *I must do the most productive thing possible at every given moment* applies with great force to your private life. The most productive thing at some moments is holding your small child and teaching him how to overcome fear; at others, it's saying to someone special, "I'll always love you." For an infinity of reasons such as these, this last chapter is devoted to how you can apply the principles in this book to enhancing your home life.

Let me clarify exactly what I'm talking about. After you internalize and reinforce the attitudes and techniques in the preceding chapters, you'll automatically use them now and then with your loved ones. But it's one thing to use them catch-as-catch-can in the daily rush of living; it's another thing entirely to put these powerful techniques to work as part of a plan to solve family challenges and achieve family goals. I'm concerned here with the deliberate use of your new sales skills in this most important area of your life.

While you've been growing fast professionally and personally, your spouse may have continued to amble along at his or her usual pace. Maybe that's fine with you. If it isn't, start now to bridge the gulf that's opening between you and your mate. Later may be too late.

There are basically only three ways that you can cope with this situation successfully: (a) You can slow down; (b) Your spouse can speed up; or (c) You can both accept that you'll be growing at different speeds and be happy about it.

Only the first alternative is completely within your control, and probably the least attractive of the three to you. The other two can't work unless your mate participates willingly. Making this happen often calls for highly skilled sales work: discovery questions, minor closes, leading questions, top-notch objection handling, major closes—not to mention lots of thought and the giving of much approval and encouragement.

If your spouse feels threatened by the new person you're becoming, have empathy. Be patient. Bear in mind that you can't dictate other people's feelings—but you can relieve their anxieties as to how you feel about them.

Early in this book, I discussed the value of learning what benefits your prospects really want before you try to sell them a specific product or service. This same step is equally valuable to the creation of an atmosphere in which every member of your family will expand in accomplishment and confidence. As you've learned here, there are no limits to your growth except the limits that you impose on yourself. Those limits, of course, are your willingness to pay the price of achievement. Do you want to fasten limits on your children by dictating what achievements they should pursue?

Never lose sight of these facts: You can't live someone else's life; you can't control someone else's emotions; you can't pay the price for someone else's achievements. As much as we love our children and our friends, each of them is a separate individual with goals, preferences, limitations, and opportunities that differ from our own. As my father and I discovered after he guided me toward becoming an attorney, success wears many different suits. Your children can't achieve your goals for you. Neither can your friends. You can only help them all achieve their goals for themselves.

The preceding chapters are loaded with techniques and concepts that can help you lead your family toward achieving whatever goals you and they want. I'll briefly recap a few of these ideas.

Tie-downs. Use them when talking with your family to reinforce the positive things you want to have happen, and to discourage the negative things you don't want to have happen. Leading people is largely the business of getting them to realize, and then to agree with, what is best for them.

Alternate advance. This technique is a real beauty in home use. Compare these two ways of handling the same situation:

1. WIFE: "Honey, do you want to go out to dinner tonight?"
   HUSBAND: "No. I want to eat here."
   WIFE: "You never take me out. I work, too—or have you forgotten?" And they're off to another argument brought on by a say-no question.

2. WIFE: "Honey, would you like to have dinner at the Blue
   Bucket, or would you rather eat at Smokey Jo's?"
   HUSBAND: "Let's go to the Blue Bucket." When an alternate
   advance will get what you want, why ask a say-no?

Porcupine. This technique is a real workhorse for clarifying do-
mestic issues and avoiding unwise family decisions. Very often,
your best answer to a question around the house is another question that's also an alternate advance toward what you want to
achieve. When you hear something like, "Dad, can we get a pet rattlesnake?" and you have a healthy fear of reptiles, don't just say,
"No way." Try this: "What makes you think a rattlesnake would
make a good pet?" Getting your kids to elaborate is the goal. Could
be they want something that'll scare their friends and make them
feel cool. Chances are good you can help them acquire the same
"cool" feeling without the fangs.

Involvement questions. When you want to invest time and
money in something for the both of you, excite your spouse about
the project with involvement questions. When you want to encourage your children to achieve, ask them involvement questions
about the goal that's under consideration.

Discovery questions and leading questions. Intense listening is the key to discovering what your prospects really want. Intense listening to your loved ones is just as important if you're
serious about strengthening your relationships with them. In many
cases, an unruly child simply wants to know that her feelings of
frustration, anger, or disappointment are understood by her parent. Acknowledging the distress is often all that a wise mother or
father has to do to relieve the child's feelings and restore calm. It
may take more. But how can you know unless you ask discovery
questions and then listen intently to the answers? When you know
precisely what the challenge is—but not before—you're fully competent to lead your child in a way that is best for her.

In Chapter 6, I talked about **catching change on the move** as
you work with prospects. This is also a key concept for influenc-
ing your family. Probably the easiest and most effective way that
you can have a long-lasting positive effect on your loved ones is to

encourage them to pay the price to achieve goals they've chosen for themselves. The first few steps beyond mere wishing are the hardest. Miss no opportunity to motivate your loved ones to act instead of watch when it's within their ability. The more they do today, the more they can and will accomplish tomorrow.

Involving emotions. Many of us have been taught that we should always go with the logical choice—that relying on our emotions is somehow bad. Logic and careful analysis are supposedly the only ways to make decisions; intuition and emotions must be left out. This destructive idea ignores reality. In the real world, we rarely have the complete facts when we have to make a decision. We're forced to fall back on our emotions and intuition. This makes us worry and feel guilty. Avoid this by guiding your children toward striking a balance between logic and emotion in decision making.

The do-nothing twins, apathy and inertia, thrive on the denial of emotional involvement. When we foster the belief that emotions are dangerous, we create frustrations that often paralyze our children's efforts. Whenever your loved ones want to do something positive, encourage them if you possibly can. Discover what rewards will motivate them and go with the best you can afford. Arouse their emotions to help them achieve their goals, and teach them how to use their emotions to psych themselves up. Success is a habit. There's no better one that you can pass on to them.

Use go-ahead terms on your family instead of rejection words. By developing positive communication within your family, you'll discover the rejection words that wound and defeat your spouse and children. Every time you hear one of these discouraging words, think of a go-ahead term to replace it, and use it from then on. Finding and saying go-ahead things instead of rejection things will have a wonderful effect on your family's happiness and ability to cope with challenges, to achieve goals, and to be happy.

You'll get a bonus for doing this, too. It's great training for your professional sales work; you can't fail to profit from becoming more sensitive to other people's feelings and needs.

I have recounted many ways this book's concepts and techniques can help you attain a richer and more fulfilling lifestyle for your family. Reread it with them in mind and you'll find new insights every time you do so. You can become a Champion of Selling, a Champion parent or friend, and a Champion wife or husband. It's all yours. All you have to do is pay the price and you can have your finest goals.

Index

Acceptance, as motivator, 100–106
Achievement, as motivator, 99–100
Activity breeds productivity, 143–44, 350–51
Activity goals, 370
Add-on sales, 325–26
Advantages of selling, 1–4
Advertisements, walking, 328
Agreement, use of term, 73
Altered, in NEADS sequence, 250–51
Alternate advance test closes, 278, 280, 374–75
Alternate of choice questions, 42–43
Anatomy of close, 285–87
Anxiety, 95, 97, 279–80
Apathy, 18–19, 364, 376
    GOYA formula for, 357–62
Apologies, 312
Appearance, 16–17, 239–42, 328
Appointments. See also First meeting
    alternate of choice questions for, 42–43
    by phone, 185–86, 195–96, 223
    to sales ratio, 140–41, 144
    scheduling time for, 346, 348
    use of term, 70–71

Arguments, with clients, 262
Arousing emotions. See Emotional appeals
Attitude. See also Positive attitude toward rejections, 124–31
Audio programs, xv–xvii
Available for (available at), use of term, 72

Bad habits, 339–40, 354–56
Balance sheet close, 295–300
Barber, Bob, xxii
Basics of selling, 6–7
Believability, of goals, 366
Benefits referrer accepted, 219, 223
Benjamin Franklin balance sheet close, 295–300
Bernstein, David, 14–15
Body language, for first meeting, 239–42
Bond, establishing with client, 53
Boredom, during presentations, 203–4, 228–29
Brady, James Buchanan, xix
Bridging, 312–13
Brochures, 144–47, 234
Bullfighting, closing compared with, 289–90
Bunches like bananas, 326–27

Burning desire, for success, 19, 23–24, 93–94

Burns, Robert, 14

Business cards, 137–38, 327–28

Business ratios, 138–44

Business slumps. *See* Slumps

Buy, use of term, 74

Buyer-client files, 341–42

Buyers
  arousing emotional response, 62–70
  decision makers, 59–62, 251
  empathy with, during closes, 17–18, 281–82, 283–84
  itch cycle and, 150–56

Buying emotions, 62–70

Buying signs, 286

By-street directories, 193

Calculators, 275

Card referral systems, 173–74, 180

Care (caring), 20–21, 63–64, 281–82

Carey, Max, 131

Catalogs, 234

Challenges. *See also* Objections
  use of term, 82

Change
  of base, 268–69
  catching on the move, 63–70
  family life and, 352–57
  fear of, as demotivator, 113–19

Characteristics of great salespeople, 16–22

Cheaper, use of term, 82

Claim-staking, 165–66

Client-buyer files, 341–42

Clients, use of term, 81

Climate. *See* Selling climate

Closed questions, 35. *See also* Tie-downs

Closing (closes), 7, 30, 273–91. *See also* Power closes
  alternate of choice questions for, 42–43
  anatomy of, 285–87

bullfighting compared with, 289–90

buyers' viewpoints, 283–84

to contacts ratio, 122–24

crash-and-burn, 280

dangerous time in, 279–80

definition of, 281

with empathy, 17–18, 281–82, 283–84

likes and dislikes, 282–83

materials for, 274–75

most important words in, 287–89

moving to, 281

in phone calls, 185, 193

porcupine technique, 44–45, 279, 280

presentations and, 208

question-asking ability and, 34

shutting up and, 287–89

test closes, 278–81

testimonial letters and, 233–34, 275–77

when and where, 284–85

Clubs, 165–69, 193–94

Cobb, Ty, 131

Cold calling, 186–89

Color, and buying emotions, 65, 66

Commercial sales, directories, 216–17

Commissions, use of term, 81

Committees, unreachable, 59–61

Community involvement, 169–70

Company files (paperwork), 153–56, 193–94, 337–40

Comparative questions, 224–25

Competitive-edge closes, 318

Computer classes, 345

Concerns. *See* Objections

Conclusions, erroneous, 278–79

Conditions, 259–61

Confidence, 13, 17, 286

Contacts, 6, 135–37, 340–43. *See also* Leads; Prospecting; Referrals
  card system for, 173–74

to closings ratio, 122–24
recontacts, 328–32
resources, 166–69, 193–94
thank-you notes for, 333
Continuing education, 21–22, 345
Contracts, use of term, 73
Corporate sales preplanner, 226
    sample form, 222
Costs, use of term, 71–72
Course corrections, 125, 127–29
Courtesy, on the phone, 194–95
Coworkers, acceptance by, as mo-
    tivator, 100–104
Craving your goals, 370
Crash-and-burn closes, 280
Creed of the Champion, 132
Customers, use of term, 80–81

Daily work plan, 346–51
Dardon, Ed, 326–27
Deals, use of term, 83–85
Dear-old-mother closes, 313–14
Decision makers, 59–62
    in NEADS Qualification
        Sequence, 251
Defense mechanisms, minor objec-
    tions as, 258–59
Delivery, moods of, 89
Demonstrations (presentations), 7,
    197–236
    17 minutes only for, 215, 228–29
    client-participation in, 197–201,
        213–14
    formats for selling interviews,
        201–4
    glamour words, 210–11, 286–87
    interruptions, 214–15
    lingo, 212–13
    models, 234
    preplanning form, 218–26
    preplanning in writing, 215–27
    printed literature, 234
    prospecting and, 144
    scheduling time for, 348–49
    steps to follow, 206–10

testimonial letters, 233–34,
    275–77
thank-you notes after, 333
triad concept for, 86–89
use of term, 83–85
video equipment, 234–36
visual aids, 227–28, 229–33
when to plan, 226–27
words to avoid, 211–12
Demotivators, 95, 107–19
    fear of failure, 108–11
    pain of change, 113–19
    security, 107–8
    self-doubt, 111–13
Deposits, alternate advances, 42
Depression, 96–98. *See also*
    Slumps
Desire, for success, 19, 23–24,
    93–94
Directories, 193–94, 216–17
Discovery questions, 50–53, 375
Documentation, 337–43. *See also*
    Forms
Do Not Call Registry, 143, 188, 194
Doubt, as demotivator, 110–11
Down payments, use of term, 73
Dubiski, H. W., xxi
Dumas, Alexandre, 322–23
Dun & Bradstreet Directory, 216,
    217, 226
Dynamic goals, 366–67

Economic truth closes, 316–17
Economy (economical), use of
    term, 83
Edison, Thomas, 126–27
Educational sales, 217–18
Edwards, J. Douglas, xix–xxiv,
    162–64, 287–88, 295, 313, 326,
    366
E-mail marketing, 144–47, 194
Emotional appeals, 62–70, 376
    closing and, 281–82
    demotivators, 95, 107–19
    logic versus, 62–63, 66–67

Emotional appeals *(continued)*
  motivators, 95, 98–106
  own (ownership), use of term,
    74–78
  positive vs. negative, 67–70
  senses that sell, 90–92
  triad concept and, 88–89
Emotional health, 347–48, 352–57
Empathy, closing with, 17–18,
    281–82, 283–84
Enjoy, in NEADS sequence, 248–50
Enthusiasm (positive attitude),
    19–20, 93–94, 96, 353–57
Erroneous conclusion advance
    test closes, 278–79
Exercise programs, 347
Eye contact, 230–31, 234, 239–42

Failure. *See also* Rejection
  as demotivator, 108–10, 363–64
Fairness, in life, 360–61
Family, 372–74
  setting goals and, 367
  as motivator, 106
  scheduling time with, 347
Fear
  as demotivator, 95, 107–19
  of rejection, 124
  selling climate and, 67–70, 92,
    238–39
Fee for service, use of term, 81
Files. *See also* Record-keeping
  client-buyer, 341–42, 349
Film equipment, 234–36
Filtering system, 210
First meeting (impression), 237–45
  appearance, 16–17
  business cards, use of, 137–38
  emotional responses and, 69–70
  in nonreferred situations, 242–45
  with referred leads, 172–73,
    241–42
  soft approach to, 238–39
  steps in, 239–41
Follow-up paperwork, 340–43

Forms, 218–26, 274–75, 337–40
  use of term, 73
Franklin, Benjamin, 22
  balance sheet close, 295–300
Fund-raising, 170

Galbraith, John, 23
Game, the (percentage game), 126,
    131
Glamour words, 210–11, 286–87
Gnomes, 60–61
Go-ahead terms, replacing rejection
    words with, 70–86, 376
Goals (goal setting), 364–74
Google News, 216
Governmental sales, directories,
    217
GOYA (Get Off Your Anatomy) for-
    mula, 357–62
Greetings, 30, 69, 240, 242, 243
Guilt, during slumps, 361

Habits, 339–40, 354–56
Handshakes, 240–41, 242
Happiness, 353–57
Harmonizing goals, 367
Higher authority closes, 318–20
History reviews, 270–72
Holds (holding), on the phone, 184
Hours worked/money earned ratio,
    141
Humor, 89, 125, 129–30, 362

"I can get it cheaper" close, 317
Incoming phone calls, 183–86
Industrial sales, directories,
    216–17
Industry news, 143
Information gathering, 193–94,
    216–18
Initial investment (initial amount),
    use of term, 73
Internalization, of skills, 10
Internal tie-downs, 39–40
Internet mailing lists, 194

Interruptions, 214–15
Interviews, 201–4
   referral-gathering, 174–80
Introductions. *See* Referrals
Inverted tie-downs, 38–39
Involvement interviews, 202–4
Involvement questions, 45–46,
   213–14, 244–45, 375
Itch cycle, 150–56
   files for, 341, 342, 349
   how to determine, 153–56
"It isn't in the budget" close, 315–16
"I want to think it over" close,
   300–304

Jargon, 212

Last resort closes, 321
Laughter, 89, 125, 129–30, 362
Leading questions, 50–53, 54, 313,
   375
Leads, 149–70
   claim-staking, 165–66
   community involvement, 169–70
   first meeting with, 241–42
   itch cycle, 150–56
   newspapers, 162–65
   orphan adoption, 157–60
   prequalifying, 149–50
   referrals, 171–81
   service departments, 169
   swap meets, 166–69, 342
   technical advancements, 160–62
Leads clubs, 166–69
Learning curve, 125, 126–27
Learning system (money study),
   8–12
"Let me make a note of that" close,
   293–95
Letters, testimonial, 233–34, 275–77
Libraries, 194, 216
Lingo (specialized languages),
   212–13
Listening, 48–50, 263, 287–89,
   313–14, 375

List price (listed at), use of term,
   72–73
Lists, 135–37, 193–94, 345–46
Logic (logical appeals), 62–63,
   66–67, 88–89, 376
Long-term goals, 367–70
Losers (losing), 355–57
Lost-sale closes, 321
Luck, role of, 370

Mailing lists, 194
Mailouts, 144–47
Marital status, for qualifying, 150
Marketing, 144–48. *See also* Leads;
   Prospecting; Telephone
Market surveys, 189–93
Meetings. *See also* First meeting
   by phone, 185–86, 195–96, 223
   to sales ratio, 140–41, 144
   scheduling time for, 346, 348
   swap, 166–69
   use of term, 71
Minor objections, 258–59
Misery (miserable attitude),
   352–57
Models, 234
Money
   as motivator, 98
   triplicate of choice for, 253–55
Money-making activities (money-
   grabbers), 143–44, 322–36
Money study (learning system),
   8–12
Monologues, 202
Monthly investment (amount), use
   of term, 73, 255
Monthly payment, use of term, 73
Moods of delivery, 89
Mother close, 313–14
Motivators, 95, 98–106
   acceptance by others, 100–104
   achievement, 99–100
   love of family, 106
   money, 98
   recognition, 100

Motivators *(continued)*
    security, 98
    self-acceptance, 104–6
Moving to close, 281
My-dear-old-mother closes, 313–14

Natural-born sales wonder, myth
    of, 4–6
NEADS Qualification Sequence,
    247–52
Needs, vs. wants. *See* Wants, vs.
    needs
Negative emotions (feedback),
    67–70, 191–92
    course corrections and, 127–29
Negative persons (neggies), 355–57
Networking, 144–48. *See also*
    Leads; Prospecting; Referrals
Newsletters, 144–47, 234
Newspapers, 162–65
Niebuhr, Reinhold, 260
Now, in NEADS sequence, 248
Nunn, Gertrude, 14

Objections (concerns), 7, 28–30,
    257–72
    comparative questions, 224–25
    conditions, 259–61
    definition of, 258–59
    isolating the, 33
    in presentations, 208–9
    questions for answering, 33, 264
    as rungs of ladder to sales
        success, 258
    shock treatments for, 266–72
    system for handling, 263–66
    triad concept for, 86–89
    two don'ts and one do, 261–63
    use of term, 82
Offered for (offered at), use of
    term, 72
Open questions, 34–35
Opportunities, use of term, 84–85
Oral closes, basic, 293
Order forms, 274–75, 293–95,
    337–40

Organizational tools, 340–43, 345
Organizations, claim-staking,
    165–66
Organized involvement interviews,
    202–4
Orphan adoption, 157–60
Outgoing phone calls, 186–89
Own (ownership), use of term,
    74–78

Pain of change, as demotivator,
    113–19
Paperwork, 337–43. *See also*
    Forms
    use of term, 73
Patterson, John H., xx
Pause, in SPR (stimulus, pause,
    and response) theory,
    25–31
Pay dirt, 327
Peers, acceptance by, as motivator,
    100–104
Percentage game, 126, 131
Performance ratios, 138–44
Performance slumps. *See* Slumps
Personal appearance, 16–17,
    239–42, 328
Personal goals, 364–74
Personal performance ratios,
    138–44
Personal rewards, 347–48
Personal sales preplanner, 218–19,
    223–26
    sample form, 220
Phone calls. *See* Telephone
Pitches, use of term, 83–85
Planned pauses, 287
Planning time. *See* Time
    management
"Playing it by ear," 202
Porcupine, 44–45, 375
    sharp-angle close, 308–9
    test closes, 279, 280
Positive attitude, 19–20, 93–94, 96,
    353–57
Positive emotions, 67–70, 92

Power closes, 292–321
  basic oral close, 293
  basic written close, 293–95
  Benjamin Franklin balance
    sheet close, 295–300
  bridging, 312–13
  competitive-edge close, 318
  economic truth close, 316–17
  higher authority close, 318–20
  "I can get it cheaper" close, 317
  "It isn't in the budget" close,
    315–16
  "I want to think it over" close,
    300–304
  lost-sale close, 321
  My-dear-old-mother close, 313–14
  puppy-dog close, 314–15
  reduction-to-the-ridiculous
    close, 304–7
  secondary-question close,
    309–12
  sharp-angle close, 308–9
  similar-situation close, 315
PowerPoint presentations, 228,
  231
Practice, drill, and rehearse
  (preparation), 26–31, 54,
  125–26, 130–31, 215
Preplan in writing, 215–27
Preplanners, 219, 220, 222–26
Prequalifying. *See* Qualifications
Presentation binders, 228, 231–32
Presentations. *See* Demonstrations
Price (pricing), 253–56, 304–7, 317
  words to use, 70–86
Pride, 17, 65–66
Primary tool, 12–15
Printed literature, 234
Problems
  handling quickly, 145
  use of term, 81–82
Procrastination, 361–62
Production goals, 370
Productivity-generating activities,
  143–44, 322–36, 350–51
Product knowledge, 54–57

Proof (testimonial) letters, 233–34,
  275–77
Prospecting (prospects), 6, 133–48.
  See also Leads; Referrals
  claim-staking, 165–66
  decision makers, 59–62, 251
  four ways to hover, 144–48
  good-guy role for, 120–22
  itch cycle and, 150–56
  newspapers, 162–65
  nonreferral methods, 149–70
  ratios, 138–44
  rejection and, 120–32
  service departments, 169
  swap meets, 166–69, 342
  technical advancements, 88–89,
    160–62
  telephone calls, 182–96
  time management and, 348–49
  use of term, 81
Puppy-dog closes, 314–15
Purchase path, 29–30

Qualifications, 6, 224, 246–56
  leads, 149–50
  NEADS sequence, 247–52
  triplicate of choice, 252–55
  uh-price technique, 255–56
Questions, 32–57. *See also* Involvement questions; Porcupine;
  Tie-downs
  3 principles of, 53–57
  12 pointers on technique, 32–34
  alternate of choice, 42–43
  discovery, 50–53, 375
  leading, 50–53, 313, 375
  listening versus talking, 48–50
  open, 34–35
  in presentations, 46–48, 208–9
  tagalong, 41
  test closes, 278–81

Ratios, 138–44
  contacts-to-closings, 122–24
Recognition, as motivator, 100
Recontacts, 328–32, 333

Record-keeping, 337–43. *See also* Forms
Reduction-to-the-ridiculous close, 304–7
Referrals, 7, 171–81, 322–25
 card system for, 173–74, 180
 caring attitude with, 20–21
 in client files, 342
 first meeting with, 172–73, 241–42
 prospecting and, 144
 role-play scenario, 174–79
 thank-you notes, 334
Reflexive responses, 27–28
Reinforcement, of skills, 10–12
Rejection, 21, 120–32
 attitudes toward, 124–31
 cash value of, 122–24
 Creed of the Champion and, 132
 rejecting negative effects of, 122–24
 words to avoid, 70–86, 376
Rejection words, 70–86, 376
Repetition, 8–9, 207
Research, 346–47
Response
 SPR (stimulus, pause, and response) theory, 25–31
 triad concept, 86–89
Retail list price, 72–73
Return on investment, 2–3
Reverse directories, 193
Review
 of account history, 270–72
 of personal goals, 367, 369–70

Sales message, 86–89
Say-no questions, 50–53
Scare words, 70–86, 211–12
Scheduling. *See* Time management
Seating, for presentations, 229–30
Secondary-question closes, 309–12
Security
 as demotivator, 107–8
 as motivator, 98

Self-acceptance, as motivator, 104–6
Self-confidence, 13, 17, 286
Self-doubt, as demotivator, 110–11
Self-interest, principle of, 77–78
Sell (sold), use of term, 78–80
Selling climate, 58–92
 arousing emotions, 62–70
 decision makers, 59–62
 senses that sell, 90–92
 triad concept, 86–89
 words to use, 70–86
Selling emotions, 62–70
Senses, involvement of, 90–92
Sequence plan, sample form, 221
Service departments, 169
Setting goals, 364–74
17-minute presentations, 215, 228–29
Sharp-angle closes, 308–9
Shoe on prospect's foot, 266–68
Short-term goals, 367–70
Shut up (shutting up), 287–89, 313–14
Sign (signing), use of term, 85–86
Similar-situation stories, 225–26, 315
Slane, Carl, 233–34
Slang, 212
Slumps, 352–62
 GOYA formula for, 357–62
Smiles (smiling), 239, 286
Solution, in NEADS sequence, 251–52
Sources of selling success, 16–22
Special districts, 217
Specialized languages (lingo), 212–13
SPR (stimulus, pause, and response) theory, 25–31
Standard & Poor's, 216, 217
Standard tie-downs, 35–38
Stimulus, pause, and response (SPR) theory, 25–31
Street directories, 193
Style, and buying emotions, 65, 66

Surveys, market, 189–93
Swap meets, 166–69, 342
Sweat (sweaty palms), 240–41

Tagalong questions, 41
Tag-on tie downs, 40–41
Tangent chasing, 202
Tax dates, itch cycle and, 152
Tax records, 343
Technological innovation, 88–89, 160–62
Telephone (phone calls), 182–96
   finding good lists, 193–94
   incoming calls, 183–86
   itch cycle and, 153–56
   keeping in touch, 145
   misconceptions about, 182–83
   orphan adoption and, 158–59
   outgoing calls, 186–89
   prospecting, 137, 145, 146
   prospecting ratios, 140–44
   referrals and, 174
   returning calls immediately, 145
   scoring system, 194–96
   surveys, 189–93
Test closes, 278–81
Testimonial letters, 233–34, 275–77
Thank-you notes, 137–38, 144, 332–36
"Think it over" close, 300–304
Thomas Register of American Manufacturers, 216, 217
Tie-downs, 35–41, 312–13, 374
   internal, 39–40
   inverted, 38–39
   standard, 35–38
   tag-on, 40–41
   waiting for positive stimulus before, 37–38
Time management, 339, 344–51
   qualifying and, 246–47
To do lists, 345–46
Total amount, use of term, 71–72
Total investment, use of term, 71–72

Traits of great salespeople, 16–22
Transactions, use of term, 83–85
Triad concept, 86–89
Tribal instinct, 78
Triplicate of choice, 252–55
   for money, 253–55
   for product, 252–53
Trust, building, 172–73, 241

Uh-price technique, 255–56
Unreachable committees, 59–61
Us-against-them instinct, 78
Utilization, of skills, 9–10

Value (valued at), use of term, 72
Verbal buying signs, 286
Video equipment, 234–36
Visits, use of term, 71
Visual aids, 227–28, 229–33
Visual buying signs, 286
Vivid goals, 368
Vocabulary. *See* Words
Volunteer work, 166, 169–70

Walker, Jimmie, 14
Walking advertisements, 328
Wants, vs. needs, 94–95, 363–64
   closing and, 284, 285–86
   demotivators, 95, 107–19
   motivators, 95, 98–106
   phone surveys and, 191–92
   qualifications and, 248–50
Watson, Thomas J., xx–xxi
What's-in-it-for me? emotion, 77–78
Wholesale prices, 72–73
"Winging it," 26–29, 228
Words (terms)
   to avoid, 70–86, 211–12
   to use, 70–86, 210–11, 286–89
Worth, use of term, 72
Written closes, basic, 293–95
WWWWWH (who, what, when, where, why, and how), 34–35

TOM HOPKINS™
INTERNATIONAL

*Tom Hopkins is
world renowned as
The Builder of
Sales Champions*

Tom Hopkins conducts live seminars around the
world. Hundreds of thousands rely on his video training programs. Millions listen to him in their cars daily
and reach for his books whenever they need a new
strategy or idea to make more sales.

If you're serious about your selling career, attend Tom's
3-day, high-intensity Boot Camp, offered only once a
year in Scottsdale, Arizona. The typical attendee
professes an average 60% increase in income after
mastering the strategies taught during those three days.

Tom also offers books and audios specific to the real
estate industry, where he got his start in sales.

Consider having Tom speak at your next conference or
create your ideal sales presentation. He is available to
develop unparalleled, customized training for your
business or organization.

For information on how Tom Hopkins can increase
your personal or corporate profits, contact us:

Tom Hopkins International, Inc.
7531 East Second Street
Scottsdale, Arizona, USA 85251
800-528-0446
48-949-0786
http://www.tomhopkins.com
Subscribe to our free monthly e-newsletter online!